OTHER WORKS BY
RICHARD KOSTELANETZ

Books Authored
The Theatre of Mixed Means (1968)
Master Minds (1969)
Visual Language (1970)
In the Beginning (1971)
The End of Intelligent Writing (1974)
I Articulations/Short Fictions (1974)
Recyclings, Volume One (1974)
Openings & Closings (1975)
Portraits from Memory (1975)
Constructs (1975)
Numbers: Poems & Stories (1975)
Illuminations (1977)
One Night Stood (1977)
Tabula Rasa (1978)
Inexistences (1978)
Wordsand (1978)
Constructs Two (1978)
"The End" Appendix/"The End" Essentials (1979)
Twenties in the Sixties (1979)
And So Forth (1979)
More Short Fictions (1980)
Metamorphosis in the Arts (1980)
The Old Poetries and the New (1981)
Reincarnations (1981)
Autobiographies (1981)
Arenas/Fields/Pitches/Turfs (1982)
Epiphanies (1983)
American Imaginations (1983)
Recyclings (1984)
Autobiographien New York Berlin (1986)
The Old Fictions and the New (1987)
Prose Pieces/Aftertexts (1987)
The Grants-Fix (1987)
Conversing with Cage (1988)
Radio Writings (1989)

Books Edited
On Contemporary Literature (1964, 1969)
Twelve from the Sixties (1967)
The Young American Writers (1967)
Beyond Left & Right: (1968)
Possibilities of Poetry (1970)
Imaged Words & Worded Images (1970)
Moholy-Nagy (1970)
John Cage (1970)
Social Speculations (1971)
Human Alternatives (1971)
Future's Fictions (1971)
Seeing Through Shuck (1972)
In Youth (1972)
Breakthrough Fictioneers (1973)
The Edge of Adaptation (1973)
Essaying Essays (1975)
Language & Structure (1975)
Younger Critics in North America (1976)
Esthetics Contemporary (1978, 1989)
Assembling Assembling (1978)
Visual Literature Criticism (1979)
Text-Sound Texts (1980)
The Yale Gertrude Stein (1980)
Scenarios (1980)
Aural Literature Criticism (1981)
The Literature of SoHo (1981)
American Writing Today (1981, 1989)
The Avant-Garde Tradition in Literature (1982)
Gertrude Stein Advanced (1990)

Books Co-authored & Edited
The New American Arts (1965)

Books Co-compiled & Introduced
Assembling (Twelve vols, 1970–1981)

Performance Scripts
Epiphanies (1980)
Seductions (1986)

Portfolios of Prints
Numbers One (1974)
Word Prints (1975)

Audiotapes
Experimental Prose (1976)
Openings & Closings (1976)
Foreshortenings & Other Stories (1977)
Praying to the Lord (1977, 1981)
Asdescent/Anacatabasis (1978)
Invocations (1981)
Seductions (1981)
The Gospels/Die Evangelien (1982)
Relationships (1983)
The Eight Nights of Hanukah (1983)
Two German Hörspiel (1983)
New York City (1984)
A Special Time (1985)
Le Bateau Ivre/The Drunken Boat (1986)
Resumé (1988)
Onomatopoeia (1988)
Carnival of the Animals (1988)
Americas' Game (1988)
Epiphanies (1982-)
More or Less (1988-)

Extended Radio Features
Audio Art (1978)
Text-Sound in North America (1981)
Hörspiel USA: Radio Comedy (1983)
Glenn Gould as a Radio Artist (1983)
Audio Writing (1984)
Radio Comedy Made in America Today (1986)
New York City Radio (1987)
Orson Welles as an Audio Artist (1988)

Videotapes
Three Prose Pieces (1975)
Openings & Closings (1975)
Declaration of Independence (1979)
Epiphanies (1980)
Partitions (1986)
Video Writing (1987)
Home Movies Reconsidered (1987)
Two Erotic Videotapes (1988)
Americas' Game (1988)
Invocations (1988)
The Gospels Abridged (1988)
Kinetic Writing (1989)
Video Strings (1989)

Films Produced & Directed
Epiphanies (in German, 1983; in English, 1981-)

Films Co-produced & Directed
Constructivist Fictions (1978)
Ein Verlorenes Berlin (1983)
Ett Forlorat Berlin (1984)
A Berlin Lost (1985)
Berlin Perdu (1986)
El Berlin Perdido (1987)
Berlin Sche-Einena Jother (1988)

Holograms
On Holography (1978)
Antitheses (1985)
Hidden Meanings (1989)

Retrospective Exhibitions
Wordsand (1978)

ON INNOVATIVE MUSIC(IAN)S

ON INNOVATIVE MUSIC(IAN)S

Richard Kostelanetz

Limelight Editions
New York 1989

First Edition August 1989

Copyright © 1989 by Richard Kostelanetz

Grid of Schoenberg's *Moses und Aron* by Milton Babbitt, copyright © 1957 by CBS Masterworks

Cover Photo Credits:
B.B. King   Photo by Jeff Sedlik
Alan Hovhaness   Photo by Jerry Saltsberg & Associates
Peter Schickele   Photo by Peter Schaaf
John Cage   Photo by Susan Schwartzenberg

Library of Congress Cataloguing-in-Publication Data

Kostelanetz, Richard.
    On innovative music(ian)s / Richard Kostelanetz. —
1st Limelight ed.
        p. cm.
    Includes index.
        ISBN 0-87910-121-0 : $12.95
        1. Music—20th century—History and criticism.   I.
Title.
    II. Title: On innovative musics.   III. Title: On innovative musicians.
    ML197.K8   1989
    780'.904—dc19   89-2813
                                                                    CIP
                                                                    MN

Especially for André Aubuchon, Jr.,
With gratitude for his taking care

CONTENTS

Acknowledgments   xi
Preface   xiii

MUSICIANS

Glenn Gould: Bach in the Electronic Age (1967)   3
Charles Ives (1967)   17
Milton Babbitt & John Cage: The Two Extremes of
   Avant-Garde Music (1967)   21
Milton Babbitt's Text-Sound Art (1987)   31
Cage's Early Piano Music (1970)   37
The Keystone of the Cagean Canon (1989)   43
John Cage: Some Random Remarks (1969)   47
HPSCHD: Environmental Abundance (1969)   61
John Cage, 75, Writes First, "Great American" Opera (1988)   67
Cunningham/Cage (1986)   77
Elliott Carter (1968)   85
Alan Hovhaness (1979)   95
Paul Zukofsky (1969)   107
Philip Glass (1979, 1988)   119
Mauricio Kagel (1988)   127
La Monte Young (1966)   135
Joao Carlos Martins' J. S. Bach (1988)   139
Peter Schickele (1989)   141
B. B. King (1979)   151
André Kostelanetz (1978)   159
Robert Moog (1970)   167

MUSICS

Rock: The New Pop Music (1968)   191
Contemporary Music (1967)   199
The New Music of the 1960s (1971)   221

MUSIC WRITING

Music Criticism and the Literate Layman (1967)   239

Blues Criticism (1968, 1963, 1968)   257

On *Perspectives* (1969)   265

Talking with John Cage About His Writings Through
    Finnegans Wake (1978)   273

AUTOBIOGRAPHICAL

On Being a Composer Who Can't Read Music (1989)   285

Notes on *Americas' Game* (1988)   293

Composing Music/Performing Words (1989)   307

Index   311

ACKNOWLEDGMENTS

The chapters of *On Innovative Music(ian)s* first appeared in the following publications, sometimes in different form:

Albany Review: "Joao Carlos Martins' J. S. Bach (1988)

American Letters & Commentary: "Composing Music/Performing Words (1989)"

Ameryka: "Alan Hovhaness (1979)"

Art Voices: "La Monte Young (1966)"

Artists Television Project, University of Iowa: "Talking with John Cage About His *Writings Through Finnegans Wake* (1978)"

Columbia Records: "Charles Ives (1967)," "Cage's Early Piano Music (1970)"

Denver Quarterly: "John Cage: Some Random Remarks (1969)"

Esquire: "Glenn Gould (1967)"

High Fidelity: "Elliott Carter (1968)"

Horizon: "B. B. King (1979)"

Labor Records: "Joao Carlos Martins' J. S. Bach (1988)," "The Keystone of the Cagean Canon (1989)"

Michigan Quarterly Review: "Alan Hovhaness (1979)"

Mundus Artium: "The New Music of the 1960s (1971)"

New Art Examiner: a review of John Cage's *Europera*

New York Times, Sunday Arts & Leisure: "*HPSCHD:* Environmental Abundance (1969)," parts of "Alan Hovhaness (1979)," "John Cage, 75, Writes First, 'Great American' Opera (1988)"

New York Times Magazine: "Milton Babbitt & John Cage (1967)," "Paul Zukofsky (1969)"

Next Wave Festival (Brooklyn Academy of Music): "Cunningham/Cage (1986)"

Northwest Review: "Notes on *Americas' Game*" (1988)

Opera News: "Mauricio Kagel (1988)"

Perspectives of New Music: "Music Criticism and the Literate Layman (1967)," "Milton Babbitt's Text-Sound Art (1987)"

The Progressive: Parts of "Blues Criticism (1963, 1968)"

Rolling Stone: Parts of "Blues Criticism (1963, 1968)"

Sonus: An early version of "Notes on *Americas' Game,*" copyright 1987 by Sonus.

Time-Life Records: "Contemporary Music (1967)"
Tri-Quarterly: "Talking with John Cage About His Writings Through *Finnegans Wake* (1978)"
World & I: "Peter Schickele (1989)"
Yale Review: "On *Perspectives* (1969)"

PREFACE

Since my ear is more intelligent than my eye, I should have been a composer; but since prose writing has become my principal marketable skill, I might have become a music critic. This began to happen in the late sixties, a few years after my literary critical career began, but only in a part-time way. Even though I have written mostly about literature, from time to time I return to music. My becoming a composer happened much later.

Collecting fugitive essays is the critic's toughest test on himself. Though individual pieces may seem sensible in the magazines in which they originally appeared (and perhaps benefit from the "reputations" or intelligence surrounding them), in a book they depend only on one another. Either a coherence emerges or there are only opportunistic judgments. I would like to think that the position defined in these essays is an appreciation of what is genuinely new, broadly considered, not only in composition and performance but in dissemination and critical understanding. In making essential discriminations between innovation and imitation, in explaining the radical nature of the new, using the common language with irony and wit, my criticism of music very much resembles my writing about other arts; the principles informing my taste and analyses here are no different. Nothing here is alien to me now, though, were I to write about similar subjects and issues today, I would probably approach them differently. Their stylistic irregularity no doubt reflects the variety of their origins—in time, in subject and in the cultural pitches of the magazines in which they initially appeared. The occasional repetition, of factual information and introductory explanations, perhaps reflects a consistency of outlook and concerns. Some of these essays have appeared before in various earlier books of mine; the one interview is here because it, unlike others with John Cage, had *not* appeared in any earlier books of mine.

I think I have learned more about Art (intentionally capitalized) through music than through anything else (and probably learned more about God as well), and it would be to music that I would always turn for revelation about mysteries unique to Art, apart from everything else. I also estimate that for my creative work I have learned more from musicians than from practitioners of other arts, often saying, as I do, that the principal influences upon my poetry and experimental prose, as well as audio and video, have been J. S. Bach and Charles Ives, the former for his aspirations toward formal perfection, the latter for his storehouse of inventions, and that among contemporaries I think most about Milton Babbitt and John Cage.

One general difference between critics predisposed to the avant-garde and conservatives is that the former eventually get around to producing their own creative work that in turn reflects principles articulated in their criticism. That is true for me as well, as my poetry came after my poetry criticism, my fiction after fiction criticism and now my music after music criticism. However, as I get more deeply immersed in an art, the perspective of my criticism changes. Instead of being a disinterested, discerning bystander, I become a polemical participant—in terms of literary models, once an Edmund Wilson, now an Ezra Pound. As I write this preface I find myself on the verge of a more intense involvement with music composition; and just as I have little sense of where this may lead, I have an even lesser sense of whatever future writing I may do about music. That's why it seemed a good time to put together this first book of music criticism. I'm grateful to many publishers for letting me reprint work initially done for them; to Susan Barron for her calligraphy; Laurie Weeks for proofreading and indexing; and to Melvyn Zerman and his colleagues for contracting and producing it.

Richard Kostelanetz
New York, New York
1 January 1989

EPIGRAPHS

Among the great techniques, music is all by itself an auditory thing, the only purely auditory thing there is. It is comprehensible only to persons who can remember sounds. Trained or untrained in the practice of the art, these persons are correctly called "musical."—Virgil Thomson, *The State of Music* (1961)

There is music wherever there is harmony, order or proportion; and thus far we may maintain the music of the spheres.—Sir Thomas Browne, *Religio Medici* (c. 1635)

[John] Cage is an extraordinary man partly because he's done things all his life that his friends have disapproved of. I always went with the greatest pleasure to anything he put on because there was always a drama that I hadn't expected, some notion of something happening on the stage that I couldn't expect. His sense of time is simply unbelievable and his pitch sense too. That he can stand the music that is made amazes me very often.—Edwin Denby, in an interview (1979)

Many sounds of nature and human activity are commonly regarded as nonmusical noises, largely because of much larger admixtures of overtones, but sometimes because of excessive loudness or monotonous uniformity. These have have been traditionally regarded as unfit materials for music, but recent composers have experimented with them as potentially musical. Any sound or noise can be treated as a theme, repeated, varied, contrasted with others, and organized into a series.—Thomas Munro, *Form and Style in the Arts* (1970)

MUSICIANS

GLENN GOULD: BACH IN THE ELECTRONIC AGE (1967)

*Always dream and shoot higher than you know you
can do. Don't bother just to be better than your
contemporaries and predecessors. Try to be better
than yourself.*—William Faulkner

"Okay, I'd like to help you," Glenn Gould told me over the telephone, "but I have two stipulations. You shan't interview any of my family or friends. They won't honor your request. Second, that we do as much of this as possible over the phone." That was the beginning of a friendship that promises to be telephonically mine for years to come. Though an impatient man, Gould is remarkably generous about time spent on the phone, even returning as soon as possible the calls his answering service collects; but he is reluctant to make face-to-face contact. We have spoken at all times of the day and night, between distances as various as a few miles across New York City to New York-Toronto (his home), from a few minutes to over two hours. "Let's talk again soon," he always tells me. "All the best."

Gould takes the cue of Marshall McLuhan, a local acquaintance, and makes the telephone an extension of himself; and he not only does as much business as possible by phone but he would sooner telephone his family and friends—extend himself literally into their ears—than visit them or even have them visit him. His parents, who live some hundred miles away, receive his calls often; but he sees them only a few times a year, mostly for brief vacations. He has a secretary whom he meets once a year for a ritual drink; but in the evening he dictates letters and essays to her over the phone, and the following afternoon she sends the carbons to him by taxicab. A telephone conversation before bedtime in tandem with Nembutal helps him get to sleep. Gould lives alone, spends most of his day at home, sees few people; nevertheless, he is constantly in touch with everyone important to him, at once, with minimum fuss.

His exploitation of the telephone is only one facet of a technologically sophisticated existence, for Gould takes McLuhan's ideas about the electronic media more seriously than McLuhan does himself. Some years ago, Gould deduced that not only was concert giving dispiriting but the performances he offered were not as perfect as those available on record. "One was forced to compete with oneself," he remembers. "Because I couldn't do as well, those futile concerts reduced my inclination to practice to nil." So, in 1964, he confirmed a decision made four years earlier and completely gave up the old-fashioned custom of concert giving in order to channel his performing primarily into the new technologies of recording machines, radio transmission and television. He frankly sees no justification for playing compromised performances before mere thousands of people when records extend his best renditions into millions of living rooms. Moreover, the act of putting a certain piece on record "frees you to go on to something else," particularly pieces unfamiliar to the conservative concert hall audience. Beyond that, the benefits for Gould are as much psychological as esthetic; for where he was once a notorious hypochondriac, now, he says, "Since I stopped giving concerts, I've scarcely had so much as a sniffle. Most of my earlier illnesses were psychosomatic—a sheer protest against my regimen. These past four years have been the best of my life."

Gould used to give live lecture-demonstrations; but since the Canadian and British Broadcasting corporations both let him do the same on television—extend his pedagogy across two countries—he has reduced his appearances before live audiences to a bare minimum, regarding the few he now gives each year as an excuse to travel to places he has not visited before and to keep the habit of facing live audiences "just in case." Whereas he once taught classes at the University of Toronto, more recently he has been expressing his "irrepressible hamminess" over the weekly, hour-long Canadian radio program *The Art of Glenn Gould,* on which he is likely to give a lecture, let the producer play his records or even dramatize a parody he wrote of a music critics' conference, where he mimicked many of the voices, sometimes doing two at once. (He rehearsed this one for me over the long-distance phone.)

If his output is, by his design, as electronic as possible, so is his intake; for he simply connects himself into a variety of inputs and they feed into him. "I'm not interested in gadgets per se, but what they can do for me." Gould watches a lot of television, exploits his hi-fi set, reads several newspapers (products of wire services), carries a radio with him all the time and at home sometimes listens to both the AM and FM simultaneously. "Quite mysteriously, I discovered that I could better learn Schoenberg's difficult piano score, Opus 23, if I listened to them both at once, the FM to hear music and the AM to hear the news. I want to stay in touch." Gould can learn a Beethoven score while carrying on a conversation; and he often reads one of the many magazines to which he subscribes while listening attentively to someone on the telephone. Afterward, he will remember details from both inputs, for Gould appears to be, as McLuhan puts it, omniattentive. Subscribing to his own preachments, he attends live concerts only to hear compositions unavailable on radio or record.

His cultural intake is various and enormous; so is his output. In our conversations, he talked knowledgeably about contemporary literature (particularly the intricate, ironic techniques of Jorge Luis Borges), theology (Kierkegaard and Tillich), electronic machinery, music both pop and classical, world problems, Canadian politics and patriotism, theories of the female orgasm, the stock market (especially Canadian mining properties), movies, the business of music and research into extrasensory perception. More professionally, his output includes records: recent and current projects being the complete Bach keyboard works, Mozart's piano sonatas, Beethoven's sonatas and all the Schoenberg pieces involving the piano, as well as his present radio shows. Like Bach before him, this noted performer also composes—so far a *String Quartet* and several choral pieces, most of them curiously romantic in ambience—and he plans to do more compositions in a wholly different mode. He contributes articles and reviews regularly to *High Fidelity* and other magazines, sometimes under the outrageous pseudonym of Dr. Herbert von Hockmeister; and everything he publishes reveals his enthusiasm for the literary craft, the musician's ear for intricate cadences and the ham's desire for a good laugh. "This curious attitude of affection for the errors of the past secures for the teaching of music more quack educators per square faculty than are the lot of any other major discipline."

The fact that he performs in a multiplicity of ways makes him a "musical personality," but his reluctance to make any social scene keeps his name out of the gossip columns. Everything he does is informed by such diverse qualities as a great eccentricity, a broad comedy, an unself-conscious informality and a high level of intellectual concern. Gould is always working on a spate of projects; and like all people passionately involved with their work, he endlessly exudes his love of everything he does—he personally conducts a relentless promotional campaign on behalf of his recent outputs. He is able to produce so much, I suspect, precisely because his intake is so high; and as a result, he functions like a revved-up machine, continually digesting all experience around him and transforming it into several kinds of manufacture. Indeed, his predominant interest is neither music nor writing but that machine, which is, after all, his primary instrument and, perhaps, his most extraordinary work of art. Its operation seems to provide his greatest visceral pleasure, and upon it he lavishes especially tender care and scrupulous attention.

We have actually met, briefly several times, mostly because I insisted that we do so, and Gould has been cordial, though more reserved than usual, probably because human contact is not his most congenial medium and I once made the mistake of warmly embracing his right hand just after a recording session. (He screamed, I heard something crack; he ran off to soak it in hot water, returned in a few minutes, apologized for his rude departure, accepted my regrets and then sent the piano tuner home.) He is politer than most of the world's eminent—he would sooner direct his attention elsewhere than tell an intruder to get lost—and young enough to treat an even younger interviewer as an equal; and he is among the few members of the serious musical profession, where nastiness seems cultivated, to make a habit of saying nice words about everyone, even the most popular targets of fashionable scorn. Paradoxically, although he is an acerbic critic of intellectual attitudes and professional positions, toward individuals he is scrupulously generous, "perhaps because I am continually amazed that anything gets done at all."

Gould is average in height, glassy-eyed in demeanor and now stockier and tougher looking than the delicate, skinny young man whose image graced the legendary, best-selling recording of Bach's *Goldberg Variations* that established his reputation. He has a well-formed face, with a broad forehead and a heavy jaw, all topped by slightly receding and rampantly thinning brown hair. As most frontal pictures of him show, he is essentially good-looking; but a few eccentric details conspire to make him look strikingly odd—his stooped shoulders, which together with his large jaw create a faintly primitive appearance; his reluctance to shave or get haircuts, which gives the impression that he might need a dime; and his clothes, which are informal and ill-matching—and every time we have met, he has managed to remove his shoes, exposing the holes in his socks. He tolerates little quarrel with his impulses toward immediate visceral comfort.

He moves spryly in an idiosyncratic manner that combines ungainly swagger with a certain grace; and instead of entirely refusing to shake hands, as he used to do, he now raises his wrist and turns his fingers down as you reach forward, so all you generally clutch are a few fingers which quickly pull themselves away. He seems as self-entrenched as he actually is; and even when revealing his most idiosyncratic foibles, he communicates the clear impression that he knows exactly what he is doing all the time (as well as what impressions he might be creating) and that, as a romantic, he absolutely insists upon his will. "The only thing Glenn likes to do more than perform is talk," at least two acquaintances told me. And he is indeed a sparkling and interminable talker. Gould regards all the world outside his house as a stage, and wherever he goes he performs with glittering words, often clowning, invariably humorous and usually dominant. His mind is as quick as his speech, and he remembers clearly miscellaneous youthful experiences (some of which haunt him) and conversations held weeks, if not months, before. Any scene with him develops a rapid rhythm which he can single-handedly sustain.

He comes to New York for a few days every few weeks, primarily to make records which still provide about one half of his income (radio, television and stocks making the rest). He takes the night train from Toronto, arriving in New York early in the morning. Since he memorizes the scores on the train and puts himself to sleep with Nembutal, he is able to go straight to work. In one hand is his suitcase, and in the other a slender wooden box about three by two feet and a few inches thick. It contains a few tapes, miscellaneous junk and, folded up, the dilapidated chair that has been Gould's constant musical companion for fifteen years. Gould discovered some years ago that he could play far better from a very low chair that happened to be in the Gould home, and his father designed its seat to be raised and lowered like a swivel stool. Since Gould is sensitive about delicate matters, he has made the chair such an integral part of his essential equipment that he has spurned offers to build him a substitute. Some years ago, the hazards of airplane travel smashed its seat; and he expended considerable effort finding pieces of green cloth and mattress rag that, he judges, "lend precisely the same tension and support as the chair originally had." When he finishes a recording session, he folds the chair into its case and lugs it back to Toronto.

His New York piano he customized from a prewar Steinway chassis, largely to simulate aural aspects of a harpsichord; and where he once made records with several keyboard instruments—one piano for Bach, another for Beethoven, a third for Brahms—now he is so devoted to this hybrid that he occasionally ships it to Toronto. "It is as close to the ideal instrument as I'll ever be able to find." Before recording, he relaxes his hands and elbows by soaking them in water he runs from warm to hot. Whenever he plays, he hums and chants, sometimes quite audibly; and although the engineers put a wall of baffle around his chair, the superfluous sound still creeps onto the final product. "It's a terrible distraction that I don't like either. I wish I could get rid of it," he says, "and I would if I could, believe me; but I can't." This is perhaps his sole confession of inexcusable weakness. Whether on the piano or not, his performances of Beethoven generally strike critics as less distinguished and even less inventive than does his Bach, while some Schoenbergians regard his recording of their master as distinctly sloppy and perversely romantic.

The hum is another symptom of his intense involvement with performing; for at his instrument, Gould is a coiled dynamo of rampant visceral energy. Nearly every part of his body moves as he plays: his large head sways from side to side, and as his right foot operates the piano's pedals, his left shifts to preserve his balance. Only his broad hips are stable and relaxed. His fingers, neither long nor stubby, are well muscled; and his famous trills are as spectacular to see as they are to hear—his fingernails literally flutter over the keys. Although he sits considerably lower than most pianists—only fourteen, rather than the usual twenty, inches off the floor—he seems to bear down on the piano, and everything he plays conveys a sense of highly tempered but incipiently overwhelming energy.

The paradox is that out of such Dionysian activities come rather Apollonian interpretations of the music. At such baroque counterpoint techniques as articulating two or more melodies at once (without subordinating one to the other), Gould is spectacularly masterful; no one else can perform this dimension of Bach so brilliantly. "In purely pianistic terms, he has an extraordinary ability to keep the texture clear at all points," writes Robert P. Morgan in *High Fidelity.* "He is able to bring everything out, not just the most important line but the subsidiary lines as well. The subject of the fugue, for example, is rarely louder than the parts accompanying it, yet is always clearly articulated." He also exhibits particular genius for phrasing—for articulating both the precise notes and the subliminal character of every passage of notes (rather than building a climax); but as a natural original, he also radically reinterprets the tempo of familiar pieces, rendering them in ways unheard before but often heard since—in rhythmic measures so original they offend, if not infuriate, before they persuade. As a result, even in Bach's superficially limited *Well-Tempered Clavier,* Gould amazingly manages to bestow on each prelude and fugue an individual identity. Achieving such precise musical articulation involves incredibly exacting rapport between the head and the hand, between the sounds the mind wants to hear and those the fingers can produce; and it is precisely by playing from the fingers that he adapts harpsichord technique to the piano. Indeed, so extraordinary and compelling is Gould's tactile dexterity that every time I watch him play I "see" thousands of synapses connecting every second, propelling dozens of signals across his circuits.

At the recording session, as soon as he finishes a complete rendition, he comments excitedly and specifically on his performance; and if these remarks are negative, the recording engineer whispers "take two" into the tape and Gould plays the deficient section again. ("I resent," he once remarked, "the one-timeness, or the non-take-twoness, of the live concert experience.") Skipping lunch and other pleasantries, he comes to the control room and goes over the tape with the record's producer. While listening to the playback, Gould watches the score, humming one of the melodies and conducting himself with a pencil baton in his left hand. From time to time, he jots down editorial notes on the manuscript or sips from a cup of tea. A perfectionist by personal taste, he rejects a section merely because an eighth note has slipped from a line; and he often instructs the tape editor that a few bars from the third take of a certain section should be spliced into an entire section of the second take, which should in turn be integrated in place of similar material in the original. Sometimes Gould will record several distinctly different interpretations of the same score and then pick judiciously among the available results, even splicing two conceptually contrary renditions into his final integral version. In the end, therefore, the record of a Gould performance that we hear is really a carefully patched collection of segments. Some performers and critics think that fiddling with bits and pieces represents a kind of artistic "cheating," particularly when incisive editing produces the kind of inspired performance unlikely, if not impossible, in a sustained recital; but more concerned with ends (the record) than means (the making of it), Gould believes that the performer is obliged not only to play as well as possible but also to edit his rendition exactly to his ideas of excellence. "A performer should treat tape as a film director treats his rushes." Actually, he splices considerably less than many performers, for when he put down his editing notes for a medium-length Beethoven sonata, the engineer who looked at them remarked, "That's minimal splicing around here. Someone else recently did fifty-two cuts in a ten-minute piece." After he finishes preparing instructions for the technician who actually reworks the tape, Gould will hear the definitive edited version of a previous recording session, and then he will either stay for another day of recording or take the night train home. He dislikes New York City and sees as little of it as possible.

His attitude to recordings is an intrinsic dimension of his enormous technological bias and sophistication; and as a writer he is, appropriately, best known as the philosopher of the recording. Indeed, his essays on the prospects and influence of recordings constitute as thorough and imaginative an exploration of this issue as has ever been done. Here Gould flatly suggests, "The habit of concertgoing and concert giving, both as a social institution and as chief symbol of musical mercantilism, will be

. . . dormant in the twenty-first century. ('For Rent: Complex of Six Acoustically Charming Auditoria. Apply, J. Rockefeller.')" More specifically, Gould argues that the development of recordings, a product of electronic technology, has thoroughly changed the musical situation in various ways. Our generation values an acoustic style characterized by a great degree of "clarity, immediacy and indeed almost tactile proximity," a sound that was neither available to nor wanted by the musical profession or public two generations ago. For instance, where orchestras once attempted to create a sound splendid enough to fill a concert hall, now the desired sound, even in concert, is more appropriate to the scale of a living room. Indeed, in his own record listening, Gould is particularly sensitive to the effects produced by various strategies of microphone placement. Second, records make continually available to the musical audience certain kinds of esoteric music, particularly Renaissance and highly contemporary, that would otherwise be heard only on rare occasions, if at all. Third, records do for music what the art book did for art; for where the latter is, in André Malraux's famous phrase, a museum without walls, so recordings create in every man's library both a concert without halls and a musical museum whose curator is the record owner; therefore, all known musical styles—indeed, all kinds of music—are, thanks to records, available to the record owner at any time. (This may explain why Gould's own enthusiasms embrace such compositionally contrary figures as Strauss and Schoenberg.) Fourth, the performer shares responsibility for the final product with the record's producer and his editors and technicians. Fifth, all the available recordings of a particular piece create a living "tradition" that forces the work's next performer to offer something distinctly original. "If there is any excuse to make a recording," Gould has said elsewhere, "it is to do it differently—as it has never been done before. If one can't quite do that, abandon the project and move on to something else." Finally, "Within the last few decades . . . music has ceased to be an occasion, requiring an excuse and a tuxedo and accorded, when encountered, an almost religious devotion; music has become a pervasive influence in our lives, and as our dependence upon it has increased, our reverence for it has in a certain sense declined."

Conjecturing about the impact of future technologies upon music, Gould not only suspects that by the time he finishes putting all his current projects on records he will need to redo them for videotape, but he also declares, "I'd love to issue a kit of variant performances and let the listener assemble his own performance. It would draw the audience into the re-creative process." Beyond that, he envisions a machine that will literally allow every man to become his own conductor. As it "eliminates the pitch/speed equation," it would enable the listener to draw from "the felicities that appeal to him as among varying performances of a musical composition" and then combine those most felicitous versions into a single, personal interpretation. The machine would have the capability of allowing the listener to become, Gould writes, "a master editor," choosing phrases "from any number of performances of the same work which may have totally different tempo predilections and dynamic relations. This would make it physically possible for the listener to produce his own Fifth Beethoven Symphony as a compote of the, to his mind, preferable features of a Mr. Karajan, a Mr. Bernstein or any other combination of interpreters that he would like to supervise." When that machine becomes generally available, Gould, I am sure, will be among the first to purchase one.

In background, the cosmopolite is indubitably a provincial; yet this isolation from cultural fashion probably endowed him with that eccentric individualism that, once the world accepted it, made him extremely cosmopolitan. He was born in Toronto, Ontario, in 1932, of prosperous Presbyterian parents; and though he is no longer a churchgoer, Protestant ideas still haunt his consciousness. His entire education took place in his hometown, much of it literally at home. His first piano teacher was, prosaically enough, his mother; and thanks to tutoring, he combined his musical education with sporadic attendance at the public schools. He entered Toronto's Royal Conservatory of Music at nine, precociously graduating at twelve but continuing to study there until his late teens. To this day his accent retains that distinctly Toronto mixture of elegant diction and anglicisms overlaid with Midwestern intonations. An autodidact by inclination and a shaper of his own destiny by insistence, Gould as a teenager discovered Schoenberg and other contemporary composers, even though his teachers had not championed them; and he now considers twelve-tone technique "the only really valid linguistic innovation in the twentieth century." Around this time, he also worked out wholly on his own that stunningly original interpretation of Bach's *Goldberg Variations* in which he successfully appropriated a harpsichord piece for the piano. Yet he was not a child prodigy in the conventional Menuhin sense; and when he first attracted public notice, at the age of twelve, his instrument of virtuosity was not the piano but the organ.

He gave two or three concerts a year in and around Toronto all through his teens; and although he was then cocky enough to send tapes of his Schoenberg performances to certain avant-garde New York composers, they denied him a precocious New York debut. (Those pieces, in New York at least, were generally the domain of the late pianist Edward Steuermann, who had been part of Schoenberg's Viennese circle.) "That was the only period of my life when I enjoyed giving concerts," Gould now judges. "Performing before an audience gave me a glorious sense of power at fifteen." Few pianists made such auspicious American debuts as Gould did in 1955, first in Washington and then at New York's Town Hall. Never one to compromise with the going pianistic fashion, in the latter concert he showed his eccentric versatility with a piece (originally for harpsichord) by the esoteric sixteenth-century Dutch composer Jan Pieterszoon Sweelinck, an Orlando Gibbons pavane, five Bach *Sinfonias,* Bach's *Partita No. 5 in G major,* a sonata by Alban Berg, one other Viennese atonal piece and the Beethoven for which he received so much praise—*Sonata in E Major,* Op. 109. Back then, as well as today, he eschewed the pianists' standard romantic repertoire of Schumann, Schubert, Chopin and Liszt. Not only did Gould's subsequent success establish a new style in piano performance but he also instituted a taste in programming that has affected younger musicians: "Ever since Gould, every young pianist feels obliged to include some 'intellectual' pieces in his recital," said the pianist Christopher Sager, then age twenty-six, "difficult works such as Bach's *Goldberg,* Beethoven's *Diabelli Variations* and Schoenberg's later piano pieces."

Those opening concerts persuaded nearly all the newspaper critics to chime their superlatives together, and before long magazine articles appeared that devoted as much space to Gould's eccentricities as to his artistry. Not only did Gould use a weird-looking and oddly low chair which, shockingly, had a back, put glasses of water on the piano, sometimes assume a posture resembling the Australian crawl, audibly hum through a performance as well as "play some passages far too fast and others outrageously slow" and look incorrigibly unkempt and wear formal dress that was noticeably oversized, but he also carried both his favorite brand of bottled spring water and an opulent cache of drugs wherever he went, ate only arrowroot cookies for breakfast, wore mittens and a coat all the time, refused to shake hands and even publicly quarreled with his elders over standards of interpretation and competence. "I think he is an absolutely inexplicable musician," another young pianist charged. "There are only two ways of doing things, very fast and very slow." "He would come," his former record producer Howard Scott remembers, "with one suitcase containing his chair, the other with scores, some clothes and a toilet kit of pills. He had a pill for everything." On tour, he established a notorious reputation for canceling concerts—

one in five on the average—and for demanding a gamut of special considerations. His behavior in those days convinced everyone he was surely out of his mind; but as he has never subscribed to psychiatry, he was probably more foxy than crazy, more uncomfortable than disturbed. In short, Gould exhibited none of the ingredients that make for musical success except sheer genius (and an ability for fomenting journalistic copy); and his artistry was at once so radical and excellent, although uneven, that the musical audience generously reclassified his excesses as artistic privileges.

Gould currently resides in a six-room penthouse that tops a late-thirties Toronto apartment building. In the living room are two pianos—one an 1895 Chickering—as well as an attractive painting by a Chinese now living in Paris and miscellaneous disarray. As Gould neither cooks nor cleans, a part-time housekeeper fights a losing battle with the mess as well as supplies him some evenings with the one big meal he eats daily. Since he generally practices the piano less than an hour a day (touching it longer only before a recording session) and often goes for days without playing at all, he currently devotes most of his time to other activities, particularly writing and broadcasting. He entertains at home infrequently and leaves the house as little as possible, usually either to perform work or dine with friends, "most of whom are in communications—with the press or the networks. They have that synoptic view of things I like."

Although a slave to his commitments, most of which he fulfills responsibly, Gould also has the instincts of a bohemian, as well as the income to finance his several-hundred-dollar monthly telephone bill; and what probably saved him from the conventions that shackle even the most adventurous of us is the fact that only once did he hold a regular job. At eleven, during the war, he was the organist at a local Anglican (Canadian for Episcopal) church; but since he would often lose his place whenever the congregation sang, his forgetfulness led to an embarrassing mistake which brought his rapid dismissal. Perhaps because he has been famous his entire adult life, he now carries himself in some respects, especially in his desperate quest for privacy, more like a movie star than an artist or intellectual.

At home, Gould does first drafts of his writing in longhand (this and his preference for trains are his two major technologically archaic habits). When he has a lot of work to do, and his parents are away, he disappears into their house near Toronto, or he drives up into Northern Ontario, where he checks into a motel or one of the older hotels in the area and works there. His favorite method for "cooling off" his machinery is driving alone through the lumber towns along the Lake Superior shore while listening to rock music on the radio. He prefers northern climates to tepid ones—London being the only city that might woo him away from Toronto; and in general, he would like to spend more time in the country. "I've got to have hills, water and leaden sky," he says. "My ability to work varies inversely with the niceness of the weather." His most enjoyable recent visits were spent in Canada's northernmost territories, and in 1967 he produced a radio show about this region—his first extended venture into nonmusical reportage. Indeed, *The Idea of North,* in which he superimposed contrapuntally various conversations and phrases into an essay on the effects of isolation, was so well received that the C.B.C. gave Gould a five-year contract solely to produce radio specials. "It's now my favorite medium."

In the past few years Gould has literally redesigned his style of life, just as he transformed his piano exactly to the specifications he wanted—rearranged his environment and ultimately himself as his own most thoughtfully created and favorite work of art. This involves not only his choices of inclusions and exclusions but also sufficient discipline to act on his plan. He claims that he can understand and judge other people far better by talking to them on the phone than seeing them in the flesh. "My eyes are always deceived," he explains. The major exclusion in his design appears to be intimate personal relationships; he lives with no one, never has (since he left his parental home) and probably never will. Nonetheless, he feels intimately involved with many public personalities, most of whom he knows largely, if not exclusively, through radio and television, simply because they are his constant companions; and his aquaintance with the pop singer Petula Clark, a favorite subject in his conversations, has been entirely electronic. Gould speaks excitedly about her, softly cackling at his own jokes. "Actually, I did want to meet her when she was in Toronto for some concerts, but I was taping at the time. I discovered her when I was driving alone on one of my northern trips; I heard 'My Love' before I heard 'Downtown.' I think she's been made to represent something enormously significant and I'm writing an essay called 'The Search for "Pet" Clark.' It's significant, in a quasi-sociological way, that there is such a dichotomy between what she's saying and the music she's given to sing it to. I'm not one, you see, who thinks the Beatles are writing great music for our time; I think it's atrocious—and atrociously produced. But Pet Clark—for one thing there's the voice, which I've called 'fiercely loyal to its one great octave,' and then her presence—what I call the Gidget syndrome. There's a detachment, a sexual circumspection: she can express the agonies of adolescence and yet demonstrate a pressing on to adulthood. She can put the adults at ease, yet get through to the teenage audience. And the thing is, she's *my age.*" When Gould had finished his Petula Clark essay, he called me up to read a longish section of it on the telephone. He read fast, acting it out, the phrasing seemingly rehearsed; and just after its final words, he sighed, "I *like* it."

The paradox is that Gould is a reclusively private person who lives, via the media, an extremely public life, in constant "touch" with the world community; for not only do his records become the intimate possessions of millions of people but the world's activities are also immediately present to him. This explains why Gould feels himself related more to the mass than to the elite; for where a truly private person loves and is loved by some*one,* Gould loves everyone and everyone in turn loves him. He writes for a public of readers, broadcasts for a mass of listeners; and even over such a functionally private medium as the telephone, he is performing—behaving as he would in public. He simply knows and has known no other way. Indicatively, the "individuals" that appear in his parodies and satires are invariably drawn upon either public figures or media stereotypes. Gould has, by a series of choices, set up a certain mode of life, and he is as much the victim as the beneficiary of his system.

Gould's eccentric procedures are far from mere gimmickry, because all of them serve particular functions in his life: beneath all the diffuse eccentricity is a consistent wisdom. He still carries several medicines, for instance, because he is accident-prone; and given his awareness of that condition, he would be foolish if he went anywhere without them. To deal with such information as he has acquired about himself, he has developed a series of strategies; and how he treats such information exemplifies the idea of a human being as a kind of cybernetic system with several dimensions of apparatus, all of which can be organized to achieve certain ends. Like all cybernetic systems, man continually adjusts to new information, called feedback, that results from his actions. For instance, say you discover that staying out in the noonday tropical sun usually produces severe sunburn; then, thanks to feedback, you realize that if you go out into the noonday sun again, another sunburn will be your fate. Every time a cybernetic system acts, it gets to consider the result of its actions and modify its behavior accordingly, and many of Gould's unusual habits and precautions are based upon informational feedback he learned in previous experiences.

Indeed, everyone continually adjusts his systems to new information he acquires about both himself and external situations, but what distinguishes Gould from most of us is a distinct difference of degree. He suffers no boss except himself and has so few social obligations that he is free enough to be wholly responsible to himself for nearly every hour of his waking day. Therefore, unlike the rest of us, he gathers more subtle kinds of information, attempts more unconventional experiments with himself, makes so many more readjustments and then makes himself systematically adhere to these new ways. He dislikes shaking hands with people, primarily because his hands are delicate and they earn much of his livelihood. He used to put a glass of water on the piano when he performed in public, because the tension of playing a live concert sometimes made him gag. He takes trains because he discovered that planes make him ill, and he drinks no alcohol because a swimming head some years ago nearly caused an accident. If Marcel Duchamp decided that he could not "work" more than two hours a day and reportedly did not, Gould recognizes that he can labor many more, and since his interests and ambitions are various, he does so. He plays the piano from an unusual angle, because that odd position is more effective for him. He purchased a new Chevrolet Impala, because that is the only brand that has seats his sensitive back finds comfortable. If extrasensory information either he or a certain friend perceives warns him that a projected trip might bring misfortune, he cancels it. For every eccentric gesture, there is invariably a legitimate reason. Gould is adventurous enough to act on his new knowledge, intelligent enough to regard his experience disinterestedly and wealthy enough to exploit the extensions the new technologies offer him. And these procedures, indeed, explain why he is such a highly individualized, extremely contented, enormously productive and maximally efficient system.

CHARLES IVES (1967)

The paradox of Charles Ives (1874–1954) is that a composer so neglected in his own time should be so unanimously acclaimed so soon thereafter. For, although his works were once so rarely played that he never heard some of his major pieces at all, his music has gloriously survived his own passing; and although he taught no pupils and founded no school, he is generally considered the father of nearly everything American in American music. What is more remarkable is that Ives was not an intentional *avant-gardist,* conscientiously aiming for a "breakthrough," but a modest spare-time composer whose innocence, of convention as well as pretense, was a shaping component of his radical originality.

Ives was a thoroughly trained musician; but more than that, he was a great inventor—the equal, in his own field, of Thomas Alva Edison or Samuel F. B. Morse—with several major musical patents to his name. Ives was the first modern composer who consistently did not resolve his dissonances. Instead of returning a piece to its tonic home base, he would end it, metaphorically, out in the field or, sometimes, as in the sharp dissonance concluding the Second Symphony, well into the grandstand. (When Ives as a youth was asked what he played, he would often reply "shortstop," significantly a position between bases.) While still in his teens, Ives developed his own system of polytonality—the technique of writing for two or more different keys simultaneously—and in a piece he composed at the age of 20 *(Song for Harvest Season),* he assigned four different keys to four instruments. Composers Henry Brant and Karlheinz Stockhausen today follow Ives's device of strategically distributing musicians over a physical space; in Ives's *The Unanswered Question* (1908), as the dominant sound shifts from one position in space to another, the place the music comes from is as important a dimension of the piece as what is played by the musicians.

In the *Concord Sonata* (composed 1909–15), Ives invented the tone cluster—where the pianist uses either his forearm or a block of wood to sound simultaneously whole groups, if not octaves, of notes. (Béla Bartók, Igor Stravinsky and Henry Cowell were among the many composers who subsequently used this device.) Another Ives innovation was the esthetics of pop art; for Ives, like Claes Oldenburg, and Robert Rauschenberg after him, drew quotations from mundane culture—hymn tunes, patriotic ditties, etc.—and stitched them into his artistic fabric. Other composers had incorporated "found" sounds prior to Ives, but he was probably the first to allow a quotation to stand out dissonantly from the text—all but waving a flag to draw attention to itself—as well as the first, like the pop artists after him, to distort a popular quotation into a comic semblance of the original. Just as Claes Oldenburg's famous *Giant Hamburger* (1962)—seven feet in diameter, made of canvas and stuffed with kapok—creates a comic tension with our memory of the original "model," so Ives evokes a similar effect in his *Variations on a National Hymn* [America] (1891, when he was 17!). In juxtaposing pop tunes like *Columbia, the Gem of the Ocean* in the same musical field with allusions to Beethoven's Fifth Symphony, Ives employed another pop strategy to create a distinctly American style that suggested that both classical music and popular, both formal and informal cultures, were equally immediate and perhaps equally relevant.

Other Ivesian musical innovations include polyrhythms—where various sections of the orchestra play in wholly different meters, often under the batons of separate conductors, all to create multiple cross rhythms of great intricacy. In his rhythmic freedom, as well as his unashamed atonality, Ives clearly fathered the chaotic, Mixmaster language of modern music, the tradition that runs through Henry Cowell and early Edgard Varèse to John Cage. Indeed, Ives preceded Cage by inventing indeterminacy—where the scripts offered the musicians were so indefinite at crucial points that they could not possibly play exactly the same sounds in successive performances. (In *The Unanswered Question,* Ives further discouraged musical unanimity by placing three separate groups of musicians in such a way that one could not necessarily see the others.)

As one of the first modern composers to develop a distinctly eccentric musical notation, Ives anticipated contemporary practices of graphs, charts, abstract patterns—manuscripts that resemble everything but traditional musical scores. He also wrote notes that he knew could not be played, such as a 1/1024 note in the *Concord,* followed by the words, "Play as fast as you can." Indeed, Ives's scripts were so unusually written, as well as misplaced and scrambled in a big notebook, that editors have labored valiantly to reconstruct definitive versions of his major pieces. There is a conceptual similtude between Ives and Gertrude Stein, who was born in the same year. While we can now identify what each of them did quite precisely, given our awareness of the avant-garde traditions to which they contributed, it is not so clear to us what either of them thought they were doing—what exactly was on their minds when they made their most radical moves—so different is their work from that which was done before or around them.

Innocent musical historians might also credit Ives as being among the first Western composers to use quarter tones, but it turns out that his own father, George Ives, a village bandmaster in Danbury, Connecticut, had during Charles's youth constructed a special instrument to produce sounds that lay, as he put it, "in the cracks between the piano keys." Nonetheless, not all of Ives's innovations were subsequently accepted: no American composer after him has followed his example of insisting upon paying for the performance of any of his compositions.

Music was hardly the only field to suffer Ives's propensity for invention. As one of the most successful American insurance salesmen of his time, Ives initiated "estate planning" as well as the current practice (replacing "hard sell") of explaining the facts of life to the customer and then letting him decide on his own that he needed a policy. The most immediate measure of Ives's inventiveness is our sense today that without him the history and style of American music as well as American insurance and perhaps American visual art, would be hugely different.

MILTON BABBITT & JOHN CAGE: THE TWO EXTREMES OF AVANT-GARDE MUSIC (1967)

Although their ideas are diametrically opposed, John Cage and Milton Babbitt are usually blamed jointly for making the composition of serious music unprecedentedly difficult: Babbitt, because he makes composing so complicated that few can emulate his methods; Cage, because he makes it so ridiculously easy that no one would dare imitate him. Cage and Babbitt, Babbitt and Cage—they are the two polar figures in American music today; each is the leader of a wing of avant-garde music so extreme that neither will acknowledge the relevance, or even the validity, of the other's work.

Both men respond, albeit in different ways, to the breakup of Western tonality that occurred at the end of the last century. For several hundred years, the seven-tone scale had been the standard mode—the dominant language—of music in the West. Although its grammar sounds "natural" to most Western ears, tonal music is no more "natural" than East Indian or medieval tonal systems. Each is a different language for organizing musical sounds, just as English and French are languages for organizing verbal sounds.

By consciously avoiding tonics and dominants, the keystones of Western tonality, several early modern composers, including Claude Debussy, Erik Satie, Richard Wagner and Charles Ives, challenged this grammar; and they and their immediate successors developed a music of freer tonal possibilities in which all notes, in any combination, would be viable components of music. Therefore, musical sounds that were characterized as "dissonance" in the tonal system would become perfectly consonant in the atonal language. Influenced by these radicals, nearly all modern music makers, from Béla Bartók to the Beatles, have exploited the expanded aural potentialities, creating a music hugely different from nineteenth-century conventions and extending mankind's sense of what "music" can be.

All serious modern composers confronted the situation of tonal possibility, but they responded to it in different ways. The most conservative response, generally attributed to Stravinsky (although he has since abandoned it), suggests that composers should exploit the new tonal freedom without relinquishing both traditional ways of constructing a musical line and classical structures such as the sonata or symphony. Such a position is rightly dubbed neoclassicism; and today its adherents include most of the "establishment" composers in America—among them Aaron Copland, Samuel Barber and Virgil Thomson.

Other composers exploited the tonal freedom to explore radically new mixtures of sound; and one of the two major alternatives encompasses an eccentric tradition whose major contemporary exponent is John Cage. If the neoclassicists want a return to classical structure, these composers favor a further exploration of dissonance, aural chaos and unprecedented sounds. The American Ives contributed to the tradition by incorporating fragments from hymn tunes into his work—by "quoting" sounds traditionally outside the domain of classical music. As early as 1915, another American composer, Henry Cowell, pioneered in the use of odd sounds, independently reinventing, for instance, the tone cluster which Ives, unknown to Cowell, had created a decade earlier—where a forearm or a block of wood sounds a whole area of the piano at once. In 1930, the Russian, Alexander Mossolov, wrote *The Steel Foundry,* which included the sounds of shaken sheet metal; and in the same year the French-born American Edgard Varèse created in *Ionisation* a totally percussive piece which employed such nonmusical sound generators as sirens, sleigh bells and brake drums.

Early in his career, Cage extended this tradition, inventing the "prepared piano," by which he first became famous. In placing bolts, nuts and strips of rubber across the strings, he transformed the piano into a multiple-voiced percussion band. Perhaps his most famous works from this period are *Amores* (1943) and *Dance* (1944), both now on record.

Cage realized that with the prepared piano he would have less control over the final sounds, and so he decided to explore situations where the resulting sounds would be similarly indeterminate with each performance. Some early pieces incorporated life sounds, such as *Third Construction* (1941), in which the instruments include "rattles, tin cans, cowbells, a lion's roar, a cricket caller and a conch shell." In a recent piece, *Variations VI* (1966), the instruments are an army of electronic sound producers—radios, tape recorders, record players, etc.

As Cage in these works is consciously relinquishing his control over the performance, so in his work since 1950 he has developed techniques to relinquish his mind's control over the piece's creation. He adopted "chance," or aleatoric, methods of composition, where patterns developed by accidental means could be translated into musical notation. To compose, for instance, *Music for Carillon No. 2* (1954), also on record,

Cage placed a sheet of graph paper behind a piece of cardboard. Then he marked the imperfections on the cardboard—discolorings, crystal glazes, accidental marks—and punched a pin through each of them so that holes were made on the graph paper. "On the graph," he writes, "one inch horizontally equals one second and three vertical inches equal any pitch range [one octave or two or three]."

Even these directions were so approximate that one performance would be considerably different from another. For most of his other chance compositions Cage used Richard Wilhelm's edition of the *I Ching,* one of the sacred books of China. It shows how tosses of coins can be translated into abstract patterns which, in turn, can dictate Cage's compositional choices. The methods seem terribly arduous; and more than one sympathizer feels it is shameful that Cage, normally a busy man, wastes so much time flipping coins. However, Cage undertakes such procedures precisely to divorce the final piece from his conscious desires. He calls it "indeterminate" or "unintentional" music, and on a record entitled *Indeterminacy* (1959), Cage tells ninety funny stories, each a minute in length (through reading at various speeds), while the pianist David Tudor plays *Fontana Mix* (1958) in another room.

Another revolutionary piece, *4'33"* (1952), suggested equally revolutionary implications, which Cage has since pursued. In that famous work, one remembers, David Tudor comes to the piano and sits silently for four minutes and thirty-three seconds; the "music" is all the unintentional sounds that occur in the performance situation during the prescribed duration. Cage's point was that silence, which can never be absolute, is as much a component of music as is intentional sound; therefore, all the unintentional noises that arise during a performance are parts of the piece. If such accidental sounds were music, one could hear music all the time, but only if one were attuned to perceive it. "If you want to know the truth of the matter," he said recently, "the music I prefer, even to my own and everything, is what we hear if we are just quiet." To Cage, the most agreeable art is not only just like life; it is life.

Following his own logic, Cage admits that he has intellectually programed himself out of a career, but he continues to create indeterminate compositions because of a promise he made long ago to Arnold Schoenberg: to devote his entire life to music in exchange for free lessons. In the past fifteen years, in fact, he has become seriously interested in other matters. In 1952, while teaching at Black Mountain College in North Carolina, Cage created the first mixed-means performance or "happening" in America, and he has since come to consider all of his own work, as well as all of life, "theater." Second, once he moved to the Gate Hill Cooperative community in Stony Point, New York, he became a mushroom fancier, even supplying a famous New York restaurant with its edible fungi; and, in 1962, he co-founded the New York Mycological Society. More recently, he has become interested in the radical futuristic social thought of Robert Theobald and Buckminster Fuller, even contributing to the little magazine *Joglars* his own thoughts on "How to Improve the World (You Will Only Make Matters Worse)."

Cage is basically an optimistic man—energetic, awesomely enthusiastic and extremely conversational. Born in Los Angeles in 1912, the son of an eccentric engineer and inventor, Cage grew up on the West Coast, attending Pomona College for a spell and also teaching at the Cornish School in Seattle. He came to Manhattan in 1942, had his first concert at the Museum of Modern Art the following year and ever since has been a recognized, though controversial, presence on the New York musical scene.

Just under six feet in height, slender and youthful in appearance (his hair, nearly entirely black, has barely thinned or receded), he lives alone in a small three-room cottage in Stony Point. However, he spends much of his time on the road as a lecturer, performer of his own music and musical director of the Merce Cunningham Dance Company.

For many years Cage was excluded from the general run of musical activities and beneficent spoils; but now that his ideas have become more acceptable, his work is at least taken more seriously (although it is hardly universally approved). Whereas he once took diverse odd jobs, in the last few years he has been able to live as a musician. His ideas and example have been an immense influence upon recent American art—indeed, perhaps no one living artist has such a great influence over such a diverse lot of important creative people. Nowadays, even those critics who disagree with him respect his willingness to pursue his ideas to their "mad" conclusions; and he was impoverished for too many years for anyone seriously to doubt his integrity.

In contrast, Babbitt descends from a countertradition, which is equally avant-garde in its esthetic distance from nineteenth-century practice. In the 1920s Arnold Schoenberg created an entirely new musical language—a revolutionary reordering of tonal possibilities. Like all languages, this has its own rules for organizing musical sounds (its own "grammar," so to speak), its own patterns of procedure (syntax) and its own kinds of structural potentialities (sentences). Essentially, Schoenberg suggested that a composer could, working within the open range of twelve tones to an octave, organize any number of tones (up to twelve), without repeating a tone, into a certain order of intervallic relations called, variously, the "row" or "set" or "series."

Once the composer chooses his row, it becomes fixed as the basic pattern for his piece, a pattern that he can then use in one of four ways: (1) in its original form; (2) in a reversed order; (3) in an inverse order (if the second note in the original row was three steps up, now it is three steps down, etc.); and (4) in an inverted, reversed order. Serial composers then observe numerous grammatical guides in shaping their compositions. Far from being as constricting as the rules might suggest—tonal music, one remembers, had its rules too—the twelve-tone system offers its own kind of possibilities. "Simple in its principles of formation and transformation," Babbitt once wrote, "it is enormously complex and deep in its ramifications." As George Perle noted in perhaps the best introduction to the subject, *Serial Composition and Atonality* (1963), many young composers find the twelve-tone system the most attractive of modern musical languages. Indeed, since the middle 1950s even Stravinsky employs serial procedure.

More important, Babbitt contends, the twelve-tone system represents "the result of a half-century of musical thought, a revolution whose nature and consequences can be compared only with those of the mid-nineteenth-century revolution in mathematics or the twentieth-century revolution in theoretical physics." Although Babbitt prefers to compose in the serial language, he does not believe that the new language will, or should, replace the old. "Ideally," he says, "composers, as well as performers and listeners, should be multilingual. However, musicians solely familiar with tonal music should no more judge a serial composition than people solely familiar with English can comment upon writing in French."

In the late 1940s Babbitt developed the concept of the total serialization of musical components—the idea through which he first became widely known. He applied serial principles not only to pitches, as Schoenberg had done, but to other elements as well—duration (which includes rhythm), register, dynamics (attack) and timbre. The result of this logical extension of Schoenberg's ideas was a twelve-tone music of unprecedented structural complexity, in which each and every note contributed to several kinds of serial relationships; and, in contrast to Cage, who theoretically hardly cared if one note should be sounded instead of another, Babbitt insisted that all notes in his pieces should be justified in several ways. Simply, whereas Cage stands for total chance, Babbitt espouses total control. Whereas Cage's music resembles much avant-garde contemporary art in exposing (and emphasizing) the processes of composition, Babbitt deals in final results or products.

From this principle of simultaneous development Babbitt developed a rather revolutionary esthetic that equated excellence with "the multiplicity of function of every event"—with the variety of serial relationships each note developed. "I want a piece of music to be literally as much as possible," Babbitt once said; and his favorite words of praise are "profoundly organized" and "structurally intricate." (A young composer influenced by this thinking once boasted that his six-minute piece contained "over 900 musical events.") Recorded examples of this phase of Babbitt's career include *Du* (1951), a song cycle, and *Composition for Four Instruments* (1948).

To describe the unprecedented intensity of Babbitt's music, the music critic Benjamin Boretz commented: "Every musical event is given a multiple function, and the resulting syntax is so 'efficient' that a single sound may convey as much information [i.e., musical action] as, say, a whole section of a Mozart symphony." The precise analogies to this revolution, in the other arts, include symbolist poetry (Mallarmé, Apollinaire), in which, ideally, each word relates to other words in a maximum number of ways; *Finnegans Wake* (Babbitt's favorite novel, as well as Cage's), in which Joyce tells several stories at once on the same page and makes many words attain several possible meanings; and the early films of Orson Welles (curiously, almost an exact contemporary of both Babbitt and Cage), where, according to Babbitt, "each event has many perceptual dimensions."

Like so many other advanced composers concerned with the precise articulation of their ideas, Babbitt became depressed by what happened to his pieces in performance. Only a few musicians were able to cope with the complexity of his scores. Rather than submit to this fate, Babbitt turned to electronic sound-generating machines, which offered the twofold possibility of achieving precisely all the complicated effects he desired and of fixing a "performance" for all time. Just as print is more efficient than a lecturer for repeating scholarly ideas, so a tape, Babbitt recognized, would always be more efficient than human musicians in precisely repeating a musical pattern. Toward the middle 1950s he began to work with the Mark II Electronic Music Synthesizer that was constructed, with Babbitt as a consultant, by the David Sarnoff Research Center.

In contrast to most electronic music, which is produced by tape doctoring, Babbitt's electronic pieces are composed directly on the Synthesizer, a wholly singular instrument whose huge cost of approximately

$250,000 discourages imitation. Some twenty feet long and seven feet high, the Synthesizer contains various sound-generating devices (tuning forks, oscillators, frequency multipliers, etc.) and about seventeen hundred tubes, all of which make it capable of producing sounds precisely to the composer's instructions. Potentially, Babbitt says, the machine can create any sound known to man; however, certain sounds, he admits, remain for the moment beyond his capacity to specify their components. The Mark II Synthesizer is housed in the Columbia-Princeton Electronic Music Center, which stands in a most unlikely place—on 125th Street, west of Broadway, in a warehouse neighborhood. As the building also houses naval research equipment, it has a guard and a sign-in book at the door.

On the face of the machine are switches that specify the following dimensions of a musical sound—frequency (pitch), octave, volume, timbre and envelope (degree of attack and decrease). When the composer assigns all the attributes of a note, the Synthesizer immediately produces the sound. If the composer finds that the result suits his intentions, he can affix it to the tape; if not, he can readjust the switches to make a new sound. "It is as if in copying the parts," Babbitt says, "you can hear them performed at the same time."

The composer can also place one sound atop another (as is standard in tape doctoring), transform live sounds and even program wholly original scales. Babbitt uses the machine for such serial compositions as *Ensembles for Synthesizer* (1964) and *Philomel* (1964). As it lacks an esthetic conscience, the Synthesizer could just as well produce rock 'n' roll. In short, unlike the tape laboratories, which require that sound be transferred from one machine to another, the Synthesizer does all its work itself. Along with other composers, Babbitt is eagerly interested in a wholly new adaptation of electronics to music composition—the use of computers—and, for a projected opera, he is toying with the idea of using a computer to compose visual patterns directly on film. (Babbitt still also creates pieces for live musicians. He recently finished *Relata I* for the Cleveland Orchestra and is working on *Relata II* for the 125th anniversary of the New York Philharmonic.)

Just as Cage's music implies a revolution in listening, where one hears everything in a performance situation, Babbitt implies that the content of a piece is not a single line of sound but a number of developing structures. Ideally, rather than perceiving only one line of development, the trained listener should be able to identify how each note contributes to the several serial patterns. To most ears, Babbitt's music sounds more interesting than Cage's. The latter's pieces invariably sound more stylized—"Cagean"—than their underpinning ideas would forecast. But Cage would respond that if we hear only the music intentionally played we suffer from narrow minds.

For both Babbitt and Cage, then, the compositional methods become the real subject of the piece; for just as Cage's music is essentially an exploration of indeterminacy, so Babbitt's subject is literally the permutations of serial patterns. Although Babbitt admits that his music is written for a specialist audience consisting largely of other composers, he still believes, optimistically, that "anyone who hears well can be educated to appreciate my music. The more you listen to serial music, the better able you are to recognize its grammar, its modes of procedure." Indeed, Babbitt's optimism matches Cage's. Whereas Cage believes that music had a new birth once man recognized that everywhere was music, so Babbitt says: "Sometimes I think that music is just beginning, reborn with such an utterly different musical language."

Like Cage, Babbitt grew up far from New York—in Jackson, Mississippi. He counts the novelist Eudora Welty among his oldest friends. "Her father was the president of the insurance company of which my father was vice president." Of his own ancestry he adds: "Nobody believes this, but one of my great-grandfathers was a rabbi; another was a metropolitan [of the Russian Orthodox Church]." Able to live with this incongruity, Babbitt blames a certain popular novel by Sinclair Lewis for "some unpleasant experiences in my youth."

He came to Manhattan to attend New York University and has lived there ever since. He now resides with his wife, Sylvia, and his daughter, Betty Ann, in a modest, music-and-book-filled apartment near Gramercy Park and commutes to Princeton twice a week, where he is Conant Professor of Music.

Gifted with the capacity to talk forever, and the talent to be continually interesting, Babbitt is a popular guest lecturer and symposiast. After years of fulfilling a horrendous variety of commitments, he has learned to carry with him a little book of staves and jot down notes, whether he is on a subway or at lunch. A Southern gentleman by upbringing, he is scrupulously polite; a radical by inclination, he can be nasty about his dislikes and disagreements.

"Having learned to read music," as he puts it, "soon after I learned to read books, about four or so," he studied various instruments, quickly specializing in reeds. "I was doing gigs at ten years old," he remembers, "and I played in high school and college bands and orchestras, even in a jazz orchestra." He began to compose before he turned ten; by 1929, at thirteen, some of his popular songs had won contests and he became a professional pop-song composer. By the time he graduated from high school, he says, "I had done so much work for Harms [the pop-song publisher] that I faced the choice of serious composition or popular." Although he opted for the former, he continued into the 1940s to write "gobs of popular songs, to see if I could make a living at it. I couldn't." He did the score for the movie *Into the Good Ground* (1949), grateful today that the print on television omits his name from the credits; and, in 1946, he wrote the score and some lyrics for a musical adaptation of Homer's *Odyssey,* tentatively entitled "Fabulous Voyager," that never got out to sea.

Mathematics has always been Babbitt's second love. He studied it extensively at college, even undertaking some graduate work in logic and algebra. During the Second World War, as he confessed in Dwight Macdonald's *Politics* magazine some years ago, he became a math teacher in lieu of combat. (Suffering from weak eyesight, he would have made a less than competent foot soldier.) He sprinkles both his lecturing and writing with basic mathematical terms ("set," "determinant," "permutation," "invariant"). Rumor has it that the music professors at another Eastern school employed a math graduate student as a tutor "so that we can talk with Babbitt." "If not for Schoenberg," Babbitt once said, "I would have gone into mathematics. Schoenberg hit upon a technique that made composition more interesting and challenging."

What Babbitt and Cage have in common is that American quality of willingness to assimilate certain European ideas and push them to their extreme conclusions. Cage allows that all sounds, even unintentional ones, are music—total chance. Babbitt extends the serial principles to all aspects of the composition—total control. So what they also have in common is an unwillingness to approve the work of the other. Babbitt in his more generous moments will say that Cage "is less concerned with musical structure than with theater." In turn, Cage, who once complimented Babbitt as the "most accomplished and adventurous representative" of serial composition in America, now says that, though he dislikes quarrels as a matter of principle, he feels that Babbitt's music represents "an escape from one's experience rather than an engagement with it." Although they exchange cordial public pleasantries, Cage and Babbitt talked extensively only once—nearly twenty years ago, when Cage had just returned from Paris with some recent scores of European composers. Today each admits that he has little to say to the other.

Nonetheless, as people, they have much in common—not only a provincial background and expansive conversational abilities but also a love of old movies on television, a highly developed sense of humor, a fondness for their own jokes. Intellectually, they regard music as both a science and an art. Neither looks upon composition as self-expression, Babbitt seeing it as purely intellectual creation, and Cage attempting to deny his intellect along with his taste and emotional proclivities. Both write essays, each having achieved a distinctive style. Cage has collected his miscellaneous writings in *Silence* (1961) and the forthcoming *A Year from Monday,* both published by Wesleyan University Press. Babbitt is compiling a collection of his.

Both are philosophers *manqués,* with Cage preferring Zen Buddhism (which he learned from D. T. Suzuki) and Babbitt favoring an opposing strain of logical empiricism. Both subscribe to the political implications of their musical thought, Cage being an anarchist and Babbitt a conservative with anarchist sympathies. Each evinces that kind of engaging charm, coupled with a messianic purposefulness, that makes him the leader of a school of composers, most of whom do not subscribe to all of the leader's extreme precepts.

Together, Babbitt and Cage may make the situation of the young composer tremendously difficult; but without these two American eccentrics, and their diametric differences, the native musical scene would be a considerably duller place indeed.

MILTON BABBITT'S
TEXT-SOUND ART (1987)

To my tastes, the best Babbitt is his compositions for the alleged Mark II Synthesizer—I say "alleged," because, as no other composer publicly acknowledges using it, there is reason to doubt its existence. Nevertheless, within that general etiology, I've always treasured the three pieces for texts and synthesized accompaniment: *Vision and Prayer* (1961), *Philomel* (1964) and *Phonemena* (1974), regarding each as an advance over its predecessor.

For the first, Babbitt took a twelve-stanza emblematic poem by Dylan Thomas. The first six stanzas are diamond-shaped, having lines with only one syllable at their top, and then increasing by one syllable for each line to a maximum of nine syllables at their midsection before returning to one; and the last six have the opposite hourglass form of nine syllables on top decreasing to one in the middle before returning to nine at the bottom.

To understand what was done to this rigorously structured text, it is best to quote Babbitt's masterful, inimitable description (epitomizing as it does Robert Frost's suggestion that true poetry is what cannot be translated):

> The temporal, sonic and pattern characteristics of this poetic structure, as well as certain interpretations of these properties in strictly musical terms, were initial determinants of both musical details and the large-scale disposition of the compositional sections. The cumulative musical progression from these details to the sections, and to the totality of which these sections are members, is achieved by trichordal and hexachordal derivation, harmonic succession through aggregates—within which the polyphony and the counterpoint are shaped by the properties of the work's third-order combinatorial set, and by the increased dimensionality—the refinements with and the compoundings of primary dimensions—easily and precisely afforded by the electronic medium.

Theory notwithstanding, this setting of the Thomas text is filled with those rapid articulations, scrupulously nonrepetitive, that I've always found superlative in Babbitt's music. There is also some gorgeous composing for language, especially in the second hour-glass stanza; and some ingenious musical clarification of the poetry's ambiguities.

What Babbitt has done is rescue one of Thomas's more obscure poems, an atypical poem Thomas did not record himself, avoiding the problem of needing to transcend the poet's own "setting." (Indeed, it was courageous of Babbitt to tackle Thomas who, among all modern poets except Carl Sandburg, was the best at reciting his own poetry, whose recitals gave his lines the sound that most of us tend to hear.) Nonetheless, I should add that to my ears the second half of Thomas's poem is more articulate, simply because of its hourglass form—language progressing from more to less to more is more comprehensible than the reverse. Also, those of us familiar with this work have become so accustomed to Bethany Beardslee's performance I question whether anyone else will ever sing this as persuasively. (In the course of researching this appreciation I learned in passing: (1) There was an earlier version for piano and voice. (2) Permission to use the poem was obtained directly from Thomas himself, around 1952, at Connolly's Bar, Third Avenue and Twenty-third Street, in the presence of the poet John Berryman, who later had to vouch for Thomas's promise.)

Philomel has a looser text, free verse composed especially for Babbitt by John Hollander, an American poet who is also an accomplished scholar; and this piece advances beyond its predecessor in electronically transforming the human voice (Beardsley's) into an entity that sings apart from the live soloist, and also in synthesizing spectacular speech choruses which would be impossible in live performance. (My favorites are the faint choral echoes that sound almost like electronic imprinting.) Again, there is a difference between words that are sung and words only spoken, but in this piece Babbitt introduces fluctuations between semantic speech and nonsemantic, or between comprehensible words and semantically indefinite vocables.

The problem here is the text. One distinguishing mark of Babbitt's settings of poetry is that, unlike too much other contemporary music in this mode, his words can be understood. Nonetheless, my ears are scarcely alone in finding the repeated refrain of *Philomel*'s third part a bit thuddish:

Thrashing, through the woods of Thrace.

And my sensory apparatus succumbs to such heavy rhymes as:

> Emptied, unfeeling and unfulfilled
> By trees here where no birds have trilled—
> Feeling killed
> Philomel stilled
> Her honey unfulfilled.

which to make the experience more cumbersome are sung once live and then, for the last three lines, repeated on tape!

Some of the loveliest writing for voice and synthesized electronic accompaniment occurs in the middle of the third and last section, around such lines as:

> I ache in change
> Though once I grew
> At a slower pace.
> And now I range

all of which is sublime until we hear again "thrashing," etc. And a few lines later, the same thing happens—a beautiful setting sabotaged by a verbal clinker. Can I be alone in wondering why there should be so many rhymes and so much else in serial music that otherwise eschews repetition? A final problem is that the recorded version isn't always clear in letting the listener know which lines are sung live and which (other than the choruses) were prerecorded.

For *Phonemena* (not "Phenomena," which is something else), Babbitt decided not to use a poet's text but to compose his own, entirely of basic speech units, phonemes, made by combining twelve vowel-based sounds with twenty-four discrete consonants, thereby making a kind of sound poem, or text-sound. Let me quote from the first sixty-two bars:

> DĒ SHĒ JĒ TĒ SHA LE RA ZHUH ĀNG SŌ THAW
>   VE THĀ Ē VI SU FŌ VŪ VU
> FU ZUH CHŪ SUH GU JĀ KŪ SHU GUH JA
> CHAH LE Ō HĀ MA LAW GŌ LE MAH DĀ THAH
>   SHĒ
> LŌ ZHU SU JAW TŌ HAH DĒ SHE
> WĀ E TŌ SHĒ MI ZA BŌ RU
> YŪ SHU RU I SHA MĀ YU ZAW
> THA GAW FE GĀ VA THA FĒ

THĒ A̱H VŪ BU WI DAW THŪ JU THU LŪ CHU HU
  THŪJ
PE MAH Ē VI CHĒ WĒ E GA̱ HI LE A̱ RŌ
VAW L YAH Ō ZO AW YŌ BAH SHŌ PǬ
LUH SAW PA SAH RA ZE RA ZHA
SHA YU KU SHU TU SHU GU ZO PO THI
MAW BĘ
VU JU Ų HU JU TĄ SU
U VŲ WŲ MU RŲ ZHUH KUH
WE NGU RU BĄ SHUH LE THE RĄ LE SHĄ LAW
  LE
GA THĪ HE SE DI̱ RAH ZHA TI DĒ AH FI DĒ WĒ
GA̱ KAH MAW PŌ WE RŪ
MA̱ NAH RA LU CHU LU NU ZŪ
LŪ GAW MA LE VŌ NU ZHE JŌ HU CHA DĒ THAH
  JAH
YĒ FU SŌ SHU DAW RI BŌ A PI VĒ
PE SHE VA̱ KUR Ē Z

Taken by itself, this is magical language, one of the pioneering poems of
the age. Not only does it reflect in vocables one of the great ideas of
modern art (seriality) but it projects that idea in linguistic materials,
semantics and syntax be damned. This is real radical poetry, pure poetry
that today's "language-centered poets," as they are called, would give
almost anything to have written two stanzas of.

    To begin to explain what is done to this text musically, I need to
quote Babbitt again, who told me that, while "neither vowels nor consonants are serialized in any independent sense, the vowels function as
instruments projecting lines in the total pitch organization as it moves
through the aggregates and the consonants project the rhythmic structure," which is to say that there is a continuous relationship between the
textual choices and musical structure. A further connection, I've been
reliably informed, is that a particular vowel, if followed through the
piece, will touch upon every class in a pitch series. The principal achievement is a text that, even though it is less accessible than those used in
the earlier piece, is every bit as *busy,* deliciously busy, as Babbitt's music.
While I admire the musical setting, and the virtuoso performances of
Lynn Webber on record and Judith Bettina live, I would also like, as an
enthusiast for sound poetry, to hear the text simply declaimed, with
comparable virtuosity and speed, to discover whether its structure would
be audible on verbals alone.

A further odd truth is that the only other composer today to make excellent text-sound from phonemes is John Cage, with whom Babbitt's name has often been paired, and more often opposed, for over two decades now!

Can my enthusiasm for these text-sound pieces be unique? Though they are frequently heard in concerts, perhaps because they attractively combine electronic tape with live performance, they are scarcely heard, for example, on my local classical music station, WNYC-FM, which is otherwise thorough and sophisticated in its programming of contemporary music.

I should add that I've known Babbitt and his ideas long enough to know that I generally hear something other than he wants me to hear, something that reflects his designs, to be sure, but in terms other than he had in mind.

CAGE'S EARLY PIANO MUSIC (1970)

The news is that within the past decade John Cage has latched on to the train of official music history. Lacking a music publisher in the late 1950s, he now finds that the august international firm of C. F. Peters is putting all his scores into commercial print. His two books, *Silence* (1961) and *A Year from Monday* (1967), have become "underground best-sellers," conspicuously displayed at every sophisticated bookshop around the world. In 1968, he was elected to that most prestigious of American cultural organizations, the National Institute of Arts and Letters.

Comparatively unrecorded a decade ago, Cage's music now appears on over a dozen discs, for almost as many labels; and those same pieces that once inspired all but unanimous critical scorn are now respectfully reviewed in the mainstream press. In short, after years beyond the fringe, Cage has become one of the most honored American composers; none today has more consequential influence on the world's contemporary art and music.

Such success might be less surprising, were Cage not a rather typical American eccentric. First of all, he originated not in that cultural "center" that runs from Boston down the coast to Washington, where everyone *au courant* in the arts today knows his name. No, Cage was born in Los Angeles, in 1912, the son of an inventor; and he attended not the "best" schools but the local public places, graduating as valedictorian from Los Angeles High School. He then went not to an Ivy League university or to a "progressive" arts school but to nearby Pomona College. However, there Cage repudiated his booming career as a top student for some rebellious intellectual gestures, and these hastened his departure to Europe, where he worked in architecture and dabbled in painting, poetry and composing.

After eighteen months abroad, he returned home and labored for a spell as a gardener and even gave housewives some modestly remunerated lectures on modern art. He showed his earliest scores (since lost) to a local pianist named Richard Bühlig, who accepted Cage as a pupil and later recommended sending them to the eminent avant-garde composer Henry Cowell. It was Cowell's enthusiasm that arranged for the first public performance of Cage's music. Cowell later advised the young man to come to New York to study with him and with Adolph Weiss.

The "contemporary" musical world at that time was divided between Stravinskyan neoclassicists, who favored tonality and traditional overarching structures, and the serialists, who advocated the new musical language invented by Arnold Schoenberg. In his first crucial musical decision, Cage opted for the latter, and in 1934 he returned to Los Angeles to study with Schoenberg, who had recently emigrated there. "Several times I tried to explain to Schoenberg that I had no feeling for harmony," Cage has reminisced. "He told me that without a feeling for harmony I would always encounter an obstacle, a wall through which I wouldn't be able to pass. My reply was in that case I would devote my life to beating my head against the wall." By that point, Cage was a committed composer, as prepared as every American eccentric to risk scorn and failure in pursuit of his predilections.

From his musical beginnings, Cage regarded the piano as his primary musical instrument; and maturing out of a childhood ambition to devote himself to performing Edvard Grieg, he later earned much of his modest income by accompanying dancers. (Indeed, many of his early piano works were first composed for the dance pieces of his closest professional associate, the choreographer Merce Cunningham.) And so, too, the piano music written between 1935 and 1948 becomes a paradigm of Cage's general musical progress in the earliest period of his compositional career.

Two pieces composed in 1935, when Cage was twenty-three, used simple structures (which Cage calls "motives") subjected to a series of variations in two pianistic voices; for if the emphasis in Western music had long been on tonal relationships, Cage resolved instead to cultivate his particular incapacity and call attention to rhythm. Few early pieces were harmonically organized; for following Schoenberg's dictum about the importance of all-determining form, Cage concentrated, instead, on structuring duration. *Metamorphosis* (1938) reveals a highly personal application of the serial principle, as both interval and rhythm are strictly fixed, though the row itself is subject to the standard serial manipulations of inversion, retrograde and retrograde-inversion.

So Cage's opening works displayed a taste for one of the great ideas of modern art—the use of imposed constraints to avoid old-fashioned habits, such as tonality and rhythm. That is, the limiting rules function paradoxically to *free* Cage's compositional decisions from conventional patterns; nothing composed by serial procedures, for instance, could possibly sound like Grieg. In fact, compositional constraints can include not only structural ideas, like serial procedures, but physical hazards, like Cage's most notorious device for deflecting habit, as well as perhaps his father's son's most famed invention—the "prepared piano," first used in *Bacchanale* (1938).

"The need to change the sound of the instrument," Cage later noted, "arose through the desire to make an accompaniment, without employing percussion instruments, suitable for the dance by Syvilla Fort for which it was composed." Cage at the time had been collecting an arsenal of percussion instruments, so that his doctoring of the piano, usually by inserting bolts or large wooden screws between the strings, connected one instrumental enthusiasm to another, that is, preparing the piano transformed an instrument of limited timbre into a more various percussion orchestra under the control of a single player.

What seemed at the time a most radical innovation now takes its place in a respectable modern tradition that extends musical atonality into nonpitched sounds or "noise." Atonal music, we remember, admitted the full range of tones—twelve between the octave scale—into a composition; and a succession of twentieth-century composers have strived for sounds between those half tones. Charles Ives was perhaps the first, in pieces composed for two pianos tuned a quarter tone apart; and Henry Cowell himself created severe pianistic dissonances, such as those made by depressing whole blocks of successive tones, that bore no aural resemblance to "atonality." Perhaps Cage's most influential precursor was Edgard Varèse's *Ionisation* (1931), a totally percussive piece which employed such nonpitched sound generators as sirens and brake drums. As aware of his own purposes as every intelligent artist, in 1937 Cage could write prophetically, "I believe that the use of noise to make music will continue and increase until we reach a music produced through the aid of electrical instruments which will make available for musical purposes any and all sounds that can be heard."

Cage's later pieces for the prepared piano extended these ideas, as he uses in *The Perilous Night* (1944), *Root of an Unfocus* (1944) and *Sonatas and Interludes* (1946–48) not only bolts and wooden screws but also glass and rubber, all to distort considerably the pitch, duration, timbre and envelope (degree of attack and decay) of the original piano sounds. The scores for these pieces, as well as others composed at this time, contain conventional musical notations; but customarily attached are some highly detailed illustrated instructions for doctoring the instrument for that particular piece. "These mutes produce a variety of timbres whose pitch and tone quality," Cowell wrote appreciatively, "suggest the sound of gamelan or the jalatarange, with some delicate buzzes, clacks, hums and sometimes an unaltered tone as well."

The piano piece *Tossed As It Is Untroubled* (1943), introduces a new rhythmic system based on numerical procedures for relating small parts to large parts; and schemes of this kind were subsequently pursued in

Prelude for Meditation (1944) and *Music for Marcel Duchamp* (1947), which was originally composed to accompany the Duchamp sequence of Hans Richter's avant-garde film *Dreams That Money Can Buy* (1948). Even radical art inevitably reveals precursors, and these pieces sound somewhat like the Polynesian music that Cage assimilated in Cowell's classes at the New School.

The composer-critic Virgil Thomson, writing in 1945, judged that all these inventions left Cage "free to develop the rhythmic element of composition, which is the weakest element in the Schoenbergian style, to a point of sophistication unmatched in the technique of any other living composer." Indeed, their distinctive rhythms and unusual tonalities make these pieces as instantly recognizable as Cage's own face and voice; for the paradox is that although his compositional constraints largely function to deny both personal habit and tasteful choice, they also create a particular style of *sound in time* that is unmistakably Cagean. *Dreams* (1948), a piano piece originally composed for Cunningham, depends upon sustaining resonances for unusually long durations; and *Suite for Toy Piano* (1948) exploits the instrument's unusual timbre and the restricted range of tones—the nine "white" keys from the E below middle C to the F above.

The historical irony is that pieces so radical at their origins now seem so obviously acceptable, if not charming, as well as a bit dated. In Nicolas Slonimsky's judgment, "it takes approximately twenty years to make an artistic curiosity out of a modernistic monstrosity and another twenty to elevate it to a masterpiece." The remarkable truth is that the avant-garde revolution initiated by Varèse and Cage has long since been won—witness both the dissonance and electronics used by rock groups. "How else can you explain a phenomenon like this," Cage recently observed, "in 1933, '34, '35, somewhere along there, it took seventy-five rehearsals to put on Edgard Varèse's *Ionisation*. Right now, with students out of the Midwest at the University of Illinois, with two rehearsals we can get a better performance." And Cage himself, needless to say, has pursued his earlier predelictions for antitonal, antistructural sounds through a succession of aurally chaotic pieces, produced by unusual instrumental combinations ranging up to whole armies of electronic sound generators.

Nonetheless, he still exhibits a special affection for his primary instrument. His single most notorious composition (or anticomposition), the "silent piece" officially entitled *4'33"* (1952), was originally composed for piano; but since no intentional sounds are made, it could just as legitimately be performed on any other instrument(s). And one of Cage's most recent works, *Cheap Imitation* (1969), is intentionally an imitation, produced by formulas of piano compositions by Erik Satie, who also favored the keyboard for his compositions. To John Cage's inventiveness, for piano and everything else, there has since 1948 been no end.

THE KEYSTONE OF THE
CAGEAN CANON (1989)

There is no question that John Cage ranks among the most prolific contemporary composers. His current catalogue lists over one hundred separate scores, some of which represent higher musical peaks than others. Since Cage, like no other major composer in history, has had a reputation and influence apart from an appreciation of his musical creations, listeners new to his work are often puzzled and disappointed. As an admirer, I'm reminded of the rule that "only the good ones count" in establishing not only an artist's reputation but our appreciation of his or her work and thus feel obliged to identify the very best compositions: in my most severe judgment, *Europera* (1987), *Roaratorio* (1979), *HPSCHD* (1969), *Williams Mix* (1952), and *Sonatas and Interludes* (1948) and no more than one other. (In several interviews, Cage himself has identified his best single work as *4'33"* [1952], his so-called silent piece; but those who concur are mostly his detractors!)

One quality that these Cagean masterpieces have in common is a grandness of conception—they take a single idea and explore it exhaustively, at length. As Cage said in another context, "What we want now is quantity; we get quality automatically." In *Europera,* the idea is an inclusive pastiche of not just a few classic operas but the whole operatic tradition! *Roaratorio* is an acoustic "adaptation" of James Joyce's *Finnegans Wake* that is as Irish and yet as universal as the original. In *HPSCHD,* the idea is the grandest mix of harpsichord music from Mozart to the present on one hand and scrupulously uninflected microtonal din on the other. In *Williams Mix,* he used the newly developed technology of audiotape for a capability unprecedented in audio storage media— it could be cut apart into small fragments that can then be reassembled into a continuous tape that, played at fifteen inches per second, realizes a rapidity of articulation that would be impossible with live instruments.

Cage's *Sonatas and Interludes* represents the culmination of his work with the solo prepared piano, which had been his initial musical invention in the late 1930s, a decade before. Essentially, into the bed of piano strings he put such objects as large wooden screws, bolts of various sizes, pieces of plastic and rubber—in short, a panoply of devices that transformed the sound of the piano strings. In retrospect we can say that by discovering alternate acoustics for a row of keys, Cage's prepared piano became a pioneering prelude to the electronic pianos and synthesizers that surround us today, with their expanding rhythmic and tonal range within a context (and keyboard) that echoes the classic instrument. (A similar contemporary paradox is that true dexterity at the personal computer depends upon the late nineteenth-century art of touch-typing!)

What makes the *Sonatas and Interludes* more significant than Cage's other prepared piano pieces from that time is not only its greater length but its completeness. It is indicative that though many works for solo prepared piano came before this masterwork, only one, and it much shorter, followed it. (Two consequential successors, *34'46.776"* and *31'57.1499"*, both from 1954, are for prepared piano in possible concert with other instruments.) The success of the *Sonatas and Interludes* partly accounts for why, in the following year, 1949, Cage received his first major awards—not only a Guggenheim Fellowship but a grant from the National Institute of Arts and Letters. It, more than anything else he had done to that time, showed his colleagues that Cage, then in his mid-thirties, should be considered an important composer.

The score for this work has notes on staves, in the great tradition of compositions for piano, in addition to an oft-reprinted chart of precise instructions about what objects to lay on the piano and where. Nonetheless, what the use of sound modifiers introduced into Cage's music was indeterminacy, which is to say that the aural results would include unexpected sounds that would not only never happen with unimpeded piano strings but probably would not happen in subsequent performances either. Only later did Cage provide graphic "scores" that were more pointedly designed to encourage not just performers' flexibility but more radical preconditions for creating aural surprise.

In their ambitious scope and the quality of individual moves, the *Sonatas and Interludes* also belongs among other exhaustive modern masterpieces for the piano—Shostakovitch's *Preludes and Fugues* (1950-51), Hindemith's *Ludus Tonalis* (1943), Messaien's *Vingt regards sur l'enfant Jésus* (1944) and William Duckworth's *The Time Curved Preludes* (1979). Listen to Cage's masterwork once, and you will recognize that it holds its own in that most distinguished company.

The truth to remember is that Cage was first a pianist, which is how the musicians union has always classified him; and to the extent that any individual instrument can be at the root of his compositional imagination, it is the piano. It is indicative that not only this earliest masterpiece but his *4'33"* should have been for piano; but just as that "silent piece" was superseded a decade later by *0'00"* (1962), which is permission for any activity for any duration ("a solo to be performed in any way by anyone"), so Cage's later masterpieces have been for other instruments.

About his *Sonatas and Interludes* Cage has made two statements which have been reprinted before and, given their appropriateness, should be reprinted again (because they cannot be adequately paraphrased). The first deals with his sense of the piece's philosophical themes: "After reading the work of Ananda K. Coomaraswamy, I decided to attempt the expression in music of the 'permanent emotions' of [East] Indian traditions: the heroic, the erotic, the wondrous, the mirthful, sorrow, fear, anger, the odious and their common tendency toward tranquility."

Then, in a 1964 catalogue of his compositions, appear these remarks about the work's structure: "The first eight, the twelfth, and the last four sonatas are written in AABB rhythmic structures of varying proportions, where the first two interludes have no structural repetitions. This difference is exchanged in the last two interludes and the sonatas nine through eleven which have respectively a prelude, interlude and postlude." On the other hand, given that nonclimactic, nonhierarchical structure has always been typical of Cage's work, one gets the impression that the sections could indeed be played in a different order.

It has long been said that Cage is a composer not of talent but of genius, and that is not untrue. As his principal teacher Arnold Schoenberg told him that he had no "feeling for harmony," his subsequent career could be seen as representing a series of inspired strategies around, or compensations for, this inadequacy. Cage has also admitted that he has "no ear for music," which is to say that his scores do not tell him exactly how his pieces will sound. Only in performance can he "hear" his work; the key to his experimental attitude is that he discovers by doing (or having it done). One reason he has worked so far outside the musical tradition was those insufficiencies that might have discouraged a lesser imagination instead became the foundation of an alternative enduring edifice. His example remains an inspiration to all of us handicapped artists.

JOHN CAGE:
SOME RANDOM REMARKS (1969)

To be unpolitical does not mean to be without politics.
Every attitude that is more than egoistic is to that
extent social, and a social attitude is a political
attitude.—Herbert Read,
"The Politics of the Unpolitical" (1943)

John Cage is one of these rare figures whom, if he did not already exist, the philistines would need to invent. Not only are his ideas so original that they all but beg to be misunderstood and/or misinterpreted, but his is the sort of eccentricity that unenlightened minds can smugly dismiss without experiencing a glimmer of revelation. It is true that some of his activities, which generate first-level newspaper copy, also arouse suspicions of fraudulence; however, many retrospectively unquestioned "breakthroughs" in all contemporary arts at first struck even sophisticated intelligences as suspect. Indeed, even beneath Cage's comedy and his propensity for unprecedented actions are eminently serious purposes. What makes uncomprehending criticism more irrelevant, if not more pernicious, than undiscriminating adulation is that Cage, very much like two of his own gurus, Marshall McLuhan and Norman O. Brown, is a fount of richly imaginative ideas that cannot be rejected or accepted in toto. Even though these ideas usually attract more comment than commentary, more rejection than reflection, he is, to increasingly common opinion, clearly among the dozen seminal figures in the arts today. Quite simply, much of what he says is valuable and digestible, though much is also chaff; yet the task of winnowing poses a multifarious critical challenge which has not, in my memory, been too eagerly or thoroughly assumed. As his new book, *A Year from Monday* (1967), a second collection of fugitive pieces, provides a propitious occasion for more comprehensive scrutiny, let me start by saying that this is rich in ideas relevant to all sorts of artistic, philosophical and social endeavors. Cage is so emancipated from professional conventions that he is free to follow his imagination into any medium and risk innovative work in areas other than music. Though his ideas invite disagreement, even from the sophisticated, I doubt if any open-minded and intelligent person would not be challenged—surely irritated, perhaps persuaded to change his mind—in the course of perusing this compendium of provocative aphorisms, intellectual flights and formulations so original they will doubtlessly make sense to some, nonsense to others. However, just as Cage no longer finds himself able to write a linear expository essay (and his book itself cannot be "read" in the conventionally linear way), so I find myself unable to compose a traditionally structured critical piece about him. *A Year from Monday* is so fertile and various that one must dip in, pick out and think about whatever strikes the mind, and that process itself informs the structure of these miscellaneous paragraphs. A further truth is that writing about Cage brings out, for better and worse, one's courage for waywardness.

One must initially acknowledge Cage's indisputable originality in an age that suspects everything has already been done; for nearly all that he makes, whether in art or life, is riddled by idiosyncratic and imaginative touches. He talks like no one else, conducts his personal existence like no one else, composes performance pieces like no one else and, as this book amply demonstrates, writes as no one else would dare. (Even its original price, $7.92, represents a minor innovation, which is perhaps part of a one-man campaign to induce 1 percent as an appropriate sales tax.) He takes even his most comic ideas very seriously and asks us to do so too, and laugh as well. His penchant for the unusual gives his writing the quality of constant surprise; and, for this reason, much of it evades immediate comprehension, though his thought is not particularly complex. Even at the beginnings of his artistic career, over thirty years ago, Cage managed to be ahead of the herds; and, as he continues to forge new frontiers, even the most aggressive younger bulls graze art-historically behind their esthetic daddy. Although fashionable to a degree, Cage continually thinks *ahead* of current intellectual pieties, including those that, to some extent, reflect his influence. True, his private enthusiasms have a way of becoming public fads, although he has no enterprise to sponsor them and collects no royalties on his recommendations. In contrast to Cage, transient fashion, in Alain Robbe-Grillet's phrase, "imitates the modern forms without feeling their necessity." Cage's essays and conversations are studded, for instance, with the names and remarks of intellectual celebrities, in addition to close friends (who are sometimes also intellectual celebrities) and several unfamiliar names; and since certain unknowns he enthusiastically quoted a few years ago are now more familiar cultural figures—McLuhan, Jasper Johns and Buckminster Fuller among them—touts on incipient intellectual fashion might be well advised to bet on Cage's new oft-dropped touchstones of wisdom. In this new book, the author of a revolution in music clearly wants to accomplish something similar for prose; and although the desired breakthrough still seems a few steps away, Cage is by now discernibly beyond literary conventions. "My pleasure in composition, renounced as it has been in the field of music, continues in the field of writing words; and that explains why, recently, I write so much." In his earlier collection of pieces, *Silence* (1961), the later essays eschewed linear organization for the structure of random comments; and, in the new book, few collections of sentences are even as approximately linear as this paragraph. The discontinuous compositional style seems an appropriate vehicle for Cage's invariably unconventional thoughts, as well as an approximate literary analogy for his scrupulously discontinuous music, yet precisely because the style continually risks obscurity, it signifies that Cage is still more of an artist than a propagandist.

One radical artistic idea that Cage has pushed beyond its previous provinces is the work of art as *primarily* an esthetic illustration. The illustrative point of *4'33"* (1952), which consists of four minutes and thirty-three seconds of David Tudor, an established musician, sitting silently at the piano, is that all the unintentional, random sounds framed within that auditorium and within that period of time can be considered "music," for "doing nothing," as the critic Jill Johnston notes, is clearly "distinct from expressing nothing." By investing a situation where sophisticated contemporary music is expected with nothing but silence (and where, as in the original performance, the well-known performer three times moves his arms in ways that suggest the piece has three distinct movements), Cage implied that in the silence was "music" that could be heard; this polemical illustration is an example of "art by subtraction" to the point that negation produces addition—in Mies van der Rohe's felicitous phrase, "Less is more."

Since Cage invariably takes the intellectual leaps his radical ideas imply, he subsequently concluded that not only were any and all sounds "music," but the time-space frame of *4'33"* was needlessly arbitrary, for unintentional music is indeed with us—available to the ear that wishes to perceive it—in all spaces and at all times. (*Variations III* [1964], he once told me over dinner, is so open, "We could be performing it right now, if we decided to do so." Another time he mentioned juvenile pieces composed by mathematical rules that "I destroyed because they didn't sound musical to me then, though I would probably think differently now.") From this, too, would inevitably follow another thesis, which holds that just as one does not naturally discern why one period of

"silence" is better than another, but rather perceives personal significances in chaotic experience, so it is likewise irrelevant to evaluate one
conglomeration of noise against another. What mattered, quite simply,
was what the perspicacious ear managed to apprehend, if not appreciate.
"Value judgments are destructive to our proper business, which is curiosity and awareness," he often says. "How are you going to use this
situation if you are there? This is the big question."

However, Cage also realized that, rather than deduce himself out
of a career, he as an artist could program sound-generating instruments
to produce an aural experience as random and miscellaneous as the
unintentional noise on the street; and most of his performance pieces
since the middle 1950s have been unstructured, indeterminate, multifarious events. It is customary to call these works "chance" music;
but since chance per se is not perceptible, I prefer to characterize them
as musically chaotic. As artistic wholes, these works differ from life in
expressing a heightened incoherence, an appropriate scale, an absence
of visual and aural focus—an ordered disorder, which is perceptibly
different from disordered disorder. (Thus does Cage allow his artistry
to compromise his theoretical position.) Most are also flat in structure,
thoroughly lacking climax, development, emphasis, pacing, contours
and variations, so that their components need merely be turned on
until turned off by a formally irrelevant decision (for example: no more
pages left in the score, the audience has completely departed, it's midnight and so on).

At the root of Cage's compositional principles is collage—the mixing of materials not normally heard together; but, because he is less
interested in barbed juxtaposition than abundant mixtures, the result is
less collage than something distinctly Cagean. That roughly explains
why an experienced ear, though it may not have heard a particular piece
or rendition before, can usually identify a certain unfamiliar piece as
Cage's work and not another's. In *Theatre Piece* (1960), he pursued an
implication of *Music Walk* (1958) by suggesting that a plethora of physical actions could, by a performer's choice, be substituted for randomly
activated sound-generating procedures; and, since he had previously
ruled that all sounds are music, this instruction eventually implied, by
analogy, that "theater" could be said to exist as soon as the perceiver's
mind wished to define it. "Theater takes place all the time, wherever one
is," Cage wrote in *Silence,* "and art simply facilitates persuading one this
is the case." Nonetheless, it is precisely in their realized inchoateness
and, in Cage's phrase, "purposeful purposelessness," as well as extravagantly spectacular qualities, that his own recent theater pieces distin-

guish themselves from both ordinary life (merely the "model" for the art) and others' "happenings" theater.

In retrospect, then, the primary significance of *4'33"* lies precisely in its inferences, which gave Cage and others "reason" or "permission" to create eventually a musical theater that is indeterminate not only in its composition but its performance too—aleatory kinetic presentational structures that are chaotic in both structure and detail. What is most conspicuously lacking in *A Year from Monday* is an analogous path-breaking gesture that could command as much suggestive influence for literature as his earlier "musical" demonstrations. The blank piece of paper is by now too obvious, if not, as we would now say, "Mallarmé's piece"; and the inferential idea of cellophane as a frame, which is perhaps the closest analogue in the visible arts to silence in music, appeared as a passing remark in my introduction to *The New American Arts* (1965), although I then lacked sufficient courage and/or professional reputation to put it on display. Regrettably, Cage has not particularly developed his stunningly suggestive assertion in *Silence:* "I have nothing to say and I am saying it and that is poetry." Maybe such a radical printed literary work cannot exist—if I could conceive it, I might do it myself; but, in principle, I hesitate to make such blanket negative statements about the future of Cage, or literary art.

Adopting the musical notion of unashamedly artificial constraints to literary purposes, Cage posits unprecedented ground rules that serve to emancipate him from conventional ways of organizing and rendering words. An instance of this is *Indeterminacy* (1958), consisting of ninety funny stories, each of which, by self-imposed rule, will be a minute in length when read aloud. When Cage performs this piece on a Folkways record of that title (1959), while David Tudor makes random noises in another room, *Indeterminacy* is very much about variations in prose tempo, as well as the random interactions between musical sounds and verbalized words. Here the form of the work expresses part of its ultimate content, as a performance illustrates (as opposed to explains) the piece's declarative title and Cage's esthetic position; therefore, the ninety funny stories, which are pleasurable in themselves and comic to various de-grees, are just the surface occasion for less obvious, but more substantial, concerns. Here, as in much else of Cage, the unperceptive spectator can be deceived into accepting the surface as the entire point—as silence is simply no sound, so stories are just anecdotes; but more significant meanings are invariably implied or inferred, by the piece, the spectator or both. However, to put these stories into conventional print, as Cage does in *Silence,* destroys much of their primary effect (corrupting their original purpose even more than recordings of Cage's recent pieces betray, as fixed renditions, their scored indeterminacy); and, in the traditions of *printed* literature, ninety funny anecdotes within a larger frame constitute no innovation at all. Similarly, another performance piece "Juilliard Lecture" (1952), published in the new book, is in its printed form all but unreadable, as is "Talk I" (1965), which, as Cage's headnote reveals, was not intended to be understood anyway.

The major pieces in *A Year from Monday* are a three-part "Diary: How to Improve the World (You Will Only Make Matters Worse)," its sections subtitled respectively the years 1965, 1966, 1967; and, in composing what he characterizes as a "mosaic of ideas, statements, words and stories," Cage posits a system of compositional constraints and indeterminate procedures (which also constrain his expression) that his headnote describes:

> For each day, I determined by chance operations how many parts of the mosaic I would write and how many words there would be in each. . . . I used an IBM Selectric typewriter to print my text. I used twelve different type-faces, letting chance operations determine which face would be used for which statement. So, too, the left marginations [*sic*] were determined, the right marginations being the result of not hyphenating words and at the same time keeping the number of characters per line forty-three or less.

In practice, these constraining procedures induce an original style with its own distinct tone and particular rhythms. The pieces of the "Diary" are "poetry," not because they manipulate poetic conventions, but because they cannot be persuasively classified as anything else. However, as a form suitable primarily for miscellaneous insights and connections, prejudices and gossip (usually to an excess), anecdotes and speculations, it is also a rather needlessly limited vehicle for verbal expression. Although it enables Cage to note unusual analogies, to make one-line suggestions, to relate one kind of position to another and to provide reviewers with numerous quotable gag lines (which are not representative of the text as a whole), this note-making format discourages the elaboration and development of thoughts, as well as granting Cage an easy escape from the necessity of pursuing the implications of his more radical ideas. On the other hand, precisely in its disconnectedness, such prose demands that the reader make his own connections. Beyond that, the form here, unlike "Indeterminacy," suggests no conceptual content that I can perceive or infer (even though previous experience with both Cage and other avant-garde materials persuades me to add that I may well be missing the significance); therefore, the primary substance of these "Diary" pieces lies not in the form but the quality of the commentary, which is inevitably erratic, instinctively radical and often stimulating. Finally, as a literary form appropriate for random remarks, this compositional process represents a successful mating of man and his makings; nothing could be more suitable, if not congenial, to an artist on the move, a man of (artistic) action, so to speak, as Cage is most of the time, as distinguished from a contemplative thinker or a professional writer. Perhaps because Cage derived an expression appropriate in form to his personal style, *A Year from Monday* is a more readable, communicative and artistically suggestive book than its predecessor.

A major theme of *A Year from Monday* is fortuitous happenstance, as the book is riddled with observations on how delightfully random both art and life can be; for out of Cage's definition of environmental reality comes his current esthetic bias. "We open our eyes and ears seeing life each day excellent as it is. This realization no longer needs art, though without art it would have been difficult (yoga, zazen, etc.) to come by." The theme of happenstance is implied in the book's title, whose spirit and significance Jill Johnston caught so well that I would like to quote it.

> [It] refers to a projected rendezvous with friends in Mexico, but who could say what would happen a year from Monday, much less a year from Tuesday, another day of interrupted designs; and so of course nobody went to Mexico, but one day Cage and Merce Cunningham bumped into Bucky Fuller in an airport outside of Madrid, which has nothing to do with the title of the book, or everything from the viewpoint of unpredictability in an ambiguous reference to time.

In another way to elaborate the theme: whatever someone plans for a year from Monday is not likely to happen, although something else will, which may be just as valuable, providing that the perceiver keeps his channels open to experience. "Only the unusual exists," runs a proverb from 'pataphysics, "and everything is unpredictable, especially the predictable." However, given the style of discourse established by Cage's philosophy and the book's title, it seems nothing but inappropriate that its pages should be chronologically numbered and then snugly bound, or that this hard-bound edition is well beyond the budgets of most avant-garde readers, or that purchasers do not need to cut open the pages (perhaps to their own designs) to read them, or that the lectures and essays and such are reprinted in more or less chronological order (as if to demonstrate some fictitious development [!] in Cage's thought) or that a tape of Cage's inimitable voice is not included; but perhaps another implicit theme is that even those artists furthest out inevitably compromise with the conventions of familiar media.

Most of the prose pieces collected in *A Year from Monday* deal with varieties of coherence in intentionally unstructured (orderly disordered) prose; and, even though Cage is more imaginative than most authors, including many of those who consider themselves "avant-garde," he neglects all the leaps his bias suggests. First of all, his headnotes to each essay are written in expository vocabulary; but, even though these notes are doubtlessly intended to make more comprehensible the material that follows, their conventionally linear form seriously compromises the revolutions in printed communications that the essays themselves imply. Second, even though each "Diary," for instance, uses an engaging variety of typefaces (thanks to IBM ingenuity), all the print is approximately of the same height; and this limitation causes another restriction in the expressive possibilities of printed words. (All the print is black—another limiting convention—although the Something Else Press has issued the third diary in a two-color edition, and the S.M.S. Press has published the fourth, dated 1968 and not collected into *Monday,* in three colors.) Third, in all the essays, not only is the type laid out in horizontal lines, but Cage also usually composes in sentences, which, though often clipped short, similarly impose unnecessary restraints. Indeed, even though he must know that precisely in syntax and linearity is the inherent conservatism of language as an expressive medium, Cage still strives for aphorisms, which are, after all, linear *bon mots.*

It seems apparent to me that, if only to follow his predilections (something he is wont to do), Cage might inevitably need to reject sentences entirely and experiment with expressively designed words, or pattern poems, which would draw upon those talents for visual composition and penmanship that are already evident in his exquisitely crafted musical manuscripts.* Nonetheless, *A Year from Monday* represents a clear stylistic progression beyond the prose in *Silence;* for, if an implicit motif of the earlier book was his quest for a literary style that would *both* express his thoughts and illustrate his esthetic ideas, now Cage has so patently forged to the frontier that I for one can see distinct territory ahead.

In the history of contemporary art, Cage functions as an antithetical catalyst, who leaps ahead so that others may move forward by steps. Late in the 1930s, he suggested prophetically that all noises, including those electronically produced, would enter the domain of serious music; and, by his use of sounds unfamiliar to concert halls, he helped establish precedents for all contemporary electronic composition. Indeed, by making art out of materials not usually familiar to art, Cage, along with his friend Marcel Duchamp, also provided antithetical precedents for pop art, found objects, industrial sculpture and much else; and Allan Kaprow, a sometime painter who originated (and christened) that performance art known as happenings, testifies that, although he personally does not subscribe to all of Cage's radical innovations, "he taught us to be free." In this respect, another implicit theme of *A Year from Monday* is that all kinds of criticism and all kinds of fiction, including critical fictions and fictitious criticism, can be put on pages, intermixed and bound between hard covers.

Cage's impact upon artists working in the musical traditions can be perceived in all aleatory composition—the works of Morton Feldman, Christian Wolff, Earle Brown, David Behrman, early La Monte Young, among many other Americans, in addition to such major European musicians as Pierre Boulez and Karlheinz Stockhausen. However, whereas all these composers adopt aleatory techniques in various ways, only Cage holds to the extreme position that regards all sounds available to the ear as music (or all movement as theater). Still, no one dares *imitate* Cage's pieces, not only because they are in some dimensions so extreme, but also because, in the world of art, a certain kind of performance event is generally known as Cage's domain. ("Others could do them," he once confessed, "but they won't.") Instead, his radical antitheses stimulate others to produce their own synthesis; for, without his radical leaps, historically there would not have been certain other steps ahead.

*Cage has since done so; in *Not Wanting to Say Anything About Marcel* (1969), the critic for once knew in advance where his avant-garde subject soon would go.

Sometimes Cage creates radical antitheses for himself to synthesize—by acting in an extreme way, perhaps with a special kind of irony, an artist can force himself to entertain new thoughts; for the fact that Cage has formally presented *4'33"* scarcely a few times persuades me to believe that he knows, first, that this piece is an ironic gesture and, second, that he sometimes takes positions finally unacceptable to sensible human beings, a category that includes himself. For instance, the first performance of *4'33"* theoretically granted him permission to explore the fullest range of sounds, both intentional and nonintentional, yet, even though *4'33"* was in a fundamental sense artless, most of these subsequent works represent a synthesis. That is, they draw, if not depend, upon the posited antithesis, as well as, of course, Cage's disciplined cleverness and his mastery of aleatory mixed-means dramaturgy. (A glint in his eye persuaded me to take the following statement ironically: "If you want to know the truth of the matter, the music I prefer, even to my own and everything, is what we hear if we are just quiet.") Similarly, although he deduces, as a radical antithesis to conventional practice, that he cannot, in principle, offer critical opinions on art or life, the synthesis is that in fact he is a very opinionated, if not dogmatic, propagandist for his idiosyncratic taste and radical esthetic positions. In *A Year from Monday,* nonetheless, there are no discernible antithetical leaps; thus, no new syntheses are likely to follow.

Critics and laymen are forever debating Cage's place in contemporary music, and part of his originality lies in continually defying the categories by which we talk and classify, if not demonstrating, by his practice, how inherently philistine might be the boundaries themselves. Historically speaking, he descended from several distinctly modern musical traditions. One was concerned with introducing sounds previously not in the language of music (for example, Edgard Varèse's *Ionisation* [1931]); a second emphasized the possible expressiveness of the theatrical space in which music was performed (for example, Charles Ives's *The Unanswered Question* [1908]); a third consistently eschewed classical tonality and structure, not for a new musical language with its own grammars of coherence, such as Schoenberg's twelve-tone system, but for more chaotic kinds of aural experiences. As a developing composer, Cage posited a succession of path-breaking stylistic positions by logical—rather, paralogical—deduction. His first discrete style was percussion music that scrupulously avoided familiar pitches and rhythms (e.g., *First Construction* [*in Metal*] [1939]), and then he invented the prepared piano, which systematically perverted, in a minimally random way, the instru-

ment's natural sounds for unusual aural effects. Particularly in the recorded *Sonatas and Interludes* (1946–48), however, Cage's pieces for his
home-brewed invention suspiciously echo the piano music of Erik Satie
that Cage has publicly praised, confirming the notion that even avant-
garde art comes out of discernibly previous art.

By the late 1940s, Cage introduced aleatory techniques into the
process of setting marks to paper, thereby abandoning premeditated
control not only over the finished score but also, in some pieces, over how
the score would eventually be performed. So far, Cage clearly remained
within musical traditions, having pursued a more or less straight path
from premeditated scores and fixed performance to chance composition
and indeterminate performance. The turnabout year was 1952, in which
he composed *Williams Mix,* a tape collage, which, I find, represents his
most valuable purely aural endeavor; presented the premiere of *4'33";*
and staged an untitled mixed-means event at Black Mountain College in
North Carolina—in retrospect, this seems to have been the first "happening" in America.

From here on, everything Cage did was, by his subsequent logical
deduction, as much indeterminate theater as indeterminate music—
Radio Music (1956) "for one to eight performers, each at one radio";
Music for Amplified Toy Pianos (1960); *Rozart Mix* (1965) for twelve tape
machines, several performers, one conductor and eighty-eight loops of
tape; *Variations V* (1965), with Merce Cunningham and his dance company, films by Stan VanDerBeek, a sensitized electronic field; the supremely spectacular theatrical environment *HPSCHD* (1969) and so on.
His "scores" for these recent pieces, though published by a music company, offer not a precise plan for articulating sound but descriptive (often
prose) instructions for generating activities that, like a football play, are
likely to run out of intentional control—that produce "indeterminate"
results. "I never imagine anything until I experience it," Cage once
declared; but this is completely contrary to one of the basic tasks of
musical training, solfège, which teaches one to regard a score and then
imagine, or hear in one's head, the finished work. In *A Year from Monday*
he defines his current art as a "process set in motion by a group of
people," a kind of activity that, in the history of human endeavor, seems
closer to noncompetitive games than esthetic artifacts.

Rather than, as some antagonists would have it, abandoning inept musical composition for "stunts," Cage became the true master of mixed-
means musical theater, perhaps the most valid American species of
"opera," that could be reviewed by the music critic or the dance critic,

by the theater critic or the art critic or, more usually, by none of them. To my sensibility, these recent pieces are far more interesting and valid as theater of mixed means, as I christened it in a book of that title (Dial, 1968), than as purely aural art; compared solely as music with Milton Babbitt's or Elliott Carter's compositions, they seem feeble indeed. For that reason, not only are records of certain recent Cage works, such as *Variations IV,* invariably embarrassing, but, in confronting a live experience of these pieces, one quickly discovers that purely musical values and categories do not provide satisfactory and/or relevant perceptual expectations or critical standards. (Also, if only to accept his pervasive Americanness, Cage ought to use the native spelling—"theater"—rather than, as he does, the European.) Indeed, in the history of theatrical events, Cage artistically descends not from literary drama but such American exemplars as vaudeville, *Hellzapoppin',* the Marx Brothers, Ives's unfinished *Universe Symphony* and the dance performance of Merce Cunningham.

Partly because of Cage's immense influence, there now exist in each of the nonliterary arts in America two avant-garde tendencies, both of which are clearly distant from nineteenth-century conventions and discernibly different from pre–1945 practice. One would isolate the intrinsic qualities of an art—serial music, minimal and optical painting, early Merce Cunningham; the second would, like Cage, miscegenate—mix in enough materials, esthetic preoccupations and structural standards from the other arts to ensure that something between or inter media is created. Almost by definition, all miscegenated art ridicules the pigeonholes of both current critical enterprise and the academic departmental system, as well as the parochial esthetic values indigenous to each art; and, perhaps until periodicals recognize that they ought to sponsor critics of mixed-means work, artists such as Cage are less likely to be widely understood, let alone appreciated. On the other hand, there is some sense, as well as some irony, in Cage's radical suggestion that, "now we have such a marvelous loss of boundaries that your criticism of a happening could be a piece of music or a scientific experiment or a trip to Japan or a trip to your local shopping market." Anything can be considered art, anything, theater; anything, criticism—although his commitments to Zen persuade him to oppose Western ideas of syllogistic logic, Cage consistently deduces an antithetical catalyst.

The news in *A Year from Monday* is that Cage has recently been renouncing music for social philosophy; but, just as he abandoned concert music for a mixed-means theater that subsumes his music, so he regards his music, which has always been about *changing peoples' minds,* as a springboard into political thought. In retrospect, we can see how much politics has always been present in his music. First of all, his music implies the abolition of archaic structures, as does his politics; and both his music and his social thought suggest that new forms ought to be built from the most essential materials:

> In music, it was hopeless to think in terms of the old
> structure (tonality), to do things following old meth-
> ods (counterpoint, harmony), to use the old materials
> (orchestral instruments). We started from scratch:
> sound, silence, time, activity. In society, no amount
> of doctoring up economics/politics will help. Begin
> again, assuming abundance, unemployment, a field
> situation, multiplicity, unpredictability, immediacy,
> the possibility of participation.

In contrast to most modern artists, who have been pessimistic about both technology and the future, Cage has, perhaps because of his "sunny disposition," always taken the optimistic side—a position that is indica-tively gaining more adherents nowadays; and his current social prophe-cies indicatively parallel his recent artistic predilections. Just as Cage's latest performance pieces shrewdly exploit various electronic media in an autonomous way, all to create a field of intentionally nonstructured activity, so Cage insists that technology can socially be considered more of a blessing than a curse. (His art is, after all, more appropriate for an age of television and take-home videotape, rather than radio and phono-graph records.)

In Cage's coherent web of related radical ideas, the major common theme is that, since great changes are still possible in both life and art, we should strive to achieve what has not already been done. Cage, in his social thought, concurs with good liberal prejudices—equality of oppor-tunity, universal civil rights, equitable distribution of economic affluence, the elimination of discrimination and segregation and so on; but, recog-nizing that liberal prejudice is not enough, he takes, as usual, several leaps ahead. As an instinctive anarchist, he favors less work rather than more, or more unemployment rather than less, as well as a guaranteed annual wage to provide for those for whom no jobs exist. "Taxation could be augmented," he remarks in passing, "to the point where no one had any money at all." Similarly, he expresses the anarchist's negative reaction to comprehensively detailed planning, noting of Le Corbusier (and, implicitly, of much modern architecture), "Art this is called. Its shape is tyranny." (Yet, he refuses to acknowledge the totalitarian tendencies in Buckminster Fuller's thought.) For situations of too much order, such as programmatic architecture and organizational bureaucracy, he champions disorder; for situations of needless disorder, he supports overall ordering, such as centrally organized and universally free public utilities. He is enough of a McLuhanite to believe that a truly global electric voltage, as well as a universal design for plugs and jacks, could have a profoundly ecumenical effect. "Alteration of global society through electronics so that world will go round by means of united intelligence rather than by means of divisive intelligence (politics, economics)." Since automated technology promises more abundant leisure, if not the possibility of endless environmental pleasure, and the obsolescence of most social and esthetic hierarchies, Cage wants to install a psychology that will allow every man to appreciate constantly the "art" around him all the time; thus do the pedagogic purposes of his musical theater link to his optimistic visions for the future. I suspect that the final vision of his ecumenical anarchism would have all of us listening to *4'33"* together.

Although his bias is "not fixing [society] but changing it so it works," what *A Year from Monday* does not offer is a practical politics—specific advice on how the golden age will come—perhaps because Cage believes that widespread mind change *precedes* social change, and he senses, not untenably, that technological development itself will initiate most of the transformations. "Once we give our attention to the practice of not-being-governed, we notice that it is increasing." This sense that the world is getting better largely on its own momentum may strike some political people as slightly naïve; but Cage's professional life exemplifies its own kind of radical activism. As a man who frequently commands audiences, spreading a certain gospel, reprogramming the heads of those who learn to appreciate his "music," offering images and proposals for a radically different future, exercising his almost Jesuitical persuasiveness—all at a time when most self-styled "radicals" offer merely negative criticisms—Cage is a harbinger-publicist for a new, necessary, comprehensive, unprecedented, unstructured, mixed-means revolution.

HPSCHD: ENVIRONMENTAL ABUNDANCE (1969)

Flashing on the outside underwalls of the huge double saucer Assembly Hall, at the University of Illinois's Urbana campus, were an endless number of slides from fifty-two projectors; and, inside, between 7:00 P.M. and just after midnight Friday evening, May 16, 1969, was a presentation of the John Cage–Lejaren Hiller collaboration, *HPSCHD* (1967–69), one of the great artistic environments of the decade. In the middle of the circular sports arena were suspended several parallel sheets of visquine, each 100 by 40 feet, and from both sides were projected numerous films and slides whose collaged imagery passed through several sheets. Running around a circular ceiling rim was a continuous 340-foot screen, and from a hidden point inside were projected slides with imagery as various as outer-space scenes, pages of Mozart music, computer instructions and nonrepresentational blotches. Beams of light were shrewdly aimed across the interior roof, visually rearticulating the modulated concrete supports. In several upper locations were spinning mirrored balls reflecting dots of light in all directions—a device reminiscent of a discotheque or a planetarium; and the lights shining directly down upon the asphalt floor also changed color from time to time. There was such an incredible abundance of things to see that the eye could scarcely focus on anything in particular; and no reporter could possibly write everything down.

The scene was bathed in a sea of sounds, which had no distinct relation to one another—an atonal and astructural chaos so continually in flux that one could hear nothing more specific than a few seconds of repetition. Fading in and out through the mix were snatches of harpsichord music that sounded more like Mozart than anything else; this music apparently came from the seven instrumentalists visible on platforms raised above the floor in the center of the Assembly Hall. Around these islands of stability were flowing several thousand people, most of them students at the university, some of whom came from far away—the museum directors from Chicago and Minneapolis, the writers, artists and film crew (doing a profile of Cage) from New York City, students who hitchhiked from all over the Midwest, and the not-young lady harpsichordist who first commissioned *HPSCHD,* all the way from Switzerland.

Most of the audience milled about the floor while hundreds took seats in the bleachers. All over the place were people, some of them supine, their eyes closed, grooving on the multiple stereophony. A few people at times broke into dance, creating a show within a show that simply added more to the mix. Some painted their faces with Day-Glo colors, while, off on the side, several students had a process for implanting on a white shirt a red picture of Beethoven wearing a sweatshirt emblazoned with John Cage's smiling face. As in the Central Park be-ins, I met friends from various places I had not seen in ages, and other people I knew before only by mail.

While co-composer Hiller checked on the machinery and its up-keep—though it scarcely mattered artistically if a few channels were lost—John Cage glided around the hall, beaming beatifically. Altogether, the sound was rather mellow and nonclimactic, except for occasional blasts of eardrum-piercing feedback that became more frequent toward the end. Just after midnight, the electronic sound machinery was turned off, the mix ran down into silence, the house lights turned on and the elated audience drifted out. At parties that night and the following day, people contrasted perceptions; and, while everyone saw the same things in general, each one registered a specific experience particularly his own.

The sounds came from fifty-eight amplified channels, each with its own loudspeaker high in the auditorium. Fifty-one channels contained computer-generated music composed in octaves divided at every integer between five and fifty-six tones to the octave (five tones, six, seven, eight, up to fifty-six, except number twelve); and since all these channels were going at once, with each operator of the four assembled tape recorders permitted to adjust their respective volumes, the result was a supremely microtonal chaos in which, as Cage's Illinois colleague Ben Johnston put it, "It was ensured that no order can be perceived."

On top of this mix, one could hear seven amplified harpsichords, for *HPSCHD* is that word reduced to the six characters necessary for computer transmission. Three were playing fixed versions of Mozart's late-eighteenth-century *Introduction to the Composition of Waltzes by Means of Dice,* in which the performer is allowed to play sections in any order he wishes. With computer assistance, Cage and Hiller realized three different fixed versions of the fragments, two of which incorporate other passages from Mozart. Two more harpsichordists, Neely Bruce and Yuji Takahashi, played through differing but individually fixed collages of harpsichord music from Mozart to the present, while David Tudor played "computer printout for twelve-tone gamut." The seventh keyboard operator, Philip Corner, had nothing more specific than blanket permission to play any Mozart he wished; and every instrumentalist received this further instruction: "In addition to playing his own solo, each harpsichordist is free to play any of the others."

In sum, then, above the microtonal din were references to Mozart, a favorite classic composer of both Cage and Hiller. "With Bach," Cage explained, "there is a tendency to fixity and unity; in Mozart, there is scalar diversity and abundance. I used to think of five as the most things we could perceive at once; but the way things are going recently, it may be in a sense of quantity, rather than quality, that we have our hope. When you use the word 'chaos,' it means there is no chaos, because everything is equally related—there is an extremely complex interpenetration of an unknowable number of centers." For all its diffusion, therefore, *HPSCHD* was an indubitably organic piece, where every element contributed its bit to the whole and which successfully established a unique and coherent ensemble of interrelated parts.

So the aural content of the work—what one should hear—is literally fifty-eight channels of sound, even though most of us can scarcely separate more than one or two from the others at any time. "You don't have to choose, really, but, so to speak, experience it," Cage added, between puffs on his filtered and mentholated cigarette. "As you go from one point of the hall to another, the experience changes; and here, too, each man determines what he hears. The situation relates to individuals differently, because attention isn't focused in one direction. Freedom of movement, you see, is basic to both this art and this society. With all those parts and no conductor, you can see that even this populous a society can function without a conductor." Cage characterized *HPSCHD* as "a political art which is not about politics but political itself. As an anarchist, I aim to get rid of politics. I would prefer to drop the question of power, whether black power, flower power, or student power. Only by looking out the back window, as McLuhan says, do we concern ourselves with power. If we look forward, we see cooperation and things being made possible, to make the world work so any kind of living can take place."

The visual material was compiled under the supervision of Ronald Nameth and Calvin Sumsion, both connected with the university, and Robert Frerck supervised the use of films. There was no dress rehearsal, nor did the piece really need one. Forty-eight people, in sum, contributed to the performance. In the course of gathering equipment, Cage persuaded an awed official of the GAF Corporation to lend eighty Sawyer projectors ("He wanted not a few but eighty!"), just as he earlier persuaded other companies to lend fifty-two tape recorders and all the amplification machinery; and art students were enlisted to paint innumerable slides. NASA lent forty films and five thousand slides (explaining the abundance of outer-space imagery) and the Museum of Modern Art extended a print of George Méliès's *Trip to the Moon* (1902). And so on and so on, all to fill up Assembly Hall with an indeterminate assembling of images, all to complement the indeterminate chaos of sounds.

Work on *HPSCHD* (pronounced Hip'-see-kid, H-P-S-C-H-D or, as Cage prefers, "harpsichord") began nearly two years ago, just after Cage arrived at Illinois as Visiting Research Professor in the School of Music and Associate of the Center for Advanced Study; on hand, he already had a standing commission from the Swiss harpsichordist Antoinette Vischer. Wanting to "make with the computer an art that has not been possible before," he sought out Lejaren Hiller, who pioneered computer-assisted composition, and together they produced the fifty-two tapes, many of which were composed with the *I Ching* randomizing procedures Cage has long favored. "Every single note was a mutual decision," Hiller declared. "It's a rather unique instance that two composers' endeavors are so intertwined that you cannot tell them apart." Nonetheless, the total conception of *HPSCHD* seems more distinctly Cage's than Hiller's, whose reputation stems from the use of computers rather than a distinct style; and, within the extant repertoire of electronic music, these tapes sound rather simple and repetitious. Cage's regular music publisher, C. F. Peters, plans to release a several–hundred–page "score," with seven different harpsichord parts, and "a particular condensation of the piece," as Hiller puts it, has just been released by Nonesuch Records (H-71224). Although only three of the harpsichord parts are included, the record offers a more intensified (and, shall we say, artful) aural chaos than the diffuse original; but that perhaps is precisely what a recording should do. Each album also includes a computer-printed instruction that, to quote Hiller, "tells the listener how to turn the volume- and tone-controls every five seconds to hear the piece properly. Every sheet is different, so you can trade it off like baseball cards." Although recording is not an appropriate medium for this aleatory and spatial art, this remains, in my opinion, the best (and most) Cagean record ever made.

HPSCHD was not just a musical light show or an extravagant multimedia display but a masterful example of that peculiarly contemporary art, the kinetic environment, or an artistically activated enclosed space. In this respect, *HPSCHD* extends Cage's continuing interest in filling huge spaces with a lifelike chaos of sounds and sights, or building an artful universe within the larger world. Here, as before, Cage prefers nontheatrical spaces, like a gymnasium or a "stock pavilion" (scene of a 1967 Urbana piece), for his multiringed, highly theatrical artistic circus. Who would believe, before Cage arrived, that Urbana's Assembly Hall itself could be transformed into a work of art? Whereas *Variations VII*, by all counts the best piece at the 1966 Theater and Engineering Festival, filled up the cavernous 69th Regiment Armory, *HPSCHD* tackles an even larger space, for an even larger audience, and makes it succumb to his environmental art.

HPSCHD is a Universe Symphony in the distinctly American tradition dating back to Charles Ives, who spent the last forty years of his life on a similarly all-inclusive but unfinished work. As Ives imagined his *Universe Symphony,* groups of musicians would be distributed around the countryside—up the hills and in the valleys—and they would sound a joyful disorder similar to the last movement of his *Fourth Symphony* (1910–16). However, thanks to technological progress, Cage and Hiller can use facilities Ives never had—tape recorders, amplifiers, loudspeakers, motion-picture and slide projectors—to distribute their chaotic art all over an enormous space; and in the increased quantity was a particular kind of quality never before experienced in either art or life. In the future, let *HPSCHD* turn on even larger spaces, like Madison Square Garden, the Astrodome or even the Buckminster Fuller dome that someday ought to be constructed over midtown Manhattan. Wish you were, or could be, there.

JOHN CAGE, 75, WRITES FIRST, "GREAT AMERICAN" OPERA (1988)

*Louis Armstrong or any other good jazz musician of
that period would take a theme and start improvising.
He would pay his respects to Aida, any number of
operas, light opera and religious music. All of this
came out in the improvisation. It assumes possession
and it recasts. There is a kind of irreverent reverence
that Americans are likely to have for materials of the
past.*—Ralph Ellison,
in an interview with the author (1965).

The news is that the New York composer John Cage, now in his
mid-seventies, has written his first opera. "I was asked to write an opera,
and I have never written one," John Cage told an interviewer a few years
ago. "It means a lot of work. It means a theater piece with all those
singers. And you see, I've come to the desire to free each person in the
performance from anyone like a conductor. Instead, what I want the
opera to be is a collage of sorts, of a pulverized sort, of European opera;
and my title, I think, is excellent. It's *Europera,* which is the words
'Europe' and 'opera' put together." As one of Cage's best verbal inventions, this coinage also sounds like "Your Opera," which is to say everyone's opera.

What Cage did, armed with a commission from the Frankfurt Oper,
was to ransack the repertoire of traditional (i.e., European) operas that
were no longer protected by copyright; from their scores he randomly
selected instrumental parts, each no more than sixteen measures long,
that could, by chance processes, be reassembled differently for each
performance. To get these fragments, Cage and his assistant, Andrew
Culver, went to the basement library of the Metropolitan Opera, where
they pulled pages at random to be photocopied. Then, in performance,
parts appropriate to each instrument were to be assigned to approximately two dozen musicians (flutists, say, getting a miscellany of flute
music), each of whom was to have music different from his colleagues'.
Thus, motifs from different operas would be heard from different instruments simultaneously.

To "write" the singers' "arias," Cage began with the information

that there are nineteen different categories of operatic voices (for sopranos alone, for instance, coloratura, lyric coloratura, lyric, lyric spinto
and dramatic), so he asked his sponsors for one of each. The nineteen
singers would be allowed to select which out-of-copyright arias they
might sing, but only in the performance itself would they find out when
and where (or if). The singers were to follow not a conductor but digital
time displays that would signal their entrances; questions of duration and
dynamics at any time were to be left to chance. It was possible for several
arias, each from a different opera, to be sung at once, to instrumental
accompaniment(s) culled from yet other operas. About recognizing such
arias, Cage writes, with characteristic wit, "Ah-hah effects will in all
probability occur more frequently here than in the case of the orchestra
parts and above all have a much stronger impact." Uh-huh.

The opera's costumes were likewise drawn from disparate sources.
From the library of New York's Fashion Institute of Technology, a few
blocks from his New York studio, Cage borrowed a multivolumed ency-
clopedia. By certain chance operations to which he remains devoted,
Cage found individual designs that were photographed; slides were then
forwarded to Frankfurt for fabrication. These clothes were assigned to
individual singers without reference to what they would sing or do
onstage. It was here, more than anywhere else, that Cage dramatized his
pulverizing objectives. As none of the performers was to wear an embel-
lished costume that would invidiously distinguish him or her as a "star,"
all performers were to be equal.

For theatrical decor, Cage extended his esthetic principle. From a
wealth of opera pictures found in Frankfurt libraries, he selected images
from various dimensions of (singers, composers, stage sets, animals, etc.)
and had them enlarged and painted, only in black/white, for the flats.
These flats were to be mechanically brought onstage from left or right
or above with an arbitariness reminiscent of the changing backdrops in
the Marx Brothers' *A Night at the Opera*. Once a flat or prop was no
longer needed, it was simply to be laid to rest beside the performing area,
visibly contributing to the chaotic mise-en-scène.

In a booklet prepared for the original performance is this further
explanation: "A computer program, compiled by chance operations,
controls the lighting process. It only makes use of the black-and-white
range [except for two passages of color] to avoid any fundamental
modification in the chromatic value of the costumes," which is to say
that the lighting could not be intentionally manipulated either to focus
the audience's attention or to give one performer more presence than the
others. One subsequent innovation that could be used in any later per-

formance is a variable computer-assisted system that can generate 3,500 separate lighting cues to 180 different lamps, which is to say an average of twenty-six autonomous lighting changes per minute, thereby making the stage illumination not only serendipitous but radically different from performance to performance.

Once Cage assembled this wealth of independent elements, he had to devise a scheme for proceeding in time. In what is perhaps his most audacious move he went to the second edition of *Webster's Unabridged Dictionary,* looking at chance-selected two-page spreads until he found listings that suggested actions. In the Frankfurt performance, one aria was sung from inside a garbage pail, others from inside a coffin and inside a bathtub. Singers arrived onstage in a jeep or inside the belly of a fish. The time available for each action was determined by chance operations; so were the moments of entrance and exit. Nothing relates to anything else, except by coincidence. This is intentional, ordered disorder, which is quite different from disordered disorder.

Since it was possible for individual performers to be assigned tasks that could not be done alone, there were several athletic supers, so-called, onstage to assist them. When a singer was stretched out from his normal height to twelve feet, a super attached the cables that executed the illusion. The supers also installed a cloud and then climbed up and down the ladder attached to it. A final pseudo-arbitrary decision was that the performance happening before the interim intermission, officially called *Europera I,* would have ten singers and be ninety minutes long; the part after the intermission, *Europera II,* would have the remaining nine singers and be forty-five minutes long.

The book-length score must be seen to be believed. After Cage's single-page introduction is a geometric chart that divides the stage into sixty-four rectangles. Then come a series of pages with times running down the left-hand margin. In "flat cues," say, across from each notation of time are shorthand indications of individual moves for the supply of flats. Similar time charts inform action. Were this score posted to a country that censors mail, it would surely be examined for months. "Music," let alone opera, was never before written like this.

"Originally I thought to have the music [of *Europera*] be the music in the repertoire of operas of that particular opera house, so that both the sets and the costumes would already exist," he told Ellsworth Snyder, the interviewer mentioned before. "They would simply be collaged in a different way from conventionally. So instead of having one opera, you'd have them all in one evening. And it's a very nice idea and relatively practical, but it turns out that operas—I was told, as I never go to the opera, of course—I was told that the opera had become quite modern, the sets were not what I imagined, and the costumes were too often not what I would think they had been in the past." From these realizations came the decisions to use music that had aged out of copyright and both new costumes and new sets (rather than those already in storage).

"Rather than have the lighting focused on the activity, I would like to have the lighting done by means of chance operations. I'll probably find out what is the minimum light, so that the singers won't fall down or something. And what would be the maximum lighting. Then to play between those, with what must be very good technology now. And that won't be too difficult. I'm disconnecting not only the lighting from the singers but the costumes from the roles and the background from the activity, and I'm going to introduce a number of what I think of as stage effects, things happening, so that the whole performance will be like not a choreography involving a dance, but still a kind of movement in this space without benefit of a plot."

Europera was designed to open at the Frankfurt Oper on November 15, 1987. However, three days before the premiere, that regal theater was gutted by a fire attributed to a vagrant looking for food. Instead, it opened on December 12 in the smaller Schauspielhaus. Tickets were so hard to obtain that I suspect, a generation from now, the number of people saying they were there will be twice the number of seats. (Several months later, in Sweden, I heard a critic for a daily newspaper there stop a conversation about something else to boast that, yes, he got a precious ticket.)

In the original performance was another innovation that would not be duplicated in New York. From traditional operatic plot summaries, Cage extracted sentences, replacing specific names with pronouns like *he* and *she*. These sentences were scrambled to produce twelve different pseudo-summaries, each two paragraphs long (to coincide with the two acts), none of which had any intentional connection to what was actually on the stage. This is the second half of the twelfth:

> He lusts after her; she had died, his only hope of redemption. In his despondency he maintains his reserve, accepts the bird. He fulfills the second part of the witches' prophecy: They rescue him quickly. He loses his power. He falls prey to another man's wife. Once more he invokes Venus (he is first to admit it); in vain; her life is over. He wishes; he refuses. Thoroughly embittered, he rails.

Into the programs for the Frankfurt performance Cage slipped only *one* of the twelve synposes. As a result, people sitting next to each other had different guides, further contributing to the spirit of general confusion.

There was also a short film, prepared to Cage's instructions by Frank Scheffer, of chance-determined, speeded-up moments from the production. As a continuous loop one minute and fifty seconds long, this film was screened in the theater itself before *Europera 1,* during the intermission and on the curtain after *Europera 2.* Leah Durner writes, "When the film became visible on the closed curtain during the curtain call, the audience remembers the performance and renews their applause and demand for 'the real thing,' creating a continuous contrast of open/ real/closed reproduction."

The Frankfurt performances of *Europera* were such a success that advanced theaters around the world have asked to restage it. Even if America did not earn the premiere, at least we had the first performance outside Germany, with all of the original stage paraphernalia and half of the original singers—on Thursday, July 14, at the Pepsico Summerfare in Purchase, New York. It was repeated, with Lord knows how different details, on the following Saturday and Sunday nights.

However, as few theaters around the world have facilities equal to those in Frankfurt and Purchase, for subsequent performances the dimensions of *Europera* may need to be scaled down, perhaps into "chamber versions," so to speak. While the work is audaciously original, it is neither hermetic nor arcane; one could imagine it becoming part of the standard operatic repertoire, mounted from time to time as a charming departure that nonetheless epitomized the opera house tradition—the comic opera to end all operas, comic and otherwise.

My sense of the key to quality in Cage's work is simply that bigger is usually better; the common mark of his greatest works has been an abundance of activity within a frame. Larger works offer Cage the opportunity to explore his tastes for imaginative constraints, alternative materials and sophisticated laughter. In size and scale, *Europera* belongs to the same class as his *Sonatas and Interludes* (1948), *Williams Mix* (1952), *HPSCHD* (1969) and *Roaratorio* (1979). For all of its contextual innovation, *Europera* nonetheless reflects a compositional principle that has been uniquely Cage's for several decades now—a principle he defines simply as "a circus of independent elements."

Like his earlier masterpieces, *Europera* has already inspired a critical literature. First off the mark were the artistic directors of the Frankfurt Oper, the official "dramaturgs" for this project, Heinz-Klaus Metzger and Rainer Riehn. In the booklet for the original performance, the former wrote, according to the translator, "Clearly, Cage has not written a Romantic opera, but indeed two 'comic' operas—in which the essence of the most European of all traditional forms of theater creates a constellation, namely, the total collage of what comprises the quintessence of those forms and at the same time sublates them critically." Respecting Cage's example of informed pilferage, Riehn composed an aphoristic text drawn entirely from quotations from an unidentified late-eighteenth-century German author (who is actually the writer known only as Novalis, 1772–1801).

The critic of the *Frankfurter Allgemeine Zeitung,* Germany's equivalent of the *New York Times,* found "an acoustical 'musée imaginaire' [referring to André Malraux's characterization of the art book], stuffed full with recitatives, arias and the meaningless phrases of the orchestra parts. Cage thinks like Goethe: 'Dig deeply into the operatic life.' " In the *Stuttgarter Zeitung,* an inspired Horst Koegler wrote, "*I* and *II* can conceivably be reversed—and without difficulty be continued by 'III' and ad infinitum [in this] gigantic operatic revue, a kind of neo-dada which, first of all, represents a test for the quiz capacity for each theater patron." In other words, a work as rich and yet indefinite as *Europera* is likely to prompt a wild variety of interpretations.

What *Europera* is finally about, to my mind, is the culture of opera, Cage's work being, from its transcriptions of phrases to its libretti, at once a homage and a burlesque, finding a wealth of surprises in the familiar; its theme could be defined, simply, as the sound of European opera after an American has reprocessed it. Nonetheless, precisely because *Europera* was initially performed in an opera house, with opera professionals (rather than amateurs), on a stage whose curtain went up, it must be judged as opera, not as just a species of anarchist theater (which it also is). Writing in *The Wall Street Journal,* the music critic Mark Swed reported, "For all its wildness, the opera proceeds with an underlying grace and a witty way with operatic clichés, putting them in unexpected contexts, that really was Mozartian in the end." In my judgment, by running innocently amok in European culture, Cage has come as close as anyone to writing the Great American Opera, which is to say, a great opera that only an American could make.

What is remarkable is that Cage, after fifty years of ignoring opera, has in this age when "everything has been done" (or "artistic innovation has expired") produced something that is by common consent truly *avant-garde,* something that makes a significant contribution to the art. It is also true that by achieving such originality in his mid-seventies, Cage, who has never doubled back (and never rejected earlier work as "too far out"), reaffirms the expectation that he will probably be a pioneering presence as long as he continues to work.

II

It is by surprise, by the important position that has been given to surprise, that the new spirit distinguishes itself from all the literary and artistic movements that have preceded it.—Guillaume Apollinaire, "The New Spirit and the Poets" (1916)

Regarding his new *Europeras I* and *II,* John Cage told an interviewer, "It's just so many things going on at once that I think you see different things each time you look at it, if you looked at it more than once." Since certain elements in the production, such as entrances and exits of the instrumentalists, would be different from performance to performance, I decided to go to all three performances at the Pepsico Summerfare, in part to see whether the differences were significant but also to discover whether my enthusiasm for Cage would remain after three viewings on four successive days.

As a grand compendium of European opera, *Europera* will test your taste for opera. What you see and what you hear are, simply, the conventions of that art—spacious stage, some typical choreography, formidable performers, costuming and singing—apart from any specific content. People familiar with opera are surprised to see familiar arias sung by performers in inappropriate costumes, accompanied by irrelevant music, against a mise-en-scène that, in Thoreau's phrase, marches to a different drummer. Those less sympathetic to opera find the work only tweaking their distaste.

The performers go about their business oblivious to the audience. By asking the nineteen singers to select their favorite arias, Cage could trust them to perform professionally what they have done before (and could perhaps do in their sleep), in spite of unusual distractions. Thanks to the Cagean principle of the autonomy of the parts, such arias become not concrete but abstract. Any opera lover trying to play the pedantic game of identifying allusions will soon be defeated by the abundance of them.

What must be seen to be believed is the degree of discontinuity. The background flats move up and down, in and out, seemingly at their own whim, making a show on their own; some images are tilted. Though several arias are sung simultaneously, the singers rarely acknowledge one another. Bouncing around the stage is another set of performers, some in leotards, others informally dressed, who go about their bits only occasionally aware of the singers. The stage lights point in all directions and change autonomously, sometimes leaving soloists in darkness. The theater's back wall is visible throughout, becoming a backdrop so neutral that anything can happen in front of it. In the pit are musicians whose platform occasionally rises to that of the stage before descending again. One recurring theme is incongruity raised to a higher level, with gags that survive repeated hearing. Especially in *Europera I* there was nearly continuous giggling in the audience.

Some of the individual moves have an obvious charm. A woman suspends a fishing pole into the orchestra pit; before long, she pulls out a cloth fish nearly half her size. An aria is sung by an alto who is seated on a plate that is dragged along the floor. As her saucer approaches a bathtub, she climbs into it, continuing her aria. In another bit, a baritone sings his aria while two dancers paint his arms. Near the end of *Europera I,* a female head emerges from a hole in the floor, her voice in song. It was a special pleasure to see a group of nineteen performers emerge in continually new guises. The crowning theatrical touch was a zeppelin that flew out into the audience, distracting attention upward while the stage action continued; every opera henceforth needs at least one flying object, I decided.

At SUNY-Purchase *Europera* was performed in a big theater which had a curtain that went up; the performers sounded and looked like opera singers; the musicians in the orchestra pit looked and sounded like professionals. It is an opera that begs to belong to the operatic canon. (Because the performance of arias amid distractions depends upon the competence of professionals, I doubt if amateurs could do it half as well.) What is missing from *Europera* is narrative, which is to say the thread connecting one incident (or aria) to another. The question implicit here is whether opera can succeed without narrative; I think it can.

Europera II differed from *I* in being denser and faster. Half the length of the first part, it seemed to have an equal amount of action, this time performed by a fresh cast. Whereas no more than four arias were sung at any one time in *Europera I,* in *II* I counted as many as seven going on simultaneously. The scene changes so fast, so continually, that someone glancing at his program, say, could raise his or her eyes to a different world. Nothing lasts too long (except, to some, the thing itself). Even on third viewing, I found myself discovering details that I'd missed before (e.g., real water dropping from a dark cloud).

The falsest moves in the opening performance came from the bass

Heinz Hagenau who, once he donned a kilt and brandished a sword, began mugging to the audience. Later some of the dancers showed off their virtuosic suppleness, drawing attention to themselves by means that were contextually inappropriate. What must be understood is that, all gossip to the contrary notwithstanding, Cage is finally not an apostle of wayward freedom, or "anything goes"; he is really devoted to disciplined constraints that must be observed. One rule is that individual performers cannot do egotistical gestures. It would have been similarly false for a singer, say, intentionally to move his or her body into a spotlight.

Elsewhere I have suggested that Cage's bigger works tend to be better than his smaller pieces; and by its abundance of materials, *Europera* begs to be compared with his other big pieces such as *Roaratorio* and *HPSCHD,* whose premiere was in a 15,000-seat basketball arena at the University of Illinois. To my mind, as a veteran Cage-watcher, *Europera* pales beside the latter, which was really an unfettered exploration of alternative performance, in a profoundly alternative theatrical space. For instance, by having more seats than spectators, *HPSCHD* allowed the audience to move around, in contrast to the experience of being imprisoned in the long rows at Purchase.

Whereas *HPSCHD* was a vision of peaceful chaos, ordered disorder, likewise without any conductor, *Europera* is essentially a reinterpretation of opera, with operatic materials, performed within the context of opera. Remember that appropriating European music, at once irreverently but respectfully, is an old American tradition, exemplified by Charles Ives, Louis Armstrong and many others; but only Cage would make a work consisting *wholly* of quotations and yet, in its rigorously uninflected discontinuous structure, reflecting his unique artistic signature.

The political achievement of Cage's art, here and elsewhere, is the elimination of hierarchy. Just as no note is more important than any other, so no quotation is honored above the others and no singer is featured over the others. Onstage the dancers have a presence equal to the singers; and when a stagehand becomes visible, he or she looks like one of the performers. When members of the company take their bows, there is no conductor to lead them. By third viewing, what seemed innovative at first had become classic, quite classic.

The question has been raised of whether *Europera* could succeed on disc? I was reminded of the 1969 Nonesuch recording of *HPSCHD* that, while only a partial representation of that piece's original performance, has nonetheless survived as an interesting record, the epitome of sustained chaotic sound. (I remember Aaron Copland, hosting a radio series in the 1970s, dismissing it as beyond the bounds of music.) While I might like to have a record or compact disc of *Europera,* what I would most of all prefer would be a videotape, preferably for a large-screen projection TV. Since productions are likely to differ from one another to degrees greater than normal in an opera's life, what would be better yet is *a set of videocassettes,* each from a different venue, so that I could enjoy the Frankfurt performance on one night, Purchase on another, somewhere else on a third, and so forth.

One innovative opera merits support for another. It seems that, having established himself as a credible opera composer, Cage has been asked to propose a sequel he would call "Nohopera," lexically combining Japanese Noh with European opera. As he explained, "Its subtitle would be 'Or the Complete Musical Works of Marcel Duchamp.' It would take another two to four years." That is to say, it could become his abundant masterpiece for the nineties (and his eighties).

We tend to think of avant-garde artists as flashy adventurers who enter new territory before retreating or retiring into more conventional work; but perhaps the most extraordinary thing about Cage is that into his seventies he has continued to be audacious and original. What the Frankfurt commission for *Europera* offered him was an opportunity to open up a genre commonly regarded as stagnant, rewarding us with pleasant surprises and incidentially creating an opera worth seeing, in my judgment, again and again.

CUNNINGHAM/CAGE (1986)

Merce Cunningham and John Cage—sometimes they are separate, sometimes together. They began separately, Cage in Los Angeles in 1912, Cunningham in Centralia, Washington, around 1919. They first met in Seattle, in the late 1930s at the Cornish School, where Cage was a dance class pianist and Cunningham a student. They came together again in New York in the early 1940s and, ever since their first joint concert in 1944, have worked together, pursuing, individually and together, similar esthetic ideas and artistic lives. Each began his own career as a favored child of a reigning establishment, and each rejected that establishment, in turn to be rejected by it, before successfully forging a professional identity based upon extreme innovation.

Historically, Merce Cunningham is best seen as epitomizing the third generation of modern dance choreography. The first generation, led by Isadora Duncan, rejected the tone and devices of classical ballet, with its fixed vocabulary of positions and movements, and put the dancer's feet flat on the floor and used freely formed gestures that appeared more expressive of human emotions than the strict conventions of ballet. The work of Duncan and her contemporaries a choreographic tradition that has developed apart not only from ballet but from folk dance, ethnic dance, social dance, jazz dance, chorus lines, vaudeville dance and "water ballet" as well.

The second generation of modern dance introduced more definite vocabularies of movement (Martha Graham, for instance, favoring contractions and releases), and its works customarily had particular subjects, such as *Appalachian Spring* or *The Moor's Pavanne* (José Limon), that evoked a plot and/or depended upon a familiar literary allusion. Like Duncan before them, these choreographers danced on standard theatrical stages to conventionally tonal music, the rhythm of their movements relating to the predictable musical beat; and their typical gestures served to mime identifiable emotions or meanings.

By the time he first met Cunningham, Cage had dropped out of college and had lived in Europe and in New York, where he studied with serial composers. Once back home in Los Angeles, he asked to study with Arnold Schoenberg, who had emigrated there. Though Schoenberg thought enough of Cage to give him lessons free, he eventually told the young man he lacked talent for harmony. In the sort of gesture that seems at once typical of avant-garde artists and indicative of his determination, Cage decided nonetheless to compose music that eschewed harmony. (Given this incapacity, it is scarcely surprising that Cage disparaged Stravinsky's neoclassicism that was also influential in the 1930s.) Initially he worked with percussion instruments, and then with a prepared piano (which transformed that traditional musical instrument into a kind of percussion ensemble). He began to explore electronic sound generation, at first through record turntables whose speed could be modulated; and transferring his allegiance from Schoenberg to the chaotic tradition of Charles Ives and Edgard Varèse, Cage thought of composing from sounds heard on the street.

In the late 1940s, Cage studied with the Japanese philosopher D. T. Suzuki and discovered an application of Zen Buddhism to art—the acceptance of all sounds, apart from intention and apart from structure, as equally valid. His most conclusive demonstration of this principle is an extraordinary work of conceptual art, *4'33"* (1952). As no intentional sound was made by the pianist, Cage's polemical implication was that all the miscellaneous sounds occuring within that time frame constituted "the music." From this principle, for instance, follows his use of chance procedures, and the *I Ching,* to make compositional decisions that discount expressionistic motives and personal taste. To this day, Cage insists that *4'33"* remains his most important single work, and also the most influential upon his subsequent compositional thinking.

Once a principal performer in the Graham company, Merce Cunningham had by the late-1940s moved outside the bounds of his profession. Not only were his performances with Cage unreviewed, they were frequently excluded from "series" anthologies where they deservedly belonged. Or, included in a series one year, he was excluded the next, "with a note I thought impolite." Cage's musical career traversed a similar wayward road well into the 1960s. The reason for their divergence was artistic, rather than personal; for at issue was not just a difference in "style," but Cunningham's and Cage's radical departures in compositional approach. Since their works "broke the rules" and thus were different in more ways than the dance and music worlds could understand, both men, separately and together, were widely dismissed as "unserious" or "absurd."

Both Cunningham and Cage were also reacting against the predominant esthetic thinking of the post-World War II years—Suzanne K. Langer's philosophy of art as symbolic representation. (It was taught to me in college as late as 1960.) The function of art, she wrote, is "the creation of forms symbolic of human feeling." The artist thus endeavors to create structures that present "semblances" of familiar emotions. If the symbolic presentation is true to a form of a certain feeling, then this formal abstraction will not only give esthetic pleasure by itself, it will also function to instigate that particular feeling in the spectator. The intellectual achievement of Langer's esthetics was a richly supported theory of art-as-emotion which avoided traditional schemes of expression and individual personality on the one hand, and explicit universal myth on the other. At the time, it seemed perfectly relevant to the representational music of Aaron Copland, the programmatic dance of Martha Graham, the poetry of T.S. Eliot and the new post-cubist abstract painting. However, Langerian esthetics did not relate to Cunningham-Cage, who have little taste for symbolism or ulterior meanings.

Not only for music, but for his visual art and writing as well, Cage has evolved a radical esthetic of nonfocused, nonhierarchical fields without definite beginnings or ends. Because he has been less interested in relationships and cohering structures than in isolated sounds, his works tend to be constellations of parts, none of them more important, more climactic or more cohesive than any other. Though his pieces necessarily begin and end, neither the opening element nor the closing element makes a firm impression. The radicalness of this kind of structuring should not be underestimated; for whereas classical notions of artistic form deal with centering and focus and also favor arclike forms that organize emphases and have firm beginnings and ends, Cage, as well as Cunningham, has been doing something else.

Cunningham had meanwhile radically reworked several dimensions of dancemaking—not only the function of gestures but the articulation of time and the use of space. First of all, he eschewed the idea of movement as meant to tell a story or articulate an emotion. Second, whereas most choreographers posited a central theme that informed all the parts, which in turn reinforced the initial concept, Cunningham's works are assembled from disparate, independently created materials that remain perceptibly separate and yet artistically complementary in the final performance. (His "events" extend this radical structural bias in assembling, fresh for each occasion, passages originally composed for different dances.) Third, whereas most ballet and even most modern dance has a front and a back, Cunningham's works are designed to be seen from all sides; and though theatrical custom has forced him to do most of his performances on a proscenium stage (which has an open front), his pieces have also been successfully performed in gymnasiums and museums.

Since their artistic moves were ends in themselves, rather than parts of intended structures or, worse, vehicles of emotional representation,

Cunningham and Cage freed themselves to explore the limitless possibilities of their materials—sound, image and language for Cage, human movement and theatrical platforms for Cunningham; and capitalizing on the freedoms they had given themselves, each has been doggedly prolific and incomparably inventive. Assimilating Cage's interests in autonomy and chance, Cunningham defied traditon by allowing parts of the dancer's body to function disjunctively and nonsynchronously. Once, in *Untitled Solo* (1953), he listed the movable parts of the body and enumerated their possible actions before tossing dice to determine theoretically possible combinations that he might be reluctant to try on his own initiative. As exploration, rather than, say, refinement has been their mutual ideal, Cunningham then took months to test all his aleatory results, until he found, after repeatedly trying, that a few hypothetical combinations were simply physically impossible.

Since his art, as well as Cage's, scrupulously eschews specific subjects or stories, his dancers avoid dramatic characterizations for nonparticularized roles, which is to say that Cunningham dancers always play themselves and no one else. Since they avoid the traditional structure of theme and variation, the dominant events within a given work seem to proceed at an irregular, unpredictable pace; their temporal form is, metaphorically, lumpy. "It's human time," Cunningham once explained, "which can't be too slow or too fast, but includes various time possibilities. I like to change tempos."

Their most radical idea was the separate creation of sound and choreography, so that dancers would not hear the music until just before the performance; for as early as 1939, Cage advocated "the simultaneous composition of both dance and music." Cunningham has always identified Cage as the principal influence upon his work, "because of his ideas about the possibilities of sound and time and the separate identities of music and dance."

Since Cunningham's nonsymbolic movements are meant to be appreciated apart from larger structures, his dance demands not the empathy of the spectator but, as Cage once explained, "your faculty of kinesthetic sympathy. It is this faculty we employ when, seeing the flight of birds, we ourselves, by identification, fly up, glide and soar." Of Cage's music, the dance critic Jill Johnston once wrote, "Each sound is heard for itself and does not depend for its value on its place within a system of sounds. Similarly, a typical Cunningham movement is a series of isolated actions, and the connection is simply that of sequence or juxtaposition, or whatever the observer wishes to make out of it." From Cunningham-Cage collaborations have come the currently popular customs of keeping apart those elements that might normally be expected to coincide, or of simultaneously offering materials that otherwise have nothing to do with one another; for their great, much-imitated idea was presentational noncongruence.

Both also challenged the traditional hierarchies of artistic practice, avoiding the format of "leader and chorus" which is typical of most music for large ensembles and much modern dance. Their performance ensembles tend to be companies of equals, who perform without a visible conductor, whose various members dominate at different times; and rather than looking and dressing alike, as is customary in most performing companies, these collaborators accentuate individuality in both appearance and activity. Unison activity, when used, is rarely sustained, as individual dancers move at different speeds and individual musicians play at different speeds, often simultaneously. In the end, what at first seems diffused and inscrutable in their work is quite comprehensible, providing one does not strive too hard to find "meanings" that are not there. What you see or hear is what there is.

Throughout the history of their collaboration, Cage has always seemed the more "offensive," his egregiously dissonant scores distracting attention from the dance, as well as offending "music lovers" even more than Cunningham's art disturbs dance regulars. I remember a performance at Lincoln Center's Philharmonic Hall in 1963, as part of subscription series with more conservative choreographers. At the time, a typical Cagean piece consisted of silences punctuated by ear-splitting amplified cacophonies (or vice versa). After every resounding crescendo, several spectators arose to march, disgusted, to the exits, effectively reducing the uptown audience to true Cunningham aficionados. It was a sight. Days later, the *New York Times* critic suggested, not unreasonably, that Cunningham might hence succeed with this Philharmonic audience if he dumped Cage. In *The Village Voice,* Jill Johnston, its dance critic at the time, responded that such bowdlerization would be comparable to "the Bible without God." In truth, Cage could have written more, and probably earned more, had he not spent so much of his life accompanying Cunningham.

One reason Cunningham appears less "free" is his acceptance of limitations, initially in the human body, but also in the responsibilities of directing a company of full-time dancers. About the former limitation, he once told an interviewer, "With dancing we're locked into the fact that it's the human body doing the action. There are two legs; the arms move a certain number of ways; the knees only bend forwards. That remains your limit." This sense of circumscription, along with a more pronounced taste for the exquisite, accounts for why most of us think Cunningham less radical than Cage. Were Cage a choreographer, he would, by contrast, probably think of how to transcend those limits and, let me speculate further, thus envision theatrical performances for puppets or objects. After all, Cage pioneered composition with audiotape, which was likewise about realizing acoustically with technology what could not be done with physically limited live performers.

Initially both men found their most loyal audience not among composers and dancers but among visual artists. The painter Elaine de Kooning tells the story that, just before a 1954 Cunningham performance, the critic Harold Rosenberg screamed in his booming voice, "Here it is almost curtain time and the Lassaws [the painter Ibram] aren't here yet." Then to top this joke, Rosenberg added, with utter confidence that his crack would not be misunderstood, "There's a stranger in the third row. Throw him out." So chummy was his audience that by the mid-1950s, Cunningham once told me, half its faces were familiar. Back in 1966, Cage told the art critic Irving Sandler, "Any experimental musician in the twentieth century has had to rely on painters, because they were the lively changers of art to begin with." In the early 1960s, Cunningham's principal patrons included the freshly successful painters Jasper Johns and Robert Rauschenberg.

Together and separately, Cage and Cunningham rank among the most influential artists of their time, affecting not only their own arts but, more significantly perhaps, others as well. In his 1971 memoir of the poet Frank O'Hara, John Ashbery recalls back in the early 1950s a Cage "piano work lasting over an hour and consisting, as I recall, entirely of isolated, autonomous tone-clusters struck seemingly at random all over the keyboard." The effect upon those poets, then still in their twenties, was "further, perhaps for us ultimate proof not so much of 'Anything goes' but 'Anything can come out.' " I see the subsequent influence of Cunningham and Cage in the unfettered exploration of materials thought unsuitable for art, whether noises in music or junk in sculpture; in extended uninflected discontinuous structures, whether in nonsyntactic prose or in dance; and in performances whose parts are not obviously complementary. (A richly varied multimedia exhibition could be assembled of work reflecting their initiative.) Perhaps the surest test of their influence is the general belief that, had they not done what they did, recent American arts would have been drastically different.

Cunningham as well as Cage speaks about art and his work with a certain unpretentious empiricism uncontaminated by prejudicial emotional words, and each is a reliable guide to the purposes and effects of his own creations. The most sustained example of Cunningham talking intelligently about himself appears in Jacqueline Lesschaeve's book of conversations, *The Dancer and the Dance* (1985). I can scarcely be alone in wanting an edition of the miscellaneous prose that Cunningham has published over his career, for in my anthology *Esthetics Contemporary* (1978) appears his single most suggestive essay, "The Impermanent Art" (1957). Cage has been more generous with interviewers. Daniel Charles's *Pour les oiseaux* (1976; *For the Birds,* 1981) is based upon conversations conducted between 1968 and 1972. The bulk of Klaus Schöning's book, *Roaratorio* (1982), is an interview with Cage about his single most important work for German radio. (It also became the sound for a Cunningham choreography.) I am currently producing *Conversing with Cage,* a concatenation of excerpts from nearly one hundred interviews Cage has given over the years, partly under the assumption that, even today, the composer remains the most authoritative commentator on both the shape and detail of his own revolution.

Cunningham and Cage have collaborated for over forty years now, in one of the richest continuing relationships in all modern art. To each has come well-earned, indisputable rewards—a Kennedy Center Honor and a MacArthur Award for Cunningham, so many commissions for Cage that he has recently needed to take a sabbatical from his traditional job as music director of the dance company. Unique though each is, their most extraordinary achievement has surely been their collaboration, not only rich in quality and influence, but sustained in duration toward, dare we say, the Golden Anniversary we look forward to seeing and hearing them celebrate.

ELLIOTT CARTER (1968)

Among the professionals of contemporary music, who constitute a scene riddled with dissension, no positive opinion seems more diversely accepted, if not more ecumenical, than Elliott Carter's excellence as a composer. To Milton Babbitt, definitely of the twelve-tone persuasion, Carter is "one of our two best composers, Roger Sessions being the other." To Aaron Copland, totem figure of the mainstream, "Everybody agrees that he is in complete command of what he wants to do. You can hear any new work of his with confidence." The young composer-critic Benjamin Boretz observes that Carter and Babbitt have "made the decisive discoveries, and have developed musical languages which are not only unmistakably their own, but which have also crystallized the musical thinking of most of their younger colleagues, as those of Schoenberg and Stravinsky did in the Twenties." And that sophisticated and discriminating audience who finds Babbitt too difficult, Copland too easy and Cage too trivial generally acknowledges Carter as the greatest living American composer. Remarkably enough, his work represents a ground that is at once between the extremes and yet artistically avant-garde.

A small and slight man, with longish, somewhat unruly gray hair, a wide smile and a broad, open and handsome face, Carter lives in a moderately spacious apartment in a Stanford White–designed building a few blocks north of New York's Washington Square. Looking younger than his fifty-nine years and flipping on and off two pairs of glasses, Carter was dressed on the day we met as casually as usual—baggy and cuffless trousers, scruffy shoes. Neither as dominating nor prepossessing as his awesome reputation might suggest, he is at turns lively and reticent, sometimes engaging but usually quite diffident. He speaks animatedly in an indefinite accent, overcoming a slight stutter; yet his sparkling blue eyes tend to turn away, as though he were too shy to look his guest straight in the eye. He frequently moves both hands in symmetrical gestures; yet he often lets the rhythm of conversation disintegrate completely. He can go on enthusiastically about certain subjects and still often give the impression that he finds talk a bit boring. More contained than outgoing, he seemingly puts blocks between himself and the world, neither communicating facilely with others nor assimilating easily the information his experience continually throws across his eyes.

"I became interested in contemporary music as a teenager, some years before I studied music in general," he reminisced. "At that time this was a very drastic thing to do, since contemporary music was not an integral part of education and culture, as it is today." It seems that one of his classmates at New York's Horace Mann prep school was the late Eugene O'Neill, Jr. Through him, as well as a few other sons of artistic parents, young Carter, then living near Columbia University, made the Greenwich Village scene in 1925–26, meeting the composers Charles Ives, Edgard Varèse and Henry Cowell, the legendary harpist-composer Carlos Salzedo and their patrons and critics. A frequent guest at the Iveses, Carter even played piano four hands with the master himself. Carter became so steeped in the avant-garde musical culture of the mid-1920s that when his father took him to Vienna in the summer of 1926, the seventeen-year-old purchased all the scores by Schoenberg, Webern and Alban Berg that he could find. Around that time, although his only musical training consisted of piano lessons, he even started to write his own pieces, mostly song settings to passages from James Joyce's *Ulysses;* and he regarded his own works highly enough to submit them to Cowell, who was then editing New Music Editions.

Carter chose Harvard in part because Serge Koussevitzky's Boston Symphony Orchestra was predisposed to advanced music. But finding the university music department too backward for his taste, he majored in English literature instead, letting music become his primary extracurricular interest. He graduated in 1930 and stayed two more years to take an M.A. in music, studying composition with the English composer Gustav Holst, a guest professor, who did not approve of the Hindemithian tastes that Carter then practiced.

That was the first of many discouragements that would have retired a less-determined composer. Thanks in part to a meager $500-a-year allowance from his father (a prosperous lace importer who throughout his life remained vehemently opposed to his son's musical career), Carter went abroad to study, choosing Paris largely because he had been able to speak French fluently since childhood. He made extra money by copying scores, singing in church choirs and even conducting a French madrigal group. "It's hard to live on the margins of life," he says today, "and it's foolish for wealthy parents to be so difficult. My teeth have been bad ever since." For three years he studied with Nadia Boulanger; and even though he conscientiously executed all the laborious exercises she prescribed and "looked for constructive criticism," she was not particularly encouraging either. Returning home in 1935, still on the small charity of his family, he labored in the compositional style most fashionable at the time, representational neoclassical American, and became musical director of Lincoln Kirstein's Ballet Caravan for which he wrote, among other pieces, the ballet suite *Pocahontas* (1939; rev., 1941).

Carter's name was at that time hardly distinguishable from others working in that hyper-American idiom—it is not even mentioned in either Aaron Copland's 1936 or 1949 survey of the native musical scene. His personal reputation was largely for multilingual literacy and financial connections above the professional norm; musically, his pieces were known to be slightly more difficult than average at the time. When he showed *A Holiday Overture* (1944) to an older, artistically similar but more established composer, the latter dismissed it as "another typical Carter piece, too complicated to understand." From New York to Harvard to Paris back to Cambridge (Mass.) for a year and then to New York again, Carter trod a rather "establishment" path, but he missed becoming the protégé of either an influential elder or a reigning clique. Indeed, his work went unchampioned, if not neglected. When asked what distinguished him from other Boulangerites, he replied immediately, "I'm a radical, having a nature that leads me to perpetual revolt."

Carter says that he was not particularly pleased with his compositions back then, and this perhaps explains why he is now neither overtly embittered about this early neglect nor especially proud of putting down his former detractors. "There were many things that I wanted to achieve but couldn't do," he remarks. "Like so many others who received the same university education, my comprehension, taste and conceptual ability were much more developed than my musical craftsmanship." His first breakthrough was the *Piano Sonata* (1946), composed on Cape Cod and in New York City on his initial Guggenheim Fellowship. There are few other examples in music history of great composers just starting to bloom in their late thirties.

Here for the first time Carter took the leap that connected his work to the avant-garde tradition he had assimilated as a youth, as well as exhibited the necessary extra dose of personal purpose that sprang him above a pack of peers. Since nearly everybody had told him that his work was not particularly good, he set about to be better than good; and as if to implicitly rebuke his pious advisers, along with their preoccupations and conventions, his work became more complicated rather than less. To the pianist Charles Rosen, the *Piano Sonata* "represents a new departure in piano writing that has few analogies in the literature of the past. The Sonata is built upon, and constructed out of, the overtone possibilities of the piano." Particularly in Rosen's recording (Epic LC 3950 or BC 1250), played on good equipment, one can hear not only the various overtone sounds that notes in combination produce, but also the ways in which the overtones create their own semblance of melodies. In this piece Carter also introduced the rapid changes in rhythm—here, Rosen estimates, one change every two or three measures—which later became a primary mark of his style.

While the ballet score *The Minotaur* (1947) seems almost a step back into the neoclassical vein, the *Sonata for Cello and Piano* (1948) incorporates a musical idea that the composer would subsequently develop—"a work that would emphasize the individuality of each instrument and that made a virtue of their inability to blend completely." The second breakthrough of Carter's compositional career was the *First String Quartet* (Columbia ML 5104), written in 1951–52 in Tucson, on Carter's second token of confidence from the Guggenheim Foundation. This piece he now regards as "the first time I really got there." The score turned out to be so complicated that Carter has since written that he feared it "might never be played."

In this work Carter bestows such individual identities on his four instruments that, as Virgil Thomson put it, the piece "sounds less like a classical string quartet than like four intrinsically integrated solos, all going on at the same time." Crediting Charles Ives's *Second String Quartet* (1907–13) for a basic conception, Carter appropriates a theatrical metaphor to characterize his technique as "the simultaneous juxtaposition of different musical characters." He adds, however, that in contrast to Ives, who sometimes let his players disintegrate into aural chaos, he prefers to control constantly the interactions of the various parts. Always eclectically literate, Carter drew upon the movies for another artistic influence. "The general plan of my First Quartet actually was suggested by Cocteau's film *Le Sang d'un poète (Blood of the Poet)* which opens with a shot of a large brick chimney being blown up and beginning to fall and ends with the continuation of this sequence. In-between takes place the entire action of the film, which appears to last for a long time but actually takes only a brief moment, as dreams always do. The falling chimney is the measure of time elapsing, just as, in my piece, the beginning cadenza for cello carried on at the end by the violin is interrupted by the 'dream' of the entire work."

In the String Quartet, as in all his later works, Carter abolishes key signatures and introduces the innovative technique that William Glock of the BBC has since christened "metrical modulation." This is, Glock explains, "the idea of having continual changes of speed and character, and linking them into a convincing and novel continuity." Carter's rhythms are neither regular nor syncopated, but rather continually rearticulated until the sense of perpetual rearticulation of the fundamental pulse becomes itself a major theme of the piece.

Although Carter composed a few other works in the 1950s, not until his *Second String Quartet* (1959) did he make his third stylistic leap. In this work, Carter imaginatively developed several principles he had broached earlier. First, he bestowed even more distinct identities upon the four instruments—indeed, the first violin he has characterized as "fantastic, ornate and mercurial"; the second violin, "laconic, orderly"; the viola as possessing a "repertory of expressive motifs"; and the cello as "somewhat impetuous." "I regard my scores as scenarios—auditory scenarios—for performers to act out with their instruments; dramatizing the players as individuals and participants in the ensemble." To those who consider performing it, the *Second String Quartet* is an awesomely difficult work, which can all too easily be done badly; to an attentive audience, it can provide an arresting and exhausting listening experience; to my mind, it is unquestionably among the greatest compositions of the past decade.

The two major works that Carter has subsequently composed—the *Double Concerto for Harpsichord and Piano with Two Chamber Orchestras* of 1961, which Igor Stravinsky judged in print "a masterpiece," and the *Piano Concerto* of 1966—have further explored this compositional idiom. In the spectrum of contemporary music, it lies indefinitely between the new serial language initiated by Schoenberg and more familiar mainstream music, combining the former's textural complexity and avoidance of repetition with the overall mellifluousness more typical of the latter tradition. It also perhaps bows slightly to the line of chaotically dissonant and spatial music that runs from Charles Ives through early Varèse to John Cage.

Though he hesitates to use the phrase "avant-garde," Carter believes that his recent work achieves something new in music—in formal structure, rather than in timbral content. "There are," as he puts it, "more possibilities of experiment in design, particularly complex designs in time, than in sound effects, which tend to be static items or very simple and obvious trajectories." To Carter, the primary medium of his music is not melody but time—not only the length of the notes but the articulated silences between them. "Pitch," he declares, his hands gesturing in unison, "is the population of time. I try to make many different kinds of temporal relations." Of classic influences, he credits "mostly Mozart and Haydn, because my music is concerned with rapid change, and it doesn't try to follow an argument point by point. It gives an impression of discontinuity while remaining coherent."

Although he aims to construct the intricate structures characteristic of the best modern music, he will still discard a realized textural intensity merely "because it doesn't have an immediate appeal to the ear; both the first impression and the deeper context must be interesting." While this might suggest that Carter may be trying to bridge the chasm between the musical profession—more or less the sole audience for quality contemporary music—and the more general public, he has hardly made the compromises that would win him greater attention. Nonetheless, some professionally respected composers do draw more interest from the nonprofessional audience, and Carter is among the few—others being Karlheinz Stockhausen and Igor Stravinsky—to command a relatively large and enthusiastic lay following.

One reason his works are so intricate stems from his awareness of the recording medium. He explicitly states, "I write for records." Not only does each of his three recent pieces run about twenty-five minutes, the length of an LP side, but Carter believes that a recorded composition should be so rich that it will offer new perceptions to the listener each time he hears it, in addition to preserving the ambiguous qualities of art in a repetitive medium. Such works should offer "bits of mosaic that the listener ought to assemble," he said, then paused and smiled modestly. "I'm not sure I'm telling you the truth." This concern for the new medium, along with Carter's reputation, may explain why his records usually sell better than the three thousand copies considered the standard quota for contemporary music—in addition to why I have played my own copy of the *Second String Quartet* at least a hundred times. Besides, as Carter himself notes of his works, "The harder a piece is, the more often it gets played"—which is also a wry comment on how different the performing scene today is from that of a decade or two ago.

Carter works at a small desk in a medium-sized room, separated only by an archway from his apartment's larger living room. Manuscript score sheets lie neatly on his desk; clipped on a cork board above are a few recent letters, reminders of appointments, and a small informal picture of Varèse. Smack in the middle of the room is a baby grand piano, but Carter uses it more as a testing machine than as a source of compositional inspiration. Shelves of books on a variety of subjects line the back wall, while scores fill an inlaid cabinet of vertically slim drawers.

Even though he tries to set aside his entire morning for composing and dabbles at his work throughout the day, Carter has in recent years hardly been a productive composer. Apparently, he lacks the physical, mental and perceptual dexterity of more facile musicians. Furthermore, the mounting levels of compositional complexity have reduced his output in the past decade to three major pieces, totaling about an hour and a quarter of playing time. (Indeed, the fact that few composers in history have won such acclaim for such brief top-notch work should testify to the persuasive excellence of these pieces.) One reason for his slowness, he explains, is that he uses contrapuntal techniques; another is that the necessities of the latest style are so demanding, and yet so unfamiliar, that Carter often feels the anxiety of an explorer in uncharted territory. "I want," he declares, "to invent something I haven't heard before." And this echoes a statement he made several years ago. "Each piece is a kind of crisis in my life; it has to be something new, with an idea that is challenging." An empathetic listener can figuratively "hear" all the work that Carter puts into his pieces.

Indicatively, the plans for writing these recent works have usually consumed more time than their actual execution, so Carter is now systematically analyzing and collating the basic rhythmic and harmonic techniques that inform his recent work. "In classical music," he remarks wistfully, "this was all given." Once he gets this "musical vocabulary" into shape, he expects that future pieces will come more easily. Current major projects include a *Concerto for Orchestra,* commissioned for the New York Philharmonic's 125th anniversary (which has already passed), a *Third String Quartet,* which the Juilliard School of Music commissioned for the forthcoming opening of its new quarters in Lincoln Center; and a cello concerto for the Russian musician Mstislav Rostropovich. On the side, so to speak, he has been revising many of his older pieces, particularly as groups saturated with the recent works have asked for more Carter to perform.

New England Spartans by background, Elliott Carter and his wife, Helen, live beneath their means—their furnishings, for instance, are more tasteful than elegant, and they exercise all sorts of frugalities that amuse, if not infuriate, their friends. On the other hand it is no secret that they surreptitiously support certain indigent musicians and generously lend their apartment or their country place in Waccabuc in upper Westchester to needy friends. "Where their wealth shows," a New York friend remarks, "is in all the parties the Carters give, and in their disconcerting habit of taking off for somewhere far away with little advance notice."

Carter is in many ways an American aristocrat, whose inherited nature forbids him from being either too conspicuous about his wealth or too assertive of his intelligence. Likewise, he does not display an overt pride in his achievements; but he does enumerate, in a matter of fact way, the considerable number of major prizes, grants, commissions and, more recently, honorary degrees he has received. One does not need to scratch too far to find his innate haughtiness, but he conscientiously tries to keep it more implicit than explicit. He does not, for instance, mention any fellow composers as either artistically or emotionally close to himself, as though he regards himself as unquestionably unique as well as detached from the routine concerns of the professional hoi polloi.

Similarly, although he will speak critically of certain positions or trends in contemporary music—serial technique, for example, he considers "basically coarse, crude and insensitive"—he refuses to make public his evaluative comments, either positive or negative, about other composers and/or their works. Perhaps because the neglect he once suffered makes him insecure, Carter prefers to remain above the wars within contemporary music, at the same time that the character of his pieces implies that he stands for certain values and compositional persuasions. "The work," he insists, "is what makes the position; the music takes a stand for me." He does, however, appear at professional meetings, where he sometimes asks the embarrassing questions that no one else dares raise, and he likes to attend international conferences and festivals, partly because he is polylingual, partly because he enjoys cultivating friendships with such rising European composers as the Russian Edison Denisov (they converse in French) and the Pole Krzysztof Penderecki (they speak German).

Over the years Carter has taught for brief spells at various institutions including St. John's College in Annapolis, Peabody Conservatory of Music in Baltimore, Columbia University and Yale, and he now goes up to Juilliard one afternoon a week. Although he does not need the money or particularly enjoy the work, he has taken these positions partly to keep in touch with younger musicians. "Students teach you an awful lot," he remarked, then twinkled; "for one thing, you can see in them pitfalls you should avoid." The example of, say, Milton Babbitt has perhaps persuaded Carter that students well taught are often the established composer's best testaments and publicists. Yet his aloof manner, together with his resistance to professional controversies (which the young invariably take more seriously than their elders), puts off pupils who might otherwise become his followers. Moreover, he has not stayed long enough at any one institution to create a continuity of influence; those who come especially to study with him often find that by the time they arrive he has gone elsewhere.

Carter is more literary than his peers. Not only is he well versed in English literature but also reads and speaks French, German and Italian fluently, a few other languages more haltingly. Carter is an insomniac who, according to a friend, "will while away the sleepless hours by conjugating irregular Italian verbs in his head." He acknowledges Proust and Joyce as the greatest influences upon his sense of rhythm, identifies the critic Edmund Wilson as his closest literary friend and keeps up with contemporary literature. Carter has written many reviews and essays over the past thirty years, and he hopes to collect some of them into a book.

A man of varied interests, of even more varied tastes, he has produced scores in a diversity of sizes ranging from those for a solo pianist or percussionist through string quartets and chamber ensembles to full-sized orchestras; yet through this diversity runs a purposeful attempt to construct a compositional language appropriate to our time—an age shaped by recordings, chaotic or chance music, the twelve-tone language and the gap between the professional composer and the larger musical audience. Although listeners can now discern how the Piano Sonata of 1945 fed into the excellences of his recent works, in looking back over his career we can also recognize how Carter made several courageous leaps above the conventional ways of composing to fashion a compositional style very much his own, yet today more widely admired and, in the highest kind of flattery, often imitated by younger American composers. The question of how Carter became a great composer deserves a profoundly American answer: he did it all by himself.

ALAN HOVHANESS (1979)

Alan Hovhaness decided four decades ago to pursue an idiosyncratic path, apart from changing fashions, that he has followed, prolifically, to this day, producing musical compositions that, in my opinion, rank among the best of the past half century. Essentially, he is a consummate melodist, who uses the modal scales and textures of Eastern music within a framework of Western counterpoint and structure. As his colleague John Cage so acutely observed in 1946, "The use of raga is Oriental; the idea of changing its tones, of letting others appear either at the same time or later is characteristic of Occidental musical thought. The absence of harmony in Hovhaness's music is Eastern. The fact that his compositions are notated and may be played more than once is Western."

No other modern composer has written for as many kinds of musical ensembles and instruments (even, in one piece, the recorded sound of large whales); and few who have worked so totally independent of professional politics are also able to live, as Hovhaness does, entirely off his compositional work. Though tonal music as such is scarcely unfamiliar, he has nonetheless created a musical style that is instantly recognizable as his own, largely because of its personal synthesis of Oriental and Occidental characteristics. Among American tonal composers, only Aaron Copland has created so much uniquely identifiable music.

Currently a resident of Seattle, where I met him early in 1977, Hovhaness was on the verge of completing his thirty-first symphony (Opus 296). Symphonies 27, 28, 29 and 30 were *all* completed in 1976. *Symphony No. 36* was performed at the Kennedy Center, Washington, D.C., by the National Symphony on January 16, 17 and 18 of 1979. (On January 22, 1979, the manuscript of his new *Symphony No. 40* was stolen from his room in a New York hotel just before he was to deliver it to his publisher.) Such output is, by itself, an unparalleled achievement for a modern composer.

Actually, Hovhaness has always been a tonal composer. His principal early influences were Mozart and Handel, and then, among the moderns, Bartók and Sibelius. Indeed, the latter he identifies as his single "favorite orchestral composer since Mozart—particularly his *Fourth Symphony, The Swan of Tuonela, Luonnotar* for soprano and orchestra." Another modern influence, more esoteric than the others, is the Armenian priest Komitas Vartabed (1869–1936), whom Hovhaness calls "the Armenian Bartók." Though he is usually generous in his remarks about other living composers, it is not surprising, given these influences, that Hovhaness strongly objects to atonality in music. "To me, it is against nature. There is a center in everything that exists. The planets have the sun, the moon, the earth. The reason I like Oriental music is that everything has a firm center. All music with a center is tonal. Music without a center is fine for a minute or two, but it soon sounds all the same."

More radically, he objects to the tempered, chromatic scale of the piano, which he finds "efficient only for playing in every key. The string orchestra is the most marvelous instrument in Western music, because it observes just intonation. Human beings will use just intonation unconsciously, because it is the scale of nature; it is what any voice will sing." Hovhaness claims for his own modal music an essential simplicity, which puts off some sophisticated listeners, but which he thinks will contribute to its survival. "Things that are very complicated tend to disappear and get lost. Simplicity is difficult, not easy. Beauty is simple. All unnecessary elements are removed—only essence remains." As a conservative, who acknowledges definable traditions, rather than a reactionary or a neoclassicist, who favors a return to anachronistic forms, Hovhaness characterizes his own music as "giant melodies in simple and complex modes around movable and stationary tonal centers." He pauses for thought. "I'm most interested in purely melodic forms of music in a timeless sense—without being tied down to any century or any place, I want to write down the best music I hear within myself."

He was born Alan Vaness Chakmakjian in Somerville, Massachusetts, March 8, 1911, the son of a chemistry professor at Tufts Medical School, Haroutiun Chakmakjian, an immigrant to the United States from Adana, Turkey. (The surname means "locksmith" or "gunsmith" in Turkish.) His wife, née Madeleine Scott, was of Scottish ancestry. When their only child was five, the Chakmakjians moved to another Boston suburb, Arlington, where young Alan attended the public schools, graduating from high school in 1929. He learned to read music when he was seven years old and immediately began to write his own pieces. An instinctive musician, he taught himself to improvise at the piano before he ever had any lessons on the instrument. So, when he was nine, his parents sent him to a local piano teacher, Adelaide Proctor, who gave him a scholarship and encouraged his composing. By the age of thirteen, young Chakmakjian had written two operas, *Bluebeard* and *Daniel,* in addition to many smaller pieces.

Unlike other Armenian Americans of his generation, he did not attend the church-sponsored after-school lessons where youngsters learned the Armenian language and culture. "My mother didn't want me to be too Armenian," the composer told me, "but my father did. He taught me secretly." Soon after her death in 1931, he changed his middle name to "Hovaness," which is Armenian for John or Johannes, in honor of his grandfather whose first name it was. Then he decided to add another *H* to his middle name and completely drop his last name, thus producing his present name, Alan Hovhaness.

He went to Tufts University for two years but then transferred to the New England Conservatory of Music, where he studied with Frederick Converse (1871–1940), a now-forgotten American composer whose most noted piece, *The Mystic Trumpeter* (1905), is an orchestral work based on Walt Whitman. In 1936, Hovhaness closely observed the North Indian musician Vishnu Shirali, who had come to Boston with the dancer Ude Shankar (Ravi's older brother). In the summer of 1942, the young composer won a scholarship to the Berkshire Music Center to study with Bohuslav Martinu but quarreled with the neoclassical establishment gathered around Aaron Copland. Unlike other American tonal composers of his generation, Hovhaness never studied in Europe. "I was more interested in Oriental music," he now remembers. "Things like that were very far from Paris." Hovhaness has no academic degrees, other than honorary doctorates. In May 1977, he was inducted into the National Institute of Arts and Letters, joining not only such lifelong friends as Cage and Lou Harrison but also his longlife nemeses.

In the 1930s, he made his living playing the piano, mostly around Boston, for choruses, chamber orchestras, violinists, solo singers, as well as social gatherings of Greeks, Arabs and Armenians. He also worked as a jazz arranger on the Works Progress Administration and as an organist in an Armenian church, where he acquired a reputation for spectacular improvisations on ancient modes. His first break as a composer came in 1939 when Leslie Heward, director of music for the BBC in Birmingham, England, aired several Hovhaness pieces and, in a public interview, identified the young American as an important new composer; but unfortunately for Hovhaness, Heward died soon afterward. In 1940, the young composer destroyed nearly all the music he had written thus far, including an undergraduate prize-winning 1933 symphony; he wanted to start the new decade afresh. In the early 1940s, he met the Boston painter Hyman Bloom, who not only influenced Hovhaness's growing interest in ethnic motifs but also introduced him to Yenouk Der Hagopian, a troubador Armenian folksinger whose music Hovhaness patiently transcribed into conventional (i.e., Western) notation. His other important friend during this period was Herman di Giovanno, a "clairvoyant" painter who stimulated Hovhaness's interest in extrasensory phenomena.

This interest in Armenian music led to his organizing a concert of his own compositions in Boston in 1944 for the benefit of an Armenian charitable organization. The successes of this concert led in turn to a series of new compositions, very Armenian in style, such as *Lousadzak* (1944), the opera *Etchmiadzin* and *Armenian Rhapsody No. 1* (which incorporates a Der Hagopian melody) among others. With these works, he initiated his first technical innovation, which he calls *senza mesura,* or "free rhythm." Essentially, in certain parts of a piece, he writes a series of notes without measure bars. The musicians are instructed to repeat these notes, at their own individual speeds, over a fixed period of time. The result is a temporarily chaotic sound or "sound cloud," as Hovhaness calls it; but in his music, unlike that of other chaotic composers, such aural disorganization is nearly always tonally resolved. "I seldom use this anymore," he added. "When everybody copies it, it scarcely belongs to me."

He collaborated with an Armenian student group in cosponsoring annual New York concerts of his music, beginning with one at Town Hall in June 1945. The composer Lou Harrison, then a music critic for the *New York Herald-Tribune,* came to review it. Having an extra ticket, Harrison invited his friend John Cage, also then a young composer, who came backstage after the concert to congratulate Hovhaness. Harrison's review was laudatory, identifying Hovhaness as "a composer of considerable interest and originality." Cage introduced Hovhaness around artistic New York and later wrote favorably about his work in *Modern Music* magazine (Spring 1946).

In 1946, Hovhaness decided to move to New York, where he lived for a year, mostly composing music for dancers, but unable to survive financially, he returned to Boston. In 1948, he began three years of regular teaching at the Boston Conservatory of Music, the smaller music school in his home city. Aside from three years of Eastman (Rochester) summer school, in the mid-1950s, that was his last regular teaching position. In 1951, he moved again to New York to work for Voice of America, making musical programs for broadcast in the Middle East and India. "When Eisenhower came in, in 1952, everyone was fired."

Around 1953, he began finally to collect on his artistic investments. The Guggenheim Foundation awarded him the first of two successive fellowships. Martha Graham commissioned a score for her dance company, and the Louisville Orchestra another piece for its own premiere concerts series. Hovhaness met the conductor Leopold Stokowski, who had been programming Hovhaness compositions since 1942; and the conductor commissioned the composer to produce his single most famous work, *Mysterious Mountain* (1955), for Stokowski's inaugural concert with the Houston Symphony.

It was Stokowski who suggested that Hovhaness ought to observe the classic custom of putting opus numbers after his works. Since Hovhaness was prolific, the conductor estimated that the new piece, *Mysterious Mountain,* ought to have the opus number of 132, and he advised the composer to count his previous works backward. Unfortunately, Stokowski underestimated Hovhaness's prior output (not including the destroyed works); and since there were already more than 150 pieces in his active catalogue, several different early works were assigned the same single opus number.

The rest of Hovhaness's current catalogue is comparably chaotic. Some works have no opus numbers at all. Many are undated, usually because they were published long after they were first written, and sometimes because the dates of composition would not correspond to their opus numbers. The undated *Saint Vartan Symphony,* for instance, was originally written in 1949–50, or after *Symphony No. 1* but before *Symphony No. 2.* However, when Hovhaness later decided that *Saint Vartan* was indeed a full symphony, the next available number was 9. Since the newly christened *Symphony No. 9* already had an opus number (80) that was considerably less than that of *Symphony No. 8* (Op. 179), Hovhaness renumbered *Saint Vartan* as Op. 180, even though it was composed a decade before No. 8. Then too, when Hovhaness revises an earlier piece that lacks an opus number, he must find one for it. Thus, "Opus 80" has since been assigned to another piece from that period. "This is like a Köchel listing," he jokes, "but Köchel was more careful than I was, because Mozart was dead."

In 1959, in his late forties, Hovhaness began the second phase of his musical education. He received a Fulbright Research fellowship to study Karnatic music in South India. Traveling all over the country for a year, he transcribed ragas (over three hundred of them, into a book he would like to publish) and even fulfilled a commission to write a piece for Indian musicians. He visited Japan for the first time, giving well-received concerts of his own works, and returned in 1962–63 to study *gagaku* music, which he describes as "the earliest orchestral music we know; it came from China and Korea in the 700s." He also learned to play Japanese instruments, such as the oboelike *hichiriki* and the complex mouth organ *shō* (which he still owns), and even performed with a *gagaku* group, in addition to transcribing thirteen pieces in Western notation. By 1965,

Hovhaness could sharply distinguish himself from his contemporaries by writing that his principal musical preferences were "Seventh Century Armenian religious music, classic music of South India, Chinese orchestra music of the Tang Dynasty, *Ah-ak* music of Korea, *gagaku* of Japan, and the opera-oratorios of Handel." Typically, one of Hovhaness's favorite modern novelists is Herman Hesse, a fellow syncretic artist who likewise assimilated Eastern thought to make Western art.

In the mid-1960s, Hovhaness lived part of each year in Lucerne, Switzerland, and part in New York, overseeing the publication of his music and its American performances. In 1972, he moved permanently to Seattle, where he was composer-in-residence with the Seattle Symphony in 1966–67. When I interviewed him, he was living with his wife, the coloratura singer Hinako Fujihara, in the southern section of the city near the airport. Their apartment is small and anonymous, with no name on the front door that opens on to a concrete courtyard. He works in the living room, mostly on two folding tables. Along one wall is a modest spinet piano; along another, a small television set which he had borrowed from a friend to see a performance of his music. On the floor was a reel-to-reel tape player which didn't work. Books filled some shelves, piles of his scores occupied others and an abstract di Giovanno painting rested on the floor, leaning against a bookcase. There was no record player, and no records other than his own. "I never listen to anything more than once," he told me, "except Indian music and Japanese Noh plays." Next door is a firehouse. "When the alarm goes off, the only music I hear is in my head. I can't hear anything else. Varèse would have liked it here." Part Armenian, part Scot, Hovhaness lives frugally. Since the composer, like myself, prefers to sleep in the mornings, we met at midnight.

Hovhaness himself is tall and slender, with stooped posture (perhaps from years of music copying), deep-set black eyes and a broad dark mustache that caps an easy smile. His appearance reminds his friend Oliver Daniel of figures in El Greco paintings. Hovhaness's face is well-formed, in a long and slender way, and handsome, his mottled skin notwithstanding. His dark wavy hair has begun to gray, especially near his ears; and he wears it long enough to fluff out from the back of his head. The gray beard he has worn these past few years is scraggly. Around his right wrist is a copper bracelet which, he believes, helps the arthritis that has been plaguing his remarkably long and large fingers (and handicapping his piano playing). He appears physically frail, but when he reveals how many push-ups he does every day, that initial impression passes. Even at home, he wears a suit and a wide tie, with pens in his handkerchief pocket. Though a shy public speaker, he is a bright, fluent conversationalist, never at a loss for answers. "Why Seattle?" I asked. "I like the mountains very much," he replied. "I don't have to go to Switzerland. I expect to stay here."

The principal mystery of Hovhaness's professional career is how he manages to compose so much. One of his several music publishers, C. F. Peters, lists over 240 separate Hovhaness pieces in its catalogue, while other publishers have other compositions, and yet more remains unpublished. "I write every day," he explained over a cup of coffee, rocking back and forth in his dining chair as he spoke. "I have so many beautiful ideas. I must write them down. I can't stop composing. I have more ideas than I can ever use." He writes all the time, wherever he is—on airplanes, in buses or cars, while walking down the street, while sleeping. Always near him is a pencil and a $5'' \times 8''$ notebook with music staves. "I don't know how to compose slowly. I correct and revise later, but composing goes in a sweep. Sometimes I just get the beginning idea, but more often the entire score, complete with orchestration, comes into my head at once." The record-jacket of *Duet for Violin and Harpsichord* says that the three-minute piece "was commissioned on May 16, 1954, composed on May 17, and given its first performance two weeks later in Frankfurt, Germany." If a conductor suggests in the composer's presence that, say, the conclusion of a certain piece is weak or inappropriate, Hovhaness, as the supremely obliging professional, has been known to deliver a new one the following day.

His standard procedure, however, is to work every night. "After feeling drowsy in the early evening, I get more and more creative as the night goes on. By dawn, I'm wildly creative; it gets stronger all the time." When inspiration is slow, he scans earlier notebooks and even old manuscripts to get ideas for new pieces. In *Mysterious Mountain,* for instance, is a fugue that Hovhaness found in a 1936 notebook. "Do you meditate?" I asked. "No, I'm too active. I take walks." When these stimulants fail, he spends the night doing mechanical chores, such as copying out previous scores for offset reproduction or publication. Since his regular copyist has recently been ill, he was presently concentrating on his last symphonies. Even at his age, Hovhaness works without eyeglasses but uses a magnifying glass when his eyes get tired. Obsessed with his work, he never failed to identify the date and place of every composition I asked about. When I inquired about other things, his memory was less sure. Hovhaness is literally a music-making machine who lives for his inexhaustible work. "I really feel that I'm doing my best work now. I'm doing more than I've done in the past few years."

He does not intend his music to be programmatic, unless the piece has a verbal text with a particular subject. Just as most of his program notes are technically descriptive, most titles for his pieces define their instrumentation, and those titles that are evocative, such as *Mysterious Mountain* (which people frequently mistakenly call "Magic Mountain" after the Thomas Mann novel), are usually coined as an afterthought. These descriptive titles usually refer to something religious or natural. "Nature is my great inspiration," he once said, "and I've always regarded Nature as the clothing of God." One could characterize Hovhaness as a transcendental composer whose principal subject is spiritual experience—or, more precisely, musical experience as it approaches spiritual domains. He once wrote, "I have always experienced from earliest childhood the sensation of traveling great distances out into the universe on what seemed like bridges or gossamer threads." That is the kind of experience, I sense, that Hovhaness wants to stimulate in his music.

Like nearly all extremely prolific composers, Hovhaness is also uneven. Typically, he is more interested in creating new works than in publicizing one or another of his previous pieces as a favorite. Nonetheless, his listeners make discriminations, his denigrators exploiting weaker works to dismiss him completely—an unfortunate practice—his advocates, like myself, claiming that *only the good ones count; the others are quickly forgotten.* To my mind, the very best Hovhaness pieces are *Khaldis,* Op. 91, *Mysterious Mountain, Magnificat,* Op. 157 and the *Saint Vartan Symphony.* All but the first are large, encompassing orchestral pieces with dramatic linear forms and rich arrangements. The last is structured like an opera with alternate textures—say, between solo arias by the trumpets and then choruses of brass instruments, as though both were operatic characters. It has marvelous instrumental writing, especially in the canons that get thicker and thicker and then thin out again. "It is like going through the universe," he remarked, "into a thick galaxy and then out the other side." He paused. "The title arose in the course of its composition for an Armenian occasion—the fifteen hundredth anniversary of Saint Vartan's death." One offshoot of his symphony was "an enormous amount of material for four trumpets," and the best of this surplus became the stunning, piano-accompanied canons of *Khaldis* (whose initial recording, now out of print, is superior to the one currently available). Few contemporary composers speak, as Hovhaness unashamedly does, of his own music as "beautiful," and indeed his best pieces are.

On second thought, a definitive critical assessment of Hovhaness is premature now. Some music is still unpublished; too much is rarely performed and never recorded. "He is a major composer in many senses," Lou Harrison told me recently. "He is a great melodist, which may arrive once every few centuries. He has a very fine sense of formal rhythm and exquisite tone color. He can produce sounds for an orchestra that very few composers can approximate. He is like Handel in this respect—an innate sense of the balance and beauty of sound." Harrison paused for breath. "He is one of my favorite composers and always has been." Henry Cowell once characterized Hovhaness's art as "moving, long-breathed music splendidly written and unique in style." John Cage, on the other hand, portrays Hovhaness as "a music tree who, as an orange or lemon tree produces fruit, produces music," which is Cage's way of saying that the music, while predictably sweet, does not confront issues outside itself. Since critical analyses of Hovhaness's music have been scandalously scanty, the most useful writings on the subject are his own, produced largely as program notes for specific compositions. As a professionally independent, awesomely prolific master of a basically traditional style, Hovhaness resembles another Armenian-American artist, the author William Saroyan.

Unlike nearly all composers of his generation, Hovhaness has lived almost entirely off his work. Back in the thirties and forties, he budgeted forty dollars a month and lived in a tiny single room. In New York, in the early fifties, he began to receive commissions. Around 1959, he started to accumulate royalties from the sales of his sheet music, mostly to churchly amateurs. In his seventeen-page C. F. Peters royalty statement for 1975, nearly all of his 240 pieces sold that year, in amounts ranging from one copy (his *Concerto for Accordion*) to 5,620 of a four-page choral piece, *From the End of the Earth,* Op. 187 (actually written in 1951). Since this work costs \$.40 in the music stores, and the composer's royalty is 10 percent of the list price, Hovhaness earned from his single most popular piece the whopping sum of \$224.80, which scarcely pays a month's rent, even in south Seattle. The largest single amount from royalties alone was \$311.40 for 1,038 copies of the vocal score of the *Magnificat.* The single piece earning the largest performance fees was *Meditation on Orpheus,* Op. 155, which was played by both the New York Philharmonic and the San Francisco Symphony in 1975, thus amassing nearly \$1,000 for the composer. In other words, Hovhaness's income comes in bits and pieces; but since he has by now produced so many pieces and bits, he is able to live comfortably from his work—or, more precisely, let his income from past music securely finance his present composing.

On the other hand, his expenses are considerable. A large portion of his gross income goes to alimony. Much of the money he gets from commissions goes into copying the parts. "Two decades ago I got $500 for doing an hour-length work for chorus and small orchestra," he remembered, as a plane buzzed overhead, "but the copyist got $1,500." In recent years, he has spent several thousand dollars annually on travel and roughly an equal amount on studio expenses for recording his own pieces, a few thousand for shipping and storage and several hundred for postage stamps. Not unlike other serious artists, he spends too little money on himself and too much on his work. So, in addition to collecting royalties and performance fees, Hovhaness must conduct concerts (nearly always of his own music), visit universities and accept commissions for new pieces, from an unsurpassed variety of patrons, including, in recent years, the International Center for Arid and Semi-Arid Land Studies at Texas Tech University for *Symphony No. 24* and the Smithtown Central High School Symphonic Band for *Symphony No. 23.* Hovhaness has also become the subject of doctoral essays, most notably by Carl Gerbrant, a baritone who teaches at the Peabody Conservatory.

Not unlike other contemporary composers, Hovhaness discovered that most recordings of his work were going out of print and that many of his best pieces were not recorded at all. Since his greatest wish is that his music be heard, he took the initiative himself. In the mid-1960s, he and Elizabeth Whittington, his wife at the time, founded Poseidon Records, initially to release tape transcriptions of his own performances, as pianist and/or conductor, that would not otherwise be publicly available. After a trial record in 1963, they began issuing a line that now contains seventeen items, including the best available recordings of both the *Saint Vartan Symphony* (Poseidon's best-seller) and the *Magnificat.*

Initially, Poseidon printed two hundred copies of each record, then five hundred, then one thousand; now they do two thousand. The records are manufactured in Allentown, Pennsylvania, by a firm which stores and mails them as well. Orders for the records are mailed to Poseidon Records, 888 Seventh Avenue, New York, N.Y. 10019, and forwarded to Ms. Whittington, who then instructs the Allentown company to fill them. It is a simple operation, with no executives, no salesmen, no receptionists and no advertising. It is also a persuasive model of what other contemporary composers could do for themselves. "We do not make money on this," she told me. "The main thing is to keep the music available for those who are really interested." Hovhaness is also thinking of forming a comparable company to publish scores of his that are not otherwise available.

I asked Hovhaness if he considered himself religious. "I feel closest to the reality of Shinto," he replied, "but my ancestral gods, or kami, are painters, writers and musicians. I believe that composers can at times join heaven and earth—can join opposites. At certain times, I have been seized by clairvoyance, but that is not a religious talent. I have also been given music suddenly, as in a very vivid dream." The finale of *Mysterious Mountain* was based on a two-stage psychic experience. "I dreamed the music and then woke up to write it down. And then I fell into another dream in which I corrected the parts." He paused. "It was a psychic experience of such strength that I would always leave the hall when it was played."

He then told me about his supernatural mental experiences—visionary, symbolic episodes, one of them drug-induced (under supervision)—that have informed his works. He once had a "vision of Prokofiev on a stage, talking to me. I had this vision just after his death. He predicted that I would write a ballet that would go around the world." And then Martha Graham asked Hovhaness to write one that did. "I once had a vision of Bartók's face on the back of my coat."

Pursuing this interest in his psychic powers, he has frequently consulted professional mediums, one of whom identified Hovhaness's earlier incarnation as "a fourteenth-century Florentine, Atalante Migliorotti, who worked as a musician, perhaps a lute player, in Leonardo's household." He suspects that other past incarnations were Greek and Oriental. I asked if he had any premonition of future reincarnations. "No," he replied. "I have too much music to finish to worry about such things."

PAUL ZUKOFSKY (1969)

Contemporary American music has not witnessed the precocious likes of Paul Zukofsky before. A prodigy who chose the violin before he turned five, Zukofsky gave his first Carnegie Hall recital at thirteen, and unlike certain other *wunderkinder,* who lose their *wunder* at the end of their years as *kinder,* he blossomed in his early twenties as a major American violinist, age notwithstanding. Moreover, unlike nearly all other successful young musicians, Zukofsky concentrated not upon the classic repertoire but—here is the crucial difference—upon indubitably modern music, particularly those pieces that other performers could not or dared not play. Thus, at twenty-five he is the master violinist of contemporary performance—without peer in America, perhaps in the world—as well as a teacher at Swarthmore College and the New England Conservatory and a presence in whose name can be founded a series of concerts, such as the three-part set at Town Hall this winter.

An activist of apparently unlimited stamina, Zukofsky zips all over the musical circuitry. During a sample week in the middle of January he played two very recent pieces at a concert on Monday night with the Group for Contemporary Music at Columbia University, after two days of intensive rehearsals (and a recital at Swarthmore the previous Friday evening); rehearsed with a cellist much of Tuesday for a Wednesday afternoon concert of Johann Sebastian Bach and Zoltán Kodály at Swarthmore; canceled an evening flight to Boston, where he would have taught his regular schedule of violin classes at the New England Conservatory the following morning; flew out in the late afternoon to Chicago, where he spent the evening rehearsing for the last time an Easley Blackwood composition that was performed the following evening. Saturday and Sunday were spent in East Lansing, Michigan, recording the Blackwood work before the educational television facilities at Michigan State University. So goes much of the academic year; and summers are mostly spent at the Berkshire Music Center in Tanglewood. "I talk about vacations," he told me over dinner, "but I've not really had one. I've always wanted to go to the mountains or back to Iceland where it is cool in summer."

Zukofsky's unbounded activity is a result of his resolve early in life to play everything he could; and instead of concentrating on only one strain of contemporary composition, such as the serial language (out of Schoenberg to Babbitt) or the mainstream (Copland, Bernstein et al.) or the chaotic music (out of Ives and Varèse to Cage), he decided to perform them all, often on very short notice and sometimes for a pittance. "There has been very little to which I've said no once and then said no a second time, unfortunately. I feel an obligation always to test myself." In the last few years he has performed John Cage works that demanded chance improvisation, La Monte Young's instruction that he play a single note at the same amplitude interminably, more conventional modern pieces by Aaron Copland and Zoltán Kodály and scores by serial composers that, like Milton Babbitt's *Sextets for Violin and Piano* (1967), are so precisely complex that no one else has been able to perform them before or since.

Each commitment becomes an opportunity to expand his range and interest. He even performed one summer night at the Electric Circus, the East Village's most extravagant discotheque. "I drove 150 miles from Tanglewood, leaving at 5:30," he explained with glee. "I arrived in time, got a queasy stomach going up that freaky stairway, practiced briefly in a small room upstairs, came down to stand on a hassock; and at my feet were [the composer] William Sydeman, [ex-*Times* critic] Howard Klein and [*Times* critic] Harold Schonberg. Each gave me a wink with either his right or left eye, we all implicitly asking each other, 'What are you doing here?' The audience was receptive, but I don't remember how large. I played, stepped down, packed up, got my check and drove back to Tanglewood that night, nearly running out of gas on the way."

Zukofsky's original training and intentions did not prepare him to concentrate in the contemporary; but since he was critically open and especially skilled, circumstances made those works his specialty, while his experience made him one of the few top-rate musicians (the soprano Bethany Beardslee is another) who can learn a recent piece as easily as an old one. Nonetheless, in programs of his own choosing, like those at Town Hall, he makes a principle of mixing classic or romantic pieces by, say, Mozart or Busoni, with the more recent works that most of his audience expects him to play; his senses of "relevance" and "responsibility," to quote two crucial words in his vocabulary, include both the past and the present. "The ultimate proof of a continuous tradition is the demonstration of composers' interest in the same material over the years. I once put a program together where every piece was involved with trills or tremolo. It included Beethoven, Stravinsky, Crumb [a contemporary] and Debussy."

Tall, thin, long-faced, less handsome than his publicity pictures suggest, Zukofsky is a lively, hypertense, extravagant but faintly forbidding presence who stares directly at one's eyes in conversation, frequently pumping his right hand and rearticulating the expression on his face. His tongue is voluble, as well as sharp, though circumspect about profanity; and in those musical circles where disdainful epithets are a cultivated art, he can hold his own, rechristening Lukas Foss's *Time Cycle* "Slime Tycle," or dismissing Béla Bartók as "the worst type of neoromantic stuff in the guise of nationalism" or referring to Philharmonic Hall as "a mortuary, where one is constrained to be silent in the presence of the holy one." His conversation is mercurial, jumping from point to point and from subject to subject; and not only does the timbre of his voice frequently change, but he displays a repertoire of stagy accents.

His skin is pale and unlined, his eyes dark and alert. His glasses tend to slide down on his long and large nose, and his dark, straight, unparted hair is messy but, by late 1960s standards, only slightly shaggy. His feet are perceptibly less graceful than his hands, for he moves compulsively with the anxious impatience of the overworked man who fears (and perhaps knows) that something will not get done unless he does it now himself. His clothes are dowdy and unfashionable, perhaps the sort one's mother would choose. On both of the days we met he favored a brown checked suit, with a light tan V-neck sweater which buttoned down the front. One time he had on a shiny brown sports shirt; the other, an orange tie with a button-down white shirt. He looks more like a graduate student or a young professor in the sciences than a Bright Young Man in the Arts.

More middle-class than his musical taste, Zukofsky lives in an unusually expensive one-room apartment on the nineteenth floor of a modernistic high rise just north of Manhattan's West Village; his parents have a similar apartment elsewhere in the same building. Bookcases full of musical scores, more classical than contemporary, run along one wall; some esoteric string instruments rest high on top of them, while other shelves full of well-used books are scattered here and there. In one alcove of the large room is a double bed; another enclave has a dining table. In the middle is an artist's drafting board, its face tilted at a slight angle; here the violinist does his sit-down work. Self-sufficient by nature, he prepares his own tax returns, and he answers his own telephone. "I almost never practice," he declared, explaining why he feels no need to rent an additional studio. "I prefer to look at a score without a violin in hand, and I won't work at anything unless it looks technically hard." Now as well as later, he works and speaks with the confidence and purposefulness of someone who knew at an early age he was destined for excellence and eminence.

The first time we met, Zukofsky was rehearsing Easley Blackwood's *Trio for Violin, Cello and Piano* (1968), with the composer at the piano and Michael Rudiakov at the cello. It was the Saturday evening before its Friday performance in Chicago, and the violinist had been rehearsing earlier that day with the Group for Contemporary Music at Columbia. He was seated on a cane-bottomed dining table chair in his parents' apartment, since the family piano is there; and his mother had turned down the heat in deference to the musicians' physical activity. The violinist sat in a chair with his legs crossed and his long feet stretched out in front of him. The expression on his face as he played was determined and concentrated, but strained only when he played loudly; his mouth opened absently during the more difficult passages. The Blackwood piece, which resembled both Charles Ives and Roger Sessions, has numerous interacting lines that are continually rearticulated and largely unresolved; and this form demands particularly precise and dexterous rhythmic manipulation.

"You know, we're faster now than when we started," Zukofsky exclaimed. "You're right," Blackwood concurred. "Let's go back." They did the passage again. "Once more," Zukofsky snorted, very much dominating the scene. "Let's go back. It doesn't set well yet." A few minutes later he punctuated the conclusion of another passage, "No, that wasn't right," and the three played again. "It needs more distinction between the 4's, 5's and 6's," he added, referring to the composer's overlapping use of sixteenth notes, quintuplets and sextuplets. His shoulders and chest bobbed as he played, as if moving on an invisible hinge in his tummy; and his head cut continual arcs in front of his body. In louder passages, his frame stiffened erectly, his arm began to vibrate; when his instrument pulled out of the ensemble, he leaned back into the chair, kept rhythm with his right hand, and then took an audibly deep breath before playing again.

Zukofsky seemed more critical of the group's rendition than his colleagues did, as well as less fatigued and less formal in his language and appearance. From time to time he would respond to a mistake by making a hideous face, or reach over to the music stand and pencil some marks on the text, his hair falling over his eyes. The three concluded their two-hour session by discussing when they would rehearse again in Chicago, eventually deciding upon the evening before, rather than the morning of, the performance. Zukofsky had all the details of flights, airlines, departure times and hotels in his head. "When do we arrive there?" Rudiakov asked; and the voice of embittered experience replied, "Depends upon what type of snowstorm they got."

There had been a piano in Louis and Celia Zukofsky's Brooklyn Heights home long before Paul was born on October 22, 1943, and his mother frequently played it. By the time their only child was four, he knew how to read and write musical notation, as well as play passages from Johann Sebastian Bach's *Anna Magdalena* books. That fall of 1947 his mother took him up to the Mannes School of Music, where the teachers discovered a competence far beyond his years—perfect pitch and an accurate sense of rhythm.

Zukofsky remembers a fateful fight with another boy for the possession of an instrument he desired, even though he did not know its name (a violin, of course); and the following spring, in 1948, he heard the virtuoso Georges Enesco give a concert of Bach's sonatas and partitas—an example of excellence that prematurely persuaded him to become a professional violinist. At the end of the academic year, the late David Mannes, director of the school, told young Zukofsky he should study piano before turning to another instrument; but as precociously confident as competent, the boy, still less than five, bargained that if he could learn a Bach partita on his own, he would then make "the quarter-size fiddle," which he borrowed for the summer, his primary instrument. Over the next months he worked on the third partita, somehow figuring out some practical fingering; and the following fall he was acknowledged the winner in his first of many battles with his musical elders.

After a succession of teachers at the Mannes School, none of whom finally satisfied his needs (and all of whom he remembers by name), Zukofsky entered the Juilliard School of Music in 1950, just before he turned seventeen, to study with Ivan Galamian (pronounced Gal-am-YAN), an Armenian born in Iran who is perhaps the most eminent of New York's violin teachers. Galamian in turn farmed Zukofsky out to his assistant Valentin Blumberg, who spent a year inculcating preparatory technique. For the following decade, the young violinist saw his master at least once a week, for no less than an hour, usually early in the morning. Zukofsky's current opinion of Galamian is reverent but qualified: "He is a great violin teacher, who can identify the needs of each student, who has analyzed the human body and knows what each person needs to develop; and he demands dedication and discipline. For another thing, he taught me how to look at a piece of music violinistically. Beyond that, he is warm and kind; he thinks he is the father of all his students."

Zukofsky smiled, somewhat sheepishly, and then spoke more personally. "He is also a very stubborn man. I'm sure he thinks I'm the most stubborn person he has ever met, and I think he is the most stubborn person I've ever met." Galamian (and most of his other students) has little interest in music written after 1940; and when in the early 1960s his maturing *wunderkind* brought him a score by John Cage, the master laughed. "In Persia, you could not play that in the summertime, because the flies would change the manuscript."

While Zukofsky's musical education progressed, his academic schooling came to an end in the second grade. He had frequently been ill (though at times able to practice his instrument in bed); and both disinclined to games and alarmingly skinny, he was shy among his classmates. (To this day, he is among the few American males not to know, say, the various positions on a baseball team.) Since his mother had a New York City teaching license, as well as a Columbia University teaching degree, she and her husband petitioned the Board of Education for permission to teach their son at home, and once this permission was granted, Paul never went to public school again. Louis Zukofsky is an eminent and influential poet and writer, as well as a former professor of English at Brooklyn Polytechnic Institute; the son freely assimilated the father's knowledge and, by the time he turned seven, had heard all of Shakespeare read aloud.

Young Paul's daily schedule involved violin practice every morning and then school lessons in the afternoons. His "substitute teachers" in the liberal arts included such family friends as the poets William Carlos Williams and E. E. Cummings. In the early 1950s, he performed before a grateful Ezra Pound, who was then incarcerated in Washington's St. Elizabeth's Hospital; and passing through the house, among his father's private students in poetry, were such subsequently eminent young writers as Robert Creeley, Robert Duncan, Allen Ginsberg and Jonathan Williams. An avid reader, young Zukofsky earned his high school equivalency diploma at thirteen, and then continued to study on his own. ("If Dad gets it, I read it.") More than once in our conversation, he displayed the literary man's flair for embellishing a point in his conversation by reading aloud a lengthy passage from a book he had just pulled off the shelf.

In addition to studying once a week with Galamian and performing now and then along the East Coast, Zukofsky took the usual courses at Juilliard. Around 1953, he met the clarinetist-composer Jacob Druckman who introduced him to the later Stravinsky and then got him to read more complicated modern scores. In 1960, the year he took his Juilliard diploma, he stopped his regular sessions with Galamian, although the two continued to meet informally, and from that year onward, he developed his instrumental talent on his own. From then on, too, he won numerous prizes, awards, fellowships and grants in aid. Formally earning a Bachelor of Music degree at Juilliard in January 1964, he quickly added an M.S. in music that May, and the following autumn he took his first regular job as a "creative associate" (which is to say a regular performer) for one year at the Center of the Creative and Performing Arts on the Buffalo campus of the State University of New York.

Meanwhile, his repertoire was conspicuously changing. For his 1956 debut at Carnegie Hall, the program consisted of Hindemith, Shostakovitch, Henry Purcell, Johann Sebastian Bach and a hyperromantic violin concerto by Julius Conus—precisely the sorts of pieces Galamian would like his promising pupil to play. The first turning point in Zukofsky's developing taste was his third Carnegie recital in 1961, where, at seventeen, he chose a program consisting of four pieces by the classic serialist Anton Webern, three pieces by the faintly disreputable progenitor of chaotic music, Erik Satie, an esoteric work by Saint-Saëns and more familiar violin pieces by Paganini, Walter Piston and, inevitably, Brahms and Bach. The critic for the *Herald Tribune* praised his "calm and collected" handling of "a recital that would have taxed a performer many years his senior in terms of both technical and musical difficulties."

A 1963 performance of Arnold Schoenberg's *Pierrot Lunaire* (1912) with the pianist Edward Steuermann, who had been Schoenberg's associate in Vienna and, by acclamation, his heir in New York City, won Zukofsky the attention and respect of many older musicians; and by February 1965, this time at the Young Concert Artists' Series, the choices were, in this order, the Mozart A-major sonata, the *Third Sonata for Violin and Piano* by Charles Ives, *Tartiniana Seconde* by the Italian serialist Luigi Dallapiccola, three miniatures by the young Polish composer Krzysztof Penderecki, *Sonata No. 6* by the Belgian Eugène Ysaÿe and a work by the Spanish romantic Pablo Sarasate. "Everyone asks why I programmed this way. Well, it seemed more interesting, while the other looked like a Levittown full of identical houses."

Nowadays, Zukofsky tends to regard an evening's program as "a building, a structure to be organized," and for his forthcoming March 26 concert, for instance, he said, "I wanted one big romantic piece, like Busoni's *Second Sonata for Violin and Piano* (1898), and it will be well balanced by J. K. Randall's *Lyric Variations for Violin and Converted Digital Tape* [1968], during which I don't appear on the stage at all. Those are the two main rooms. Furthermore, those pieces are both involved with counterpoint, and both are variations." He flexed his eyebrows over the tops of his glasses. "The opening piece, Brian Fennelly's *Divisions for a Violinist* [1968] is also a set of variations, and an antechamber; and as for the music by Donald Harris and Emmanuel Ghent [both contemporaries]—well, those pieces are ornaments. I think they should be played." Zukofsky derives a particular pleasure from envisioning possible programs; and like all knowledgeable instrumentalists, he can enumerate, as enthusiastically as endlessly, the works he would like to perform.

Indicatively, the master of such a personal repertoire developed his career without the pushing of an elder benefactor or the established impresarios; excellence and persistence, along with personal generosity and a liberal taste, were the major reasons for his rapid rise. But not all turned to success, as he did not, for instance, capture top prizes in the major European competitions—a misfortune that he now rationalizes: "Had I won the Tchaikovsky competition, I might have played the same five concertos for the rest of my life."

Not only have less adventurous violinists and their critical henchmen objected to his up-to-date repertoire, but his catholic enthusiasms within modern music have drawn disparaging words from the parochial figures at the extreme positions. Those who praised his performances of John Cage or his concert at the Electric Circus invariably would not approve his reverence for Babbitt, and vice versa. But all this bothered him less than seeing "incompetents win competitions and get managers. I would get so fed up," he explained, very late one night, "that I thought of going into science. One wishes that music like science blew up now and then, so that incompetents would be washed out."

Partly because his professional standards are so high, he does not own a record player or listen to the radio, and he rarely goes to concerts. "Most performances to which I have listened," he snorted, "are torturous and perverted. I feel inclined to get the hell out of there." The few times he has gone to concerts with his pretty strawberry blonde fiancée she testifies, "He nudges me and says, 'See, see. See how terrible the whole thing is. I told you so.'"

Instead of listening to a record or attending a performance, he likes to purchase the score. "I prefer to hear what I want to hear in my head—my version of the performance"; and when asked if he could literally "turn on" an interpretation in his skull, he nodded, "So can any musician who's worth his salt."

Though Zukofsky continually distinguishes himself from the "necrophiliacs"—those violinists who exclusively perform a repertoire that was old hat fifty years ago—he does not, in the end, regard himself as a dogged avant-gardist. Middle-class in background, he looks and lives an upwardly mobile bourgeois life, with a five-figure income, a compact car in the basement garage of his apartment house and credit cards in his wallet. "I like good food, good cigars and good brandy." Scarcely an enthusiast for rock and other forms of youth culture, he chooses to perform in the traditional costume of tails with white bow tie and very much prefers the company of academics to bohemians; actually, young professional musicians are his closest friends, most of whom are inevitably a few years older.

"True, I may be avant-garde compared to Isaac Stern and Nathan Milstein," he said between puffs on his after-dinner cigar, "but I'd like to see a return to the nineteenth-century examples of Franz Liszt and Busoni, who were both performers as well as composers and who played the classic repertoire as well as the music of their own time. If Liszt did not exist, how would we know of people like Berlioz? I consider myself a forward-looking conservative, who believes in things only conservatives espouse, such as the continuance of live performance, even though it is often unfeasible; the acting out of a historical sense; passing on to the next generation of what is best today; and recognizing where I now stand, along with the acknowledgment of where I came from—identity, with antecedents. I'm more like Paul Klee, who was regarded as an avant-gardist but really wasn't."

His taste in contemporary music is eclectic and perhaps capricious. Among the current composers "whose next piece I want to see," to quote his evaluating phrase, he listed, "alphabetically, Babbitt, Cage, Elliott Carter, Luigi Dallapiccola, Olivier Messiaen, Luigi Nono and Roger Sessions, of the established generation; and Donald Harris, Philip Rhodes, Michael Sahl, Ralph Shapey, Seymour Shifrin and Charles Wuorinen, among the younger Americans. I'm not too impressed by what's happening in Europe."

Regarding the elder violinists, he is knowledgeable, but less than awed; the figure he admires most today is Yehudi Menuhin, likewise an American prodigy who became a mature master. "I heard him perform the Beethoven concerto with Leinsdorf and the Boston Symphony," Zukofsky said. "Nobody draws a line like that. It was so beautiful you were moved to tears, which is something I don't easily do."

In the future, Zukofsky would like to have more time to cultivate other interests such as composing, writing, teaching and conducting. Over the past decade he has composed a number of scores for various groups of instruments; and although he continually revises earlier pieces and has hardly settled upon a definite style, he has a number of ideas he wants to pursue. "Composing," he declared, "has been a private matter which I would like to make less private." His essays on musical subjects have appeared in magazines ranging from such hip poetry journals as *Kulchur* and *Joglars* to the hyperprofessional *Perspectives of New Music;* he also has been writing a book entitled *The Contemporary Violinist: Technique and Repertory* that he hopes to finish soon. "It's harder to master the techniques necessary for contemporary music," he explained between puffs on his cigar. "There is no place to learn; that's why I'm doing my book."

He expects to associate more with academic institutions than musical conservatories, mostly because the former are more predisposed to contemporary music (except for the composer-conductor Gunther Schuller's New England Conservatory, where Zukofsky already teaches). His work at Swarthmore, which requires both performance and instruction, has succeeded to the point where his classes in instrumental technique increase every year, and he is getting musicians "at the middle and lower levels of competence" to perform such moderately difficult modern pieces as Charles Ives's *The Unanswered Question* (1908), Aaron Copland's *Sextet for String Quartet, Clarinet and Piano* (1938) and Elliott Carter's *Eight Etudes and a Fantasy* (1950). At the New England Conservatory, where most of his pupils are aspiring violinists, he is a strict taskmaster who pays close attention to technical detail and subjects his students to strict routines, such as an established order in which pieces should be studied in order to master a certain technique.

In the past few years, Zukofsky has conducted several pieces, mostly contemporary, at various minor league occasions; and, characteristically, he can itemize the pieces he would like to conduct sometime soon. Beyond that, he is organizing a string quartet which will be in part-time residence at Temple University in the fall.

It is inevitable that anyone who has risen so quickly, along such an unconventional route, should attract both genuine criticism and jealous sniping; as the young master says, "I'm arrogant enough to suspect that I have made enemies." The more conventional younger violinists, which is to say Zukofsky's "necrophiliacs," are likely to put down his taste in music. Romantics sometimes fault his performances as "too cold, too impersonal and too technical," but such epithets, which are likewise hurled freely at all contemporary music, usually reveal the critic's ignorance or an unwillingness to understand. One admiring composer regrets that sometimes Zukofsky "plays roughly, or imprecisely, particularly in his timbre; and he often evades decisions of phrasing and dynamics."

Some fellow musicians find him too imperious, too inconsiderate and too egotistical for effective ensemble relationships (and thus, rumor has it, a few refuse to play with him); and this is one reason why older performers, who charitably attribute Zukofsky's prickliness to the generational gap, are usually more congenial collaborators than his chronological peers. (Particularly competitive toward his own generation, the violinist will in turn allow his elders certain sins he would not tolerate in his contemporaries.)

A more sympathetic impression comes from the pianist Gilbert Kalish, thirty-three, perhaps Zukofsky's most frequent professional associate: "Paul is quicker than anybody I've ever collaborated with. He can read a fresh score—a piece he has not seen before—note-perfect the first time through, regardless of what period the music is; and then our rehearsals can be devoted not to rhythmic and other mechanical problems but striving toward a satisfactory interpretation." To the pianist Paul Jacobs, who has performed with Zukofsky, "He is certainly the most interesting violinist of his generation. He is the only one investigating a repertory outside the standard fifty pieces."

Negative criticisms of Zukofsky rarely appear in print, where reviewers are all but unanimously laudatory; and more than one regularly interrupts his general discourse to proclaim Zukofsky's excellence. "It was still an occasion," writes the *Boston Globe*'s Michael Steinberg of a recent performance of Busoni's *Concerto for Violin and Orchestra,* "for superb playing by Paul Zukofsky, whose astonishingly complete violinistic equipment is at the service of a most remarkable musical intelligence." Even the indomitable Galamian is persuaded by his wayward pupil's achievement. "He has one of the finest intonations I have ever known," he said recently. "Paul is always in tune. He has a very fine sound and a very good head, which does more than hold the fiddle. But I would like to see him go back in music; he plays earlier things well, too."

What is probably as remarkable as Zukofsky's competence and his conception of a contemporary repertoire is the fortuitousness of his arrival. Many works of recent composition demand technically proficient and yet supremely adventurous performers; but because such musicians often do not exist, certain notoriously difficult pieces go temporarily unplayed, if not permanently unfinished. However, when Zukofsky appeared to fill this prior need, professional success was his inevitable fortune. "We can hardly imagine the New York contemporary scene existing without him today," Paul Jacobs said. "There he is in every other concert."

"I am the only one that does what I do," Zukofsky told me frankly, mixing conceit with concern. "For the sake of the age, it would be better not to have a monopoly." His singular achievement inevitably transforms him into a conspicuous symbol, not only to even younger, aspiring musicians but also to older composers. A few months ago, the morning after conducting the first European performance of Milton Babbitt's *Correspondences for Strings and Tape* (1968), Gunther Schuller wrote the composer, "It will probably take ten years before your work gets a proper performance—until our string sections are made up of Paul Zukofskys."

PHILIP GLASS (1979, 1988)

Back in 1971, Philip Glass realized that his music was too advanced for commercial record companies; so rather than restrict the performance of it to increasingly popular chamber concerts, he joined a sympathetic art dealer in founding a personal record label named *Chatham Square,* after the principal intersection in New York City's Chinatown. The first record issued by Chatham Square Productions, Inc., was Glass's own *Music in Changing Parts* (1970), which soon became an underground classic that graced the collections of everyone interested in advanced American art and music.

The year that *Music in Changing Parts* was originally written, Glass was moving out of one compositional phase and into another. His initial music of distinction—a sequence of pieces that included *Strung Out* (1967), *Music in Similar Motion* (1969), *Music in Contrary Motion* (1969), *Music in Fifths* (1969)—was monophonic. These compositions have lines of individual notes, with neither harmonies nor counterpoint, conceptually resembling Gregorian chant. These pieces are tonal without offering melodies; they are pleasant and accessible without being seductive.

Nonetheless, such music seemed unacceptably radical at the time, as it avoided the principal issues that nearly all contemporary composers discussed through the sixties—issues such as chance and control, serialism and atonality, improvisation and spontaneity. Indeed, given how different these works were, it is scarcely surprising that they were mostly performed not in concert halls or in the music conservatories but in art galleries and in art museums and sometimes in churches.

Initially, the audience for Glass's music consisted largely of people connected to the New York avant-garde art world. Later, especially in Europe, his audience would include pop musicians like David Bowie and Brian Eno and, still later, music students. To this day, American music conservatories and university music departments regard Glass as an errant ex-student, and only recently have some of the latter come to sponsor his concerts. "Even then," he mused recently, "the students come, while the professors stay away." Every step of his career, Glass won his own audience of people not prejudiced by fashionable ideas of what should or should not be thought interesting in contemporary music. By now, he has the kind of loyal, expanding following that every independent artist envies.

With *Music in Changing Parts* Glass introduced music that moved progressively from monophony, in its opening moments, to a greater polyphonic complexity and then, toward its end, into the kinds of modulations that would inform his next major work, *Music in Twelve Parts* (1974), an exhaustive encyclopedic piece that epitomizes Glass's music in much the same way that *The Well-Tempered Clavier* (1744) epitomizes J. S. Bach. Glass also remembers that *Music in Changing Parts* was the first piece of his that was long and weighty enough to fill an entire concert program too; it was the first ever to receive a favorable review—from Alan Rich in the *New York* magazine.

Music in Changing Parts was also the first Glass to be recorded, and through that process the composer learned about the special advantages of audiotape mastering. "I began to see that it was a completely different medium from a live concert," he says. "The record doesn't sound like what we were playing. It's a sixteen-track recording, which means that at the end of *Changing Parts* we're listening to eight flutes, five organs, two voices and a piccolo. We have on the record something I can never play in public with an ensemble of six or seven musicians. So I decided to exploit the new medium and do things that I couldn't have done before. I wrote some new parts that I overdubbed. The tapings took about twenty hours, but three of us spent over two hundred hours mixing. That was the most crucial part, and it took us all winter. When it was finished, I said to a friend, 'Maybe someone can do better, but I can't.' "

The son of a music store proprietor, Glass was born in Baltimore, Maryland, on January 31, 1937, 140 years exactly to the day after Franz Schubert. (His sister, Sheppie, is now to married Morton I. Abramowitz, a career diplomat whose name appears from time to time in the newspapers, most recently as ambassador to Thailand.) As a child he studied flute at the local Peabody Conservatory and attended Baltimore City College, a selective, competitive boys high school comparable to Bronx Science in New York and the Latin School in Boston. From working part-time in the family store, he can rightly boast, "I grew up in the record business." At fifteen he skipped both his junior and senior years of high school by obtaining early admission to the University of Chicago, where he took a liberal arts degree. From there he moved to the Juilliard School, a profession-centered Manhattan conservatory, where he studied composition for four years. Here his classmates included two bright young men who would likewise become prominent, if errant, composers—Peter Schickele ("P. D. Q. Bach") and Steve Reich. By most measures, Glass had the best music education America could offer.

After a year as a Ford Foundation-supported composer-in-resi-

dence in the Pittsburgh school system, Glass received a Fulbright scholarship which took him to Paris for two years. Here he studied composition with the legendary Nadia Boulanger, who had previously taught a
whole string of American composers, including Aaron Copland, Virgil
Thomson, Walter Piston, Roy Harris and Elliott Carter. While in Paris,
he also worked with Ravi Shankar, annotating a score for a film, and this
experience prompted him to visit India before returning to the United
States.

Once back in New York, Glass decided against pursuing the academic career for which his extended education had prepared him. Instead, he worked initially as an artist's helper and then as a plumber, a
furniture mover and finally, until 1978, as a cab driver. ("You know," he
once confided, "you can earn sixty dollars a night driving a cab in New
York City.") In 1967, he founded the Philip Glass Ensemble with Steve
Reich, Arthur Murphy and himself on keyboards and both Jon Gibson
and Dickie Landry on horns. (Reich left in 1970 and Murphy a few years
later, while new members have since been added. As the melodies of this
music incorporate a strong rhythmic quality, Glass has never felt the
need to add a percussionist.) By 1970 or so, Glass had become, along with
Reich and Terry Riley, a prominent exponent of what is sometimes
called "minimal music" but can more accurately be called *modular
music* because it is based upon comparatively elementary musical structures (modules) that are repeated and modified into surprisingly complex
aural experiences.

The handwritten, photocopied score of *Music in Changing Parts* has
eight lines of eighth notes, equally distributed over four staves, two in
the treble (G) clef and two in the bass (F) clef. These lines are divided
into eighty-eight numbered modules (or "figures" or "phrases") which
vary in length from eight to twenty-four eighth notes. Two parallel
vertical lines separate each section from its predecessor and successor.
At several points above the vertical lines are the letters *CF,* which
indicate that at these points the figures (or parts) change drastically.
There are no other markings on the score—nothing about interpretation,
nothing about instrumentation, not even any indication about how long
each section or the entire piece might be.

"It is an open score," Glass explains, reminding us of Bach's *Art of
the Fugue;* "I assign the parts." At the beginning of a performance, the
group customarily plays only one and then two of the six lines; but as
more of the scored lines are incorporated into the playing, the musical
texture gets thicker. While the keyboards are playing the notated lines,
the horns and the singer either duplicate the keyboards' riffs or improvise

harmonically appropriate sustained tones for as long as possible. (That accounts for the long unwavering notes that are almost continually audible.)

Everyone *repeats* his part until Glass as the organist-conductor silently nods his head, indicating that the current section must be repeated two more times before everyone goes on to the next notated module, which usually differs only slightly from its predecessor. (The exceptions are, of course, those modules following the *CF* notation.) Since Glass's nods are determined largely by how the piece feels in each performance, *Changing Parts* can vary enormously in total length—from an hour and ten minutes on the record to an hour and forty-five minutes in live performances.

Glass has been known to speak of this early piece as "intentionless music," by which he means that it does not program "a calculated effect. It does not paint a picture." One could also describe it as *pure music,* much like abstract painting is pure, in representing nothing other than musical sound itself, existing primarily as sounds in euphonious combination. This explains why this music is nonrepresentational and nonsymbolic and also why Glass's titles are characteristically more descriptive than evocative.

However, one crucial difference between *Changing Parts* and the earlier monophonic work is that the composer is, as he says, "less interested in the purity of form than in the psychoacoustical experiences that happen while listening to the music. Music is able to create emotional content because of the ways in which the language is built," he continued, "rephrasing his idea for emphasis. "Emotional content is built into the language of music. Musical grammar has always been responsive to physiology."

Part of this emotional impact comes from the fact that, in concert, Glass's music is customarily played at high volume, and one member of the ensemble, Kurt Munkasci, sits in front of the group, facing them, much like the conductor in conventional music. Actually he is "playing" the knobs of his electronic board to ensure that the group's sound is both loud and free of distortion. Glass recommends that his records also be played loudly, or be heard over earphones. "It brings out the psychoacoustical phenomena that are part of the content of the music—overtones, undertones, difference tones. These are things you hear—there is no doubt that you are hearing them—even though they may not actually be played."

In the past decade, Glass has since progressed on to other music—not only *Music in Twelve Parts,* soon to be issued as a six-record set, but the score for the great contemporary opera, *Einstein on the Beach* (1976), and more recently the music for the opera *Satyagraha* (1980), which is based upon Mahatma Gandhi's early years. His current major project is a third opera, which he regards as completing the trilogy begun with *Einstein.* Just as the titles of his works are not different in kind, so his latest music represents a departure in style. "I'm now more involved," he explained succinctly, "with dramatic music that paints a picture that is overtly theatrical."

A slender, almost wiry man of medium height, with a familiar face and unusually close-cropped hair, Glass presently lives sparely with his young children in the Gramercy area of New York. His living room contains not couches or coffee tables but rugs and a piano, a harpsichord and an electric organ. Most of his composing is done in his stocking feet on that organ, which is connected to the record player's amplifier. His house has remarkably few records, fewer books and even fewer scores. The truth be known, Glass is not particularly interested in contemporary music and hears little of it, aside from rock. "The composers I studied with Boulanger are the people I still think about most—Bach and Mozart."

II (1988)

Philip Glass's earliest music was acknowledgeably difficult, not only for its minimal musical materials but for his use of excessive repetition. In *Two Pages* (1966), for example, each musical figure is, to quote Glass's own program notes, "repeated from six to sometimes as many as thirty times before the player(s) proceed to the next figure. The succeeding figure is the same with the addition (or subtraction) of one (or a group) of note(s)." In a version once available on record, Glass and the pianist Michael Riesman extend such minimal materials through thirteen and a half minutes, for one characteristic of Glass's work at the time was working out radical ideas to an extreme, regardless of audience appeal. There were hints of sacredness in the use of repetition; one heard of Glass's consorting with refugee Tibetan monks. While the professional music world shunned his work, those on the outside could recognize that he and other composers working in similar ways at the time (Steve Reich, Terry Riley, Meredith Monk) were making fundamental contributions to the history of tonal composition. The apex of this first phase was Glass's *Music in Twelve Parts* (1974), a four-hour masterpiece that has, unfortunately, never been fully available on disc.

In the mid-1970s, Glass became involved with making music for a larger public. His audience was no longer just the art world, attending concerts in lofts which mostly had other uses; by this time his music was in opera houses, initially in Europe, but also here. The music became more obviously beautiful—more lyrical, more charming, though devoid of those characteristics that made it problematic. When artists now about fifty were coming of age, they heard a myth about "selling out," which portrayed an artist, once beloved by a few, simplifying his work to make it accessible to a larger public. Now that we have all been around for over a quarter century, I realize that this has become less frequent. Simply, the gulf between the noncommercial and commercial, between art made initially for the approval of one's peers and that made for the larger audience, has become so great that crossing it is nearly impossible. In all the arts I know of only two figures other than Glass who have success-fully made that leap—Twyla Tharp and Walter Abish.

In Glass's case, the result was commissions to make more operas, all of them containing beautiful music, to be sure, but none as rich in musical invention as the first one—*Einstein on the Beach.* Success also earned Glass a contract from Columbia Records, which nonetheless refuses to issue everything offered to it. Too, celebrity brought, first, invitations to do advertisements for products other than music and then the publication of books like *Music by Philip Glass* (1987), not from a small press but from the sort of commercial publisher who thinks it has made a science of measuring celebrity.

Mostly Glass's monologue, this book shows that he knows what he is doing, not only in fabricating music but in redirecting his career. From time to time he slips into such sloppy platitudes as, "[We] decided to audition several other principal parts in New York [because] American singers are among the best-trained and best-prepared in the world," which means that among the "best-trained, etc." are Americans, but *not,* as I think he wants to say, that Americans are better trained than others or that all American singers are well trained.

Music by Glass also reprints the librettos of the three major op-eras—*Einstein on the Beach, Satyagraha* and *Akhnaten,* the first done mostly by Robert Wilson, the second by Glass in collaboration with Constance de Jong, the third principally by Glass. While the first is a masterpiece of textual innovation, the next two are successively less audacious. *Music by Glass* concludes with a list of compositions, in addition to a discography that is scarcely definitive. When I read that the complete *Music in Twelve Parts* would be available from Virgin Records in 1988, I wrote its New York office, but a publicity person replied it is "not available through Virgin in America"!

What the book reveals is that Glass has become the Aaron Copland of his generation. Thirty-seven years younger than Copland, Glass likewise studied with Nadia Boulanger, eschewed a teaching career and initially composed works respected by small audiences. Both picked up spare change as keyboard players and conductors. Likewise around his fortieth year, Copland got involved with making music for theater and then for film, composing slicker pieces that won him not only a larger audience and a Columbia Records contract but a reputation as the most famous "serious" American composer among those who couldn't name any other composers. This accounts for why fellow musicians are coming to regard Glass with the same ambivalence, mixing envy with genuine criticism, that their predecessors displayed toward Copland some thirty years ago. *Plus ça change, plus c'est la même chose,* as we say.

The truth is that for Copland, as for Glass, all this success came at the expense of certain qualities admired in the early music and the loss as well of earlier admirers. Those who think, as I do, that the *Piano Variations* (1930) represents Copland at his best are likely to share my opinion that *Music in Twelve Parts* is the best Glass, while admirers of Glass's pop music arrangements would be no less shocked by the harshness of *Two Pages* than Copland fans hearing *Vitebsk* (1929). One crucial professional difference between the two men is Copland's care for his colleagues, as a masterful politician within his art, perhaps the best ever in America at apportioning spoils to younger composers who would therefore be eternally indebted to him.

Glass's latest Columbia records are beautiful, to be sure, but beautiful in roughly the same obvious ways that Copland's *Red Pony* (1948) was beautiful, and certain Glass compositions may have an equally long life with popular audiences. The trouble is that music listeners claiming greater discrimination have hailed composers other than Copland as more consequential among his generation. Elliott Carter, Milton Babbitt, John Cage and Roger Sessions all have admirers whose claims cannot be extended to Copland. As Glass's music ceases to have influence upon other musicians, he takes the risk of becoming a celebrity to the many and a nonentity to the self-chosen few. My own hunch is that as he approaches sixty, Glass might, following Copland's example, return to composing a more difficult music, to defining a third phase to his compositional career. The ultimate question is whether anyone who has jumped over the gulf in one direction can later come back?

MAURICIO KAGEL (1988)

The name Mauricio Kagel has been familiar in contemporary music for over three decades now. Since he writes articles and lectures, in addition to working in other arts, he has long been ranked among the more interesting, prolific figures in contemporary European culture, and his work has appeared all over the Continent. Nonetheless, Kagel's work is rarely heard or discussed here. When I asked the New York office of his music publisher for clippings about him in English, I got only copies of the listings in *The New Grove* and *Baker's Dictionary.* When I asked Kagel himself, he offered me only articles in French and German.

In my mind and memory, Kagel has long been more of a myth than a reality. I knew of him as the composer who produced prize-winning films and radio plays in addition to live theater and gallery exhibitions—a *polyartist,* to use a term I initially reserved for John Cage and Moholy-Nagy, or an ironic Wagnerian in his devotion to the idea of the elaborate *Gesamtkunstwerk* with comic elements. I had heard about such spectacular performances as a requiem that he conducts, collapsing on the podium while the chamber ensemble plays on (*Finale,* 1980–81), and *Pas de cinq* (1965), in which five performers wearing different kinds of shoes walk over a stage floor composed of various textures, their steps making beautiful percussion. In one of the rare New York performances of his work, at a "Horizons" concert at Avery Fisher Hall a few years ago, the performers in *Pas de cinq* reportedly had canes as well.

I had meanwhile acquired two German collections of his fugitive writings, one book issued a full decade after its predecessor, the latter with one of the most appropriate of all back jacket photographs—Kagel dressed as he was ten years before, in a similar stance, but holding in his right hand a pencil in place of a cigarette and in his left hand a copy of the earlier book, its picture turned outward, revealing how he looked a decade before. (The photography credit reads "Ursula Burghardt," a fellow Argentinean whom he married before coming to Germany.)

Meeting Kagel for the first time in 1981, at a West Berlin party after the final performance of *Aus Deutschland* (1977–80), his "Lieder-Oper" about nineteenth-century Germany, I was struck by his burliness—at least six foot four, with a broad chest and shoulders—and then by the resounding depth of his laugh. No lightweight, he. The next time our paths crossed, in his car leaving the Pro Musica Nuova concert in Bremen in 1984, he told me a marvelously funny story about an American tour in which he was imprisoned in a small airplane with Milton Babbitt telling him that Charles Ives was "not a professional composer." I noticed that Kagel's wife was driving, because his eyesight wasn't what it had been. Earlier in the evening, he admonished a photographer not to use flash: "My eyes are ill."

Pronouncing his name Cog-ull (rather than Kay-ghel or Kay-jell), Mauro, as he is called, was born in Buenos Aires on Christmas Eve in 1931, the son of Russian-Jewish parents who had emigrated to South America in the early 1920s. By his own account, he had childhood lessons in piano, cello, organ, singing, theory and conducting, but none in composition. At the local university he studied philosophy and literature, where one of his strongest teachers was the fiction writer Jorge Luis Borges. Remember that the Buenos Aires of his youth was not the problematic city it is today; it sheltered such distinguished European refugees as Erich Kleiber and Manuel de Falla. Professionally precocious, young Mauro cofounded the Cinemathèque Argentine in 1950 and in 1955 was appointed a conductor of the Colón Chamber Opera and Teatro Colón.

For 1957 he applied for a grant to live in Paris. Turned down, he accepted an invitation to Cologne instead and commenced a career full of local successes: conductor of concerts of contemporary music with the Rhineland Chamber Orchestra in the late 1950s, visiting lecturer for the Darmstadt summer course from 1960 and 1966 and then at the Berlin Film and Television Academy in 1967. In 1969, he was chosen director of the Institute of New Music at the Rheinische Musikschule, Cologne, and in 1974 he was appointed professor of new music theater at the Cologne Musikhochschule. He has also received an abundance of those prizes that European cultural organizations, unlike American, are predisposed to give.

We met again this past June, at Skinnskatteberg (pronounced shin-skahtteh-bery), a lakeside town two hours north of Stockholm, which sponsors an annual Elektron Music Festival, perhaps the most avant-garde gathering in the entire country. Kagel had just arrived from Turin, where he had conducted the first Italian performance of his *Sankt-Bach-Passion* (or St. Bach Passion, 1983–85), which he describes as a portrayal of the life of J. S. Bach as resembling that of Christ. "Even if all composers don't believe in God," he explains, "we believe in Bach, a god who serves all musicians." The following week, Kagel went to Oslo for the premiere of his third string quartet. On June 19, Swiss television broadcast *Mitternachtstük* (Midnight Music, 1980), a film he scripted and directed, in addition to composing its music. This last work is based upon four fragments from the diary of Robert Schumann. In a preview, the critic for the *Neue Züricher Zeitung* wrote, "The performers are for the most part silent; it is primarily their movements, their mime, their faces that 'speak,' but so do the director's imaginative images. He interprets, by means of surrealistic-expressionistic optical visions, one of Schumann's nocturnal texts."

Later that month, Kagel was in London for the star-studded Eighth Almeida International Festival of Contemporary Music and Performance, where several events devoted to his work incidentally illustrated the range of his activities: *Ensemble* (1967–70), an opera without words (or orchestra) which is described in *Grove* as "a satirical look at the previous history of opera" but is also about sexual confrontations among the singers; *Oral Treason* (1981–83), which the brochure describes as "a music-epic based on the devil, in a new English translation by Christopher Logue"; *Hallelujah* (1967–68), "a staged version of Kagel's exploration of religious gesture drawn from innumerable rituals throughout the world"; all three string quartets in a pioneering performance by the Arditti Quartet, which is developing a reputation for being able to play *all* of everyone; *Ludwig van,* "a Kagelian montage of Beethoven motifs"; and two evenings surveying shorter pieces. Meanwhile, his films were shown over Britain's Channel 4 Television. To say that his work is "all over Europe" is an understatement.

At Skinnskatteberg, with an audience of less than one hundred, most of them professionally involved in the arts, Kagel would be the only star, showing a selection of his films on Saturday evening, giving a lecture on Sunday morning, then conducting the Kölner Ensemble für Neue Musik in a performance of his *Acustica* (1970). The idea of a composer making films in his own name, rather than just contributing scores, is itself impressive. For two of the four films, however, Kagel's work consisted mostly of composing a sound track to classic silents—F. W. Murnau's *Nosferatu* and Luis Buñuel's *Un Chien Andalou,* the former retitled *MM 51* (1976), as Kagel cut clear new footage of a contemporary piano player (Alois Kontarsky) into a blurred print. The best film was *Hallelujah* (1968–69), a spectacularly swift montage that is memorable more in terms of style than specific subject or images. Impressive both visually and acoustically, *Hallelujah* won the Scotoni Prize of the City of Zürich in 1969.

In introducing his retrospective, Kagel began to speak German, pausing to ask if the audience would prefer English. This was greeted with applause, so he continued in English that was perfectly clear, if eccentric. "I reject to learn any language," he explained, "but I agree to speak any language." The next morning, when he was scheduled to give a "seminar" about his films, he asked the festival emcee if he could speak German, which he did. Educated Swedes were too polite to object, though most understand English far better than German (and better than Germans do, in part because the American films shown there are subtitled, rather than dubbed); but some of those unable to follow instead dozed off as he talked. (Here Kagel's eyesight failed him.)

Later that Sunday afternoon his group performed *Acustica,* which is a spectacle for a huge variety of percussive mechanisms, including rocks dropped into pails of water, tools of various kinds, a tape of previously recorded sounds and much else. He handed me an inventory printed in someone's English; it read in part: "*Nail-Violin,* a form of the idiophonic fiction-instrument invented in the mid-18th century, with 16 iron rods of equal width but of different lengths. . . which vibrate transversally when played with a cello or double-bass bow; two sets of *Bull-roarers* (one with an aerodynamic profile, the other out of plain pieces of wood), which are wielded by hand and worked by twisted rubber band; *Scabella,* clapper sandals worn by ancient Roman choirleaders, but fitted with a hinge in the middle of the sole, so that the performer can achieve audible results with a minimum of effort; *Gas blow-lamp,* to produce vibrations in pipes, the fundamental frequency of which is reached by altering its total length; *Hinged-board* (crepitacolo), a flat piece of wood with various handles attached which the iron parts hit according to the force with which it is shaken back and forth (a new version of the original church bell)" and so on.

Not uncharacteristically, *Acustica* concludes with Kagel himself speaking unintelligibly through a long, thick hose, one of his colleagues manipulating the scabella to make a wood-cracking sound and the playing of an old record. What made the piece interesting were the quick transitions between comedy and terror, between moves that were funny and sounds that were threatening. Its theme appeared to be the range of emotional expression available through percussion alone.

Kagel himself sat in the back, running a mixing board and playing an audiotape of prerecorded sounds. Whereas the other performers were dressed uniformly, in clean white open-necked shirts and black tuxedo trousers, he wore a denim jacket over a colored shirt. Had you not known he was the piece's composer, you might have thought him a technician or even a stagehand. Once he stepped forward to blow his hose, so to speak, he looked more like a mad genius.

It was not easy for me to interview Kagel. Saturday evening he wanted to give to the Swedish reporters who would be writing about his concert in Stockholm the following Monday. Over breakfast the following day, when I hoped to interview him alone, we were surrounded by others. As the day progressed, he had other business to attend to. Just before the concert, when I asked him to sign my copies of his books, he wrote, in a thick black marker, "I am in stress." He promised me a tape of an English interview at the Almeida festival, but it turned out to be inaudible. All I have are bits and pieces of an unfinished interview he promised would be continued, yuh betcha, the next time we met.

His new stage work for the Vienna State Opera was commissioned initially for the Styrian Autumn festival in Graz. "*Tantz-Schul,*" he explained, "is based on an absolutely extraordinary book, written in 1716, by a Venetian choreographer, Gregorio Lambranzi, who worked in Dresden for thirty years. This *Neue und Curieuse Theatricalische Tantz-Schul* is a source of Surrealism. He wrote a book about dance, with pictures, and for each picture he found a short melody. It is truly extraordinary that he saw no difference among court dance, the country dance of the peasants and play or games using dance. His theory was that all in the world can be put onstage as dance. He published the book without the help of the king, because he was absolutely free of subventions of the money to publish. There are only three copies left— one in Munich, one in London and a last in Berlin. I found a reprint of 1975. I took each melody and developed it into this new piece, *Dance School.*" What was revealed in this evocative summary were two characteristic Kagelian strategies—an esoteric source and the use of someone else's artistic material.

Though he customarily conducts his own premieres, on September 18 he will be in Paris instead, preparing his *Quodlibet* (1987–88) for a festival in Metz. "Quodlibet," he explains, "is a musical term from the late Middle Ages; it is the musical term for fricassee. The piece is based on poetry of the late fifteenth century. I made a fricasee of this poetry. The themes are codified, you know, for chanson—love between human beings or for God. I found in the poetry of the time a kind of ubiquitous chauvinism that is interesting. I wrote a piece for one woman and orchestra, changing the voice all the time between man and woman, making a dialogue using either a woman's voice or the man's voice." This last touch typifies Kagel's extravagant inspiration.

Many of Kagel's pieces are elaborate commentaries on an existing cultural artifact. In this respect they resemble, more than anything else, the work of his fellow Argentinean Jorge Luis Borges, who, we remember, wrote stories in the forms of critical articles, stories about fictitious entries in the *Encyclopaedia Britannica* and so forth. When I suggested that Borges should be seen as a *major* influence, Kagel replied that this principle reflects the Argentinean culture in which he grew up. "One of the first pieces I made, when I was really a child, was a kind of nonharmonic harmony. I had a book of the chorales of Bach and at the beginning of this book was one measure of each chorale: to say this is the key, the tonality and the beginning of the works. I was so fascinated that I made my own composition using only one measure each from this table of contents. The result was a kind of promenade into the kingdom of tonality, but the essence of this was atonality. This is not pastiche. This is in a way what afterwards I have called *metacollage*. The essence of collage," he continued, "is using heterogenous sources and mixing them together, and you have a new entity. The collage is the sum of its sources. But, if you make a collage using only one source, you have a metacollage."

To explain this last principle, so unique to his esthetic, he refers to *Ludwig van* (1969) which was once available here on a DG record. In its liner notes is an interview with someone identified only as "Karl Faust," who is told by Kagel (in translation), "The listener, hearing a composition in which musical quotations occur sporadically, is often forced into a position similar to that of someone sitting at a window; people walk past him while he stays in the same place. If he happens to know a passerby, there is a courteous nod of greeting. My idea was to do the opposite—by means of careful inbreeding to make up a closely integrated montage of more or less well-known [chamber] pieces—without the addition of any alien material; the listener's attention could thus be directed towards the musical substance of the context, instead of being distracted by anecdotal flashes of recognition." In other words, a metacollage is not a parody but an examination, an interpretation that begins with selective appropriation.

"When a pianist gives a Beethoven recital today he should not necessarily announce certain piano sonatas as his programme but simply 'Beethoven.' If he were capable of allowing his music to flow through his fingers for two hours, without, perhaps, playing any movements in their entirety, I would prefer this experience to the 'commercial-ethical-musical-society' pressure that compels a pianist to present complete works for the hundredth time. *Ludwig van* is intended to prove this point. Its overall form is based on the thirty-three *Variations on a Waltz by Diabelli,* [Beethoven] Op. 120. I have transferred Beethoven's variation technique to the problems of my composition, altering Beethoven's own music in a manner similar to that in which he altered Diabelli's theme." Though he continually refers to his Argentinean background, it is this submersion in German music, in German culture and in the German language that makes Kagel a supremely German composer, which is to say, someone who could succeed only in Germany, with its tremendous pride in its culture, his career demonstrating that a Jewish *auslander* can do as well in Germany today as six decades ago.

Over cold breakfast cereal, he spoke of his interest in "random bibliography. I don't think culture can be a systematic chronology. Even before I met Borges I discovered that a man of culture should not be systematical. Then I was really free to make my promenades in this universe; there were really no closed doors at all. Borges used to give lectures in the Free University of Buenos Aires—on the Zohar, the Kabbalah, very different things. But I studied English literature with him, and he was a very Latin critic of Anglo-Saxon literature. The American tradition of criticism of literature is, for me, rather boring— it's too scientific. I'm not interested in these matters.

"Because Borges had such a very broad vision of literature, he could put this in relationship to other literature. He could speak of Ben Jonson and immediately after make a parallel to Kafka, which was absolutely logical and nonhistorical. In my field of music I am very much interested in history, but not linear history. I prefer to go with a fishing net. Also, testimonies are very good but they can be enormously boring, and nonartistic." Not unlike Borges, Kagel has a taste for inventing semblances of authentic history (e.g., collapsing on the podium during a performance of his *Finale*); like Borges, Kagel can be profoundly funny.

Why isn't Kagel's world-class work more familiar in America? The problem is scarcely his devotion to pre-Nazi German culture, most of it equally familiar here; the problem is not his wit, for which there is probably more taste in America than Germany. In part he has been a victim of a sort of tokenism that allows only one of any alien category to be acknowledged here—as Karlheinz Stockhausen has been the German composer for the avant-garde, so Hans Werner Henze has monopolized the presentation of contemporary German music in the opera houses. (Günter Grass and the late Heinrich Böll have similarly monopolized American literary attention for over two decades now.)

A further problem with Kagel's reputation is the absence of any universally acknowledged masterpieces that can be commonly associated with his name. That perhaps accounts for why only a few of his records have ever been available here at any time. Yet another cause for neglect is that America has little of the avant-garde opera culture, and even less of the radio culture, that not only contributes to his celebrity in Germany but permits the painstaking rehearsals required by his pieces. Then too, there have been tales of perverse incidents, of his insulting American benefactors, of his failing to keep commitments, of his requiring fees and considerations (such as rehearsal schedules) comparable to those in Europe, where avant-garde work and artists have always been better paid than here (which is a major reason most American innovators have gone there).

It is unfortunate that Mauricio Kagel is still more of a myth than a presence in America; for if his operas and other musical-theatrical works are half as good as descriptions suggest and half as imaginatively intelligent as he is, they deserve to be presented here more often.

LA MONTE YOUNG (1966)

We are slowly beginning to recognize the new art form in our midst. Its situation is basically theatrical—performers project upon an audience—but it differs from traditional theater in several respects, particularly in eschewing literary reference. Some critics have called the new form "happenings," from a coinage by Allan Kaprow; but this term implies unplanned results that characterize only certain strains of this new development. The epithet Theater of Mixed Means seems more useful to me, because it isolates the central characteristic—the use of elements as various as music, dance, sculpture and film—that unifies the entire new theater.

The criticism of the new form has been negligible, some of it written by people who have witnessed scandalously few performances; and most of what has appeared has been inadequate. The major problem is that critics' sensibilities are too specialized. The dance critics who write about the new theater tend to reduce pieces to a sequence of movements; art critics deal more in a succession of images; critics originally trained in theater offer plot summaries; and the music critic concentrates upon a piece's sound. Instead, the new theater of mixed means demands of the critic, as well as its audience, a more generalized sensibility, responsive through the total sensorium.

My own sensory bias, I must confess, tends to favor aural perceptions; indeed, sometimes I enjoy hearing movies more than seeing them. (I would, for example, recommend Michael Cocyannis' *Electra* for its score.) This bias may account for why I am particularly enthusiastic about La Monte Young's Theater of Eternal Music. For a piece called *The Tortoise, His Dreams and Journeys,* Young, along with three other musicians, produces a continuous, barely changing, harmonic (consonant) sound that is amplified through a prodigious system to the threshold of aural pain. One musician, Tony Conrad, continually plays a chord of two notes on a contact-miked violin, while Young's wife, Marian Zazeela, reinforces either one of these two notes. Other positions on the basic, unchanging chord are filled in by Young himself, as drone voice, or Terence Riley, who projects his droning sound through his nose; like the other singers, he performs directly into a microphone. These two lead voices initiate changes in timbre that would be nearly imperceptible in conventional performance; but in Young's piece, the slightest shifts become perceptibly momentous. In most performances, this sound is sustained for one hour and fifty minutes for each of two sessions.

As a multi-sensory conception, this Theater of Eternal Music also contains visual and olfactory dimensions. Because the level of sound must be carefully controlled and the loudspeakers strategically placed along the auditorium wall opposite the performers, this theater needs a rather small enclosed space, which must be as darkened as possible. Slides of Oriental calligraphy flash on the performers and the wall behind them; and the four musicians offer a faintly ironic image of Oriental dress and hipster glasses behind a wall of distinctly Western electronic machinery. More often than not, an odor of incense infuses the room.

The epithet Theater of Eternal Music raises the critical question of whether this performance should interest us more as music or theater. Personally, I find it more satisfying as mixed-means theater. True, the piece induces us to perceive minute shifts in a constant sound, teaching us to appreciate better such noises as automobile motors, buzz saws and airplane engines; for like so much of the new theater, this educates us to be more receptive to the "art" in our normal environment. There is, I am told, a revolutionary and significant musical explanation for the sound, but I have yet to assimilate it and am not sure that understanding this esoteric rationale is fully relevant to the spectator's experience.

To me, as I said, *The Tortoise, His Dreams and Journeys* is more effective as a theatrical conception—as Artaudian theater—which capitalizes on electronically produced sensory overload to move its audience, in Antonin Artaud's phrase, "with the force of a plague." Like the Living Theatre's production of *The Brig,* which is similarly Artaudian in style and purpose, this Young piece has various and unusual effects upon its audience. Some people find the sound unbearably loud and leave. The more tolerant stay, the sophisticates gravitating as close to the loudspeakers as tolerable; and they let their senses openly respond to the sound. Some find the timeless situation so relaxing that they would like to have a roomful of the tortoise sound at home as therapy for anxiety. Others report that it so awakens the senses they later have trouble falling asleep. Like such modern painters as Piet Mondrian, Young employs highly objective and predetermined methods to induce complex, various and unexpected subjective responses.

More than theater simply of the stage, *The Tortoise* creates a kinetic environment within a fixed space and an unfixed time; and like all realized environments, it wholly envelops the spectator's attention. Although Young and his troupe terminate the piece when they become tired, in theory it could last forever. Indeed, in a mimeographed manifesto distributed before one performance, Young envisions the creation of "Dream Houses where many musicians and students will live and execute a musical work." Here they shall create pieces similar to *The Tortoise* that "after a year, ten years, a hundred years or more of constant sound, would not only be a real living organism with a life and tradition all its own but one with a capacity to propel itself by its own momentum. This music may play without stopping for thousands of years." What Young wants to do, then, is make this sound an eternal component of our existence; and not only is such a prospect conceivable, given electronic devices, it may also be desirable. If one steps just outside the immediate performance situation, he can converse over the Young sound; and when it stopped, in a recent performance, I noticed that several people talking just outside exclaimed at once that they missed its presence.

I have seen *The Tortoise, His Dreams and Journeys* five times now, in three different performance situations, and the resulting sound, I have noticed, does not have a pleasurable consistency equal to its intention. In a recent performance, in a tent in Easthampton, Young employed for the first time two electrical frequency-generators to establish the basic drone notes; but sometimes the superfluous noise of the machinery— static, white noise—overwhelmed the vocal sound, creating a loud cacophony of slight dissonance that, unlike loud consonance, is painful to nearly all ears. Another time, one of the loudspeakers went haywire, producing a slight burping sound that, in turn, created a dissonance too hard to bear; for Young is not yet entirely the master of his technology's volatilities. Finally, it is regrettable that most of the recent performances have been open only to invited audiences—indeed, there were only two nights of public presentation in the past year, both sparsely publicized— for La Monte Young's Theater of Eternal Music is as universally accessible as it is artistically both imaginative and unprecedented.

JOAO CARLOS MARTINS' J.S. BACH (1988)

Many of the most ambitious modern composers have produced long keyboard pieces that are designed to explore exhaustively some highly particular compositional ideas. Among the most familiar are Paul Hindemith's *Ludus Tonalis* (1943), Olivier Messiaen's *Vingt regards sur l'enfant Jésus* (1944), John Cage's *Sonatas and Interludes* (1947) and Dmitri Shostakovitch's masterful *Preludes and Fugues* (1950-51, which is about as good as his work can be); but there are such lesser-known, more contemporary examples as La Monte Young's five-hour *Well-Tuned Piano,* Terry Riley's *Harp of New Albion* and the *Opus Clavicenbalisticum* by Kaikhosru Shapurji Sorabji.

The latest of these modern masterpieces is *Well-Tempered Clavier* (1988), an exhaustive keyboard work by the young German composer J.S. Bach, reportedly a reclusive artist who has never before made his music publicly available. (Rumor has it that since this Bach uses only initials instead of full first names, he may be a woman. He/she does not allow himself/herself to be photographed; his/her whereabouts are, like those of the American author Thomas Pynchon, always unknown.) It should be made clear that this new piece is not the classic work incidentally of the same title, by an eighteenth-century church composer who put a space between the two initials of his name (Johann Sebastian), but something else—a thoroughly contemporary composition, richly eclectic, challenging and secular in the ways that only modern music can be.

This new J.S. Bach work was discovered by Joao Carlos Martins, an accomplished Brazilian pianist whose name is incidentally identical to that of a precocious keyboard artist, deceased in the wake of a tragic sports accident, who recorded the classic J. S. Bach work as a young man, some twenty years ago. (In the U.S., this six-record *Well-Tempered Clavier* appeared under the imprint of the Connoisseur Society.) No, this other, extant Joao Carlos Martins is a Brazilian businessman, a successful construction executive, who resembles the American composer Charles Ives in taking his music just as seriously as his business. It really shouldn't be confusing that all these names recur, because once you get beyond superficial similarities, anyone hearing the two sets of records will observe how different they finally are. Similarly, anyone hearing this contemporary *Well-Tempered Clavier* will understand how only Martins, among contemporary pianists, could have played it.

The soft opening phrases of the new *Well-Tempered Clavier* not only contrast with the more percussive openers of the classic piece, but they also announce that we are in the presence of music that reflects the tradition of exhaustive modern keyboard pieces I mentioned before—the tradition of Shostakovitch and Hindemith and Cage, as well as Young and Sorabji, with dashes of Terry Riley, Philip Glass and, of course, Bach's countryman, the formerly preeminent Karlheinz Stockhausen. In the grandeur of the conception and the composer's obsessiveness in pursuing a radical idea through all its ramifications, we find the hallmarks of avant-garde modernism at its finest.

Not only does this *Well-Tempered Clavier* reflect modern music, it additionally incorporates contemporary advances in instrumentation. In Martins's dextrous playing we hear an impressive variety of attacks upon the piano's keys—not only the example of the harpsichord but also that of the organ in his use of the piano's pedal. Listen carefully and you will also hear tones that distinctly resemble those of such late-twentieth-century instruments as the electric piano and the ubiquitous synthesizer.

It has been speculated that this *Well-Tempered Clavier,* coming as it does from a composer who otherwise has no public existence, was actually written by the late Glenn Gould, the Canadian pianist, who until now was uniquely successful at bringing Bach into the twentieth century. There is no question in my mind, as Gould's sometime friend, that the composer of this contemporary *Well-Tempered Clavier* is someone else, in all probability this mysterious Mr./Ms. J.S. Bach, and that this is the sort of music that many contemporary composers would have sold their grandmothers to have written two minutes of.

Several years ago, Jorge Luis Borges, the great Argentinean writer, wrote a classic story, "Pierre Menard, Author of *Don Quixote.*" Ostensibly an obituary for a writer recently deceased, this tells of Menard, a turn-of-the-twentieth-century literary gent whose greatest achievement was to write out of his own head, word by word, the ninth and thirty-eighth chapters of *Don Quixote* (1605). The author of the memoir points out that Menard's contemporary text is really quite different from the Cervantes classic because it reflects a different culture. Therefore, a sequence of words that is "a mere rhetorical eulogy of history" in seventeenth-century Cervantes becomes, in Menard's version, something else: "Menard, a contemporary of William James, does not define history as an investigation of reality, but as its origin. Historical truth, for him, is not what took place; it is what we think took place. . . ." Let me suggest that it is in this spirit, with a twentieth-century head, that this new Well-Tempered Clavier is best heard.

PETER SCHICKELE

*[Saul] Steinberg's role automatically disguises itself,
and his performance continues to prompt people to
ask, 'But is he really an artist?'—the question by
which each legitimate avant-garde has been
greeted.* —Harold Rosenberg, *Art on the Edge* (1965)

P. D. Q. Bach has been such a successful innovation that he has all
but obscured the existence of its creator, a composer named *Peter Schickele,* who scarcely resembles his alter ego. Whereas P. D. Q. is portrayed
as a sot, Schickele himself is virtually abstemious; whereas P. D. Q. was
self-defeating, Schickele has been industrious; whereas P. D. Q. was
reportedly too incompetent to receive music lessons, Schickele had an
elaborate education not only in music but the liberal arts. If the pseudo-
historic Bach was a jerk, his creator is anything but. Whereas P. D. Q.
was born in Germany, "the 21st of Bach's 20 children," Schickele was
born in Ames, Iowa, July 17, 1935, the son of a German-born professor
of agricultural economics. Whereas P. D. Q. is famous, Schickele himself
is not.

Nonetheless, P. D. Q. Bach is a unique figure in the history of
classical music, a pseudo-eighteenth-century composer whose works
were "discovered" in the twentieth century. Under his name have appeared over seventy-five individual pieces, for various instrumentation,
all of them comic, some of them, like *The Seasonings,* quite classic. The
records issued under his name, over the past quarter-century, are all in
print; so is *The Definitive Biography of P. D. Q. Bach* (1976). Every year
there are dozens of concerts of his work across the U. S. His pieces can
be heard again and again, not only because the gags are good enough to
stand rehearing, but the music as music is mellifluous as well. Not only
does P. D. Q. Bach have a distinct compositional identity; but looking
back, I think there is every reason to regard him as the most substantial
comic composer in the history of classical music.

Before there was P. D. Q. Bach, there was Peter Schickele, whose
father had come to Ames, Iowa, in 1933, on an academic fellowship from
the German government. The son of Rene Schickele (1883–1940), a
peripatetic Alsatian poet (pronounced Schick-uh-luh), Rainer Schickele
soon met Elizabeth Wilcox and married her the following year. Peter
came a year later; his brother David two years after that. In 1947, the

family moved to Fargo, North Dakota, where the father taught at the North Dakota Agricultural College, as it was then called, while the brothers built a basement theater. They also produced radio comedies, taped their musical performances and shot films. It was back here that the moniker "P. D. Q. Bach" was born, his initials referring to an obsolete euphemism for "pretty damn quick."

A whiz at school as well as the bassoonist in the local symphony and a performer in local theater productions, young Peter graduated from the public high school and then went to Swarthmore, as tough a college as America knows. Graduating as the only music major in the 1957 class (just two years behind Michael Dukakis), Schickele came to Juilliard, which was then considered to offer the best professional training for the budding composer. Among his Juilliard classmates were Philip Glass and Steve Reich, two young men who have since become well-known composers.

Schickele is best remembered as the most proficient student in the class—the one who could finish all the assignments with the quickest dispatch. "If we were asked to write a symphonic movement in the manner of Stravinsky," Glass once told me, "Peter could do it over a weekend." For his final year, he was invited to teach an advanced class, and to this day Philip Glass attests that his best course at Juilliard was "Peter's, in ear training." It was back in Juilliard, in the spring of 1959 to be exact, that Schickele produced his first concert of pseudo-classical music.

In 1962, he married Susan Sindall, then a dancer, now a poet. Soon afterwards the family purchased a Brooklyn brownstone where they and their two adult children still live. Just under six feet tall, thickly built, Schickele has twinkling eyes, an easy smile and the booming voice of a summer camp music counselor. He has fully recovered from the polio that put a brace on his leg in his early twenties. A charming, funny guy, he speaks about his activities with great, almost relentless enthusiasm, pronouncing his name in an American way: Schic-kell-lee. Aside from a few years of teaching in the early sixties, he has lived entirely off his music.

In 1965, Vanguard Records released an album *P. D. Q. Bach (1807–1742)?* that introduced many of the jokes that, classic as they were, have survived to this day. The basic conceit was that disheveled Schickele, purportedly a "Professor" at the equally fictitious "University of Southern North Dakota at Hoople" had discovered P. D. Q., "the last but least of J. S. Bach's twenty-odd children." As the dustjacket explained:

Fifteen years ago musicologists completely ignored
P. D. Q. whose existence had only been deduced from

> police records, tavern I. O. U.'s and the like. But in
> 1953, while visiting the lovely Lechendochschloss in
> Bavaria, Prof. Schickele discovered—quite by
> chance, in all fairness, a piece of manuscript being
> used as a strainer in the caretaker's percolator. This
> turned out to be the 'Sanka' Cantata, the first auto-
> graphed manuscript by P. D. Q. Bach ever found.

which is to say that the "Professor" is thick in ways that the real *Peter
Schickele* is not (just as the stage "Jack Benny" was stingy in ways that
the real *Mr. Jack Benny* was not). To put it differently, P. D. Q. is a
dummy "discovered" by another dummy—literally a dummy-within-a-
dummy—and you laugh at them both.

The first piece on the 1965 record was *Concerto for Horn and Hardart,* its title an allusion to a chain of New York City restaurants more
plentiful then than now (though Schickele would later claim this as "the
first example in history of a restaurant chain being named after a musical
piece"). This Hardart turned out to be a collection of noisemakers, each
tuned to a different pitch. The second was a cantata, *Iphigenia in Brooklyn,* in which a professional counter-tenor and an equally professional
harpsichordist did their jobs while another musician played only a trumpet mouthpiece and Schickele himself tooted a wine bottle. Back in 1965,
who would have thought that these gags, as well as the P. D. Q. conception, would be just as funny a quarter century later?

The concerts are a delight, full of a variety of jokes. The one I saw
last year at New York's Carnegie Hall, just after Christmas, opened with
the Professor dressed pseudo-formally, his hair askew and one front
shirttail hanging down, intimately delivering a monologue in which he
proposed a new Presidential cabinet entirely of celebrities, including
Leona Helmsley for Secretary of Interior and Don Rickles for Secretary
of State. "How many Californians," he asked, "does it take to play a
trio?" The Professor divided P. D. Q.'s career into three periods—"the
initial plunge," "the soused, or brown bag, period (the only creative
person surrounded by two other creative periods)" and "contrition."
When the audience applauded his return to the microphone, he quipped,
"Same to you."

In *Minuet Militaire,* a kind of Mozartian exercise, the orchestra
paused twice to recite "hut, two, three; hut, two three." For the *Bach
Portrait,* purportedly about P. D. Q.'s father, Schickele sat in a chair
reciting authentic J. S. Bach texts, much as Carl Sandberg did for Aaron
Copland's *Lincoln Portrait* (1942)—"This is what Jack Bach said . . .";

and the acoustically witty music combined imitations in the manner of
Bach with orchestrations of the same American folksongs quoted by
Copland. For *The Preachers of Crimetheus,* Schickele played a variety
of noise-makers, including balloons and a "tromboon," which had the
body of a trombone and a reed for a mouth piece. When the audience
screamed for an encore, Schickele advanced to the center of the stage and
opened his mouth to say nothing, as the house lights went up. As always
in these concerts, some jokes were simple; others, so awful they were
good; yet others, quite sophisticated, which is to say appreciated only by
those who are musically literate. Given the success of such concerts, it
is scarcely surprising that Schickele spends much of the year touring,
mostly to colleges and provincial concert halls, and then that audiences
return year after year.

A principal mark of this wit is the twist or displacement in contexts
previously filled with meaning. Thus, the four human voices of *The
Stoned Guest,* "A Half-Act Opera (S. 86 proof)" are defined as "mezza-
nine soprano, off-coloratura, bargain counter tenor and basso blotto." A
fifth performer, a St. Bernard dog, is classified as a "houdentenor." The
technique extends especially to his titles and subtitles: "*Serenude* for
Devious Instruments (S. 36-24-36)," *Pervertimento* for Bagpipes, Bicycle, and Balloons," "A Ballet in One Selfless Act," "*The Safe Sextette,*"
"*Traumerei,*" "*Sonata for Viola Four Hands,*" "*Toot Suite.*" The performing groups are called the Semi-Pro Musica Antiqua and the New
York Pick-Up Ensemble. And so on and so on. On this verbal level alone,
Schickele's comic talent shows no signs of flagging.

In musical terms the favorite jokes are having pitched notes coming
from unexpected sources (such as the Hardart), the mixing of eighteenth-
century music with contemporary (Bach with Copland, Mozart and
rock), instrumentalists deviating from a familiar musical structure and,
of course, excess, sheer excess, as in his recent take-off on his friend
Philip Glass, *Einstein on the Fritz,* where Schickele took the opening bars
of J. S. Bach's *Well-Tempered Clavier* and simply repeated them interminably, until he moved onto the next bars, much as Glass himself would
move from one "figure" to another. Perhaps because Schickele's humor
is so American, he has rarely performed abroad.

Another technique appropriate to the crossing of centuries is verbal updating: *I. in Brooklyn, Hansel and Gretel and Ted and Alice.*
One of my very favorite bits has the pretentious title of "New Horizons
in Music Appreciation." Here Schickele and his sidekick describe a live
orchestral performance of Beethoven's Fifth Symphony as though it
were a sports event and they were radio announcers, each enthusiasti-

cally confirming the other's interpretation of the musicians' actions. A final signature is the abundance of German jokes, even though Schickele scarcely speaks his father's language. Indeed, in its persistent reworking of German culture, as well as his instrumental inventions, his compositions resemble those of the Argentinian-born German composer, Mauricio Kagel.

"New Horizons" originally appeared on the album *P. D. Q. Bach on the Air,* which is also the best testament to Schickele's skill as a producer of records. Whereas the first album records a live concert, this was made entirely in the studio. The Professor is a Hoople morning radio announcer unable to master his disk-jockey machines. After electronic distortion, we hear an explosion, purportedly knocking down the radio studio's walls; so that farm animals in the background are audible. Fumbling to keep his listeners, the Professor offers a prize—"the complete Vivaldi on 45 rpm records, to come one per week for thirty-five years." And so on for a full hour. This is marvelous acoustic comedy that takes its place in the great tradition that Schickele heard in his youth. To Reynold Weidenaar, professor of film and television at New York University, *"P. D. Q. Bach on the Air* is a terrific example of studio work, of building tracks and editing; we use it in my class. He's a conduit from comedy heaven to us." Another media classic is the videotape of P. D. Q.'s full-evening opera, *The Abduction of Figaro,* though once you get beyond the Professor's comic introduction the satire has more presence, in my experience, if you turn off the picture and listen to its sound alone. Whereas the earlier records were on the Vanguard label, the new ones will come from Telarc.

Funny titles and other verbal plays would not be enough; Schickele's music is comic as well. What he did was bring to classical music the sonic disruptive techniques of Spike Jones (1912–1965), whom Schickele has always generously identified as the major influence on his work. However, because he is working with classical music, rather than the cocktail pop favored by Jones, Schickele produces music that works best with audiences familiar with classical music, in part because it *is* classical music, with the lengths and instrumentation of classical music, as well as comparable sonic textures (except for aberrations). It is not for nothing that the scores of P. D. Q. Bach, along with instrumental parts, are available from a major music publisher for performance by musicians other than himself.

His compositional trick, reflecting that Juilliard-trained competence, is not to quote the classical composers but *to write in a similar manner,* with melodies of similar structure and texture (just as Stravinsky and Bartók did not steal folk songs as much as imitate them). Ask him about this, and he will hasten to point out that he's writing in the late twentieth century, making his music sound fresh with a contemporary sense of harmony and a musical literacy that reflects the availability of recordings. P. D. Q. Bach represents, as he says, "a musical style as well as a cradle for gags." That style could be characterized as eighteenth-century music that reflects the influence of Stravinsky, exemplifying the Kagelian principle of "random bibliography."

The difference between his work and that of Gerald Hoffnung, a German-born British musician, whose similar records preceded P. D. Q. Bach's, is that Schickele composes his own music (unlike Hoffnung, who recruited other composers); and he is also its principal performer. Perhaps because of the distancing implicit in the pseudonym, Schickele, in my opinion, also takes his humor more seriously; and because the works published under P. D. Q.'s name have a signature unique to themselves, they also make a more substantial contribution to the history of music. Indeed, remembering that the esthetics of Dada was based upon the comic disruption of conventional forms, it could be said that Schickele has produced a genuine Dada music, which is a notion that escaped the artists in the early modern movement, confined as it was to literature and the visual arts. In my own judgment, the most serious critical treatment of this music would consider the implications of Jorge Luis Borges's masterpiece, "Pierre Menard, the Author of *Don Quixote,*" which is a fictional critical appreciation of a twentieth-century author, Menard, who tried to write out of his head, word for word, certain chapters of the Cervantes classic. The story deals ironically with the peculiar status (and opportunities) of classic texts in modern times.

Perhaps because the idea of a persona is more literary than musical, the very best single Schickele work for me is his book, *The Definitive Biography of P. D. Q. Bach* (1976), which likewise depends upon the ironic possibilities of double framing. Whereas the book's author (and holder of its copyright) is the unknown Peter Schickele, its narrator is the better-known *Professor* P. Schickele of U of SND at H; and in his biographical preface, the dutiful professor takes all of P. D. Q.'s achievements as gospel. The professor also annotates a sequence of illustrations that look as though they came from the eighteenth century, all of them purportedly relevant to P. D. Q.'s life. (This structure of a self-deluded professor commenting madly on an internal text is reminiscent of Vladimir Nabokov's very best novel, *Pale Fire* [1962].)

On the book's cover is a picture, a pseudo-painting, of a portly, bewigged eighteenth-century man holding music paper in one hand and an overflowing mug of beer in the other. Played (or posed) by Schickele himself, this is, of course, meant to represent P. D. Q., though, as we discover in the book, he also resembles Prof. P. S. In the book's third section are pseudo-documents, including photographs of that university at Hoople, which turns out to be a single building on an otherwise empty horizon. The fourth section has pseudo-professorial notes on individual musical works. There are even discographies, footnotes and other scholarly paraphernalia, contributing to what ranks among the great pseudo-autobiographies of all time, which is to say a highly detailed work of visual-verbal fiction.

II

Musical humor is very tricky in the sense that there isn't much of it at any time, and even then it's mostly words.—Peter Schickele, in conversation (1989)

The anomaly of Schickele's otherwise successful life is that he has tried under his own name to become known as a composer of serious music, extended compositions in the tradition of Stravinsky and his teacher Roy Harris. This *Peter Schickele* has composed film scores; he contributed songs to *O Calcutta;* he has written full-length theatrical musicals that have never been produced. Some of his compositions have appeared on the standard labels for classical music (Louisville, CRI, RCA, Leonarda); perhaps the best of them are the *Quartet* recently released on a compact disc and the bassoon quartet on Wagnerian themes, *Last Tango in Beyreuth,* released on an anthology from the New York Bassoon Quartet. For much of his recent life, Schickele even vowed to devote half a year to this endeavor (letting P. D. Q., his sugar daddy, so to speak, take a vacation, so to speak), but nothing of equal significance has come of it.

The odd thing is that while P. D. Q.'s music is instantly recognizable, even after only a few measures, Peter Schickele's is not. The latter is charming, if not slick, and perfectly serviceable for background purposes, say; but what is lacking is the quality we call *signature,* which is to say the individual mark. He insists his style is based upon "certain kinds of dramatic fast lines that owe a bit to bebop, especially Lenny Tristano, and certain kinds of accompaniment textures." To most of us, however, such characteristics are less audible, such ideas are much smaller, than those marking the music attributed to P. D. Q. As one colleague put it, "You'd have to announce it with bright lights for anyone to know it's a Peter Schickele piece. He's like a baroque composer displaying the standard effects in an era when originality wasn't particularly valued." Another is yet more severe: "He hasn't added a note that anybody needs."

My own sense is that the ingenious double framing, the separation of both P. D. Q. and his discoverer (the "Prof") from himself, became a device enabling Schickele to do what could not be done under his own name—to exploit not only his legendary facility but his rich capacities for humor and theatricality, creating an *oevre* apart from his own. Once he discovered the possibilities of such an alter ego, he had, thankfully, the courage and artistic sense to pursue them without embarrassment. (More than one other composer known to me has, after discovering humor in his work, retreated from the possibility.) In this respect, Schickele's pseudonyms have been as useful, as successfully useful, as, say, "Isak Dinesen," "George Eliot" and Marcel Duchamp's "Rose Selavy": the ironic extrapolation of himself as a Professor has been as useful as other contemporary ironic narrators bearing the author's name. As Schickele put it, "I've always said that P. D. Q. Bach is as real to me as Santa Claus and Howard Hughes."

Simply, as a fertile conception, the tandem of P. D. Q. and the Professor enables Schickele to be a more significant composer, in both sound and language, than he has so far been under his own name. To get a sense of the difference in personalities, just consider Mr. P. S.'s prose introduction to a work recorded under his own name two decades ago: "A garden is the half-way point between the house and the forest. We create it, but we can never be sure exactly what's in it." The irony is that P. P. S. would never have introduced musical work with sentences so prosaic. (A further irony is that Schickele's problem is scarcely unique—Spike Jones also did "straight" cocktail music that was far less successful than his comic work! Similarly, both Scott Joplin and Eubie Blake, among others, wanted to compose straight classical music.)

Schickele thinks his own compositions are very good. As we talked, he offered me claims that I could not in all honesty write down. I came to think that the comparative failure of his own music has become the biggest problem not only in his professional life but for his imaginative sensibility. P. D. Q.'s success is not sufficient for him; I sense he felt at times angry enough to want to kill him off. Acknowledging his disappointment in my disappointment in the P. S. music, as well as the uniqueness of his problem, I left him with the challenge of writing a P. S. composition, probably of some length, that would include quotations from P. D. Q.'s music, much as the Borges story includes quotations from the fictional Pierre Menard, thereby exploiting (and perhaps resolving) the different sides of oneself.

The only other example known to me of a theatrical creation more famous than its creator is Edgar Bergen's Charlie McCarthy, which some might remember from the 1940s as a little dummy more resonant than his ventriloquist creator (who is also Candace's father). Bergen became the straight man to a pseudo-child who generally appeared in formal dress (much like Schickele's Professor) and would make outrageous remarks forbidden to a well-groomed adult. Though Bergen sometimes performed on his own, his success came from speaking through a uniquely attractive fiction who had, alas, literally stolen his master's show.

B. B. KING (1979)

I don't think there is a better blues guitarist in the world than B. B. King.—Eric Clapton, in an interview in *Rolling Stone*

By 1967, B. B. King was known to Afro-Americans as one of the very best blues men. He had had his first hit record in 1949, and he had toured continually since 1954, playing an unsurpassed 342 one-night stands in 1956; but by 1967, his name was scarcely familiar to white audiences. True, some whites had bought and treasured his records, and some at times even ventured into black neighborhoods to see him perform; but he had not yet played before an audience that was predominantly white. Perhaps because he had not diluted his blues with jazz or pop, he had never sung in a folk club, he had never been invited to a jazz festival, he had never gone to Europe. The places in which he played made up the "Chitlins Circuit, U.S.A."

Early in 1967, he received an invitation from a familiar San Francisco hall. "We used to play the Fillmore before Bill Graham bought it," he recalled recently. "I was booked out there by the agency. When I got there, I didn't know that it had changed. It used to be about 90 to 95 percent black. This time it seemed to be 98 percent white, so I thought maybe we had gone to the wrong place. I knew we were liked by some whites, but I didn't know that our popularity had reached the position where we could play an audience where we'd have mostly whites and go over. Bill carried me into the same old dressing room we used to go to, and I was very nervous—very, very nervous. I was kind of frightened, because I was considering how I would go over, whether the people would like me this time.

"Bill Graham introduced me himself. He said, 'Now, ladies and gentlemen,' shortly, just like that, 'I bring you the chairman of the board, B. B. King.' That was the first time I heard that. And at that time, when everybody stood up, it was the first standing ovation I ever had in my life. And I cried, because I'd never had it happen before. It was very touching to me. Everybody was honoring me so much I was hoping I really deserved it. It's a feeling I can't describe to you. It's almost like going to another country where people don't understand what you are trying to say and maybe you might need to call for an emergency of some kind, and you can't make anybody understand. Well, I felt lost. It is kind of like looking at a baby that's crying, and you want to help it but you don't know how to."

That concert was such a success that King was booked into the Fillmore East, which he played in early March 1968, and a month later at a private concert, in tandem with Janis Joplin, in Greenwich Village. A few days after the assassination of another King, Martin Luther, Jr., it was a performance to remember. A rounded, middle-age black man of average height, with a broad smile, advanced to the middle of the small stage. His hair was processed high on his head in a "conk" style which resembled a prosthetic crown. Behind him were five musicians: a drummer, an organist, a bassist, a trumpeter and a saxophonist.

After making some now-forgotten remarks about a premature death, he took a deep breath, closed his eyes and plucked a riff that made his audience gasp in awe. No one they had ever heard before could play guitar like that, and no one has done so since. The notes were clear and crisply played, in a bouncing sequence; and they were played more slowly than most electric guitarists would, the fingers on King's left hand bending each note for its particular resonance. It was truly beautiful; it was sublime. After a few more runs, he began to sing "Every Night I Got the Blues" in a voice that was neither sweet nor harsh. Its one distinction was that his lyrics were enunciated with unusual clarity—more clearly than most of the blues singers or even rock singers that we had already heard.

Since those career-turning concerts, B. B. King has played in colleges both white and black, in Central Park, in open-air festivals, at Radio City Music Hall, at night clubs both fancy and plain and on national television. He has traveled around the world and played even in Africa and Asia. The Moscow news service, Tass, reported that over a hundred thousand people attended his concerts in a month-long tour of Russia early in 1979. In the past dozen years, he has traveled beyond the Chitlins Circuit without, in certain respects, ever leaving it.

He was in Manhattan again, as the top act on a golden bill that also included Bobby Blue Bland and Muddy Waters, two friends and colleagues for over two decades. Even though tickets cost an average of ten dollars apiece, they sold out a large Manhattan theater for two shows on a Friday night and then sold out Symphony Hall in Newark the following night—all thirty-four hundred seats. He had enlarged his backup group, so that it now had, in addition to the bassist and the keyboard man, a rhythm guitarist and six horn players, all led by a conductor-arranger whom King introduced as "Mister Owens, Mister *Calvin* Owens." It is now called the B. B. King Orchestra.

His audiences at these concerts consisted largely of middle-aged blacks, elegantly attired, complemented by a few younger whites, informally dressed. It was apparent that most of them had seen B. B. King perform before. He had only to pluck an opening riff before the audience cheered its recognition of the song to follow. He rocked from side to side as he played, his eyebrows arching high and his face going through grimaces and smiles as he executed spectacular crystalline runs; and then he pulled the guitar way down to his right hip while he sang into a microphone across his left shoulder.

On both evenings, near the end of his set, he promised a brand-new song, "one I just wrote. I'm sure most of you have never heard it before. I'm almost scared to try it." After an opening phrase on his guitar, the audience knew that he would again sing his masterpiece, "The Thrill Is Gone." Even in the wake of Bland and Waters, I sensed that everyone knew this man was still the King of the Blues.

We met in his Newark dressing room, just before his set. Unlike performers who prefer to keep to themselves before they go onstage, King was affable and relaxed. He wore gold-rimmed glasses, bifocals; since he takes them off only when he goes onstage (because they slide down his nose as he plays), most of his fans would recognize him on the street less by his face than by his left-hand ring of diamonds set into the letters "B B." He spoke slowly and somewhat formally, in great control of what he was saying, only his elongated vowels betraying his Mississippi origins.

Even though he had been interviewed hundreds of times before, he evidently liked doing it again, much as he enjoyed playing his guitar night after night. Ever hospitable, he offered his guests fried chicken from a large tin and canned liquids from his portable cooler, and he asked his valet to keep other guests away from the door until we were done. He is the kind of engaging man most of us would like to befriend, because he is so cordial, considerate and aristocratic. In a business full of instability, he has remarkable loyalties—the same record company for eighteen years, the same business manager for a dozen years and an arranger who worked with him back in the 1950s.

As American royalty, this King arose from a lowly birth—on September 16, 1925, in the countryside between Itta Bena and Indianola, Mississippi, a few miles west of Greenwood—notorious Greenwood, right in the heart of the Mississippi delta region. His mother left his father when he was four, taking her only child, then named Riley B. King, back to her own hometown, Kilmichael, in the Mississippi hills east of Greenwood. When she died five years later, young King inherited her plantation hut and lived alone amidst an extended family. "I stayed there mostly because that was home to me, instead of living with a relative here, a relative there. Some of them I didn't like anyway. That's one thing about those little places. It's kind of like a little village, a little area where everybody knows everybody. Everybody else in the area was my mom and everybody my dad. You had guardians all around you. You couldn't play hooky from school, like the city kid does," he remembered, "because if you were supposed to go to school and you didn't go, it would get out that you didn't. Anybody could chastise you about it, anybody. You had no way out, really. Usually most of the people in the area knew you and liked you—white, black and what-have-you."

It was here that he learned singing in the church and guitar from a minister uncle, and before long he was regularly performing in a gospel quartet. When school wasn't in session, he worked twelve hours a day in the fields, mostly walking farm implements behind a mule. "My education ended in the tenth grade. I didn't finish high school."

During World War II, farm workers were excused from military service if they stayed on the farms, and they were paid more than the $5.15 a month that King had previously received as a hired hand. For the first time in his life, he had enough money to break the economic stranglehold that would otherwise have kept him on the plantation. He could afford to take public buses to the Mississippi cities—Jackson, Greenville, even Hattiesburg in the south—where he played the blues on street corners, "making more money on a weekend than I could in a week." At the end of the war, he moved north to Memphis and lived for a while with a cousin, the bluesman Bukka White. (King's mother's mother and White's mother were sisters.) "There was a lot I had to learn when I moved to the city. I'm still learning."

His first professional break was a ten-minute daily program on a local radio station. He played the blues and wrote jingles advertising Peptikon Tonic. This show was so popular that it was expanded to fifteen minutes and moved to lunchtime, and King was given an additional hour-long disc jockey program, which had yet a second hour on Saturday. He also formed a trio that included on piano a young man named Johnny Alexander, Jr., who was later known as Johnny Ace. Their first hit was "Three O'clock Blues" (1949). Before long, Riley King was known as Blues Boy King, or B. B. for short and just plain B to his friends.

Meanwhile, he was beginning to tour outside of Memphis, taping his radio program in advance of his absence; by 1954, he decided to make touring his principal activity. "I noticed that my popularity and income would be better if I started moving about. I'd been to New York by then, and a lot of the major cities, and I came over pretty well." In his book, *Urban Blues* (1966), Charles Keil reprints an itinerary for late November 1962 that includes, on eight successive nights: "Rhythm Club, Baton Rouge, LA; Stardust Club, Longview, TX; High School, West Helena, AR; Fairgrounds Night Club, Muskogee, OK; Stevens, Jackson, MI; Club Handy, Memphis, TN; Madison Night Spot, Bessemer, AL; Club Ebony, Indianola, MI." Every day King and the band drove, and every night they played the blues.

Even now, he is still performing at least three hundred nights a year. A full sixteen weeks of each year are spent in extended residencies in Nevada hotels, and this is one of the reasons why King moved his permanent residence from 10 West Sixty-sixth Street, off Central Park in Manhattan, to Las Vegas six years ago. However, if you ask him where his home is, he'll point to the floor of his dressing room and say, "Here." Behind him were stacks of unanswered letters; beside him was a bag with his composing notebook and a portable tape recorder. The night after the performance would be spent in a chartered bus journeying from Newark to Buffalo.

King's music is the blues, which is not gospel and not jazz. Essentially, the blues is songs, customarily composed in a twelve-bar unit, whose lyrics fall into four-bar lines. The first line is often repeated, and the third line generally completes a rhyme. The lyrics of the blues are generally about disappointment (and thus about feeling "blue"), and the subject and symbolism of a blues song are usually sexual. The melody runs through a harmonic chord progression that typically goes from tonic to subdominant to dominant to subdominant and back to tonic (e.g., I, IV, V, IV, I). Most blues singers accompany themselves on the guitar or piano, usually with the help of a backup band. Within this comparatively strict form the blues singer creates his own variations.

With this definition in mind, we can see that the blues differs from gospel, which is songs in praise of the Lord; and blues differs as well from jazz, which is an expressionistic, freely formed, mostly instrumental music. The blues also differs from work songs, which are meant to sustain body rhythm, and from pop songs whose sentiments are contrary to the blues. The grandfathers of the blues were solo singers, both known and unknown, including, among the best, Robert Johnson and Blind Lemon Jefferson; their most familiar descendants were the British rock groups of the early and middle sixties—the Beatles, the Rolling Stones, Cream and the Bluesbreakers. In fact many of these pioneer rockers learned their instruments from listening to the records of B. B. King.

King himself is self-taught. Had he actually been drafted into World War II, he would have qualified for the postwar GI bill and thus could have gone to music school at government expense. That he did not get such education is more of a regret to him than one might think; for, before any discussion of art turns technical, he will tell you that the principal tragedy of his professional life is that he does not have a musical education. "Wouldn't it be a sad thing," he said, while looking at the floor, "if a person could speak but could not write down what he'd want to say and pass it on to someone else?" To compensate, King took correspondence courses. However, he still does not consider himself sufficiently adept. He says that he can hear a printed score in his head "slowly, but I read, I've been reading, trying to, since the late fifties, but I cannot write down what I want, the way I want. That is sad, very, very sad. Any person who doesn't get educated to the point that he can write down what he wants to say is sad. In my case, musically, it's awful, it's terrible."

King has literally devoted his adult life to performing, and there is no other subject he would rather talk about. Sooner than boast of his competence as a singer or a guitarist, he will tell you, "I'm supposed to be the entertainer—the guy who goes out there to make the audience feel good, to make them enjoy what I have to present. I think I know my job pretty well. You get out, and you work hard as you can. You try to play as many tunes as you can with as much care in doing it as possible. You can't satisfy all the people. You know you're not going to; you know that everybody isn't going to like it. Some people want you just to get up there and sing and play. Others want you to move.

"Let's say we'll split the audience into four groups. One group wants to hear only the old songs, all the hits you've made; but you've made albums that had tunes on them that weren't hits. Another group wants to hear those hits, too, but they're open-minded and want to hear what else you have. Then you've got another group that comes to hear somebody else that is along with you, another act in the show, and they want to hear things that are moving. And you want to keep them too. Then you have another group that doesn't want to hear any of the older stuff you've done. They want to hear something that's happening. All right. You're thinking about the whole audience. When people come out to hear you with someone else, I fix my program so I'll have something that will make them remember B. B. King. I can make friends. That is what I think of when I'm onstage—an entertainer trying to make friends. And I think I've done pretty good through the years."

Even as he sings, King listens to his audience, partly to hear which songs go over best. He is prepared to change his program in midconcert to win its allegiance. "I'm concerned about them. Those are the people that caused me to be on the stage, and they can take you off the stage. It's kind of like in any business. Are you listening to them, pro or con? Each audience is kind of like, excuse the word, a lady. They have a right to change their mind, and they do. You have to be alert enough to tell that if you're not going very well in this direction, change it, abruptly. There are times when you imagine you have long rubber arms and can envelop the audience and make them move, or not move, with you." When King talks about live performing, he speaks with the authority of someone who has performed three hundred days a year, often with two or three shows a day, for thirty years—*for at least fifteen thousand audiences.*

Even though he has also been making records for over thirty years—a few dozen albums and scores of singles—King has yet to make a disc as superlative as his live performances. Records can capture his guitar playing, which remains inimitable, so that anyone turning on the radio, say, can usually tell after a few plucked notes that the guitar they hear is his. However, some of the awe is lost when you cannot see the expressions on his face and the agility of his fingers; some of the communication is lost when the audience doesn't respond with you. King has not yet learned to compensate, as, say, the Beatles did, by exploiting the radical possibilities of recording technology. Most of his recordings are unedited transcriptions of his live performances. The best of these is probably a disc he made fifteen years ago, before the B. B. boom—*Live at the Regal* (a Chicago blues palace).

In *Listen to the Blues* (1973), Bruce Cook observes, "As booze [is] to bluesmen, so heroin is to the jazzmen, so amphetamines to country and westerners," and in blues songs there are far more references to alcohol than to any other drugs. But King eschews all stimulants, not on religious grounds but for practical reasons: "If you spin around many times you can't stand straight. I know that, because I've been drunk. I'm not trying to be a preacher or a priest. After the show, a man can do what he wants to do in his own room. I can see a man drinking because drinking is socially acceptable. I'm not against guys smoking grass, if I don't see them. I don't think smoking grass is any worse than smoking cigarettes, but it's not socially acceptable. But onstage, no drinking, no smoking, no drugs, no pills, no booze, no nothing else. I'll fire a man if I catch him using them."

Charles Keil quotes one Chicago disc jockey in the mid-1960s, introducing him as "the president of the Amalgamated Blues Association,

Incorporated!" while another referred to King as "the boss hoss—like Sea Biscuit, he never lost a race!" By the time Bill Graham introduced him to white audiences, he was known to be the living master of an acknowledged tradition. As an artist, he has been less of an inventor than a perfectionist, less of a mixer of musics than an extender, who has brought a particular style to its unsurpassed culmination. He is the blues singer who has no egregious faults, other than the absence of them (which some think betrays the funky origins of the blues). B. B. King is not a Stravinsky or a Charles Ives—a volatile, fecund innovator—but a daily-working, prolific master, like Johann Sebastian Bach. Indeed, he is the Bach of the Blues.

ANDRÉ KOSTELANETZ (1978)

Few of the world's performing musicians have accomplished as much, as widely and as continually, as André Kostelanetz, for he has been conducting orchestras for fifty years in concerts, on records, in films and over radio and television. Since 1928, he has given nearly three thousand concerts to audiences around the world. In addition, he has produced over one hundred different record titles, which have sold over fifty million copies. His name has become internationally familiar sheerly on the strength of musical produce that has survived economic recessions, world wars, changing fashions and generational conflict—the whole panoply of historical developments that have prematurely terminated other artistic lives. Even now, late in his eighth decade, he is scarcely retired, for few cultural figures have sustained uninterrupted fifty-year careers in the U.S., or anywhere else in the world.

He was born in Russia, in St. Petersburg, as he calls it, late in 1901, the second child and elder son of Nachman and Rosalia Kosteljanetz (as the name was then pronounced, with the accent on the third syllable, more audibly connecting it to its Hispanic origins as "Castellanos"). Through his mother's family, he was the nephew of the constructivist sculptor S. Dymschitz-Tolstoya (1889–1963) and first cousin of the Soviet critic A. L. Dymschitz (1912–1975). A precocious child, Kostelanetz began studying music at five, initially mastering the piano; he continued musical lessons through high school. From 1920 to 1922, he studied with the composer Alexander Glazunov at the St. Petersburg Conservatory. He also became, in 1920, an assistant conductor and vocal coach of the Leningrad Opera.

However, by 1922, he decided to join his parents and siblings, who had already settled in America. Initially, he made his living here has a vocal coach for the ill-fated Wagner Opera Company (fresh from Germany, it folded in Pittsburgh) and then as an accompanist to opera singers. His first opportunity to distinguish himself came with the development of radio. Most classical musicians at the time deprecated the new medium, deploring its inability to reproduce fully the sound of, say, a live orchestra. As a younger man, who had already traversed the U.S. by train, Kostelanetz recognized that radio, its acoustic limitations notwithstanding, would be the most effective medium for the national dissemination of music.

So in 1928, he took a menial musical job at the newly renamed

Columbia Broadcasting System, initially doing miscellaneous work, such as arranging and accompanying. The first orchestra he ever conducted in America was in a radio studio; once a month he also conducted an opera. In 1932, Columbia asked him to do a weekly one-hour, unsponsored program called "André Kostelanetz Presents," which was instantaneously aired over the entire network, from coast to coast. "Suddenly," he recalls proudly, "distance was conquered completely."

It was for this program that Kostelanetz developed his characteristic programming style of mixing romantic classical music with full orchestrations of lighter music, such as show tunes and even currently popular songs. Since the format of the show required that the titles of the entire program would be announced at the beginning, Kostelanetz had to tie separate pieces together, moving from one to another with scarcely a pause in between. "It was like a tapestry that didn't have any seams."

In 1934 came a second major break. Chesterfield cigarettes decided to sponsor, in the "prime time" of the early evening, a half-hour program that would be broadcast every Monday, Wednesday and Friday; and by the end of its run, in 1938, this thrice-weekly program had been extended to forty-five minutes. Guest soloists included Jascha Heifetz, Arthur Rubinstein, Rosa Ponselle and Lily Pons. The program had millions of loyal listeners, most of whom, do not forget, were hearing pieces that *they had not heard before.* Indeed, never before in history did so many Americans hear as much classical music. Because he wanted to make this music accessible to a large public—because he wanted to make classical music more popular than it had ever been before—Kostelanetz was very much an appropriate orchestral conductor for this new age of mass media. "If I can leave an inheritance of a growing audience for the concert hall," he once told a reporter, "I'll have accomplished everything. All the rest are second-class accomplishments."

One by-product of radio's success was the development of electronic audio equipment, and Kostelanetz was among the first classical musicians to explore these new technologies. "In the beginning of radio," he remembered, "there was no one who knew how to microphone music. Everything had to be experimented, and learned." One discovery made at the beginning was that the microphone should be placed not directly in front of the violins, say, but several feet above them. "You suddenly had a sea of violin tone that blended well. It was unbelievably beautiful. It was something you never heard before." The sound of sixteen violins could then be amplified to sound like an army of eighty. Kostelanetz learned to spend much of his rehearsal time in the control room, working with audio engineers on how best to place the microphones and at what levels to set amplification volume.

"Music was no more what we hear in the halls, but what comes out through the speakers," he continued. "What we played had very little to do with what went out over the air. We discovered that the microphone could be a medium for creative sonorities we have never heard before. We could take a few instruments and have them play softly; but if they were amplified, the result would be an orchestral color never heard before. I don't think there was one broadcast in which we did not do something we had not done before. Each piece deserved to be microphoned differently. We rehearsed five hours for every half-hour program. I was busy." All through the late 1930s, other musicians, and orchestra conductors especially, listening to these broadcasts, would later ask Kostelanetz what techniques he used to produce particular acoustic effects.

At first, he resisted invitations to make records of his performances, fearing that they would compete with his radio programs; but once Columbia entered the record business actively, around 1939, he began to produce discs prolifically, bearing in mind that, since a single 12-inch record at 78 rpm could accommodate only four and a half minutes of music, he could record only short pieces or edited versions of longer works. Later, after World War II, when long-playing records were perfected, he was among the first conductors to make them, producing a few new titles each year, nearly all for Columbia, for the next three decades. More recently, he has made videotapes for national distribution through the Public Broadcasting System. Indeed, one key to his popular success is keeping abreast of new technological developments.

During World War II, he gave up his radio program to organize an orchestra composed of American soldiers and then conducted them in concerts throughout the Allied Theater—Europe, North Africa, the Middle East, China, Burma and India (even performing for Soviet troops in Persia). Before the war's end, this military orchestra had played before several hundred thousand people. After the war, Kostelanetz did a weekly radio program for a year—one hour every Sunday afternoon— and then began the practice he has continued to this day of guest-conducting orchestras around the world. Unlike the resident conductor who is also the musical director of his own orchestra, Kostelanetz has conducted other musical directors' orchestras, so to speak, in Germany, Israel, England, France, Australia, New Zealand, Japan and in every major city of the U.S. and Canada. Everywhere he goes, all over the world, he is addressed as "Maestro."

Even in 1978, in his own late seventies, he meets a prodigious schedule. After a New Year's Eve concert with the New York Philharmonic, he conducted the National Symphony in Washington, the Phoenix Symphony, the Florida Symphony in Miami, the Kansas City Philharmonic, the St. Louis Symphony, the Victoria Symphony in British Columbia and then the National Symphony again—all before May. With most orchestras, he does only a concert or two; but with the New York Philharmonic, every May through June but one for the past fifteen years, he has organized three weeks of "promenade" concerts. In these, the rows of seats in Avery Fisher Hall are replaced by tables and free-standing chairs, alcoholic beverages can be purchased at the beginning of the concert and during the intermission, and the performances customarily include visual phenomena, such as dancers and light shows. In between his live concertizing, Kostelanetz also makes new recordings with the "André Kostelanetz Orchestra," which is not a permanent group but approximately sixty free-lance musicians whom he has regularly used over the years.

When summertime comes, Kostelanetz conducts an elaborate series of out-door concerts in Philadelphia, Washington, Detroit, Chicago, Toronto, San Diego and Los Angeles. He also takes the New York Philharmonic on its annual tour of New York City's major parks, giving a free concert apiece in each of the five boroughs. (The 1975 concert in Manhattan's Central Park attracted an estimated 150,000 people—at that time a record attendance for that venue.) "By conducting many orchestras," he explains, "rather than the same orchestra for a faithful group of the same people who would come every week, I am doing more for music." Since his summertime audiences consist largely of people who already know his records (and perhaps remember his radio broadcasts as well), he continues to reap the rewards of adventurous decisions made decades before.

As most orchestras have severely limited rehearsal time, he has had to develop methods of meeting an orchestra new to him and getting it to perform his interpretations with only a few hours' practice. This preparation is an art in itself. First of all, Kostelanetz travels not only with his own scores but with his own copies of *all* the musicians' individual parts, which are heavily marked with interpretative signs that are internationally understood. Thus, musicians seeing them for the first time will immediately know *how* the notes should be played. The violinists, say, will know whether they should bow up or down and exactly when their bow motion should change, or the horns will know precisely how loudly or softly they should play. "Everything is marked," he declares proudly, "that can be marked." The principal reason why Kostelanetz and his assistants go through all this preparatory work is to ensure that, during rehearsals, time-consuming questions and interruptions are kept to a minimum and yet that, during the performance, the music will have the characteristic "Kostelanetz sound."

These annotated parts are themselves the product of Kostelanetz's lifetime of involvement with the music he plays; without them, his kind of generous touring would simply be impossible. If a forthcoming concert includes a piece he has not performed before, he will begin marking his own conductor's score months in advance and then reconsider his annotations at a later date. (Assistants will later transfer these markings to the musicians' parts.) During rehearsals, he is the epitome of efficiency, giving general instructions, correcting specific mistakes, until he is sure that the piece will be performed appropriately. "The most crucial thing about rehearsals," he says, "is that time should not be wasted." If the parts need more markings, he will wait until that night or the following morning. Few other conductors prepare their musicians' parts as meticulously as Kostelanetz, and few, indicatively, tour as widely.

Kostelanetz has kept a permanent residence in or near New York City for his entire American life. His current home, in which he has lived for thirty years, is a palatial Manhattan duplex penthouse overlooking the East River and Queens to the east and Gracie Mansion to the north. On its downstairs walls are original paintings by Miró, Renoir, Pisarro, Braque and Matisse, as well as prints, Oriental sculptures and photographs of himself with Carl Sandburg, Yehudi Menuhin and Moshe Dayan, among others.

Upstairs is his workroom, a cluttered personal space, perhaps thirty feet square, facing the river, lined with record albums, his annotated conducting scores, his piano, his record player, his tape machine, his metronome, his stopwatches as well as personal mementos collected over the years. (The musicians' parts are kept in his office near Lincoln Center, in specially made containers ready for shipment to future venues.) In this workroom, too, are his notebooks, alphabetized by city, of typed lists of the pieces he has played in live concerts and a second set of notes on the hundreds of soloists with whom he has worked. In the middle of his desk is usually an envelope with the score and orchestral parts of a piece he intends to perform several months hence—a fresh score ready for his markings.

Kostelanetz is a small and slightly built man, with legendary beautiful light blue eyes, a ready smile, a reserved manner and a determined energy that particularly focuses upon the task before him. He speaks English with a slight, indefinite European accent, in a naturally soft voice which is sometimes hard to hear. His comments about nearly everything tend to be generous; one exception is "the critics," which is his typically flattering epithet for newspaper reviewers.

Married in 1938 to the coloratura soprano Lily Pons, he frequently toured with her, giving many concerts that are still remembered, and made records that remain in print. Even though they divorced in 1958, they stayed friends, and it was under his aegis, at a promenade concert, that the late soprano gave her last New York performance in May 1972. A second marriage, to Sara Gene Orcutt in 1960, ended in divorce a decade later. Neither marriage produced children. His principal recreation has been travel, as every year he visits at least one place he has not seen before. In 1976, it was Malaysia "very thoroughly"; in 1977, it was small islands in the Caribbean.

Perhaps his most extraordinary mental attribute is his memory—not for everything, to be sure, but for certain things. Although he easily forgets people's names, he remembers music, rarely looking at the score he conducts (which he can scarcely see without his glasses anyway); and he can hear in his head nearly all of the three thousand different orchestral pieces he has ever performed. He can also remember where and when he first heard a particular piece (which may be decades ago). As a veteran traveler, he has encyclopedic recall of the world's finest restaurants and hotels, even remembering his favorite dishes and his favorite rooms.

In his musical tastes, Kostelanetz is predisposed to the romantic classics of the last three centuries. Acknowledging no particular favorites, he plays nearly everyone—Tchaikovsky, Chopin, Berlioz, Glazunov and Glazunov's teacher, Rimsky-Korsakov, as well as Mozart, Beethoven and Brahms. Though he may occasionally conduct Boccherini or Bach, Kostelanetz never programs any music written before the eighteenth century. Among the moderns he prefers the tonal composers, such as Shostakovitch and Benjamin Britten. Although colleagues may conduct one or another of these composers better, no one to this day can rival Kostelanetz's orchestrations of George Gershwin and Richard Rodgers. Among the recent compositions he has personally commissioned are Aaron Copland's *Lincoln Portrait* (1942), William Schuman's *New England Tryptich* (1956), Jerome Kern's *Mark Twain* (1942) and Alan Hovhaness's *Floating World—Ukiyo* (1968).

Reflecting his St. Petersburg education, Kostelanetz believes that "music" is *music* only when it is tonal—a position most contemporary theorists would dismiss as ineluctably conservative. Finally, however, his defense of this bias, as well as his practice, returns to the fact that, yes, his records and concerts are popular and, yes he has survived not only his competitors but his imitators. "I was born totally unknown," he once told a reporter, "and somehow or other it seems that now everybody knows me. I also think that most people like what I'm doing."

ROBERT MOOG (1970)

*The artist has always employed new tools and
knowledge, though never so readily as now, when he
haunts the factory as often as the museum. In the
past the gap in time between the new product and its
use in art was far wider.*—Douglas M. Davis,
"Art & Technology—the New Combine" (1968)

The Moogs have been coming these past few years, they have gone
nearly everywhere, and there is no end in sight to their proliferation and
purpose. As everyone attuned should know, the Moog is that new electronic music-making machine, its name rhyming with "rogue"; and its
capabilities are extraordinary and various. Not only was a Moog the
featured instrument on that best-selling classical album of recent years,
Switched-On Bach, but the Beatles, the Rolling Stones, the Beachboys
and other rogues of rock have obtained their Moogs, as have many
university departments. Its sound, often disguised, can be heard in innumerable television commercials; and on local classical-music radio is
repeatedly heard an advertisement promising new records for piano,
orchestra, rock ensemble, "and that newest recording phenomenon, the
Moog" (invariably mispronounced to rhyme with "frug"). Soon will
appear Mini-Moogs, their trademark copyrighted, for under a thousand
dollars—for your home, or mine; and who would dare foretell the next
steps in their advance.

Technically, the Moog is a music synthesizer, which is to say a
maker of sounds; and in this respect it is clearly an extension of earlier
musical instruments, which were also, each in its own way, machines for
making desired tones. The difference, however, is that the Moog can
produce a far greater variety of sounds, generally with more precise
articulation than any precontemporary instrument; and again in contrast
to strictly manual music-making machines, all sounds made on a synthesizer are electronically generated and electronically modified. If the electric current were turned off, no amount of cajoling could induce a bleep
out of a Moog.

As a synthesizer in the purest sense of the word, the Moog works
by combining discrete parts into an aural whole, a sound, that represents
a synthesis of elements. It is not by any means a composing machine, as
it can make no crucial compositional decisions, instead merely executing

its performer's musical designs, like any other reliable instrument. Nor is it a "computer," as it computes nothing in its present form; nor can it perform as thoroughly automatically as a player piano. Take away the human hand that operates the Moog, and it lies silent. Perhaps because of musicians' traditional dependence upon instrumental machines, they have generally been more disposed to electronic technology than other kinds of artists.

The typical Moog machine has a piano-like keyboard that is usually tuned to a conventional tonal scale (though other tunings are possible). Above the keyboard is a patch panel full of holes, plugs, knobs and switches which become standard electrical hardware offering access to tone-generators and modifiers, all of which can be called upon to contribute to producing the final musical sounds. For instance, merely by turning a knob the performer can vary the speed of attack—the rise of a sound from silence to maximum amplitude—from two milliseconds to ten seconds, and the speed of decay, or a sound's fall into silence, can be independently programmed to vary within a similar range of rates. Among the attachments available are a sequencer with which a performer can repeat a particular riff until the sequencer is turned off. The keyboard is included as "the most obvious and efficient interface between man and machine," but a performer can bypass it to generate tones directly on the switch panel. On certain synthesizers is stretched, between two points on a board, a metallic ribbon that responds to fingertip manipulations.

A fully equipped Moog runs about four feet square and weighs over two hundred pounds. Most Moogs currently in use are *monophonic,* or able to produce only one sound (or one programmed cluster of related sounds) at a time; but several very new machines contain *polyphonic* keyboards. Therefore, in its simplest form of operation the Moog resembles an electric organ, limited however to only one note at a time, but with the advantage of a greater number of attachments for controlling and transforming sounds that are begun by depressing a key. For that reason, anybody who knows how to play a keyboard instrument has the elementary prerequisite for sitting down before a Moog. Its more sophisticated performers, however, know how to use other equipment for maximum musical effect.

What can a Moog do musically? It has the potential to produce virtually any audible sound; but in practice a musician's ability to imitate, or generate, a particular sound is limited by his capability for specifying its components. That is, to recreate the middle-C of a clarinet, say, the performer must know not only the pitch (middle-C) but also the characteristic timbre of a clarinet's sound, its typical nuances of acoustic attack and decay, the possible degrees of loudness, and perhaps the likely overtones of the original instrument sound. Moreover, this knowledge must be so accurate, as well as precisely applied, that it soon becomes clear that imitating the middle-C of a live clarinet is not an especially profitable way to use a synthesizer, particularly if there is a live clarinetist around.

It is not quite true that the Moog "can produce any sounds"; for as even its inventor admits, "There are more conceivable sounds that it can't produce than it can. There are certain classes of spectra it can't produce, such as a cymbal or piano, where there are a great number of frequencies related together in complicated ways." Nor can the Moog "do anything" for although simple live sounds, such as a heartbeat or a violin, can be imitated accurately, more complex conglomerations, such as a richly symphonic orchestra, still remain beyond even the master Moogists' capacities for imitation. Indeed, some live sounds are so complex that current knowledge of their components is often less than comprehensive; and whereas the Moog's operations are fairly precise, sounds made by live musicians are generally inimitably imprecise. Even the most skillfully realized Moog music strikes the experienced ear as perceptibly different from live sounds. *Switched-On Bach,* for instance, used only a Moog to play a score originally for chamber orchestra (J. S. Bach's *Brandenberg Concerto No. 3*); yet the faithfulness of the transcription notwithstanding, no musician alive would mistake the result for live performers. "There is no point in conceiving an instrument that can do everything," Moog judges; "nothing can."

What does make the synthesizer radically different from pre-electronic musical instruments is that no sounds are "natural" to it; but certain musical gestures are characteristically synthesized. One of these would be continuous vocal-like tones (e.g., a clarinet or a trumpet) sustained far beyond the capacity of human breath, especially if their timbre or pitch is radically rearticulated; and more subtle examples of synthetic sound would be well-defined attacks and decays that are either unprecedentedly quick or extremely and evenly delayed. Finally, the Moog can be used in the old public art of live performance before a live audience, or in the new performance art of recording (where the result is not to be mistaken for a live performance).

The Moog synthesizer is the latest important development in the various and continuous history of electronic music, which has existed, in one form or another, since Thomas Edison's time. The earliest achievement was, of course, the first recordings, where live sound was transformed into impulses on cylinders and discs, and then reproduced as sound by a playback machine. In this respect, all subsequent recordings, as well as music played over radios and television, or during movies, can be regarded as elementary forms of electronic sound. Another early form of electronic assistance was amplification, so that a live performer's sound can be extended far beyond its normally audible levels; and not only has amplification been used with a human voice, but a so-called "electric" guitar would go unheard in a blackout. The loudspeaker is another early aural technology that remains with us, in roughly its original form.

It is more customary, however, to define *electronic music* as sound that is either electrically generated or radically modified by electrical means. In that case, electronic music is not a specific style but a set of new media that can be adapted to various musical styles. The classic technique is sophisticated tape-doctoring, where a sound, which can be mechanically or instrumentally produced, or purely natural (voices of humans or birds or waves, etc.), is recorded on magnetic tape and then manipulated through several tape recorders in various ways. For instance, if the composer plays the tape at twice its original speed, the frequency of vibrations per second doubles, which means, musically speaking, the sound rises an octave. At one-half its original speed, the sound decreases an octave. The tape can be run through filters which can amplify or modify (or completely erase) certain components of a sound, radically changing its quality; or other electronic technologies can be used to add echo and/or reverberation.

In these tape studios, one sound can also be mixed with another, or several sounds can be affixed to tape in a precisely staggered succession, or tape can be looped, end joined to end, to repeat itself over and over again. The working tape can be cut and spliced, sounds from one tape can be mixed with sound from other tapes, and so forth. Beyond that, the composer can create each of several tracks of tape separately, and then re-mix the tracks with one another into a two-track tape suitable for *stereo* playback. (The writer J. Marks reports, for instance, that the screeching seagulls sound in the background at the beginning of the Beatles' "Strawberry Fields" was made by first recording the laughter of Paul McCartney and then speeding up and looping the tape.) The masterpieces of tape-manipulated music include John Cage's *Williams Mix* (1952), which is a collage wholly of live sounds; such entirely electronic tapes as Edgard Varèse's *Poème élèctronique* (1958) and Bülent Arel's *Music for a Sacred Service* (1961); and Karlheinz Stockhausen's *Gesang der Jünglinge* (1956), which combines live voices with sounds that were electronic in origin. The important points for further history were that the tape system does not synthesize its original sounds and that, since most of these pieces mix pitched sounds with nonpitched, the conventional distinction separating "noise" from "music" became irrelevant.

The evident limitations of tape technologies, particularly in producing musically accurate pitch, inspired a further technological development—a machine that generates synthetic sounds precisely to the composer's specifications. Earlier electric instruments included the Theremin, a tone-generator with two sensitized antennae, one for pitch and the other for volume, that respond to hand-motions in the space around them by producing a single sustained tone (of unfixed pitch, however), and then the Hammond Organ (1934), whose electrically generated sounds (made by depressing keys that are fixed in pitch) imitated those of a nonelectric organ with uneven success (until its performers realized it was more profitable to exploit effects wholly indigenous to this new instrument).

The first *synthesizer* to carry that name grew out of the RCA Laboratories at Princeton, New Jersey, in the early fifties; and the Mark I, as it was called, was superceded by the Mark II, a singular machine subsequently loaned to the Columbia-Princeton Electronic Music Studio located in New York City. A huge musical instrument— some eight feet high, seventeen feet across and three feet deep, filled with innumerable sound generators and some 1750 tubes (an archaic technology implicitly revealing Mark II's birthdate)—this synthesizer has numerous sets of switches that allow the composer to specify accurately five dimensions of a musical sound. These are pitch, octave, timbre, amplitude (volume) and envelope (characteristics of attack and decay). Only when all these dimensions are specified will the RCA Mark II produce the desired note.

If that aural result does not fulfill the composer's intentions, he can readjust the specifications to generate a revision; and once that note is satisfactory, he then records its sound on tape. As in tape-doctoring, the composer can mix one note with another, as well as distribute his sounds over all the available channels of a tape. The primary disadvantage of the Mark II is that each sound must be comprehensively programmed—a painstaking procedure that makes the composition of an original piece a most time-consuming process.

At this point in the development of electronic music enters Robert A. Moog. Born in New York in 1934 and reared in Flushing, the son of first-generation parents—a Swiss father (whose name was Dutch) and a Polish-Jewish mother—he grew up in a largely Irish neighborhood, to which he attributes his penchant for profanity. He studied the piano between the ages of five and fifteen, even journeying twice each week to the Manhattan School of Music, where he also took courses in music theory and sight-singing. He toyed with attending the High School of Music and Art but decided instead upon Bronx Science, "spending half of my teenage on the subways."

The only child of an engineer, he took to tinkering quite early; and in 1949, at the age of fifteen, he "abandoned all those stupid piano lessons" and produced his first electrical musical instrument, a Theremin made by following instructions in a magazine article. A few years later, while a student at Queens College ("a good school"), he wrote an article about a more advanced Theremin, which used newer tubes, and then sold a few made by his own hand. Moog finished a physics course at Queens College in 1955 and then went on to Columbia to take his bachelor's degree in electrical engineering, receiving that degree in 1957. His lab instructor there was Peter Mauzey, who had been a primary technical advisor to the Columbia-Princeton studio since its founding in 1951; and this friendship made him aware of the pioneering efforts in American electronic music. Moog then moved to Cornell to complete his doctorate in engineering physics (that he eventually obtained in 1965 with a thesis on crystals).

In 1958, he married Shirley Leigh, whom he knew at Queens. Partially to support his family, he revived the Theremin business with a new transistorized version which, much to his surprise, sold $50,000 worth of kits and assembled instruments in 1961. "It was really, like, too much." Shirley remembers, "Most doctoral students went back to the labs at night; Moog [as she calls him] went to build his Theremins." He took his instruments to music educators' conferences, among other gatherings, and met in this way several young musicians who influenced his future development.

One was Herbert Deutsch, a composer now teaching at Hofstra University, who visited Ithaca in the summer of 1964; and together they concocted what Moog calls "the germs of the synthesizer." It was Moog's brilliant idea to make both a voltage-controlled oscillator and a voltage-controlled amplifier, and then attach these components to a keyboard, producing, in effect, a primitive version of the current system. There was at this time, Moog now remembers, no sense of artistic or technical breakthrough, and even less ambition to found a business around this machine. "It was just something amusing." In retrospect, it is clear that Moog's great invention lay not in a new discovery but in integrating various existing technologies—synthesizing the whole, so to speak, out of various elements. "Any one aspect of our synthesizer," he acknowledges, "can be traced back to something else."

A fortuitous circumstance that autumn enabled him to obtain gratis a booth at the Audio Engineering Society Convention; and although his makeshift, unimposing equipment looked terribly amateur beside all the gleaming professional machinery, it was here that Moog sold his earliest synthesizers. The first went to the famed choreographer Alwin Nikolais, who had previously been using a tape process to compose electronic accompaniments for his dance-theater pieces. "I saw I could make my life much easier if I had a Moog," he recalls, "and a recent Guggenheim put me in enough chips to buy it." The second went to Eric Siday, a highly successful composer of advertisements and other commercial music. A third went to the University of Illinois, while Vladimir Ussachevsky, a co-director of Columbia-Princeton, ordered parts. Recognizing artists' need for cheaper and accessible electronic musical machinery, Moog wanted at first to supply just kits, as with his earlier Theremin, because both manufacture and shipping would be easier that way; but most customers wanted an assembled system.

Disregarding the advice of good friends that "no market existed" for his machine, Moog took the synthesizer destined for Illinois to Dallas the following spring, for the Music Educators National Conference; and although the machine received much unfavorable publicity in the local newspaper, Moog made a few more sales. That summer he ran the first of several three-week seminars for composers, his wife feeding all the participants; and this too led to the founding of a few more studios with custom-made Moog machinery. These demonstrations, along with modest advertisements and recommendations by satisfied customers, enabled Moog to hire a few assistants; but early in 1967 he thought of closing the business and becoming a professor.

The turning point came that spring when Moog journeyed to Los Angeles to another musicians' convention, where, to his surprise, word-of-mouth communications brought out numerous Hollywood composers to inspect his machines. They discovered that this Moog could be played in "live time" (as distinct from "studio time," where sounds are made primarily to be recorded on tape). Since they usually work against a pressing deadline and thus desired more rapid means of composing "sounds that were both 'sound-effects' and music," Moog was swamped with orders. In retrospect, it was his practical achievement to build a far more accessible means of generating "electronic" sounds, making it available to musicians who found the earlier technologies impractical. By

1969 Moog was able to incorporate his burgeoning business, as that year appeared not only *The Well-Tempered Synthesizer,* a more various sequel to *Switched-On Bach,* but also the two-record *Nonesuch Guide to Electronic Music,* which, its erroneously general title notwithstanding, is really a rather fuzzy lesson in using the Moog.

Establishing an enterprise of this sort posed innumerable problems. Though Moog had always cultivated the notion of founding an advanced technological enterprise, he was scarcely prepared for all the responsibilities and resulting crises. With only shoestrings to his name, and no beneficence (to this day) from either foundations or the government, Moog had to borrow extensively. His patron here, providing as much as $75,000 at unusually favorable terms, was Mr. A. W. Chamberlain, who recently retired as vice-president of the Tompkins Country Trust Company. "If a hardnose had been in charge of my account," Moog conjectures, "we would have gotten nothing." Until 1969, Moog was also chief researcher, builder, tester, installer, repairman, salesman, and greeter of his enterprise. Although he worked all the time, and always looked exhausted, it was many months, often after many postponements, before the company could deliver a finished machine. "It took a lot of work and money," he explained, "to break open a market that hadn't existed before."

The next turning point came in 1969, when he expanded the physical size of his factory, hired four degreed engineers, a draftsman-designer and a traveling repairman-installer, appointed his first "composer-in-residence," and took on business-types as general manager and sales manager; so that a new machine could be produced, inspected and sold without Moog's seeing it. In 1969 he also obtained a loan from the Small Business Administration "that provided money to continue." The payroll, currently for twenty-five people, is now processed by computer (instead of by Mrs. Moog, as before). The gross volume of business has officially doubled every fiscal year since 1965, except for the most recent (largely because of the Nixon recession), which still witnessed a 25% increase to sales of a half-million dollars; and nearly three hundred complete Moog synthesizers are now in use.

His company is now producing approximately one hundred synthesizers a year, deliverable within a few weeks of the original order. The boss takes a salary of $20,000, the maximum allowed under the S. B. A. arrangements; and the young professional staff earns wages slightly substandard for their credentials. The major problem now is increased competition from other machines; so that most of the profit cleared last year has gone into further research, technological sagacity merging with commercial necessity. The recent expansion, he says, "forced me to become more of a businessman—more rational and objective about general business considerations. Four or five years ago, if anything interesting came along, I'd jump at it. Now I consider financial expenses and benefits, although these may be long range; and I ascertain agreement of other people. Our situation is still precarious." As sole owner of all the stock, Moog has considered takeover offers from electronic and music companies but rejected them largely because of insufficient control over research and development.

The R. A. Moog Co. started in an abandoned furniture store on the main street in Trumansburg, New York, an otherwise unremarkable hamlet (pop. 2,000) about ten miles north of Ithaca; and it has since expanded into adjacent space and the floors above, becoming the biggest business in town. The ground floor is a fifteen-foot high cluttered space. In one section is a short production line running around both sides of a long table. Behind skilled laborers on one side are boxes of sorted electrical parts, which are assembled on boards and then placed in metal casings, completing the construction of a basic module. (Since individual units can be replaced and reorganized in the Moog, the system is called "modular.") On the other side of the table, keyboards are produced by hand. In the back is a metal press where the modules' casings are cut and marked. "Report all accidents immediately," reads a sign.

In newly acquired space is now an inspection area where about one hundred synthesizing functions are extensively tested before shipping (as is customary with expensive precision equipment); and beyond that is paraphernalia for packing. (The young engineer showing me around banged a module hard upon the table to show that nothing moved or bent, and whole Moogs are dropped a few feet before shipping, "because everything goes out of here by air freight.") In the back is the only studio containing all the equipment sufficient for making electronic music. Upstairs are the higher-ups, crowded into inadequate space. The boss himself shares a room with his general manager, whose experienced neatness contrasts with the mess on Moog's desk; and the research engineers work in the back.

II

I would like to use 'invention' to mean the process of bringing new technology into being, or again, the new technology created in the process. 'Technology' will mean any tool or technique, any product or process,

*any physical equipment or method of doing or
making, by which human capability is extended.
'Innovation' will mean the process of bringing
invention into use, and 'diffusion,' the spread of its
use beyond the first instance.*—Donald A. Schon,
Technology and Change (1967)

Moog came to meet me at the Ithaca airport, an act of personal generosity I learned was typical; and he was thereafter a most gracious host. His manner is modest, unpretentious, informal, beloved and friendly, in spite of nervousness at the beginning; and his memory for acquaintances, both professional and personal, is strong and sincere. He talks in simple, dispassionate, almost colorless language, his accent revealing his New York upbringing. About six feet tall and slender, thanks in part to a recent diet, he has a narrow, clean-shaven face capped with prematurely grey curly hair that waves a couple of creases upward, though clipped high around his ears; it probably looked rakish ten years ago, when Moog first styled it that way. His nose is long, his mouth slightly puckered, his fingers thick, his complexion fair, his eyes grey and his expression alert; in general, he looks and sounds half-Jewish. With narrow cuffs and desert boots, a restrained and informal demeanor, and pens clipped into his sport shirt pocket, Moog would scarcely pass as the boss of one of America's hipper enterprises. "The crunch is," one friend judged, "that he's too nice and honest to be a true businessman. He's not the kind to hurt anybody."

Around the shop, he wanders chaotically, with an unfocused eye on surrounding activity; and from time to time he renders casual advice. Lacking haughtiness, he took the liberty at one point in our conversation of lying supine on the studio's carpeted floor. When deadlines arise, Moog tends to meet them in a last-minute rush, very much like a college student; and at a live concert at the Museum of Modern Art in the summer of 1969, he could be seen, just before the music began, desperately finishing the wiring and tuning of a brand-new machine. In principle, he claims no special authority in judging music produced on the Moog. "I'm not an artist or a critic. I don't feel strongly about any modern music, although I don't much like the romantics." Ever since some composers complained about derogatory critical statements Moog made in public, he tries to withhold judgments more musical than technical. "How do you expect to stay in business," one friend advised, "if you insult your customers? Don't forget that you are primarily an instrument-maker."

The Moog family—now including three daughters and a baby son—live in a farmhouse on fifty-two acres, which they purchased a few years ago (having rented places until then); and just last year some government conservation money helped them build a private pond. The area is lush with greenery; and the small river across the road becomes, a mile later, the spectacular Taughannock Falls, at 215 feet the highest waterfall in the East. A handy man around the house, Moog recently installed his own heating system, thereby saving his family five hundred dollars; but they have not yet acquired a hi-fi set. "Moog won't have anything but the best," Shirley explains, "so we have nothing now." There is a piano, rather poorly tuned, which Moog confesses he has not touched in years. The only visual art in the house is a small kinetic sculpture with flashing lights, done as a gift from the electronic artist James Seawright; in it Moog, whose sensibility is more temporal than visual, finds "the most beautiful thing is the proportioning of time divisions."

Particularly in the summer, Moog entertains an endless stream of visitors, including, the weekend I was there, the company's Southwest representative and his vocalist wife, the musician Dick Hyman, Herbert Deutsch, research scientists from Bell Labs, a former employee, a television crew from Rochester, and an engineer desiring a job; for nearly everyone involved in electronic music has, at one time or another, passed through the Moogs' hospitality. Over dinner, for which Moog had thoughtfully purchased a gallon of wine, conversation turned mostly to anecdotes about the machine and its practitioners. "Women find it very masculine," one man remarked. "It represents magic to them." Someone else suggested that, "Feelings of wonder and music come with any new instrument." As the evening went on Shirley Moog became more demonstrably affectionate toward her husband, seated not at the end of the table but on its side, right beside her. Their life-style mixes New York bohemianism with country ways, integrating high cultural tone with modesty and informality. Should the business encounter catastrophe, or the recession become a Nixon depression, Moog told me he would reduce family expenses "and become a bum to think and write, maybe teach."

Electronic music has progressed so rapidly, in numerous studios, that it is hard to determine who did what first. Nonetheless, there is no doubt that Moog's great innovation in electronic-music technology came from adapting the process of voltage-control; this, as noted before, was the key engineering idea in the development of his synthesizer. In brief, voltage-control is the capacity to transform the operation of a circuit by electrical, rather than mechanical, means, and this change comes from changing the amount of electrical pressure (measured as voltage) flowing through the circuit. This principle capitalizes upon the convenient fact that externally applied voltage can be easily amplified and diminished. In a theatrical dimmer board, for instance, voltage-control allows the dimming or heightening of the lamps merely by pressing a button, rather than physically shifting a calibrated lever; and changes set in motion by this button are inevitably more accurate than those mechanically calibrated to the moving hand. In sound, voltage-control creates the capacity to contour in live time, electronically, the degree or intensity of each musical element, such as pitch or loudness, instead of having to specify in advance, as in the earlier Mark II synthesizers; or to readjust manually the "gain" of an amplifier, as in the amplitude-control of the Hammond or a home radio. More crucially for sound-generation, voltage-control offers the capacity to change pitch within a single oscillator, thereby superceding the innumerable oscillators in the Hammond. Every Moog oscillator is "variably pitched," which means it can vibrate to any frequency between 0 and 15,000 cycles per second; and in each oscillating module are five distinct kinds of standard sound-waves—sine, triangular, sawtooth, square and pulse.

The advantages of voltage-control extend even further, into more complex audio phenomena. For instance, as one signal can be connected to modify another, an oscillator programmed at five cycles per second, which alone would be heard as merely a regular series of individual clicks, can be applied to control another oscillating sound that is, say, tuned at middle-A (or 440 cycles per second); so that the latter tone would audibly fluctuate at a rate of five fluctuations per second. Or one could oscillate a filter, thereby periodically fluctuating certain transformations in harmonics.

To put this crucial but difficult idea in another way, all physical moves on the face of the synthesizer generate electrical signals, which are the Moog's internal language, carrying directional information through the system. Therefore, each module in a voltage-control system can be connected to control any other module; but the electrical signals passing between modules do not become audible sounds until they are transformed by an amplification system that completes the synthesizing process. Since, to repeat, all switches produce voltage signals, rather than particular sounds, the keyboard, say, can be connected, by patchcords, to a filtering module, so that by depressing keys one can change not the pitch (as in the conventional kind of patch) but, say, the timbre of the resulting sound. To get a "wah-wah" sound, for instance, the performer need merely connect by patchcord the keyboard oscillator to an envelope filter, tuned in an appropriate way; and whatever sounds are played on the keyboard will wah-wah until that connection is removed.

With the Moog, changes of musical pitch are also determined by voltage-control. An increase of one volt in the control input doubles the frequency of the tone; similarly, in diatonic tuning, each half-tone, of which there are twelve in an octave, results from shifts of 1/12th of a volt. With an attachment called "a scale programmer," the physical octave on the Moog's keyboard can be retuned (again thanks to voltage control) merely by flipping a switch to represent aurally only half a musical octave, say, or two musical octaves. In addition, each key of the keyboard can be individually tuned. A knob to the left of the keyboard dials degrees of "portamento," so that the sound slides slowly from one tone to another (as in a slide trombone). Depending upon how the controls are set, the note can resonate (and be modified) until the performer's finger is lifted, or until another note is pressed. If two keys should inadvertently be pressed at once, the Moog automatically sounds the lower tone.

It should be clear by now that the patchcords, both ends of which are plugged into holes, resemble those cords on an old-fashioned telephone switchbord. Here they serve to connect one module to another (each labeled "R. A. Moog Co."); so that a performer customarily makes the desired interconnections (for where the signals flow) before he starts to play a note. One can also preset a fixed series of variations off the basic input, or have these variations repeat themselves (thanks to the sequencer) while the player adds new material. In certain patchings, more than one note can be generated at a time—say, a parallel third (or anything else harmonically related to a fundamental tone); but the machine will continue to generate parallel thirds until that patch is terminated. Possible inputs include live instruments, or recorded tapes, where sounds can then be modified, or resynthesized, through the system. In the Moog synthesizer, nothing is fixed, not even the effects of the keyboard, as noted before, because every element can be modified by voltage-controlled signals. As everything can be interconnected into everything else, the basic elements can be combined in almost innumerable ways—in one calculation, three million discrete possibilities for modifying a single tone with the knobs and the patchcords alone, in sum making the system fantastically flexible.

In some respects, as noted before, the Moog can be compared to its primary predecessors, the electric organ and the RCA Mark II; but in other respects, it is a radically different instrument. In the organ, the pitch for each keyboard key is fixed, so that attacks, decays and amplitude are subject to touch control (that is by nature imprecise). Although the organ's "stops" can modify timbre, often quite radically and usually with accuracy, there is little capacity for contouring a sound, and no capacity at all for changing a sound after the key is depressed. The electric organ's primary comparative advantage is, of course, its polyphonic keyboard. Since the Mark II, on the other hand, can be externally programmed, by punching specifications on a paper sheet that is then fed into the machine, there is no relation to real-time processes (that have, of course, their own limitations), or even any need to touch the machine. Furthermore, the RCA Mark II has more precise pitch, as well as greater power at realizing subtle degrees of durational accuracy; but its huge cost, well over $100,000, makes a successor prohibitive. One basic advantage of the Moog is its possible use in live-time performances or processes (such as rapidly laying lines in multi-track recordings). Thanks to the keyboard, one Moogist rationalizes, "The interface with humans is direct and traditional." The Moog is also much cheaper, more compact and more portable.

Since the Moog has no particular sounds, while its capacities for articulation are so immense, it has been used by composers of diverse artistic persuasions, each of whom finds it the best instrument for his musical ideas. The sometime tuba player and Thereminist Walter Sear, who is also the Moog sales representative in New York City, specializes in sound effects for commercials, which demand not only "electronic" noises but also the simulation of live sounds. It would be difficult to get an aurally clean recording of such sounds as a heartbeat, or stomach rumbles, or shower water hitting the body (to mention three Sear achievements), because the natural source is full of too many extraneous noises. The Moog, according to Sear, "is incomparable for sound effects, but we are not trying to promote it that way."

The veteran, highly dextrous keyboardist Dick Hyman has made pop records on a Moog, mostly in collaboration with Sear (who mans the patchboard); and Hyman attests, "It has sounds you couldn't do on either piano or organ. I have no desire to imitate the sounds of other instruments." Despite his experience with piano and harpsichord, as well as organ, Hyman finds the Moog a different instrument, in part because of its monophonic limitation. "It requires you to think differently," he judges, "in a linear way, and not in terms of chords."

The first step in Alwin Nikolais's method, by contrast, is improvisation, "until I find a sound area I want to use," which he records on tape; and he then considers and edits these tapes, occasionally overdubbing, into a sound collage appropriate to his choreographic needs. "To me, the music is the sound dimension of the same subject as the dance." A composition about a half-hour in length takes Nikolais an average of four weeks to realize. By contrast again, the Moog studio's composer-in-residence, Jonathan Weiss, avoids the keyboard entirely, preferring to generate sound directly on the controls for the oscillating module. His pieces could be characterized as densities of nonrhythmical developing sound-textures—a style reminiscent of Iannis Xenakis's recent compositions. "What Jon Weiss is doing," Moog testifies, "is radically different from earlier electronic music—the sort of complex 'sculpturing' of sound that cannot be done in a controlled way by classic tape techniques."

The most swinging rock for synthesizer comes not from rock groups, whose uses of their Moogs have been rather modest (and, as in a recent Beatles album, unacknowledged)—an exception being the Beachboys' "Good Vibrations"—but from Chris Swansen, a sometime jazz musician who first passed through Trumansburg out of curiosity, but later moved into a house nearby. "Bob heard what I did in an afternoon; and he knew, as I did, that the synthesizer and myself would get along just fine. Even though I'd just walked in off the street, he turned his studio over to me as a place to work. He's beautiful that way." A tall, bulky, pony-tailed, grey-bearded musician in his early thirties, Swansen found that his musical ideas were beyond the capability of instruments, as well as instrumentalists (not to mention organizational hassles); so he came to the synthesizer with the idea of playing all the parts himself, most of them from the beginning to the end of a short piece. He plays new parts against a taped background of those already recorded, laying on track after track until his "orchestration," as he calls it, is finished. The result, still unavailable on commercial recording, is the first Moog-produced rock that sounds like rock (that, like, can be danced to), rather than just a cute imitation. Moog regards Swansen as the machine's most adept performer so far in live concerts, where he customarily plays the lead part against a background of either live instrumentalists or other parts previously synthesized on tape. Though not employed by Moog, Swansen has become a key figure in Trumansburg's growing community of engineers and musicians.

Walter Carlos's *Switched-On Bach* is similarly indebted to multi-tracking, a tape-recording technology that has nothing to do with the Moog; and this enables him to overcome the synthesizer's monophonic limitation. Capitalizing on his Ivy League education in physics and musical experience, particularly in arranging and sound-engineering, Carlos similarly lays down tracks, about one minute at a time, until all the notes that Bach assigned to linear (i.e., monophonic) instruments are included. His success with Bach, which he now characterizes as a "rather simple album technically," illustrates that, for intrinsic reasons, multi-tracking is especially suitable for contrapuntal music; and one virtue of Carlos's musically faithful transcriptions of *Brandenberg* concerti, in comparison to performances with live instruments, is the awesomely clear enunciation of contrapuntal lines that were previously muffled. "When was the last time," notes Glenn Gould, "you heard keyboard fugues realized with that contrapuntal autonomy that only electronic segregation can provide?" Moog's judgment is that Carlos shows "you can use the medium in ways equivalent to traditional musical instruments and not sound 'mechanical.'" Nonetheless, his transcriptions inadvertently established a characteristic "Moog sound" for classical music.

"A lot of nuances in my interpretation have nothing to do with the synthesizer," Carlos explained in a high-pitched voice, "but with other hardware that gives me my particular style. Overdubbing is an art in itself, and a tape isn't finished until the final mix is made." Exemplifying this point, Carlos has been known to record particularly fast sections at reduced speed and pitch, electronically transposing the music by raising the playback speed; and the painstaking preparation of both sides of each of his long-playing records takes about a year. "I hate to take short cuts," he explains. "For every detail and parameter you *can* control, you *must* control."

In his opinion, the Moog machine has "a huge vocabulary of color, but nuance doesn't come naturally to the instrument. I can also play a Steinway more rapidly. I'd say that the instrument is always in my way, but it's the best to realize my ideas on." Serving as his own arranger, keyboard player, synthesizer patchman, recording engineer and mixer, Carlos has also added so many ingenious adaptations to his Moog chassis that his instrument has grown to twice the original size. "There is no doubt," he says, "that this Moog is an early generation in the development of a real musical instrument," and he has recently purchased custom-made Moog attachments that will, he hopes, enable him to synthesize sounds resembling those of the human voice.

Artists other than composers have been able to turn Moog machinery to their special uses, usually with the master's personal assistance. In *Variations V* (1965), which Merce Cunningham did in collaboration with John Cage, the stage is filled with Moog-manufactured Theremin that produce sounds whenever a dancer's body comes close enough to stimulate its signaling. The sculptor James Seawright incorporated a small, digitally controlled synthesizer into his kinetic environment, *Elec-*

tronic Peristyle (1968), where sounds are generated in response to the presence of spectators (as perceived and thus digitally signaled not by Theremin but by the breaking of beams aimed at photocells). Seawright finds himself frequently asking Moog's advice. "If I have a question about using electronics, Bob is the first person I go to, because he can teach you more in five minutes than you could learn in six months by yourself. He knows what new products can do, just as soon as they are available. Most engineers won't understand why an artist wants to do a certain thing, but Bob understands the *why* immediately. Besides, everybody knows how nice he has always been about helping people." And so too do colleagues try to help Moog—particularly engineers with an amateur interest in music (and, thus, electronic music) and musicians and writers with pipelines to the publicizing media.

Needless to say, Moog's success has also generated competitors, such as Donald Buchla in San Francisco, whose synthesizer uses, in place of a keyboard, a metal plate responsive to hand pressures. Some of Buchla's components are thought to be superior to Moog's; but for general durability and other usefulness, especially in live performance and in conjunction with other pitched instruments, the complete Moog system is unquestionably better. (Jonathan Weiss insists that an experienced ear can usually discern which brand was used to synthesize a particular recorded sound. "It's like the difference in violins between a Stradivarius and a Guarneri.") New companies, such as Putney in London, Synket in Rome and Tonus in Newton Highlands, Mass., manufacture live-time machines that are, like the Moog, fundamentally monophonic. The first is closer to the Theremin, as the oscillators are neither calibrated nor stable in tuning (and thus cannot be used to realize accurately a tonal score). The Synket, in contrast, has limited voltage-control of the oscillators, but more complete voltage-control of other elements.

The Arp synthesizer, manufactured by Tonus, closely resembles the Moog in concept and detail. A modular system with a keyboard, the Arp has more recent components and a technical advance of interior switching, so that connections are dialed, instead of patched, as in the Moog. However, some musicians experienced on the Moog prefer the spaghetti-like cords as enabling them to *see* the current lines of interconnections. "Were I to start as another manufacturer, with a new line of products now, particularly to exploit a market someone else had created," Moog said, with visible annoyance, "I'd try to explore a new area of electronic application to music. I can see at least a dozen types of systems basically different from the Moog synthesizer." He paused to weigh his words. "They'll discover that the market for large machines, which is mostly universities, large recording studios, and commercial musicians, is not unlimited." Nonetheless, the Arp's arrival has lit a fire under Moog. "I suppose we were lucky," he mused, while lying on the floor, "to have no competition for several years."

If the brand-new Mini-Moog represents a popularization of the earlier concept, the next step in synthesizers—the new "generation," as they say at IBM—will be the integration of a computer with a synthesizer. As Moog envisions it, the computer would be particularly useful in quickly setting all the flows and levels for electrical signals, thereby eliminating the need for patchcords and other manual operations that are currently necessary; and this advance would save considerable nuisance in establishing desired controls in live time. The keyboard would remain, but the most appropriate input medium for presetting the other controls would be a typewriter that is customary in computers nowadays, thereby enabling typed instructions to become a code for internal communications. The computer would also be particularly useful at remembering complicated patch and dial settings; so that if a composer wanted to reproduce a particular sound used before, he need merely program the code for that complex combination which would in turn electronically set specific levels for each of the elements. In this respect too, the system would perform real computations, such as a rapid conversion from equal-tone tuning to just-tone intonation of the keys. The computer could also store time-varying patterns, emancipating musical results from the sequencer's current repetitiousness. Moog contends that since this computer-assisted compositional method does not require as many raw computations as the other technique (whereby musical signals are implanted directly on tape, without an audible sound), smaller computers would be adequate. An early version of this system, developed under the name of GROOVE at Bell Laboratories at Murray Hill, uses Moog machinery. His ultimate vision for electronic music, for say a decade hence, has a computer at the "control center" of a studio using the synthesizer as only one of many sources.

Another new project has educational purposes—to employ the synthesizer as a medium for involving students in the compositional process. This first of all requires the manufacture of special equipment— three modules, each costing between $200 and $400, that can be used separately or added together. Herbert Deutsch has been particularly involved in this project, founding an educational consulting service named Pulse and placing pilot projects in five Long Island schools this coming fall. The idea is to encourage children to bypass conventional instruments in making sounds; for by working first with raw aural material, so its sponsors claim, children can better learn ideas of form and creative process. "Breaking out of preconceived notions of musical composition, which even children have," Deutsch conjectures, "gives you the opportunity to discover what music is about." Over dessert Moog added, "Kids nowadays take easily to the electronic media; it's natural to them. They're not afraid of machines. The reduction of sound to its parts also leads kids to work physically with real elements, and to think in compositional terms. Also, musicians cannot function today without knowledge of electronics, and here is the best place to start." It is indicative that Moog himself has also returned to academia, teaching one course each semester in Cornell's engineering department—the first in "Music and Electronics" and the second in "Electronic Processing of Audio Material."

A critique of the Moog must first acknowledge that so much awful music—awful as *music,* not electronic technique—both pop and not, has been fabricated on the machine. While supine on the floor, Moog reluctantly confessed his objection to the titles of certain records carrying his name, his *bête noires* being "The Plastic Cow Goes Moog" and "Music To Moog By." He continued, "Then there are some where the name is innocuous but the music obnoxious," before remembering his corporate obligation. "But don't mention anything specific. Just say we've helped both good musicians and bad." Walter Sear insists that just as Mr. Steinway cannot be indicted for all the atrocities perpetrated on his pianos, so "how the Moog is used cannot be blamed on the instrument."

Nonetheless, as a musical machine designed to overcome earlier difficulties and laborious procedures, the Moog makes "electronic" (or "freaky") sounds available to those musicians who could not possibly cope with more problematic musical machinery and processes. Sear concurs, "Reasonable proficiency on the Moog can come in a few weeks, but it does not give musical intelligence. That takes a lifetime." By opening up the young art of "electronic music" to lower-level, inexperienced and impatient talents, the Moog is inadvertently responsible for the recent flow of crummy electronic music, particularly spaced-out sound effects and corny arrangements of familiar tunes that old instruments do well enough already, thanks. (No one in his right mind would swap an original Beatles for any of the many versions realized on a Moog.) Some apocalyptic critics fear that, in a musical Gresham's Law, all the bad electronic music will smother any taste, or audience, for the good.

The next crucial question asks why none of the masterpieces of contemporary electronic music have been composed on the Moog? And then why the Moog, in contrast to both tape-doctoring and the Mark II, has not inspired any stylistic innovations in electronic composition? These answers too ultimately reflect upon the machine itself. The Moog has never been brilliantly used alone in live performance, partially because in addition to sounding the keyboard the performer must manipulate the patchcords to generate anything more multiple than, say, a saxophone's linear sound. Any further musical complexity would necessarily depend upon super-human dexterity, if not three heads and several pairs of hands. That is among the reasons why the Maxi-Moog alone, without live instrumentalists or taped background, is fundamentally limited as a performance instrument. (It has also been hard to keep Moogs in precise tune, a deficiency that critics perceived both in live performance and on Walter Carlos's first record; and internal corrosion due to environmental pollution remains a persistent problem, especially in New York City.)

This absence of musical innovation may have something to do with the fact that for all its technical advances the Moog does not suggest a radically new approach to organizing sound. It seems that the only compositional technique indigenous to it is the "sculpturing" Moog noted before of extremely extended sounds. One composer favoring another medium insists, "The Moog is essentially a compact, portable and elaborate set of sound-sources for a tape studio. To do anything at all sophisticated you are back to splicing tape. What the Moog produces, therefore, is first-stage material; it should neither be the sole source nor the final end. You see that a Moog alone does not give you an 'electronic studio.' Even the much-heralded sequencer is like looping tape in the classic procedure." It is more likely that the next stylistic change will come from the next new technology of electronic music—computer-assistance in its various forms (including that system in tandem with a live-time Moog).

Regarding Moog music realized through tape processes, I can risk certain critical generalizations. Successes cannot be credited to the Moog alone, for the quality of the musician's recording machinery and tape-manipulation techniques invariably influences the result. Secondly, many "avant-garde" pieces for synthesizer are so embarrassingly repetitious that one imagines that their "composer," in an obvious short-cut, simply let several sound-generators and/or sequencers run their riffs far too long—for example, certain simplistic, over-extended pieces recorded by Morton Subotnick (technically done on a Buchla). Although perhaps thousands of original compositions (as distinct from interpretations) have been realized on the Moog, few have commanded attention for their musical excellences—the best in my hearing being Andrew Rudin's *Tragoedia* (1968), available on a Nonesuch recording, and perhaps the unrecorded scores of Alwin Nikolais. None of these rank artistically, however, with such compositions for the Mark II synthesizer as Babbitt's *Philomel* (1963) or Charles Wuorinen's Pulitzer Prize-winning *Time's Encomium* (1969).

Vladimir Ussachevsky blames all those Moog "snake-dances of nine minutes" upon the compositional ease and speed possible on the machine, comparing the decline in the quality of electronic music to the deleterious effect upon cloth caused by the transition from hand-weaving to the mechanical loom. "But of course some very beautiful fabrics came from it," he judges, "eventually." Moog himself attributes the scarcity of excellence to the composers' general inexperience with the new medium. "The composer must work with it for years," he rationalizes. Indicatively, nothing better has been produced so far on an Arp, a Buchla, a Putney or a Synket.

There is no doubt that, thanks in part to Walter Carlos's success, the general listening climate has become more susceptible to Moogian magic, and the cultural reasons for this change are intertwined and complementary. They include the impact of radio and records (which provide electronic signals heard through loudspeakers), the increasing appreciation of nonpitched noises in the environment, and the amount of a melodic electronic dissonance (fuzzy tones, hum, pure feedback) found in highly amplified rock. J. Marks shrewdly attributes this, as well as sales of Moogs, to "an experimental mood which has always surrounded rock and roll in particular and amplified music in general." Indeed, just as the Lutheran Mass, some centuries ago, served to popularize the "new sound" of post-Renaissance tonality, so distinctly contemporary celebratory rituals accustom the populace to electronic atonality. The present Moog is less likely to replace any instrument, except perhaps the electric organ, than to add to the current repertoire.

The bad eggs hatched through Moogs are, in the end, quickly discarded; for the first rule in judging any new art, or in this case any new instrument, is that *only the good ones count.* So far the machine seems most conducive to sound-effects, eccentric performances of simple music (such as pop tunes) and, in collaboration with multi-tracking, enormously precise and clearly contrapuntal interpretations of baroque music. The real question facing any Moog composer now is not how to use the machine, but how to make extraordinary music with it. I suspect that since electronic music today is an adolescent enterprise, everyone shall recognize, say a decade from now, that even today's masters simply failed to exploit certain fruitful possibilities. The irrefutable truth is that so much we take to be new and significant in contemporary art stems from technological advance; and just as the sixties in pop music was the era of the electronic guitar, so the seventies may witness the vogue of the Moog.

MUSICS

ROCK: THE NEW POP MUSIC (1968)

We're in science fiction now. All the revolutions and the old methods for changing consciousness are bankrupt.—Allen Ginsberg

The show begins with five or so young people, mostly male, coming on to a darkened stage filled with faintly visible microphones, instruments and rectangular gray amplifiers. One of them sits among the drums, another straps a guitar over his shoulder, a third straddles the organ bench, a fourth takes up an electrified four-string bass that is held not like a cello but a guitar, while the last man comes to the microphone at center stage. The spotlight isolates, stage right, another informally dressed young man who hastily introduces the musicians, while a diversely garbed audience, almost entirely under thirty, applauds politely. Then out of the auditorium's large loudspeakers comes a gigantic wave of sound which is amplified to (and perhaps beyond) the threshold of aural pain. The backdrop screen springs to life with a rich and animate profusion of brilliantly colored, kinetic pictures which are apparently projected from behind—a "light show" whose images constantly change in rhythm with the music and the gyrating musicians. The scene is a rock concert; the place I have in mind is the Fillmore East in New York City, itself modeled after a companion Fillmore in San Francisco. And there are hundreds of other comparable rock palaces around America.

This kind of presentation exemplifies the new pop music that has swept America in the past few years. What conclusively separates this new music, generally known as "rock," from the old (and from the old's current heirs) are several crucial differences. The old pop music was decidedly sentimental—about falling in love at first sight, about emotions divorced from sexuality, about syrupy sweet feelings—while the new pop music strives to be realistic about a greater range of attitudes and experience, including such previously taboo subjects as seduction, promiscuity, alienation, politics, psychedelic euphoria, frustrated sensuality, the terrors of violence and, most especially, sexual intercourse. No one hearing it once can forget the Rolling Stones song that declared, with both its title and its refrain, "Let's Spend the Night Together"; other songs weave more thinly veiled narratives of sexual pleasure. One group calls itself the Fugs, another the Mothers of Invention, while a recent piece by a group known as the Ohio Express has this blatant opening couplet: "Yummy, yummy, yummy,/I got love in my tummy."

The new songs are also musically different from previous pop. They flirt more with unusual harmonies, if not outright dissonance (that is usually resolved, nonetheless), as well as the possibilities of feedback afforded by electronic amplification; the loudness is partially an attempt, analogous to much environmental art and psychedelic drugs, to overwhelm the spectator's sensory systems with unusual extrinsic stimuli. The new pop music has largely rejected the rhymed couplet for a less restricted "free" verse, as well as eschewing the decade-old conventions of pop-musical phrasing, mostly derived from the sonata form, for more freely formed structures. It has also overthrown the three-minute limit on pop songs established first by the ten-inch 78-rpm record and, later, the commercial radio station, for pieces running seven minutes and beyond.

Also intrinsic in this new music is an emphasis on groups, rather than on individuals, partly because more than one performer is needed to project the ear-shattering volume. That voluminous sound is one reason why a large theater is a more appropriate setting than a smaller night club (where, incidentally, the old live pop music continues to draw an audience). In the new pop, the predominant instrument is the guitar, usually accompanied by drums and a bass, sometimes by an electric organ, and occasionally by horns, a tambourine or other percussion instruments, all of which are either attached to amplification equipment or played directly into microphones. Also, most of the new musicians write their own melodies and lyrics. All these differences immediately distinguish the new pop music from the performing of, say, Frank Sinatra, who has come to exemplify the old pop music in its currently most persistent form.

Similarly, the performers of the new pop hardly resemble their predecessors, as nearly all the singers wear outlandish costumes (and in white groups, unlike black, no two performers dress alike); and their collective names strive for outrageousness. Compare the calling cards of successful groups of the 1950s—the Crew Cuts, the Ames Brothers or the Kingston Trio—with such current monikers as the Grateful Dead, Creedence Clearwater Revival, Pearls Before Swine, Jefferson Airplane, Vanilla Fudge, H. P. Lovecraft, Steppenwolf, Ars Nova and even the United States of America. Moreover, the performers of this new pop music are nearly all under thirty; they wear their hair long, often letting it fall below their shoulders. Most have sideburns; a few have mustaches or even full beards. By the standards of 1962, before the new pop music began, they look socially disreputable; to American audiences of the late 1960s, they are heroic (and sometimes wealthy) figures, epitomizing life-styles worthy of imitation.

If the old pop music came from superficially sweet and clean guys who might be libertine in their private lives (again think of Frank Sina-tra), the new music comes from men who make no pretense of being straight and clean. (An analogous cultural figure is the bearded poet Allen Ginsberg, a friend of the Beatles and an early enthusiast for rock, who became respectable in the same years as the new pop music's suc-cess.) These new singers boast of their lechery or their quarrels with established authority; they get arrested for using illegal drugs and bear illegitimate children, all to the admiration, if not emulation, of their fans, rather than the reprobation which would have been the reaction only two decades ago. (Think, by contrast, of what happened to Ingrid Bergman in the late 1940s, after public revelations about her love affair with Roberto Rossellini.) The refrain of a Bob Dylan song underlines the root of it all: "Times they are a-changin'."

One major reason the new pop music is so different from the old is that rock grows out of different musical traditions. Whereas the old pop, again epitomized by Frank Sinatra, came from neoclassical composition, Broadway show tunes and advertising jingles, the new pop, in its singing styles and unsentimentality, descends primarily from Negro-American music, which is to say urban folk blues, to which has been added a dash of gospel and a pinch of jazz, all as evidence of implicit Black Power. The first era of rock came in the mid-fifties, with Elvis Presley, a white singer-guitarist who appropriated (perhaps *imported*) the earthiness of Negro blues for a white audience, and Bill Haley and the Comets, whose best-selling single "Rock Around the Clock" helped bring into the com-mon language a new phrase, "rock 'n roll" (that, true to the new times, was even more blatantly sexual in its origins and implications than "jazz"). This fifties music was very conducive to dancing, usually rather fast in modified versions of the Lindy—a graceful bobbing dance dating back to the 1930s; and both this early kind of rock, as well as its expo-nents, coexisted amicably with the older style of pop music all through the late fifties.

The early 1960s witnessed the increasing popularity of both guitar-oriented folk music, represented at its best by solo singers like Bob Dylan and Joan Baez, and by piano-playing black "rhythm and blues" perform-ers like Ray Charles and Antoine "Fats" Domino. About that time also came a new dance called The Twist, invented by the black singer Chubby Checker, spawning a new kind of dance hall where the Twist was emphasized and informal (if not unconventional) dress was allowed, if not encouraged. However, not until 1963 did the new music really begin to flourish.

There were two complementary developments, one in England and the other in America—one associated with the unorthodox appearance and the highly amplified instruments of the Beatles, the other with several new black groups sponsored by a Detroit-based, black-owned record company, Motown. Both the Beatles and the Motown groups— among them, the Supremes, Mitch Ryder & the Detroit Wheels, Martha & the Vandellas, Smokey Robinson & the Miracles—won their earliest successes not with the established commissars of popular music but with that newly affluent audience of teenagers. By current standards, both the early Beatles and the Motown groups favored slickness in their melodies and harmonies, their instrumentation and arrangements; however, out of marginal breakthroughs came a stream of influence that eventually generated the revolution that became rock.

To think in terms of academic years, one could characterize 1963–64 as the beginnings of new rock, then 1964–65 witnessed the arrival of a second wave of new groups—the Rolling Stones and the Who in England, the Beachboys and the Lovin' Spoonful, among many others, in the United States. In the following year came the Beatles' shift (followed by others) away from hard-driving rock with a regular beat to a music that would be rhythmically more free, more repetitious and, at base, more psychedelic. The signposts in the Beatles' repertoire were songs like "Norwegian Wood" and "Strawberry Fields Forever" (in which changes happen so slowly that small shifts are exaggerated), as well as the beginnings of a pop-related enthusiasm for Indian music, popularized particularly by the sitarist Ravi Shankar. In 1966–67 came the first great American rock groups—the Doors, Jefferson Airplane, Big Brother and the Holding Company, and so on. It was precisely on this issue of psychedelics (and, concomitantly, of Indian music) that white rock began to diverge drastically from black music.

The academic year that has just passed, 1967–68, represents, in this compressed history of rock, the public flowering of white rock: with big articles in all the major American magazines, a network of concert and dance halls around the country, the rise of experienced and sympathetic producers and managers, appreciation of the new music by serious critics and musicians, the founding of magazines devoted largely to rock music and its performance, the beginnings of a considered rock criticism, and the arrival of two new groups who, though their membership is mostly black (the Chambers Brothers, Sly and the Family Stone), produce a music that, indicatively, seems more indebted to the new white rock than black "soul" music.

But perhaps nothing more firmly signifies the increasingly spectacular impact of rock than both the flourishing business and the proselytizing culture that have grown around it. Since the established record companies were initially too entrenched in the old pop music to care much about the new rock, into the record business came both new free-lance producers, who could deliver finished, replica-ready tapes to the established distributors; into the biz came entirely new labels like the supersuccessful Motown and a host of names founded by Phil Spector, perhaps the first American to become a rock millionaire mogul in his early twenties. (As the social commentator Tom Wolfe perceptively wrote of Spector, "It was never a simple question of his taking a look at the rock and roll universe from the outside and exploiting it. He stayed within it himself. He liked the music.")

Rock has become one of the few cultural domains made almost entirely by young people—mostly owned by, managed by, bought by, publicized by and criticized by them. The rock revolution has brought about a new set of social dances, which were less regular in movement and more permissive of individualized expression; new styles of clothing, such as stretch-pants, tight dungarees and then outlandish costumes, as well as the ubiquity of long hair, on men as well as women.

Several new magazines have been founded out of a genuine passion for rock, *Crawdaddy* in New York and *Rolling Stone* in San Francisco, while other new youth-oriented journals, such as *Cheetah, East Village Other* and other members of the "Underground Press Syndicate," have abundant coverage of the new media. Many already established magazines have hired very young writers who specialize in rock—Richard Goldstein in *The Village Voice,* Robert Christgau in *Esquire,* Ellen Willis in *The New Yorker.* This highly organized system of disseminating news and criticism means that reputations in rock become established rather quickly, as the excellence of a particular new group or new song usually becomes rather rapidly known.

The informal hierarchies of reputation are so accurate that, in a typical concert of three successive groups, the second is invariably superior to the first and the third much better than the second. The audience of rock does have genuine critical standards, even if it often seems less articulate than professional critics; for not every well-promoted song, or even every song by a popular performer, becomes a best-seller. Nor in a concert does the audience applaud wildly after every group or every number.

There must be literally thousands of rock groups in America, all with several instrumentalists, a panoply of expensive amplifying machines, perhaps a manager who tries to get them jobs, a collection of tapes they will eagerly lend or play for anyone who might employ or even publicize their work. Yet just as in contemporary painting, where all new works tend to resemble one or another of the established styles, so most new rock groups fail to differentiate themselves from the morass of familiar ways of sounding. Still, reputations for excellence, based though they are upon as little as fifteen, or eight, or sometimes even four minutes of acclaimed music, do eventually emerge from this highly competitive scene.

Beyond that, one cannot help but think there are some mysterious fates governing the entire scene of this new rock—one of which ruled that a music of guitars and keyboards, rather than of horns and reeds (perhaps the more fashionable instruments for teenagers in the late fifties) should become so prominent in the sixties. Another fate must have determined why one group of four men, rather than another bunch, who dropped out of the workaday world and then happened to come together a few years ago, should, within time so brief for art, become musically and commercially successful, and then why one rather than another group should produce a succession of popular records. To put it differently, pop music has always been a competitive domain with success at the mercy of fortune, but with the new rock the chanciness of efforts, along with the sheer unexpectedness of results, seems to multiply.

Critics have from time to time raised the question of rock's place in the larger world of contemporary music. One occasionally hears that rock is "the only valid music for our time," but in nearly every case that opinion comes from people either professionally involved in rock on one hand and/or ignorant of contemporary "classical" composition on the other. To my mind, rock in performance may make excellent theater— few examples of literary drama exploit the performer-audience relationship so successfully; but considered solely as music, not even the best rock is as artistically adventurous or as intrinsically rich as avant-garde music in either the serial or even the aleatory tradition. The reasons are that by contemporary musical standards the compositional ideas are too elementary, the techniques too repetitious, the pieces too short and the means too obvious. (The only idea indigenous to rock that could influence contemporary composition would be the use of amplified instruments; otherwise, rock musicians have always been stealing from Karlheinz Stockhausen and John Cage, rather than vice versa.)

It is more valid to say that rock stands to contemporary music as journalism stands to literature, for the former of each pair is un-ashamedly transient and stylistically derivative (rather than innovative). Moreover, both journalism and pop music strive for an immediate im-pact, their commentary is strictly current in focus; both are more inter-ested in communication than in art. As both are heavily implicated in the cultural commerce, they are more inclined to pander to the preju-dices of their audiences than to challenge them; both shamelessly exploit the clichés of the current moment for pragmatic ends, and so forth. Just as some journalism is better, as well as more honest in its methods and serious in its intentions, so is some rock music better, as rock, than other. To extend the analogy in two ways: while rock lyrics are a kind of poetic journalism, so the new pop music is very much the *illustration* art of our time.

What makes the success of this new pop music so spectacular is its current pervasiveness and increasing influence. At most parties of people under the age of twenty-five (as well as older artists, filmmakers and even intellectuals, among others), the only music ever played is rock. It has recently been infiltrating the background of movie scores (whose produc-ers know that sound tracks should not seem embarrassingly out of date in the future). Nearly every American city has at least one radio station devoted to rock, rather than the old pop music (which, needless to say, still commands an audience, largely over thirty).

Indeed, the songs and stars of rock have become an intimate part of nearly every young American's imaginative life, much as the old pop music was for an earlier generation, as movies have long been for many Americans. Indeed, perhaps the most immediate sign of whether some-one's sensibility is either aural or visual lies in whether he remembers all the pop songs (as I do), or all the old films; or the names of the individual pop singers, or the movie stars. Perhaps because America lacks an aris-tocracy, either social or intellectual, which feels the need to insulate itself and its children from the mainstream, pop culture affects almost every cultured American; and just as Charles Ives incorporated nineteenth-century hymn tunes into music written early in the twentieth century, so the superhighbrow contemporary composer Milton Babbitt, born in 1916, proudly claims to remember every song (old style) popular between 1925 and 1935, not because they were artistically important to him (they weren't) but simply because their melodies actively inhabit his acoustic memory. However, the argument of solipsism, based upon the audience's purported culture, does not bestow artistic status—just because the new pop group haunts the minds of genuine artists does not, per se, make rock a genuine art.

The persistence and success of rock owes something to the new music's virtues—it is a better pop, in the ways that one kind of pop music can be better than another—in addition to its more appropriate and more respected implications and attitudes. Primarily, the new songs are musically more complex, which is why they generally cannot be hummed, and intellectually more realistic and relevant, which is to say less sentimental, in their comments and advice, as well as more ambiguous and perhaps more poetic in their lyrics. These songs, too, are concerned with such unprecedented American realities as more accessible and (thanks to the contraceptive pill) safer sexual experience and the increasing use of hallucinogenic drugs, as well as possible styles of life in a post-industrial society of increasing leisure. Beyond that, the politics of rock music epitomizes the power of youth, which has not only changed the consciousness of millions of their peers and gained control over a large segment of the record industry but also has designs on periodicals, publishers, universities and other institutions. The young today feel an unprecedented sense of distance between the realities they see and the pieties of the powerful, between the world they envision and the politics of established institutions; and the difference between the old pop music and the new is symbolic of this divergence, as well as perhaps an intimation of an immanent world.

CONTEMPORARY MUSIC (1967)

Looking back over recent music history, we can see that since the 1930s there have been three distinctly different languages for serious composition—three completely different ways of organizing musical sound—which I christen chaotic, serial and mainstream. Since composers, as generally the most rational of artists, are clearly aware of the relationship between artistic intention and effect, nearly every composer today knows in which camp he belongs, which is to say, what language he speaks. As a result, the quarrels between school and school, as well as among composers, invariably progress along clearly demarked lines.

Historically, each of the three major languages represents a particular approach to the breakup of classic, post-Renaissance tonality—a disintegration that occurred at the end of the nineteenth century. For several centuries, the seven-tone scale had been the standard language of musical sound in the Western world. Mozart used it, as did Vivaldi before him and Beethoven after him. Although post-Renaissance tonal music sounds "natural" to most Western ears, the harmonies of its scales are no more "natural" to nature than East Indian or medieval scales. Each language represents, quite simply, a different system for organizing musical sounds, just as English and French are systems for cohering verbal speech.

The greatest early modern composers created pieces that consciously avoided the tonics and dominants—the firsts and fifths—that were the keystones of harmonic tonality. (*Tonic,* remember, refers to tonality.) As these *atonal* composers did not resolve their dissonances into a basic key, their works seemed to end not, metaphorically, at "home," as previous music did, but up in the air, in an apparent nowhere. As such technique freed music from a primary classical structure, the composer Claude Debussy, at the end of the last century, could justly assert that all notes in any combination were the viable stuff of music; and along with such contemporaries as Charles Ives and Erik Satie, Debussy developed compositional styles that exploited greater tonal possibilities. As a result, instrumental sounds that were characterized as "dissonant" in the harmonic tonal system became legitimately consonant in the atonal language, just as certain verbal sounds that are meaningless in English can have great significance in French. Influenced by these radical developments, nearly all major modern music makers, from Béla Bartók to the Beatles, have exploited this expanded aural vocabulary, creating music that not only differs hugely from nineteenth-century conventions but also expands our sense of what "music" can be.

II

As this revolution in musical tonality freed, if not encouraged, composers to create unprecedented musical combinations, subsequent revolutionaries took the next step of creating structures so outrageously different they were indisputably innovative; and others employed individual sounds (or noises) previously unheard in musical contexts. Born in 1874, Ives, for instance, incorporated such "found sounds" as American hymn tunes into his classically conceived works; and in his *Second Symphony* (1902), he mixed them with snatches of Beethoven's Fifth, all to demonstrate that American popular material could be as viable a source of quotations as European classical music. In "Putnam's Camp, Redding, Connecticut," one of his *Three Places in New England* (1903–11), Ives reproduced in a concert context a series of sounds he had found in the world around him—the chaotic noise that resulted when two separate marching bands approached each other on a Connecticut street; for out of aural chaos, Ives created magnificent art. In *The Unanswered Question* (1908), Ives was also among the first modern composers to experiment with distributing musicians over a space, the location of the sounds contributing to its effects. He was also probably the first to divide the musicians into several groups, giving each section a distinctly different tempo (and its own subconductor) and then instructing them to play concurrently. In his Fourth Symphony, written between 1910 and 1916 but first performed in 1965, Ives divides and redivides the orchestra into constantly forming and reforming groups; and in an opening section, while percussion, brass instruments and flute play in 6/8 meter, a piano is heard in 2/4, a clarinet, a second piano and a triangle in 5/8 and the bassoons in 7/4. On top of this, according to Henry Cowell, "The upper strings have a measure equal to twelve of the eighth notes previously mentioned, but written as a whole note to a measure." Since the notes assigned to such a variety of meters could not possibly be executed in precisely similar ways, we can say that Ives's score contained not an exact plan for determining what would occur but general instructions for an indeterminate result. This principle of intentional indeterminacy became an important contribution to the tradition of unusual musical sounds.

Another American inventor in this history of aural chaos, dissonance and unprecedented sounds was the composer Henry Cowell, who was born in California in 1897. Beginning in his late teens, Cowell initiated a number of radical steps that similarly increased the techniques available to musical practice. He independently reinvented the pianistic tone cluster that Ives, unknown to Cowell, had created a decade earlier; here the pianist uses his forearm or a block of wood to sound a whole area of keys at once. Cowell also plucked piano strings with his fingers, discovered esoteric instruments and experimented with the Theremin, an early electronic sound-generating instrument which presaged more sophisticated contemporary synthesizers. Cowell's book *New Musical Resources,* published in 1930 but actually written in 1919, as well as his example, persuaded subsequent composers that the sounds available to music were no less limited than their possible use.

Although this atonal development had exponents in Europe, where the Czech composer Alois Hába (b. 1893) composed quarter-tone and even sixth-tone music for specially designed instruments, and where the Russian musician Alexander Mossolov incorporated the sounds of shaken sheet metal into *The Steel Foundary* (1930), it was American composers who were more totally devoted to the radical redefinition of musical sound. The year after Mossolov's work, the French-born American composer Edgard Varèse created in *Ionisation* a wholly percussive piece that employs such nonmusical sound generators as sirens, sleigh bells and brake drums; and even though trained percussionists could strike them at precise times, the resulting noises had indeterminate pitch. Indeed, the interaction of such large blocks of unusual percussive material produced a chaotic sound so distinctly unlike any previous musical experience that laymen and critics condemned the piece as merely noise (that was "not music") and even professional composers feared that the apocalypse—the end of music—had come.

In more recent American music, the foremost proponent of this chaotic tradition has been John Cage, who was also born in California, in 1912, but who, unlike Cowell, actually studied with established composers. Early in his career, Cage invented the "prepared piano" by placing bolts, nuts and strips of rubber across its strings, distorting pitches while emphasizing the instrument's percussive possibilities. At this time, back in 1937, Cage prophesied, "I believe that the use of noise to make music will continue to increase until we reach a music produced through the aid of electrical instruments which will make available for musical purposes any and all sounds that can be heard." In short, not only did Cage assert that noise was as viable for music as instrumental sound, but he also imagined electronic machines whose sound-generating capability would exceed that of human musicians.

Not only musically inventive but philosophically inclined, Cage discerned significance in the fact that with the prepared piano he would have less control over the final sounds. As bolts and nuts cannot be so precisely placed that the resulting sounds can be accurately predicted in advance, the relation between the notes prescribed in the score and those heard by the audience must be as indeterminate in pitch as Varèse's sirens and brake drums. Pursuing these implications, Cage commenced to explore situations where the performed sound would be similarly indeterminate. Some of his early pieces, like *Third Construction* (1941), followed Varèse's example by incorporating such nonmusical sound generators as, to quote Cage's list, "rattles, tin cans, cow bells, lion's roar, cricket caller and conch shell." By the early fifties, one of his pieces, *Imaginary Landscape IV* (1951), consisted entirely of the random sounds that happened to emerge from twelve live radios. In *Williams Mix* (1952), Cage created a tape collage of sounds gathered from miscellaneous sources in the environment. By the mid-sixties, in *Variations V* (1965), Cage's instrumentation had escalated to a small army of electronic soundproducers—not only radios and tape recorders but also record players, amplification systems and miscellaneous apparatuses.

This exploration of indeterminate sounds parallels another development in John Cage's thought—the use of indeterminate procedures in composition; for just as his preference for such unpredictable machinery signified that he relinquished his control over certain dimensions of the final performance of his piece, so he began to develop techniques that would minimize his mind's control over the piece's creation—that would intentionally reduce the impact of any intentions. To this end, Cage adopted "chance" or aleatory procedures of composition, where happenstance methods produce abstract patterns that he then translates into musical notation. Further to deny his conscious designs, such notation might itself be so approximate that two performances of the same score would be extremely different. To compose, for instance, *Music for Carillon No. 2* (1954), Cage placed a sheet of graph paper behind a piece of cardboard. After he marked on the cardboard such imperfections as the discolorings, crystal glazes and other accidental spots, he punched a pit through each of these places. By this procedure he made holes on the graph paper, the sheet as such then becoming the "score" of the piece. Cage's instructions for playing the graph paper were as follows: "On the graph, one inch horizontally equals one second and three vertical inches equal any pitch range," which is to say that three inches could, at the performer's discretion, be interpreted as either one octave or two octaves or three. Around this time, Cage also turned to the American edition of Richard Wilhelm's translation of the Chinese classic *I Ching,* which he uses to show how tosses of coins can be translated into abstract patterns that, in turn, can help Cage make one of several compositional choices. Paradoxically, although Cage undergoes such arduous processes precisely to divorce the final piece from his conscious desires, his individual pieces sound characteristic enough to reveal a personal signature that is acoustically recognizable. The reason for such a distinct artistic identity is the fact that certain parameters of his work, such as the range of musical materials, are selected—determined—often quite cleverly, before he subjects subsequent decisions to chance procedures.

In another revolutionary work, *4'33",* Cage suggested equally revolutionary implications which have influenced not only his later work but musical thinking around the world. In that notorious work, the accomplished pianist David Tudor comes to the piano and sits silently for four minutes and thirty-three seconds, three times moving his hands to the piano as if to suggest that this silent piece has several movements. As a stunt, this would be a pleasant joke; but since Tudor was known as a performer of avant-garde music, while *4'33"* was performed in a concert situation, before an audience that expected musical sounds, the piece implies, by deduction, that the "music" consists of all the *un*intentional noises that occur in the performance hall during the prescribed duration.

From his philosophical inference follow several corollaries. First, silence can never be absolute; outside noises always intrude into every supposedly silent situation. Second, as silence or intentional nonsound is as much a component of music as intentional sound, in any musical performance all accidental noises become intrinsic parts of the piece and, it follows, have a status equal to sounds that are prescribed. Third, "music" is available to the listener, all the time, as long as he simply attunes his ears to recognize it. "If you want to know the truth of the matter," Cage once said, "the music I prefer, even to my own and everything, is what we hear if we are just quiet." With that sentence Cage rejects the whole Western tradition that presumes Art (intentionally capitalized) represents an enhancement of experience; for he regards the most agreeable art as just like life not only in its forms but like it in actual fact—to Cage the line traditionally distinguishing one from the other no longer exists. Nonetheless, no one needs to agree with Cage's extreme position to appreciate the fact that he has single-handedly established a musical situation in which, in theory at least, anything is possible, including nothing at all.

III

If Cage represents one radical tendency of recent music, the other revolutionary direction, equally distant from nineteenth-century conventions, extends from Arnold Schoenberg's creation, in the 1920s, of a
wholly new language for musical expression. Whereas Cage found in
aural chaos a new musical language—a kind of sensible nonsense—
Schoenberg and his followers developed an entirely new way of coher-
ently putting notes together; and this technique was as radically different from nineteenth-century conventions as the music of Varèse and
Cage. Like all new languages, twelve-tone or serial music, as it is
called, had to discover its own rules for organizing musical sounds
(its own "grammar," so to speak), its own patterns or procedures (syntax) and its own kinds of structures (sentences). In brief, Schoenberg
(1874–1951) postulated that the composer, working within the open
range of twelve tones to an octave, could organize any number of
tones (up to twelve), without repeating a tone, into a certain order
of intervals which we now call, variously, the "row" or "series" or
"set."

Once the composer chooses a row, it becomes his basic pattern for
the piece; and he can then use this pattern of intervals in one of four
ways: (1) in its original form; (2) in a reversed or retrograde order; (3)
in an inverse order (if the second note in the original was three steps up,
now it is three steps down, etc.); (4) in an inverted, reversed order. Now
this row, we should remember, is less a series of specific musical notes
than a pattern of intervalic relations; therefore, perhaps the best way to
graph a particular row's essential nature would use not musical notation
but a chart:

```
11  -------------------------------------------X----------
10  ----------------------------X----------------------
 9  ----------------------------------X---------------
 8  --------------------------------X-----------------
 7  --------X-----------------------------------------
 6  -----------------X--------------------------------
 5  -------------X------------------------------------
 4  ------------------------X-------------------------
 3  ---------------------------------------------X-
 2  --------------------------------------X-----
 1  ----X---------------------------------------------
 0  X-------------------------------------------------
    0    1    2    3    4    5    6    7    8    9   10   11
```

This chart outlines the relationship, in terms of intervals, that one note in the row has with the others. When such a row is imposed upon a G clef, while C sharp is chosen as the first note, the row produces the following notes:

When the row is reversed, it gives us these notes:

When the row is inverted and D natural (above high C on the G clef) is then chosen as the basic note, the row assumes these pitches:

The row can also be transposed, up or down, as long as the pattern of intervalic relations is maintained. Here is the same row transposed up two steps, to D-sharp:

As traditional musical notation is inadequate in outlining a row, the composer Milton Babbitt, perhaps the foremost contemporary theorist of serial procedure, proposes instead that we represent the above set in the following terms:

0,0; 1,1; 2,7; 3,5; 4,6; 5,4; 6,10; 7,8; 8,9; 9,11; 10,2; 11,3

with the first number in each pair marking the individual note's position in the entire set. Therefore, as the left-hand numbers in each pair escalate from o to 11, the second number in each pair refers to that particular note's intervalic relation to the first or base note of the row. Whereas the second note (1,1) is one step away (up in the original form, down in the inverted form), the third note is seven steps away, the fourth only five and so forth.

If we transpose this row up two intervals, we would then mark it as follows:

0,2; 1,3; 2,9; 3,7; 4,8; 5,6; 6,0; 7,10; 8,11; 9,1; 10,4; 11,5.

This kind of notation illustrates the nature of the row, as well as how the elements relate to one another, more clearly than musical notes; but these numbers, don't forget, are like notes on the staff, which is to say, instructions for producing musical sounds. Also, whereas note number 6 in the original form had the interval designation of 10, now it becomes 0. What adds up to 12 becomes 0 (as 13 in note number 9 becomes 1), because once the row's pattern is imposed upon musical notes, the numbers refer not just to specific notes but also to what Babbitt calls "pitch classes." That is, if note number 6 in this row produces C sharp, then the serial composer can use any of the C sharps available to his instruments. Second, just as the notes of a row can be strung out in a line:

so any succession may be bunched into a single chord:

These are among the elementary grammatical principles informing the serial composer's manipulation of the row.

Perhaps the most definitive way of illustrating the manifold possibilities of a single row of intervalic relations that we have been discussing is the following charts constructed by Milton Babbitt for his analysis of Schoenberg's opera, *Moses und Aron* (1932), first in entirely numerical form and then with the more conventional pitch classes:

```
 0  1  7  5  6  4 10  8  9 11  2  3
11  0  6  4  5  3  9  7  8 10  1  2
 5  6  0 10 11  9  3  1  2  4  7  8
 7  8  2  0  1 11  5  3  4  6  9 10
 6  7  1 11  0 10  4  2  3  5  8  9
 8  9  3  1  2  0  6  4  5  7 10 11
 2  3  9  7  8  6  0 10 11  1  4  5
 4  5 11  9 10  8  2  0  1  3  6  7
 3  4 10  8  9  7  1 11  0  2  5  6
 1  2  8  6  7  5 11  9 10  0  3  4
10 11  5  3  4  2  8  6  7  9  0  1
 9 10  4  2  3  1  7  5  6  8 11  0
```

	I	II	III	IV	V	VI	VII	VIII	IX	X	XI	XII
1	C♯	D	G♯	F♯	G	F	B	A	B♭	C	E♭	E
2	C	C♯	G	F	F♯	E	B♭	G♯	A	B	D	E♭
3	F♯	G	C♯	B	C	B♭	E	D	E♭	F	G♯	A
4	G♯	A	E♭	C♯	D	C	F♯	E	F	G	B♭	B
5	G	G♯	D	C	C♯	B	F	E♭	E	F♯	A	B♭
6	A	B♭	E	D	E♭	C♯	G	F	F♯	G♯	B	C
7	E♭	E	B♭	G♯	A	G	C♯	B	C	D	F	F♯
8	F	F♯	C	B♭	B	A	E♭	C♯	D	E	G	G♯
9	E	F	B	A	B♭	G♯	D	C	C♯	E♭	F♯	G
10	D	E♭	A	G	G♯	F♯	C	B♭	B	C♯	E	F
11	B	C	F♯	E	F	E♭	A	G	G♯	B♭	C♯	D
12	B♭	B	F	E♭	E	D	G♯	F♯	G	A	C	C♯

"Each row of this table," Babbitt continues, "read from left to right, contains one of the twelve transpositions of the prime set, and read from right to left one of the twelve transpositions of the retrograde form of the set. Each column, read from top to bottom, contains one of the twelve transpositions of the inverted form of the set and, read from bottom to top, one of the twelve transpositions of the retrograde-inverted form of the set." Conceptually similar charts could be made for other serial pieces. The fact that Schoenberg could successfully transform this basic material into continuously various structures illustrates, quite conclusively, that the serial language is not as constricting as all the rules superficially suggest—tonal music, one remembers, had its rules too. Instead, just as twelve-tone procedure discourages the kind of repetition endemic in tonal music, so it creates its own kind of syntactical and grammatical possibilities.

The history of the twelve-tone language has been rather checkered and its development uneven. Soon after Schoenberg invented it, the idea quickly spread through Europe; and by the late 1920s, Schoenberg was invited to succeed Ferrucio Busoni as professor of composition at the Berlin Academy of Art. However, once the Nazis assumed power in Germany, Schoenberg, born a Jew but raised a Christian, resigned his post and reassumed his Jewish faith, emigrating first to England and then to America, where he eventually taught at the Los Angeles branch of the University of California. When the Fascist cultural authorities condemned twelve-tone music as "degenerate," other musicians devoted to that technique either left German territories or moved culturally underground: whereas the pianist Edward Steuermann eventually settled in America, the Spanish-born composer Roberto Gerhard (b. 1896) moved to England and Nikos Skalkottas (1904–49) returned to his native Greece. Anton Webern (1883–1945), deprived of his conducting jobs, nonetheless stayed in Austria, where he concentrated on composing and eventually become a copy editor and proofreader for the same firm that earlier published his music.

After Schoenberg immigrated to America, this serial language converted several important composers who were previously counted among its opponents. By the late forties, Igor Stravinsky (b. 1882) had also settled in Los Angeles; and although he had once been considered Schoenberg's arch antagonist and his "neoclassicism" an "answer" to the new serial language, Stravinsky himself came to incorporate twelve-tone procedures into such pieces as *Canticum Sacrum* (1956) and *Agon* (1957). His most recent pieces, *Thereni* (1958) and *Requiem Canticles* (1966), are thoroughly serial. The Austrian-born composer Ernst Krenek (b. 1900), previously famous for his popular opera *Johnny spielt Auf* (1926), also adopted the twelve-tone language soon after his own immigration to America. By the late fifties, the converts included such American-born composers as Roger Sessions (b. 1896) and Arthur Berger (b. 1912); and even Aaron Copland (b. 1900), previously known for his mainstream ways, adopted twelve-tone techniques for several of his later major concert pieces, such as *Connotations for Orchestra* (1962).

Not until the postwar period did the twelve-tone language revive in Continental Europe. Because of the efforts of such prominent young composers as Karlheinz Stockhausen (b. 1928) and Pierre Boulez, Webern's posthumous influence began to exceed that of Schoenberg, the former being credited as more consistent and rigorous (and thus more radical); and the serial language became the established discourse in many of the major European conservatories. Once in America, Schoenberg himself set the example that most serial composers have since adopted of earning his living primarily not in music academies but in liberal arts universities. Indeed, because aspiring composers today are more likely to attend the latter sorts of institutions (while instrumentalists favor the conservatories), most composers today who make their mark while young—while still in their twenties—exhibit twelve-tone techniques.

Two of the leading figures in the postwar twelve-tone revival are Milton Babbitt and Pierre Boulez, one an American composer born in 1916, the other a Frenchman born in 1925; and each has been as passionately committed as the other to the new language. Whereas Babbitt once said, "Sometimes I think that music is just beginning, reborn with such an utterly different musical language," so Boulez once declared, "Since the discoveries made by the Viennese, all composition other than twelve-tone is useless." So in addition to being influential exemplars and propagandists—the former as a teacher, the latter as a conductor—both Babbitt and Boulez attempted to extend serial principles to dimensions of sound other than pitch. Babbitt christened his procedure "combinatoriality"; others call it "total serialization." To this end the composer applies other kinds of serial organizing procedures not only to pitches, as Schoenberg had done, but to other elements as well: duration (which includes rhythm), register (octave), dynamics (the degree of attack and decay), volume and timbre.

The result of this logical extension of Schoenberg's ideas is a twelve-tone music of unprecedented structural complexity, in which each and every note of a piece contributes simultaneously to several kinds of serial relationships. This technique is, as a compositional structure, similar to that of *Finnegans Wake*, where every phrase in Joyce's prose ideally suggests several phrases and contributes to several stories. Similarly, every note in a totally serialized composition develops several musical "stories." The principle of simultaneous development leads Babbitt, for one, to posit a rather revolutionary esthetic that equates excellence with "the multiplicity of function of every event"—the number of serial relationships each note develops. This compositional procedure achieves such an unprecedented intensity of musical activity that, as the composer-critic Benjamin Boretz wrote, "A single sound may convey as much information [i.e., musical action] as, say, a whole section of a Mozart symphony." The considerations required for writing such music are so unprecedentedly numerous that many trained musicians are surprised to learn that Babbitt can actually finish anything that fulfills his ambitious designs; yet all these pieces are so short in duration that Babbitt's complete work, like the complete Webern, can fill only a few records. Among the other contemporary composers who have extended serial procedures to dimensions of musical structure other than pitch are Stockhausen, the German I mentioned before, the Italians Luciano Berio (b. 1925) and Luigi Nono (b. 1924), and the Americans Peter Westergaard (b. 1931) and Donald Martino (b. 1931).

IV

Whereas both the chaotic and serial traditions were revolutionary in creating wholly unprecedented languages for musical notes, proponents of the mainstream of modern music integrate all sorts of new elements into traditional ways of structuring tonal sound. For instance, though a composer working in this middle stream uses snatches of harmonically dissonant material, the entire section invariably resolves into a traditional grammar of tonics and dominants; and while a few passages may exhibit the jerky, discontinuous rhythm typical of most avant-garde styles, the progress of the whole work is basically linear. Whereas the middle-stream composer might even draw upon certain serial procedures for the manipulation of pitch, these are incorporated into a context of basically traditional structures. Indeed, nothing more immediately signifies a middle-stream piece than titles that include such genre words as "sonata," "fugue" or "symphony."

Mainstream music is more accessible to the general audience, not only because its texture is filled with "melodies" whose variation and development can be followed by most musically experienced ears but also because such works generally embody the classical form of introduction, exposition, development, recapitulation, climax and conclusion. Therefore, as individual sections are aurally resolved into a traditional format, so is the entire piece. Largely because this music combines the familiar with the unfamiliar, middle-stream music draws a far larger audience than either twelve-tone or aleatory; and as serial music has become the international language of the university music departments, so middle stream is the international style of the larger concert halls around the world.

Whereas both avant-gardes created music compositions that exist primarily for themselves and with reference only to themselves, the "subject" of an individual piece becoming literally the arrangement of sounds unique to it, those working in the middle-stream, in contrast, compose music that often expresses or represents something outside of music. This ostensible subject could be either a place, an emotion, an abstract quality or even a call to arms. For instance, Ferde Grofé's *Grand Canyon Suite* (1931) represents a tour of that national park; Leonard Bernstein's *Third Symphony—Kaddish* (1963) is a prayer for the dead; Roy Harris's *Third Symphony* (1938) portrays an American mystique; Dmitri Shostakovitch's *Fifth Symphony* (1937) likewise seems designed to patriotic ends. Within this general mainstream language exist many individual and national styles; for although Copland and Shostakovitch, say, usually speak the same musical language, the former achieves a style that reflects his American heritage, while the other's music continually acknowledges Mother Russia. (Indeed, no characteristic seems to divide composers of this persuasion into distinct groups as clearly as national origin.)

Mainstream music is also capable of expressing a composer's emotion and of instilling similar feelings in the audience. In drawing upon a tradition, such music exploits a backlog of awareness; it gives the audience sounds evoking specific qualities, a frantic tempo standing for excitement, downwardly sweeping phrases signifying sadness, upward musical movement announcing joy and so forth. Indeed, precisely by communicating in a familiar idiom, a middle-stream piece can echo, as well as create, specific references to phenomena outside the music itself.

V

The three major languages of modern music have produced works so clearly different from one another that the audience for contemporary music also divides into several camps. As commitments of taste are invariably parochial, listeners who prefer one kind of music rarely have contact with any of the others. The tradition of eccentric sounds, for instance, tends to attract creative professionals in other fields, perhaps because an artist in paint or words can extend the esthetic freedom implicit in aleatory procedure to their own practice. This accounts for why John Cage's esthetics have influenced recent works by prominent painters, theater-creators, writers and other artists, while the professional music community as such has comparatively less interest in his ideas. While the largest public for serious composition gravitates to the middle-stream tradition, most concerts of twelve-tone music, particularly in such cosmopolitan centers as New York, draw upon audiences consisting largely of professionals—composers, musicologists, critics and musicians. The character of these audiences implicitly illustrates

Schoenberg's famous dictum: "I write the kind of music which does not appeal to those who understand nothing about it. But one must admit that it appeals to those who understand it."

Another story illustrative of the divisions in contemporary music's audience tells of an eminent concert hall conductor invited to direct several pieces in an established concert series of serial music. Just before the music began, he made several defensive and somewhat patronizing remarks about music so original the audience might not understand it, etc. Several people began to snicker, a few chuckled and then many laughed; and when the famous conductor halted his speech in surprise, he was informed that he was probably the only person present at that concert who had not attended the series before!

The further some kinds of music drift away from traditional practice, the less adequate the old systems of notation become, either because they do not adequately specify the kinds of complex relationships demanded by certain new music or because notes are too constricting a format for the kind of operational freedom upon which aleatory music, say, insists. If a composer desires unusual sounds, he generally writes directly on the score such instructions as "play with both forearms" or "play with flat of hand," etc. An aleatory composer who intends that his score have as few specifics as possible leaves to the performer the choice of whether to play one note or another. A page like the following from John Cage's *Music for Piano 64* (1956) consists of eight fragments which, he writes, "may be performed, in whole or part, by any number of pianists":

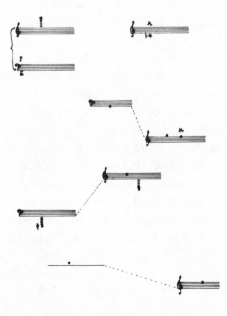

In those Cage pieces where individual pitches are indeterminate, the score appears more like a work of art than a plan for music (and, indeed, an art gallery once offered an exhibition of Cage's scores):

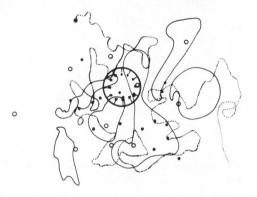

Finally, as radically new music often needs new notation, so too it demands new musicians who are able and willing to execute such unfamiliar scoring, which is to say newcomers to the performance profession; however, until musicians predisposed to new music become more plentiful, composers recognize, first, that the smaller the number of performers necessary for a piece, the more likely it will, in general, be played—only fools and madmen would write for a full orchestra, it is joked—and second, that as composers they would inevitably become their own most reliable performers.

VI

As the development of new technologies influenced general social change to an immeasurable degree, so did the new machinery also influence the practice and even the composition of recent music. Whereas 78 rpm records allowed four and a half minutes per side (and forced certain five-minute pieces to be speeded up), the postwar techniques of 33 rpm and smaller grooves permitted nearly a half hour to each side. As a result, certain long pieces, which were once annoyingly interrupted every few minutes, now confront the listener as more continuous works. Moreover, long-playing records were, minute by minute, considerably cheaper than their predecessors, as well as less breakable; and these factors, along with the general increase in standards of living, persuaded many music lovers to accumulate record collections of unprecedented size.

More important, the development of records reshaped the general audience's musical literacy in a variety of ways. Precisely because records made available to the musical audience certain kinds of esoteric works that would otherwise be heard only on rare occasions, records have expanded the general awareness of both music history and the multiplicity of musical styles. Long-playing records enable us to hear abundantly long stretches of primitive songs, early Renaissance operas, Gregorian chants, oratorios and, most important, contemporary compositions. Moreover, all this "history" is as immediately available to record listeners as the books on their shelves; for whereas the concert goer or even a radio listener was not able to hear a work until it was offered to him, the record owner can on his own initiative listen to his favorite pieces whenever, and sometimes wherever, and at whatever volume (if not bass and treble) he wishes. The record rack becomes an auditorium without walls, filled as it is with the stuff of music history.

The availability of musical variety influences both the performance of music and its composition; for where the nineteenth-century interpreter or student of a certain piece depended upon the score, coupled with the memory of an earlier live performance, now both interpreters and students can test their understanding of a score against actual performances. While the general availability of such precedents may cause certain uniformities in the performance of a work, it also creates the opportunity for an imaginative interpreter to be truly original. From this situation comes Glenn Gould's esthetic ethic: "The only excuse for recording a work [in the traditional repertoire] is to do it differently."

In the past, unless a composer resided in one of those few cosmopolitan centers where modern music was regularly performed, his contact with contemporary composition would be minimal; for just as Johann Sebastian Bach had small awareness of his musical contemporaries, so most of them had no knowledge of his work. Now, thanks to recordings, as well as self-produced audiotapes, composers can have a more accurate sense of recent achievement than published scores alone would allow. Although a thoroughly trained musician can guess from the score how a certain piece might sound, he cannot be sure until he hears the piece actually performed. Indeed, the more eccentric the composer's notation, the less likely is the musician's preperformance estimate to be correct. Recently, as Milton Babbitt put it, "I don't think one can possibly exaggerate the extent to which the climate of music today is determined by the fact that the total Webern is available on records, and the total Schoenberg is becoming available." A final point to make about this theme is that recordings enable today's composers to extend their influence over subsequent musical history in an unprecedented way; for when a major composer conducts recordings of his own works, as Stravinsky or Copland have done, he then leaves for posterity, as Bach or Beethoven could not have done, his own ideas about how his notation should *sound.*

One distinct advantage that a record offers over a concert hall is that music can be played at the listener's discretion, and this advantage functions in several ways. First, it costs nearly as much money to buy a record of a certain piece as to attend a concert; but once the listener makes the basic investment, all subsequent performances are free. Second, as noted before, records permit one to hear whatever he has, when he wants, where he wants (providing his equipment is portable enough), at whatever volume he wants. If he prefers to work or read to a musical background, the record listener can choose his own accompaniment, rather than rely on the taste of a radio disk jockey; and if a certain passage is too loud for his taste, he can readjust his acoustic environment with the flick of a switch. Thirdly, if the listener either likes a piece enormously or perhaps finds it puzzling, records allow him to hear it again, immediately, wholly on his own initiative. A comparison is the difference between hearing a lecture and reading a book; for in the former, if the listener misses important ideas the first time around, he is not likely to hear them again. With the latter he need only to reread the page. Finally, recording technology also permits music to become our constant companion, in most cities for every hour of the day and night; for as the continuous performance of live music would be exhorbitantly expensive, most radio shows, as well as Musak and other sound-piping systems, depend upon prerecorded sound.

The proliferation of records means that individual radio programs, as well as individual stations, can develop a reputation for one kind of music—rock, pop, classical, modern—and never fear running out of fresh material. "It is my view," writes the pianist Glenn Gould, "that in the electronic age the art of music will become more viably a part of our lives, much less an ornament to them, and that it will consequently change us much more profoundly."

Recordings represent a marriage of art and technology, in which complex machines and skilled technicians become the hidden servants of art; and the complicated production processes demanded by most recordings make the record's producer a de facto coauthor, with the performer, of the final product. Most recordings nowadays represent not the taping of a live performance but the careful reconstruction of a performance (actually, the semblance of a performance) through a succession of processes. "There is no excuse at all for recording live concerts," the record producer John Culshaw once said. "It is a lazy—and cheap—way to make records."

First of all, the recording engineer, in taping a performer, adjusts the microphones in various ways, not only to amplify sounds that might otherwise be inaudible (or cut out extraneous noises) but also to give the recorded sound a particular texture. That is, a sound recorded with a microphone near the performer differs from the same sound entering from a distant mike, even though the volume levels have been equalized. Beyond that, after sound enters a microphone, technicians can doctor it in various ways before affixing it to tape. Then, when the performer finishes, that tape is played back, usually in the presence of someone ultimately in charge (i.e., the record's *producer*); and if a certain passage or even a phrase is thought or found deficient, it can be recorded again, or a more perfect version spliced in place of the deficient one. Sometimes, such a switch can be made several months after the original recording date; sometimes as well, talented engineers can later successfully integrate additional units as small as a single note. In sum, with the aid of new technologies, the performer can offer the record listener the best performance that he and his colleagues can possibly create; and it is highly unlikely that any musician could equal this perfection in a live concert. This new reality poses problems for the performing musician today. Either he must offer visual interest unavailable to record listeners, making them forget that live performance might be comparatively deficient or he can, as Glenn Gould has recently done, refuse to "compete" against his recorded self and give up live performances entirely.

"Dial-twiddling is in its limited way an interpretative act," Glenn Gould once wrote; for all those switches on the new amplifiers allow the listener to shape aspects of the performance that he is currently hearing, and to shape them in live time. The more dials the listener has on his machines, the more of a fine interpreter he can be. Future technology, Gould predicts, will endow the listener with greater power over the sounds his records produce, for scientists are currently working on machines that will literally allow him to edit his own favorite version of a particular piece from the recorded interpretations available to him. That is, by equalizing the pitch-speed equation, such machines will enable the listener to take the opening passages from, say, Hermann Scherchen's recording of J. S. Bach's *Brandenberg Concerto No. 1,* then splice in some sections from Thurston Dart's and a few bits from Pablo Casals', then draw some phrases from Yehudi Menuhin's and finally close the piece with Scherchen's rendition. Because it allows the record listener to create his own ideal performance, such a machine would make him, so to speak, his own conductor. Though certain cultural critics characterize modern machines as repressing human instincts, recording technologies allow both the performer and the listener to extend their esthetic taste to dimensions far beyond previous limits.

VII

As new technologies have immensely influenced the performance of music, so too have they affected its composition. For one thing, the composer can now regard electronic amplifying equipment as an instrument that, since it is usually reliable, can be integrated into compositional designs; for not only are the new machines capable of transforming sounds initially produced by either instruments or the human voice, they can also generate their own sounds. That is, electric guitars and electric organs nowadays do not amplify sounds made by strings but, instead, produce musical notes within the mechanism itself—notes that the performer can then electronically adjust to make more suitable to his needs. Second, nearly all live concerts today depend enormously upon amplification systems to spread musical sound evenly over the entire concert situation; and even during a performance, such sound systems can be adjusted to make one sound source contribute more to the blend than it otherwise would. For that reason, the vocalist commands the microphone, while the band keeps its distance. Similarly, John Cage sometimes tapes a contact microphone directly to his throat and then eats a sandwich; so that sounds that would otherwise be barely audible are amplified throughout the hall. This principle is expanded in such recent theatrical creations as La Monte Young's *The Tortoise, His Dreams and Journeys* (1964), where the composer uses amplification equipment and several loudspeakers to raise vocal music to the threshold of aural pain and then circulate the overwhelming sound throughout an enclosed space. With the aid of such machinery, Young can produce a musical effect that would otherwise demand a thousand voices to duplicate.

Composers turn to the new electronic systems for purposes nearly as various as their compositional practice. The earliest forms of so-called electronic music stemmed from sophisticated tape doctoring, where the composer takes a sound, produced by either a live instrument or a machine (for instance, an oscillator), and then manipulates it in various ways. If he plays a note at twice its original speed, say, it sounds an octave lower. Morever, with tape, one sound can be imposed upon another, literally to make a chord; or different sounds can be presented in a staggered succession far more rapid than anything human beings can do on any instrument. The tape artist can also arrange and splice as well as transfer all the sounds from his spliced tape onto virgin tape which can then be endlessly duplicated; so that all available "versions" of his piece are as identical as phonograph records. Using such techniques, the composer can make a collage of noises initially recorded on the street and elsewhere, as John Cage did in his *Williams Mix* (1952); or he can combine human voice with electronic sound and manipulate the resulting mixture in various ways, as Karlheinz Stockhausen did in *Gesang der Jünglinge* (*Song of Youths,* 1956). Or he can work entirely with electronically produced sounds, as Edgard Varèse did with *Déserts* (1954) and his *Poème élèctronique* (1958). (In the last work, the drumming sounds, for instance, can be traced to a pulse generator.)

After several years of such experiment, many critics and composers sympathetic to the new electronic medium feel that tape doctoring alone is too limited a process, simply because the number of ways a composer can manipulate tape are so few that the resulting pieces sound too identical; therefore, composers look toward even newer technologies that offer greater aural potentialities. One example is the Mark II Synthesizer, a unique instrument built at a huge cost by RCA and later housed at the Columbia-Princeton Electronic Music Center in New York City. A huge machine, some twenty feet long, several feet high and a few feet deep, the synthesizer contains various sound-generating devices (tuning forks, frequency multipliers, etc.) and seventeen hundred tubes. Capable of producing sounds precisely to the composer's instructions, the synthesizer has a face filled with switches that can precisely program the following dimensions of an individual sound: frequency (pitch), octave, volume, timbre and envelope (degree of attack and decay). When the composer assigns all the attributes of a note, the Mark II immediately produces a sound. If the composer finds the result suiting his intended design, he can flip another switch and thereby affix the sound to the tape; if the sound is not quite what he wants, he can readjust the switches and produce a slightly different sound. The synthesizer also allows the composer to place one sound atop another (as is standard practice in tape doctoring) to transform live sounds in various ways and even to program wholly original scales. In using the Mark II, the composer works at his instrument; and as soon as he programs his notes into the machine, he hears them performed. Its principal user, the composer Milton Babbitt, insists that the machine can make any possible audible constructs, although, he adds, there exist sounds whose specifications (frequency, timbre, envelope, etc.) he has not yet been able to discover. Unlike tape doctoring, which requires that a sound be transferred from a source to a machine and then from one machine to another, the synthesizer does all its work by itself.

Like so many other composers of highly complex music, Babbitt found that performances of his work were enormously disappointing; for not only were most musicians ill-prepared for the unprecedented demands made upon their skills, but sometimes a performing ensemble would completely disintegrate in the course of a performance. Therefore, Babbitt turned to the electronic medium first to produce the aural precision he desired and then to fix on tape an "interpretation" that would be valid for all time. Whenever any performance organization wants to play any of his pieces wholly for synthesizer, he needs only to send it a copy of the tape. Therefore, too, Babbitt regards electronic machinery as a mean of realizing ideas that he originally assigned to human musicians; partly because they were unable to reproduce his designs he turned to electronic machinery. (Similarly, when human beings cannot tote figures as quickly and accurately as adding machines, most of us would sooner exploit technology.) The synthesizer he therefore regards as an accomplice that realizes and extends his preelectronic compositional purposes. In this respect, the synthesizer resembles all instruments, even the simplest ones, which are basically machines that respond to a performer's, as well as a composer's, instructions. "As for the future of electronic music," Babbitt once wrote, "it seems quite obvious to me that its unique resources guarantee its use, because it has shifted the boundaries of music away from the limitations of the acoustical instrument, or the performer's coordinating capacities, to the almost infinite limitations of the electronic instrument. The new limitations are the human ones of perception."

VIII

Primarily because musicians a century ago could hardly imagine the stylistic inventions of modern music and the technological developments of radio, television and high-fidelity sound-reproduction systems, and because only a few could believe a decade ago that recordings might actually provide an adequate substitute for a live concert, any predictions about the future of music in an age of such rapid artistic and technological change are apt to be too modest. Nonetheless, let me suggest, first of all, that records will soon become technologically obsolete, because musical performances will become available on videotape, which everyone will be able to program at his discretion over his high-fidelity television set. Second, concert halls will become obsolete for everything except brand-new music; for once we can see and hear a musical performance at home, only certain kinds of highly theatrical spectacles will ever persuade us to come to a performance space. Third, as the twelve-tone language becomes more thoroughly integrated into the general musical curriculum and more musical laymen can appreciate its unusual qualities, the serial tradition will probably coexist equally with other musical languages. Both composers and listeners will need to be bilingual, so to speak; and just as we do not expect a French author to make sense in English, so we shall not expect the obvious mellifluousness of mainstream music when a serial composition is offered. Similarly, electronic sound-generators will coexist with traditional instruments, as composers can draw upon one, the other, both or (if Cagean) neither.

Constancy and change is the theme of this history; for whenever there have been new developments comparable to those seen within our lifetimes, even the most innovative music nonetheless retains certain characteristics of earlier work. As we have become accustomed to aural dissonance as acoustically pleasurable and the new electronic high-fidelity media as satisfactory replacements for both earlier sound-making machines and live acoustic experience, so we shall discover ourselves accustomed to more kinds of new phenomena, both musical and technological, than we can now imagine—contemporary compositions that nonetheless reflect the great tradition of Western music.

THE NEW MUSIC OF THE 1960S (1971)

Between 1930 and the present, three distinct compositional languages matured side by side in Western music, each with its own standards of structure and propriety—grammar and syntax, so to speak; and the work of nearly every major composer marked him as speaking in one or another language. Given the absence of generally accepted names, let me call them *mainstream, chaotic* and *serial.* The most conventional of the languages, mainstream composition, deviates little from the tradition of classical forms, post-Renaissance tonality and familiar harmonies; and although dissonances both tonal and rhythmical are introduced, these are eventually resolved. "Neoclassicism" was once mainstream music's term for itself, particularly in extolling the thirties and forties pieces of Igor Stravinsky; but by the 1960s this conservative term passed out of fashion, while Stravinsky himself adopted the serial language. In the post–World War II period the major practitioners of mainstream composition were Samuel Barber, Aaron Copland, Gian-Carlo Menotti, David Diamond and Leonard Bernstein in America; Benjamin Britten and William Walton in England; Dmitri Shostakovitch and Aram Khachaturian in Russia; and Paul Hindemith, who abandoned a professorship at Yale to return to his native German-speaking Europe. Most of the living composers performed in major concert halls of both America and Europe spoke in this idiom. However, in the history of significant art, mainstream music became inconsequential by the sixties, as nearly all its major proponents failed to offer new works significantly different from or better than their earlier successes (an exception being Aaron Copland, whose *Connotations for Orchestra* [1962] followed Stravinsky's example in appropriating the serial language); and few of the respected young composers were working in the mainstream mode.

The tradition of "chaotic" music, which is largely American, descends from the radical atonality of Charles Ives and Henry Cowell (in his earliest period) and then Edgard Varèse, who not only abandoned classical structures but also used nonmusical (or unpitched) sound generators such as sirens and anvils in his *Ionisation* (1931). Varèse spoke of "sound as living matter" and "musical space as open rather than bounded." He referred to himself as "a worker in rhythms, frequencies, and intensities," as well as calling his pieces "organized sound" rather than subscribing to such "musical" criteria as pitch; and his subsequent works define themselves as chaotic by thoroughly repudiating all known modern conventions for ordering tone and structure. Of contemporary composers, the most consistent and influential exponent of atonal and astructural music has been John Cage, whose work progressed from the use of pianos with strings doctored to distort their original qualities (particularly pitches), to chance compositional procedures derived largely from the *I Ching* and designed both to discount habitual ways of structuring and to isolate individual sounds, to scores so approximate that performers would need to choose the exact pitch and duration on their own, to tape collages like *Williams Mix* (1952), which incorporates an intentionally disordered library of noises from the environment. Indicatively, it is back to Ives, in addition to Zen Buddhism, that Cage has traced his "faith in the harmonious coexistence of disparate elements."

Historically, it was chaotic composers more than others who insisted upon the esthetic validity of all sounds, which is to say that all available noises (including, especially, electronic ones) could be viably incorporated into musical purposes; and by now nearly every advanced composer offers previously unheard sounds, which are achieved as often by new forms and combinations of instruments as by unusual ways of playing old instruments. "In fact," writes the critic David Hamilton, "almost every mechanical noise previously regarded as objectionable has now found employment in a musical work," and certain recent pieces freely combine live sounds with electronic notes. No significant composer, however, is interested in new sounds alone, for such aural materials are customarily incorporated into larger structural ideas.

John Cage's most resonant musical gesture was *4'33"* (1952), a classic example of Inferential Art, in which the eminent pianist David Tudor sat at the keyboard but made no musical sounds, implying (in this meaningful context) that the "music" consisted of all the accidental noises heard in the auditorium during the piece's duration (four minutes and thirty-three seconds). Since accidental noises by definition cannot be planned, the piece represented at once an apparent dead end to the chaotic tradition and yet esthetic license for a thoroughly indeterminate music in which absolutely everything (including sounds not prescribed, or simply nothing) is available to the art. Rather than accept the first implication and forsake his chosen career, Cage embarked on a series of works designed to represent in musical art the aural chaos of life, where the miscellaneous sounds have no particular relationship to one another. Nonetheless, as chaotic as Cage's atonal and astructural pieces are, they still differ from life itself, which merely provides the model, so to speak, for his art; for whereas cacophony on the street could be characterized as disordered disorder, Cage's best recent pieces achieve the perceptibly different quality of highly ordered disorder.

All through the fifties, Cage's material became more spectacular and his means more abundant, so that by the sixties he was using whole choirs of electronic sound generators—in the premiere performance of *Variations VII* (1966) there were telephones, food blenders, radios, fans and other machines—to achieve the artful chaos his esthetics demanded. By this time, too, his pieces realized another quality merely implicit in that earlier work—a theatrical spectacle that made Cage one of the most reliably accomplished creators of mixed-means performance. (Incidentally, the common characterization of this music as "chance" is critically inept, because that refers not to the perceptual experience but the procedures Cage sometimes uses to realize compositional choices from a preselected range of possibilities; and although aleatory or chance procedures, if strictly observed, should produce truly atonal and astructural music, not all chaotic sounds necessarily stem from aleatory composition.)

Other composers in this tradition include Alan Hovhaness, Henry Brant, Harry Partch and three musicians commonly grouped with Cage—Morton Feldman, Christian Wolff and Earle Brown. Hovhaness, an extremely prolific individualist, favors non-Western instruments (and their unusual timbres and tonalities as well) and risks looser structures, if not more passages of improvised chaos, than the mainstream composers with whom his work is customarily performed; yet even his most occult pieces embody representational figures and dramatic motifs. Certain Brant works distribute sound sources all over an audible space, so that groups perform the same or different materials autonomously and, thus, somewhat nonsynchronously—the sound in *Millennium II* (1953), for instance, ideally coming from twenty-two spatially separate groups. Harry Partch, an eccentric Westerner born at the turn of the century, became a self-taught musician who repudiated his earliest endeavors and then, in the 1930s, developed a forty-four-tone scale. Patiently building new instruments, mostly percussive, on which to play his microtones, he christened his inventions with such appropriately outlandish names as ZymoXyl, chromolodeon, kithara, cloud-chamber bowls, etc., as well as eventually training musicians to play them. The microtonal scales produced interesting relationships and his instruments fresh timbres; yet the forms of Partch's music seem ridiculously archaic and his rhythms are too regular, while his arrangements are perhaps too reminiscent of Indonesian gamelan bands. In short, the innovation in one dimension of tonality does not induce comparable revolutions in others.

Cage's oldest compatriots are more integrally radical than Partch, and yet different from one another. Only Earle Brown is as scrupulously committed to indeterminacy in both conception and execution; but none equals Cage's willingness to incorporate anything that sounds, if not to generate (and accept) aural chaos. The scores Earle Brown included in *Folio* (1952–53), written prior to his first meeting with Cage, pioneered aleatory ensemble activity; and his more recent works, such as *Available Forms I* (1961) and *Available Forms II* (1962), respectively for chamber ensemble and full orchestra, continue this style, containing pages of fixed but eccentric notation, or "available forms," which may be sounded in any order, repeated, combined or played in varying tempi, all to the spontaneous choices of the performers. "Performers make their decisions by reacting, within a specified technique, to each other as well as to the flexible character of the music at hand," writes the composer-critic Eric Salzman.

> When everything is working well, there is a sense of lively, organized spontaneity, a kind of controlled incoherence of great vitality, and, from time to time, a real impression of "discovered" form arising from the interaction of an effectively conceived musical action and gesture.

Feldman's characteristic scores, in contrast, are graphic notations of fixed pagination that merely approximate dimensions and relationships of pitches, registers and attacks, all of which the individual performer may again interpret to his taste. In practice, as in the percussionist Max Neuhaus's rendition of *The King of Denmark* (1961), the sounds of Feldman's music are soft and isolated. This aural pointillism, indebted in part to Feldman's interest in contemporary painting, superficially sounds like Webern's music; but the compositional choices owe more to personal intuition and thus a sense of *taste* (a key word in Feldman's vocabulary) than either serial systems or strictly Cagean indeterminate procedures. To Feldman, "sound itself can be a totally plastic phenomenon, suggesting its own shape, design, and poetic metaphor." Finally, European composers over forty who acknowledge Cage's influence customarily allow atonal and astructural passages within their more definite structures; but the assimilation of radicalism remains inevitably less than complete.

Cage's most important musical piece of recent years, done in collaboration with the composer Lejaren Hiller, has been *HPSCHD,* or "Harpsichord," whose chaos emerges from fifty-eight distinct channels of sound. Fifty-one contain tapes made beforehand of computer-synthesized music, composed in successive scales divided equally at every integer between five and fifty-six tones to the octave (except the conventional twelve). On top of this chaos of microtones Cage puts seven harpsichord soloists, some of whom play scored transcriptions of Mozart's putative composition with interchangeable parts, *A Musical Dice Game,* several fixed versions of which were realized in a computer-assisted process. Two more keyboard performers play a previously prepared collage text of harpsichord music from Mozart to the present, while one harpsichordist is granted permission to play any Mozart music he wishes. The sheer number of autonomous sound sources ensures that *HPSCHD* is, in short, a gloriously astructural and atonal chaos with references to harpsichords and Mozart because, so Cage explained, "Bach is committed to unity, Mozart to diversity"; and even though certain components of the score are fixed, the overall scheme for ordered disorder ensures, as always in Cage's works, that no two realizations will be alike in anything more than means and general effect.

The serial language descends from Arnold Schoenberg's radically original method for structuring pitches; for while he admitted the entire chromatic range (of twelve tones to an octave) established by atonal music, he subjected the tones to a rigorous ordering process considerably different from prior procedures. Essentially, the composer sets those twelve tones into a fixed order, where no tones are repeated, and this ordering becomes the "set" (also called the "row" or "series") defining the entire piece. In practice, this is a structure not of specific notes but of intervals, and this set can then be used in its original forms, in a reversed form, in an inverted form and in an inverted-reversed form. The notes can be bunched together into chords, or strung out individually; and the entire row of intervalic relations can also be transposed up and down to the composer's taste. (Significantly, as Roger Sessions writes, "The current trend is to refer to such vertical conglomerates as 'densities' rather than 'chords' or 'harmonies.' ") In short, the original set of intervals is permuted into various forms in the course of the piece, and this makes truly serial music more permutational in structure than classic music, with its harmonic combinations.

Schoenberg, Alban Berg and Anton Webern were the original masters of the serial language; but just after World War II several much younger American and European composers assumed artistic leadership—Milton Babbitt in America, the German Karlheinz Stockhausen, the Belgian Henri Pousseur, Alberto Ginastera in Argentina, the Frenchman Pierre Boulez, the Englishman Humphrey Searle, the Italian

Luciano Berio, among others. Most of these composers not only appropriated the serial language but, in a radical innovation, also extended its new organizing principles to other dimensions of musical experience, such as duration, timbre and dynamics, so that every note produced changes in several serialized sets. At first this supremely polyphonic procedure was christened "total serialization," which was inappropriate since considerably less than the totality of musical expression was subject to serial ordering. True, Stockhausen at one point claimed to serialize such dimensions as the density of sounds in space and the degree of the composer's control over the performed material; but since his selection procedure disintegrated into a musically arbitrary numerology, while his works eventually failed their pretenses, Stockhausen subsequently pursued other enthusiasms.

Babbitt was historically the first composer to extend, systematically, serial organization to dimensions other than pitch, including register, timbre, dynamics (or phrase rhythm) and durational rhythm; and he subsequently named this procedure "combinatoriality." Not only has he adhered to this pioneering position for over two decades, but he eventually formulated appropriately revolutionary esthetic criteria which measure quality and interest by the "multiple function of every musical event"—each note's simultaneous relation to several sets of developing serial structures; and his earlier endeavors at multiple serialization— *Three Compositions for Piano* (1947) and *Compositions for Twelve Instruments* (1948)—evoked a more Schoenbergian (hyperactive) field than the Webernian pointillism (spare sounds with pauses between) of Stockhausen and Pierre Boulez.

Babbitt's opening innovative pieces suffered such a chilly reception that he all but retired from composing during the fifties, instead devoting his abundant energies to teaching an even younger generation of composers and musicologists at Princeton; and this activity eventually contributed to several revolutions in America's modern music society—composers teaching not in the musical conservatories but in the liberal arts universities, the development of a criticism based upon empirical statements and verifiable perceptions, the founding of *Perspectives of New Music* in 1962, the influence of such Princeton-trained younger critics as Benjamin Boretz, David Hamilton and Eric Salzman and the practical principle of the avant-garde composer creating not for the larger artistic public but for the very few, consisting mostly of his professional peers.

Babbitt did not return to extensive composing until the late fifties with his *Composition for Tenor and Six Instruments* (1959), which he considers his most difficult piece—it has been performed fewer than five times and, as yet, never recorded. Dominated by a tenor part that requires sustaining vowel sounds for awesomely long durations, the piece is supremely intricate in texture; and although the untrained ear can hardly identify all the permutational orderings (and even the professional's comprehension is often less than complete), the attentive listener can nonetheless perceive as well as appreciate the relational intricacy, multiple density and scrupulous avoidance of repetition.

Since Babbitt's scores were too difficult or unfamiliar for most performers, if they dared to attempt them at all, Babbitt turned increasingly to the RCA Mark II Synthesizer, a singular instrument built in the middle fifties with the composer as a consultant and subsequently housed in the Columbia-Princeton Electronic Music Center in New York City. This machine enabled him to specify precisely up to five dimensions of a single note (pitch, register, duration, timbre, dynamics), affix the production to tape, immediately test the resulting sound against his intention (and respecify the components if necessary) and pile notes on top of one another on up to four different tracks of tape. When finished he could rest assured that all his intended designs would be accurately realized in the final performance, which is to say the duplicate tape that Babbitt releases to concert producers. His two major pieces wholly for electronic means are clearly among the best of their kind, *Composition for Synthesizer* (1961) and *Ensembles for Synthesizer* (1963); and he also wrote two scores where a prepared synthesizer tape accompanies a live soprano, *Vision and Prayer* (1961) and the especially brilliant *Philomel* (1963). Despite the obvious advantages that the machine offers his compositional ideas, Babbitt continues to create incomparably intricate and inevitably difficult pieces for live performers, including *Sextets for Violin and Piano* (1966), *Relata I* (1966) and *Relata II* (1968), both for orchestral ensembles. All this achievement and influence made him the father figure to a new generation of professor-composers (most of them now approaching forty), most of them working out of the serial tradition, the best of whom—Henry Weinberg, Donald Martino, Peter Westergaard, James K. Randall and Benjamin Boretz—were once Babbitt's students.

Jazz has continued to change, rather independently of other kinds of music, despite vain efforts by composer-performers such as Gunther Schuller, William O. Smith and John Lewis to develop a "third stream" between jazz and modernist. The most interesting individual jazz performers of this post-Charlie Parker period, the saxophonists Ornette Coleman and Albert Ayler and the pianist Cecil Taylor, have been defining a music of chaotic atonality and harshly wailing lyricism; and although this new style is stunningly original and dramatic in live performance, it seems limited in both its expressiveness and its capacity to earn an audience—two symptoms of a cul-de-sac. The tradition of imaginative improvisation has been enriched by Sandy Bull, whose intricate, varying and unclassifiable pieces are indebted to skillful use of recorded overdubbing of Bull himself on several stringed instruments.

The rock music of the sixties is decidedly different from the pop songs of the fifties—less sentimental and more dissonant, less slick in its lyrics and harmonies, considerably louder in volume and longer in duration and less subservient to the sonata form—all these things still distinguishing rock from the current performing of, say, Frank Sinatra. Though this new species of pop music is more interesting and more contemporary than its predecessor, it nonetheless represents a kind of journalism. That is to say, its supposed lifelikeness notwithstanding, by contemporary standards the musical ideas of rock are too elementary, the structures too repetitious, the pieces too short, the means too obvious; its progress belongs less to the history of musical art than to popular fashion. There is not one musical idea born in rock (other than the use of *amplified* instruments) that has influenced, or probably could influence, other contemporary composition, partly because the rock musicians have always derived ideas from Varèse and Cage, rather than vice versa. Nonetheless, just as some journalism is better than other journalism, so certain rock groups are musically superior to others, largely because they acknowledge some of the creative adventure of more serious modern music—the Beatles in their *Sergeant Pepper* album, the Mothers of Invention, Silver Apples and a short-lived combine called the United States of America. Moreover, in live performance, against a background of light shows, rock groups inspire some of the most exciting mixed-means theater of recent years.

Whereas both the aleatory and the combinatorial persuasions of American music were clearly defined by the late sixties, each to achieve more elaborate realization largely with the help of electronic machinery, a more amorphous position, not quite either serial or mainstream but lying between, has since become more definite and consequential. The primary figure here is Elliott Carter, who began as a rather unremarkable mainstream composer; and not until the mid-forties, in Carter's late thirties, did his work take the leaps that distinguished him from his contemporaries. The *Piano Sonata* (1946) is not only intricate in texture (and difficult to perform as well) but it also explores the instrument's capability for producing overtones. His *First String Quartet* (1951) presents an innovative technique subsequently christened "metrical modulation," where the basic rhythmic pulse is continually changing, so that the articulation of duration is as important as the ordering of pitches, and this constant redefinition of musical time (as distinct from real time) becomes the primary interest, if not the "subject" of the piece.

> This is caused [writes Carter] by an overlapping of speeds. Say, one part in triplets will enter against another part in quintuplets, and the quintuplets will fade into the background and the triplets will establish a new speed that will become the springboard for another such operation. The structure of such speeds is correlated throughout the work and gives the impression of varying rates of flux and changes of material and character, qualities I seek in my recent works.

This technique also defines Carter's *Second String Quartet* (1959), where the four instruments play less in unison than separately, all seated farther apart than usual, each articulating its own personality in conversation with the others; and the piece deals in instrumental contrasts and contests in real space. His *Double Concerto* (1961) divides the musicians into two ensembles, each performing an intricate text; and the *Piano Concerto* (1966) completes the current canon of Carter's masterpieces. Though not at all a serial composer, Carter nonetheless acknowledges in his work the esthetic values generally associated with the serial tradition—precise pitch, intricate relationships, textural density, associational structure, detailed notations of complex manipulations, accurate rendition of scored materials, elimination of repetition and instrumental virtuosity that challenges the performer's optimal competence; and these qualities probably explain why his works, though not strictly serial in structure, should sound so much like serial pieces.

Much of this semiserial music in America comes from composers who, unlike Carter, are also the most adept performers of difficult contemporary scores—the conductor and French hornist Gunther Schuller, the conductor Ralph Shapey, the pianist Easley Blackwood, the pianist and conductor Charles Wuorinen and the flutist Harvey Sollberger, among others. Shapey's *Evocations* (1959) deals in blocks of sustained sounds that are intricately formed and dramatically rearticulated—a style indebted to the best works of Stefan Wolpe (perhaps the most neglected and unrecorded older composer); and Schuller's compositions, though invariably too thin for their length, are remarkably sensitive to the particular capabilities of individual instruments. Wuorinen, the most prolific younger composer, at his best creates rapid disjunctions in timbre and amplitude that are controlled by some serial structuring in pitch and, less often, in rhythm. His most recent pieces were written largely for members of the Group for Contemporary Music at Columbia University, which he cofounded and codirects; for they intend to exploit the virtuosities of its regular performers—the percussionist Raymond DesRoches in *Janissary Music* (1966), the oboist Josef Marx in *Chamber Concerto for Oboe and Ten Players* (1965) and his codirector the flutist Harvey Sollberger in *Chamber Concerto for Flute and Ten Players* (1964). Indeed, most composers working in this way avoid electronic machinery (Wuorinen excepted), instead exploiting a new generation of unprecedentedly skilled performers of new music—the sopranos Bethany Beardslee and Cathy Berberian, the pianists Robert Miller and Alois Kontarsky, the violinist Paul Zukofsky, the trombonist Vinko Globokar, both as individuals and in a variety of live ensembles.

The chaotic tradition implies artistic permission to make musical collages, which is to say works that pull together in a less than integral manner an unlikely diversity of aural materials. What was called *"musique concrète"* in the early fifties did precisely this, as tape composers spliced together sounds made not on electronic sound generators but recorded in the environment; perhaps the best American sample of this technique is Cage's *Williams Mix* (1953). The idea of collage is so fertile in possibilities that it attracted composers around the world; but if Europeans like Dieter Schnebel and Giuseppe Giorgio Englert customarily weave motifs from the classics into indubitably contemporary structures, American composers creating musical collages—Stanley Silverman, William Russo, Lejaren Hiller, Michael Sahl, Eric Salzman— characteristically incorporate passages of popular music. Probably the most intelligent of these stylistic pastiches is Salzman's *The Nude Paper Sermon* (1969), which successfully eschews obvious juxtapositions (the primary fault of simplistic collages) to mix a huge variety of both historical styles (including faked Renaissance compositions) and musical articulations, as well as a spoken narration (which provides, or parodies, a bass continuo) and electronic sounds, all around the unifying theme of "the end of the Renaissance—the end of an era and the beginning of another." Although sometimes performed "live," as a kind of "opera," *The Nude Paper Sermon* was originally written for stereophonic tape to exploit opportunities peculiar to recording, as well as revealing a compositional sensibility shaped by the sheer abundance and eclectic repertoire of available recordings; perhaps its only peer in this style is Karlheinz Stockhausen's overloaded (and humorless) anthology of fragmented, distorted and overlapping national anthems, *Hymnen* (1967)—a "global" piece designed to emerge from eight surrounding speakers.

Perhaps the most spectacular collage of all—so spectacular it continually courts esthetic vulgarity—is Krzysztof Penderecki's *The Passion According to St. Luke* (1965), which mixes fragments of all sorts, in ways less inventive than derivative, if not simplistic—in sum, making the piece highly congenial to that lay audience that does not like much modern music, an updated *Carmina Burana,* so to speak. The *Passion* seems pretentiously impure in comparison to Penderecki's earlier *String Quartet* (1960), where old instruments are effectively resonated in new ways; and his successfully moving *Threnody for the Victims of Hiroshima* (1960), where fifty-two strings realize smoothly modulated frequency bands, mostly at their highest possible pitches, creating a highly controlled atonality. (Incidentally, this technique of frequency bands, which comes from sounding the spectrum of available frequencies *between* fixed notes, dominates Gyorgi Ligeti's stunning *Atmospheres* [1961] and *Lux Aeterna* [1966], both of which realize his professed ideal of "a static self-contained music, without either development or traditional rhythmic configurations," in addition to providing background music to Stanley Kubrick's film *2001.*)

Stockhausen, in many ways the most imposing of the major European composers, has radically changed his style in recent years, partly to acknowledge chaos and collage; and he continues to compose prolifically, in contrast to Pierre Boulez, likewise a dominant figure in the fifties, who decided in the sixties to devote most of his energies to conducting. Stockhausen first became known in the early fifties, before turning twenty-five, for trying to serialize practically every dimension of sound—particularly in *Kontra-Punkte* (1953); and he later produced one of the first genuine masterpieces of tape composition, *Gesang der Jünglinge* (1956). His next exploratory interest lay in the spatial effects of live music, exemplified in *Gruppen* (1959) for three separate orchestras and *Carré* (1960) for over one hundred musicians divided into four orchestras and four choirs, each section with its own subconductor. Recognizing that such a diffusion of sound sources and performing responsibilities would inevitably randomize his systematically serial scores, Stockhausen soon became more thoroughly involved in aleatory procedures. *Zyklus* (1961) is a graphed plan for a single percussionist to realize as he wishes; and his later work, *Solo für Melodie-Instrument mit Rückkopplung* (1966), allows the solo trombonist (usually Vinko Globokar) to react spontaneously to played-back sounds recorded only a few moments before. In a more complex conception of random unpitched sounds, like

Mikrophonie I (1964), the score consists of passages from earlier compositions, and Stockhausen programs the following activities:

> With various materials, two players excite the tamtam; two other players pick up the vibrations with directional microphones. Distance between the microphone and tamtam (which influences the dynamics and timbre), relative distance between the microphone and the point of excitation on the tamtam (influencing pitch, timbre, and above all determining the spatial impression of the sound, ranging between distant, echoing, and extremely close), and rhythm of microphone movement are prescribed in an appropriate notation. Each of two more players activates an electronic filter and potentiometer (which controls volume). They again shape the timbre and pitch (through a combination of filter adjustment and volume control) and the rhythm of the structures.

In the sequel, entitled *Mikrophonie II* (1965), the original sounds come from a chorus of twelve singers, who declaim into microphones, complemented by a Hammond (or entirely electronic) organ and four ring modulators. However, a conductor controls what sounds in the available mixture, and in what measure, will emerge from the auditorium's speaker system. For example, *Momente,* composed in the early 1960s but definitively revised in 1965, employs a variety of live sounds, both pitched and nonpitched, generated by a spatially distributed group of instrumentalists and performers instructed to sing and speak, clap their hands and stamp their feet, click their tongues and fingers, slap their knees and shuffle about. The result as could be expected is an atonal and astructural theatrical collage of miscellaneous sounds.

The more interesting composers in the chaotic tradition are mostly a generation younger than Cage's first set of epigones, Feldman and Brown, who accepted the availability of all noises and structures but scarcely realized the implicit license afforded by this position; in contrast, these younger chaotic musicians have extended the Cagean bias into radically unprecedented ways of generating and organizing sound. Within a decade, La Monte Young moved from experience in jazz improvisation through serial composition to the antithesis of extravagant Cagean gestures, including pieces where he drew a line back and forth across a floor for several hours, where he beat a pan a thousand times and where he released a jar of butterflies into an auditorium; but his masterwork, which both synthesized the antitheses and developed tendencies implicit in his earlier music, is *The Tortoise, His Dreams and Journeys,* first performed in 1964 and, officially, still "in progress." Here Young and several other musicians (or, more recently, a number of sound generators) project a constant harmonic chord amplified to an extremely loud volume, so that its overtones become more clearly audible, particularly when the chord's strictly specified components are recombined or individual voices change their timbre. Although this summary makes *The Tortoise* seem musically negligible, the work is genuinely interesting, not as just an unusual aural experience that hones the ear to perceive change in superficial constancy; but especially in a darkened room filled with incense and Marian Zazeela's contemplative slides, *The Tortoise* is the base of a supremely effective environment.

Another exploration in the chaotic tradition is the time-lag pieces of Terry Riley, who feeds a live instrumental phrase, played on either an organ or a soprano saxophone, into one tape recorder with immediate playback, and the tape travels into a second recorder that echoes the original sound several seconds later. This echo is continually (and electronically) recycled back into the moving tape until the riff progressively dies away. In creating *Poppy Nogood's Phantom Band* (1966), Riley pours more intuitively improvised riffs into his recycling system, which becomes filled with aggregates of sounds similar in timbre—compellingly repetitious on the surface but in fact continually rearticulating the pitch, pulse, phrasing, amplitude and decay of the mixture. (Tape delay as a musical device is hardly Riley's invention, instead dating back at least to Otto Luening and Vladimir Ussachevsky's wholly electronic experiments of the mid-fifties.) Riley's works for live performers similarly exploit rather simple means for complex ends and express parallel structural ideas, as the eleven performers in the recorded version of *In C* (1964), for instance, play through fifty-three discrete measures (or "figures," as the composer calls them), each at his own speed; and each performer is encouraged to sensitively interact on his own impulse with the ensemble. "A good performance," writes David Behrman, himself a composer of aleatory scores, "reveals a teeming world of groups and subgroups forming, dissolving, and re-forming within a modal panorama."

The chaotic tradition also seems the primary exemplar behind such varied activities as the sophisticated indeterminacy of Roger Reynolds and Toshi Ichiyanagi; Max Neuhaus's *American Can* (1966), where cans are distributed to an audience which is then instructed to bounce or slide them along the ground; the Ivesian theatricality of both Henry Brant and George Crumb, the otherwise unclassifiable improvisations of Larry Austin and the extravagant collages of Michael Sahl, in addition to three works by Salvatore Martirano: his remarkable *O O O That Shakespear- ean Rag* (1958) and two spectacularly theatrical pieces, *Underworld* (1965) and *L's GA* (1967), all of which, curiously, used twelve-tone rows for their musical material.

Although the major avant-garde styles in contemporary music are diverse, not to say opposed, on the crucial issues of chance, coherence and control, nearly all persuasions and practitioners hold certain atti- tudes in common. One is that structure itself is a major theme of a work, as a piece's singular mechanisms establish its particular subject or iden- tity. If Cage's works are primarily about aleatory processes evident both in the creation and in the perception of discontinuous, unpitched sounds, Babbitt's are primarily about the permutational ordering of precisely programmed pitched materials, and even Carter's define their theme as the continual rearticulation of musical time; and appreciating the multi- ple intricacy of Babbitt's structure need not prevent anyone from admir- ing the artfulness of Cage's chaos. What the listener hears in both cases is a particular texture—swift, abundant and extravagantly disordered in Cage, sustained and minutely varying in Young, complex and unresolv- ing in Carter and so forth. At any rate, music for this age of minimal personal expressionism is created less from feeling or psychological his- tory than from prior esthetic premises; and though these may change in the course of a composer's career, his objective attitude toward his work generally remains constant. Second, the existence of new instruments, mostly electronic, and new artistic freedoms instill a concern with appro- priateness of medium and music, so that the composer need not try in live performance what can best be realized on machines (i.e., outra- geously complex scores) and vice versa (i.e., improvisation or theater).

Third, in nearly all persuasions, the notation of music has changed drastically, so that a working score by Milton Babbitt, say, contains not bars or clefs but just numbers specifying the degree of each musical dimension, or John Cage's recent scores have nothing more than prose instructions for creating an atonal and astructural field, or La Monte Young's specify frequency ratios, or Terry Riley's *In C* contains just one page of separated but numbered measures in standard musical notation, or Silvano Busotti provides transparent sheets of notes and lines to change radically the underlying preprint and so forth; as John Cage and Alison Knowles's anthology of *Notations* (1968) demonstrates, today's avant-garde music *looks* as well as sounds different. Furthermore, at both extremes of new music—in, say, both Babbitt and Cage—is a commitment to quantity as a measure of quality; for as one school would literally count the number of discrete musical events within a certain piece, the other regards an abundance of autonomous sources as the best means for generating the desired chaos. At this point it should also be mentioned that many recent pieces of reputation are not available on record or in published scores, though, thanks to recent technologies, both photocopies and tapes can privately circulate; and many indisputably important pieces—even some recent Stravinsky—have gone rarely performed.

In all strains of new music, there is a constant concern with unfamiliar and difficult perception—with comprehending unprecedented aural material in similarly unprecedented ways. As Eric Salzman put it, "The new music is 'about' the quality and nature of heightened experience, perception, thought and understanding communicated throughout the range of human capacities." One reason music must continue to be new, as well as express itself in so many languages, is to ensure that those of us who love sound do not allow our honed perceptual equipment to lie unused in habitual ruts.

MUSIC WRITING

MUSIC CRITICISM AND THE
LITERATE LAYMAN (1967)

*In too many areas today, the people who write don't
know, and those who know don't write.*

"Amazing" and "shocking" are insufficient epithets to characterize
what passes for serious "music criticism" among literate people in this
country. Just as they rightly judge that newspaper music criticism must
be as generally ignorant and tasteless as nearly all daily writing about
literature, so they presume that commentary on music in the more
highbrow press must be of a caliber equal to its literary criticism. Closer
examination suggests, however, that this piety is hardly justified; instead,
the level of critical discourse is as low as the degree of concern about
musical matters. For an index of the latter, consider that when Meredith
Willson, composer of *The Music Man* (1957), was the only musician
appointed to the National Council of Humanities, there was nary a word
of protest in the literary press, although I am sure that if, say, either
James Michener or Herman Wouk, writers of comparable ambition and
stature, was appointed as the sole representative from literature, the
howls of outrage would have been loud and long.

A monthly magazine with the highbrow aspirations of *Commentary,* for instance, has not to my memory printed a word of intelligent
writing about music. True, a recent issue had a literary gent's warm
remembrance of the late Noah Greenberg; and another recent number
had an interview with Igor Stravinsky, in which he talked less about
music than miscellaneous matters. Also, a few years ago, *Commentary*
published a noxious article by an English professor named Albert Goldman who reargued Richard Wagner's notion that Jews have contributed
to music more as interpreters and critics than as composers—a thesis
that incorporates a rather untenable interpretation of Arnold Schoenberg as "not so much a great composer as a great thinker," as if the two
were necessarily contradictory, as well as curiously echoing Constant
Lambert's assertion, in *Music Ho!* (1934), that "Negro talent [is] on the
whole more executive than creative." (Why is it that critics who believe
Jews are "different" must draw so many of their themes from anti-
Semites?) I have noticed that musicians, in contrast, seem more immune
from ethnic and geographical preoccupations than writers, probably

because they presume, correctly I believe, that these sociological factors count for little in the creation of art. For instance, whereas literary folk find great significances in Stravinsky's attitude toward Mother Russia, musicians I know are invariably more concerned with his attitudes toward Schoenberg. The fortnightly and pretentious *The New York Review of Books* has its music volumes covered primarily by Virgil Thomson and B. H. Haggin; and not only did it once invite W. H. Auden to publish an ignorant derogation of Otto Erich Deutsch's painstaking scholarship on Mozart, but a recent issue contains another one of those Stravinsky interviews that far too many people regard as high gospel. Whereas Stravinsky speaks with varying degrees of irony, his unsophisticated readers accept everything with equal seriousness, so that, say, a passing favorable mention in these chats can do more for a young composer's popular reputation than all the fellowships in Christendom.

In other quality magazines, the coverage of music, particularly modern music, is in general just as bleak. Martin Mayer in *Esquire* chats more about performers and recordings of classics than the compositions performed, and Winthrop Sargeant in *The New Yorker* specializes in covering recent performances of premodern works; both of them evade essential dimensions of critical responsibility. My friend Benjamin Boretz simply has not written enough for *The Nation,* and now that the composer Dika Newlin's occasional music column no longer appears in *The New Leader,* the modern musical scene goes unnoticed in its pages. The regular man in *The Village Voice* loves Philharmonic Hall; but its second stringer, Carman Moore, specializes in contemporary work, sporadically publishing reasonably informed but critically inscrutable commentaries on recent concerts. As for *Ramparts, Commonweal, The Progressive, Congress Bi-Weekly,* and *Christianity and Crisis,* their conception of cultural coverage simply does not extend to music. Indeed, no general cultural medium in America seems as concerned about contemporary music as New York's subscription radio station, WBAI, which not only broadcasts numerous recordings and tapes but also airs lectures, interviews and symposia. Alas, it lacks resources sufficient enough to sponsor an American equivalent of BBC's *The Listener.*

One might expect to find more serious concern about music in those intellectual quarterlies supposedly committed to a general understanding of all significant tendencies in contemporary art and thought; but few of them publish music criticism regularly and most print it not at all. What musical discussion there is often either gravitates to matters peripheral and/or ancient, or the writer displaces critical focus by speaking of music as though it were expressive of literary meanings. *The Partisan Review,* for example, has in the past several years printed nothing more substantial than B. H. Haggin's attack on the editors of *The Nation* and his umpteenth praise of Ernest Newman. *The Kenyon Review* has published essays eclectically—by both Robert Parris and John Cage; but the editors, having nobly let diverse sides utter their messages, do not wish to encourage the arguments their articles suggest. The only mention of music in *The Sewanee Review* in the two years I followed it, 1963–65, was a paragraph reviewing F. W. Sternfield's *Music in Shakespearean Tragedy;* and in the two years (1962–64) I subscribed to *The American Scholar,* whose fifteen-man editorial board includes no professional musicians, it published, in sum, George Steiner's heavy-handed attack on the New York Metropolitan House's neglect of modern work, B. H. Haggin's polemic against musicologists, Edward T. Cone's extensive review of Stravinsky's literary efforts and Peter Maxwell Davies's reasonably perceptive essay on extreme tendencies in American composition today, a piece that the editors inexplicably entitled "The Young Composer in America." To its credit, *The Hudson Review* at least prints a regular column on music; and where the critic was once Joseph Kerman, who had at least the minimal advantage of an education in music, the seat is now warmed by Mr. Haggin, who, though not a practicing musician, has long been the American literary editor's favorite music critic. His opinions appeared regularly, for nearly thirty years, in *The Nation* and then, for a shorter time, in *The New Republic;* and they continue to show up in other places from time to time.

Haggin's high reputation has always mystified me, even though his latest collection of journalism, *Music Observed* (1964), is puffed by blurbs from such prominent literary folk as Mark Van Doren, Stark Young, Randall Jarrell, Dwight Macdonald and Irving Howe. Haggin's most obvious deficiency, which even a literary critic should have detected, is his extremely narrow range. Nearly all his notices cover performances of music composed between 1700 and 1900, a scope whose smallness might be more excusable if Haggin claimed to be an academic specialist; and with pedantic zeal Haggin customarily evaluates each new performance of a work against past performances. Although he offers little reason for neglecting music composed before the eighteenth century, back in 1944 he cavalierly dismissed all recent work as "hideous and feeble" (p. 53), and he has scarcely sampled it since. Not only are modern composers such as Berg, Webern, Carter and Bartók mentioned not at all in *Music Observed,* but also the major performances of new music escape Haggin's interest.

Even in the areas he favors, he consistently evades such essential critical questions as whether the performance reflected either a particular interpretation or a scholarly discovery, or why one piece of music should strike him as significantly better than another. Impressionistic judgments rarely receive any analytic support, as Haggin eschews explaining what within the music causes "the power" he continually feels. (Did not Kenneth Burke's debunking of that magic word long ago rule it out of serious critical discourse?) He usually wastes lots of space dismissing a newspaper critic's responses to the performance they both heard, offering rebuttals which are neither more complex nor more knowledgeable but merely disputatious; and although he dishes out cartloads of opinions, no discernible overarching ideas inform these criticisms. In short, even within his chosen turf, Haggin is critically inadequate, hardly realizing that a performance of a classic piece can be a more complex phenomenon than his approach can explain; but unlike the newspaper critic, he cannot attribute his simplemindedness to journalistic "lack of space." Indeed, precisely because both his perceptual equipment and musical interests are so meager, Haggin tends to write the same notices over and over again; and even though this book draws upon the work of nearly forty years, its pages are incorrigibly repetitious.

In his crotchety attacks upon the journalistic critics, Haggin boosts his pretentions by knocking his hastier and less serious inferiors; but even if the arrows are directed at such obvious targets as Jacques Barzun's anthology *The Pleasures of Music,* Haggin exhibits a genuine critical courage that deserves admiration:

> What he has done in this collection is to demonstrate
> again . . . the enormous amount and range of his
> reading and his astounding lack of discrimination.
> And one begins to see the process which produced
> both books: a lifetime of indiscriminate collecting of
> bits of material into files, then an equally indiscrimi-
> nate emptying of the files into books.

However, since Haggin looks down the cultural ladder rather than up, he is rarely disposed to tackle critics more knowledgeable than himself; and his few forays in this direction are more treacherous than not. Haggin's deepest problem is clearly that he cares more about Schonberg than Schoenberg, precisely because he moves in the same musical universe as the *New York Times'* principal critic, merely interpreting the same material in a different way; therefore, his weaknesses are more symptomatic than interesting. His equivalent as a theater critic, say, would scoff at nearly all plays written after 1900, emphasize the efforts of actors and directors, regularly pounce upon newspaper critics and never approach such questions as the influence of scholarly or critical ideas upon contemporary performance of classic works and the criteria for evaluating one playwright as better than another. Of course, no serious literary editor would ever hire such a theater commentator, and there is no excuse for his musical equivalent receiving such unbounded praise.

The nagging question is why Haggin should be accorded such respect in the literary community. To suggest an answer, let me quote in full the critic Irving Howe's rather lengthy blurb on the back of *Music Observed:*

> I have long admired Bernard Haggin's criticism. He writes with a forthrightness, courage and independence; he's a man utterly devoted to the highest standards of craft and seriousness; he makes one feel that the business of the critic, be it literature, music or any other art, is an exacting and worthy task. Whether he is right or wrong about this composition or that performance doesn't to me matter nearly so much as the fact that, as a critic, he is preeminently that rarity: *the real thing.*

Aside from the infelicitous phrasing in the last sentence, aside from the subjective criteria ("makes one feel") in a supposedly objective estimate, this statement says that if the writing resembles criticism—if the critic exhibits an independent and courageous stance and writes polemical prose—therefore it must be criticism, regardless of whether or not the judgments are perceptive. Surely Howe would never allow such irrelevant criteria—the quality of a man's style, rather than his insight—to shape his evaluation of literary or political criticism, for then he would need to take William Buckley as seriously as Leon Trotsky. Why, then, should he tolerate such indulgence for his comments about music criticism? One explanation might be that Howe's intelligence is less important to him than either his subjective feelings or his emphatic enthusiasm; another, that he does not realize what he is saying. A third might be that he presumes, as so many literary people do, that if a critic's writing on a nonliterary subject appears in a respected place, it must be serious and perceptive and significant. (Editors of these journals, in choosing a music critic, often depend upon the judgments of their literary critics—a custom that, alas, perpetuates a cycle of ignorance.) A fourth possibility is that Howe is simply uninformed about music; and indicatively, although I have read much of Howe and, for that matter, Dwight Macdonald, I cannot remember either of them remarking on music (aside from Howe's passing 1954 complaint against Olin Downes) or using a musical reference with any intelligence. The fact that he should feel the temptation to blurb a book about music, or even that he should be asked to do so, suggests the need for some intellectual hygiene that might curb such irresponsible activity. As for Haggin himself, he is very much the music critic for people who, though they "enjoy *Hamlet*" and know how to read, but do not understand very much about music.

II

I know of more than one contemporary musician who will consign all literary intellectuals, even the most tenaciously curious of them, to a hell of eternal ignorance; for there is indeed much truth in Aaron Copland's assertion that when "the literary man . . . puts two words together to characterize a musical experience, one of them is almost certain to be wrong." (For a sustained performance that illustrates this principle, see Brigid Brophy's *Mozart the Dramatist* [1964]). More than any other modern art, music requires a knowledgeable listener for minimal understanding; painting, by contrast, needs little more than tolerant curiosity. Nonetheless, I know of several artists and writers, all under forty, who are more informed and discriminating about contemporary music than some critics who appear in print; and for this reason, I have come to believe that even if the classroom musicological education offered most of us was terribly deficient, it is possible for a good reader to learn, albeit imperfectly, from books about contemporary music. Conversations with composers can be a supplementary aid, particularly in clarifying difficult concepts; a familiarity with contemporary tendencies in the other arts can also be useful. Friendship with musicians is an incentive; for when in Germany, it helps to speak German. I for one think I have learned quite a bit about contemporary music without attending classes; but before I discuss those books I have read, it might be wise to offer my own credentials as a reader.

I am by trade an unaffiliated writer, specializing in contemporary art and thought, both of which I consider encompassed in "cultural history," which I identify (only when asked) as my "field"; I hold an M.A. in American History from Columbia University. (I have not been able to find any work written by a cultural historian that treats music in an intelligent way. The closest exception is Roger Shattuck's chapters on Erik Satie in *The Banquet Years* [1958], but Satie is not a difficult composer and Shattuck is a professor of French.) As a writer, I have published both journalism and criticism in magazines as varied in intellectual level as *The Partisan Review* and *Holiday* and in announced interest as *Art Voices, Plays and Players,* and *Les Temps Modernes.* Despite possessing a musical name (that "rings bells," as they say), I received a meager musical education—perhaps four years of piano; in high school I sang in the choir, even earning a selection to the All-State (New York); and I taught myself to play folk guitar. I joined no music courses or activities in college or after; and although I have been taught to read music, I cannot today, to my regret, either hear a simple score in my head or *exactly* reproduce it on a piano. When buying records, I prefer, for reasons not entirely clear to me, Johann Sebastian Bach and recent music more or less in the tradition of Schoenberg; and in concert-going, I have favored the Group for Contemporary Music at Columbia and certain Cagean performances (e.g., Cage's *Variations VII* and La Monte Young's *The Tortoise, His Dreams and Journeys*), which I generally enjoy and admire as mixed-means theatrical events in which the composer's sounds are a partial contribution to the total experience. Among my favorite recent pieces is Elliott Carter's *Second String Quartet,* in which I perceive intensity of activity, precision of execution, variousness of syntax within a unified structure, continuously interesting relations among the elements, originality of conception. (These values, I think, also shape an appropriate characterization of both Willem de Kooning's *Woman I* and William Faulkner's *Absalom, Absalom.*) As a critic of critics, I pass over prose that states what was "thought but ne'er so well expressed" in favor of analysis that tells me things I either did not know or only vaguely perceived.

The first book about modern music I ever purchased, probably because it was the cheapest, was *Modern Music,* by John Tasker Howard and James Lyons (1957); and as an introduction for teenagers, it has its virtues. It is short, simply written and catholic in interest; its biographical discography is useful, although sometimes inaccurate (such as listing "Stepan Wolpe" as "b. New York, 1924," rather than Berlin in 1902). True, the authors neglect some aspects of the basic task, failing, for instance, sufficiently to distinguish between atonal and serial music; and they needlessly minimize how different modern music is from that of the nineteenth century. Still, Howard and Lyons are good cultural journalists who talk more about the music than the composers, thereby transcending the central evasion endemic in such elementary introductions.

A Short History of American Music (rev. ed., 1967), by Tasker Howard and George Kent Bellows, is similarly informative and yet limited in both critical discrimination and intelligence.

Unfortunately, many of the better-known names in modern music produce prose I found of little use. Too many literary people I know think of Virgil Thomson as an important music critic, perhaps because his prose is so elegant and witty and his references to art and literature so plentiful; but upon closer examination, his language seems coy and evasive. From its title to its tone, *The State of Music* (rev. ed. 1962) pretends to confront important matters; but if Thomson has quite a lot to say about the composer's life and times (gossip), he has almost nothing to say about modern music (criticism). At the base of *The State of Music* is an evasive principle that characterizes much popular writing about difficult matters in modern art: if the critic avoids explaining the stuff itself, he thereby keeps it from being forbidding. "The function of criticism is to aid the public in digesting musical works," but Thomson would be a more considerate dietician if he offered less saccharin and more forks. As a writer, the composer Ned Rorem places himself in the Thomsonian tradition; and while his *Paris Journal* (1965) is far more impolite and salacious as gossip than Thomson's disclosures, Rorem's *Music from Inside Out* (1967), a collection of essays, lectures and journal jottings, talks more substantially about song, that genre for which he is most noted, than about music in general, contemporary or otherwise.

Other American composers who have collected their fugitive essays into books include Aaron Copland and John Cage; and one quality both men have in common is a writing style similar in character to their music. *Copland on Music* (1963) exhibits supremely cunning prose whose singular flair is elegantly doing contradictory things at once. His style is both engaging and condescending, tough and tolerant, pretentious and popularizing, enthusiastic and yet apologetic; it is continually on the verge of saying something important or unfamiliar, invariably to disappoint. Perhaps because he thinks of himself as addressing the great audience—the buyers of *What to Listen for in Music* (1939)—Copland makes a defensive case for modern music, even when more unashamed enthusiasm might have been more effective for the cause. In his Charles Eliot Norton lectures to a Harvard audience, which were published as *Music and Imagination* (1952), Copland reveals how intelligent a critic he can really be; but even this book tells more as a series of miscellaneous remarks than as a structured argument of exposition—a factor that limits its value to the reader who wants to know more about the subject at hand than what Copland happened to be thinking or saying at the time.

John Cage's collection of pieces, *Silence* (1961), is a disappointing book, for he presents his ideas in such scrambled and indecipherable forms that the persistent reader can hardly fathom either the notions or their immense impact upon so many important artists in other fields. Cage once ingeniously decided that a lecture should embody his radical esthetic principles, rather than explain them; to this end, he illustrates "indeterminacy" by reading aloud ninety stories at various speeds while David Tudor, in another room, plays *Fontana Mix*. Whereas this might be a reasonable idea for a live concert or even a Folkways record, the ninety stories in print do little more than consume many pages of an expensive book. Cage's few unaffected expositions of his compositional practice, all reprinted within the first sixty pages, are slightly more helpful; but his summary of how he uses the *I Ching* to guide his decisions escapes my comprehension, even though it is, laudably, more technical than mystical, and I have read that Chinese classic. His pretentiously entitled essay "History of Experimental Music in the United States" turns out to be a step-by-step summary of how modern American music leads to Cage himself, and his relentless promotion of those composers trailing in his wake is eventually tiresome. One would be more critical of his curt dismissal of composers moving in other directions if not for the fact that this sort of haughty parochialism seems generally customary within the profession. Unlike Copland, Cage conceives of himself as writing for an elite public; but, unwilling to make compromises necessary for the medium of bound print, he creates a book in which precious little is communicated.

These books by composers raise the question of whether a composer makes the most propitious music critic. In most of the arts, I have noticed elsewhere, the practitioner-critic generally lacks that broad, catholic perceptiveness that marks the best of committed critics—a breadth best defined by the willingness to understand and explain works his taste finds abhorrent. Instead, most creators make meager efforts to comprehend a style they judge disagreeable, if they tolerate it at all; and this custom explains why their criticism is usually extremely biased. Indeed, a practitioner-critic is generally more perceptive about his own work or one stylistically close to his own (or, sometimes, close to his image of his own pieces); therefore, efforts quite different he neglects, dismisses, distorts or, with missionary fervor, rhetorically converts to his own persuasion. Severe limitations in critical sensibility, I would judge, afflict most of the above composer-critics. A further fact is that some strains of analytical criticism can become an implicit polemic for a particular creative approach, especially if the critic employs a vocabulary of discourse effective only with a certain style of artistic work. Taste tends to create a critical language that, in turn, justifies taste; and as the critic's style shapes his sensibility, he can perceive and explain only what his words can define. Examples of this include not only criticism predisposed to programmatic music but, in more subtle ways, the kind of analysis developed in *Perspectives of New Music.* Another problem is that some composers employ a language ineffective in critical discourse; and whereas so many of the essays Gilbert Chase collected in *The American Composer Speaks* (1966) traffic more in platitudes than in critical insight, other criticism as various as James Tenney's *Meta + Hodos* (1964) and, say, Peter Westergaard's essays in *Perspectives of New Music* are couched in a lingo that I for one cannot fathom. Nonetheless, what in music separates the critic who also composes from the experienced observer, to quote Haggin's definition of himself, is that, to a degree far greater than in the other arts, the practitioner can discern and explicate the hard technical matters that, particularly in contemporary music, remain imperceptible to the underequipped critic. In short, if modern music requires a more knowledgeable audience than any other art, so it also demands of an aspiring critic greater sophistication than appears necessary for criticism in any other field.

III

One might expect that volumes of more general musical interest—historical surveys or ersatz textbooks—would offer a substantial understanding of modern music; but I have read several I would judge as hardly useful at all. *Contemporary Music in Europe,* edited by Paul Henry Lang and Nathan Broder (1965) is largely reportage, where journalists list composers, works and dates, as well as enumerate reputations—the purposes of the book are more informational than critical. Most of the essays Howard Hartog commissioned for his *European Music in the Twentieth Century* (1961) exhibit that marvelous British mixture of elegant prose and critical evasion. Marion Bauer's *Twentieth Century Music* (2d Ed., 1947) is poorly organized, badly written and critically negligible; and all those deficiencies plague Peter Yates's book of precisely the same title (1967), which has in addition both a virtue in some gossip and a failing in its repetitiousness. Indeed, this book is so hopelessly disorganized that only someone very familiar with the subject could figure out what Yates has to say. Ineffective organization also plagues William Austin's 708-page *Music in the Twentieth Century* (1966), which covers so many more names and territories, both musical and geographical, than either Yates or Bauer—indeed, Austin seems to have attempted a definitive introductory textbook—that the sense of chaos increases proportionately with the amount of information processed. Several major composers appear under the strangest rubrics; Stravinsky's work is split into three chapters, each of which is pages distant from the other. The intentional refusal to discuss composers born after 1910 (except Charlie Parker, because Austin identifies him among the modern greats) means that not only are contemporary controversies unmentioned (it's a textbook, you see) but recent stylistic innovations also neglected. Moreover, Austin's style is so congested that I found several explanations impenetrable; and the patter on composers familiar to me, such as Elliott Carter, I found unilluminating. The saving virtue of the book is a huge bibliography that unearths many items that others seem to have missed.

A considerably more adept and sophisticated musical historian is Wilfrid Mellers, who has long been "England's foremost interpreter" of music to the literary public, first as music editor of F. R. Leavis's *Scrutiny* and currently as a regular contributor to *The New Statesman.* He possesses the authoritative style, the broad erudition, the comprehensive stance and the catholic interest that generally signify intelligent criticism; and these virtues establish considerable confidence even with liberal, educated, skeptical readers. Unlike Haggin, who appeals to a similar audience in this country, Mellers is a trained musician, a composer of pieces which are sometimes played, as well as the author of several scholarly histories. In sum, he is a hybrid of B. H. Haggin, Virgil Thomson and Paul Henry Lang—and nearly as productive as all three combined.

His history of American work, *Music in a New Found Land* (1965), covers everything from the classical tradition to jazz and popular music. That Mellers should have churned so much ground is, of course, to his credit, for Clio, rather than Pan, is his tutelary deity. Among the book's virtues is a clear definition of the large lines of the classical tradition— who belongs where and why and how important everyone is; for Mellers' judgments in this area would seem to coincide with the Standard Opinion that, say, most graduate students assimilate. What is curious, however, is that Mellers does not divulge that his present judgments are considerably different from those in earlier articles on American music, published in *Scrutiny* and *The Kenyon Review.* As an inveterate reader of old little magazines, I discovered that in 1939, for instance, Mellers spoke condescendingly of jazz as neither modern, American nor interesting; condemned Varèse's music as "close to gibberish"; judged that Ives is "not so much art as material out of which art might be made"; and doubted that any of this American music would survive more than fifty years—all of which were, I suppose, standard opinions in Anglo-European musical circles at the time. By 1943, however, Mellers had discovered that Ives was "the first really American composer" and that Copland and Marc Blitzstein were creating in their music genuine products of industrial civilization. What Mellers seems to have done in this new book is to have incorporated the current prejudices (depreciating Blitzstein, for instance); and indicatively, although his numerous judgments strike me as generally sympathetic, I find it hard to discern precisely what principled criteria might shape them.

Although Mellers is by trade a professor of music, his criticism seems curiously informed by literary notions. His major values are pro-life and anti-life, a dichotomy that probably reflects the influence of F. R. Leavis; and one can perversely admire how Mellers stubbornly foists these extrinsic criteria upon recalcitrant evidence, even offering the absurdity that electronic music is intrinsically inhumane. (Animals can't do it. Nor can vegetables.) Moreover, in his use of literary analogies, Mellers continually insists upon identifying programmatic literary content where it is more likely that none exists. His figures of speech become ridiculous when he describes Ben Weber's Symphony for William Blake's poems as "neurotically acute" or asserts that "empty distances" in Ruggles's work "powerfully suggest man alone in the prairies."

Moreover, in interpreting artistic forms as necessarily embodying their creators' beliefs, Mellers presumes that composers are intellectuals before they are artists, whereas even "intellectuals" as different as John Cage and Milton Babbitt seem to draw their political and philosophical positions from musical predilections. Mellers's approach leads him to see all contemporary music as reflecting a crisis in intellectual belief, rather than the post-tonal compositional situation. Likewise, a cultural historian truly aware of the actual processes of artistic creation would identify Whitman and Ives as similar, not because of their common faith in democracy, as Mellers would have it, but because of the similar character of their formal departures from traditional syntax and rhythm; and from an analysis of these characteristics a historian could indeed derive common political ideals. In short, rather than work from form to content— surely the only intelligent approach to music—Mellers moves the other way, even prefacing each of his chapters with quotations from literature. (His selections are so tasteful, incidentally, that sometimes I think Mellers is missing a more propitious vocation as a literary critic.) Finally, the book is riddled with factual errors and, as some reviewers have demonstrated, an opportune crib or two. Nonetheless, *Music in a New Found*

Land is a useful history of American music that has more to tell the literate layman (or the cultural historian, for that matter) than the two other mammoth volumes on the subject: Gilbert Chase's informative, prodigious but critically befuddling *America's Music* (1966) and John Tasker Howard's telephone book of names, addresses and numbers, *Our American Music* (4th ed., 1966). Still, the history of American music, as well as the historians of American culture, deserve a better book than any of these.

Mellers has also written two books primarily about contemporary music. The first, *Studies in Contemporary Music* (1947), I cannot find and thus have not read; but the second, *Caliban Reborn* (1967), lacks his prime virtue—detailed comprehensiveness—and accents his deficiencies. Since his concerns are "humanistic", which is in this context a pretentious word for *literary,* Mellers devotes most of *Caliban Reborn* to modern opera, which seems hardly the most propitious key to unlock the important secrets of modern music. He draws his insights as much from the plots as from the music; and he frequently explodes his perceptions into grandiose generalizations. "In Wagner's *Tristan and Isolde,* the identity between love and death is the beginning of the end of humanism." The base of Mellers's critical remarks seems to be his quarrel with the contemporary revolt against traditional forms of hierarchy; and rather than explore critically the new significances in the new ways of ordering—after all, Cage's devotion to natural existence surpasses both D. H. Lawrence's and F. R. Leavis's—Mellers hews his polemical point. Finally, as the book is neither an introduction nor a thorough critical interpretation nor a scholarly contribution, for whom is *Caliban Reborn* intended?

IV

André Hodeir's *Since Debussy* (1961) I found the most useful introductory paperback on contemporary music, but I always feel reluctant to recommend it to anyone without enclosing an addendum of warnings. In general, Hodeir's descriptive statements are more valuable than his evaluative comments. His summary of basic twelve-tone procedure, in the Schoenberg chapter, struck me as the most comprehensive introductory explanation that I have ever come across; and his chapters on Anton Webern and Pierre Boulez are effective surveys of their contributions to the serial tradition. To his credit, Hodeir is not reluctant to make generalizations about technical matters, though he sometimes forgoes the next step of specifically demonstrating how these ideas function in a particular composition. For instance, he points out that one consequence of row technique was "the identity established between the vertical and the horizontal," which I interpret as explaining a crucial surface difference between the new music and the old. However, Hodeir's evaluations are more often than not contentious and unsupported, sometimes reflecting a vulgar Hegelianism that sees composers as either in the stream of history or out of it. Stravinsky in this historical drama becomes "one of those exceptional creators who, because they are born during the last stages of a civilization, must necessarily hasten its downfall." Later, after praising Webern for extending Schoenberg's discoveries, Hodeir reverses his field and compares Webern's music to Mallarmé's poetry "in that its influence is probably greater than its intrinsic worth." Warrior Webern, it turns out, fought for the correct side; but his work did not complete the synthesis. Then, in the chapters on Boulez and Jean Barraqué, Hodeir's Parisian rhetoric, which is implicitly an evaluative instrument, eschews skepticism entirely and becomes unashamedly enthusiastic, if not agressively patriotic.

These ideological and nationalistic biases probably account for the factual errors and outright contradictions that even this amateur could detect. Since France, thanks to Boulez, has reassumed that avant-garde historical spirit that it only briefly relinquished to the Germanic world, everyone else must be lagging behind. So Babbitt's contribution to total serialization is not credited, and Stefan Wolpe is pigeonholed as a "neo-classicist" and his name omitted from the index. (Cannot some foundation supply Wolpe with a press agent to correct all the published errors?) Even worse, on page 139, after discussing Cage and Varèse, Hodeir writes, "No major composer has followed in the footsteps of these two independent artists." However, on page 222, we learn that their "uneven works may be considered 'traditional achievements,' valid only insofar as they are transcended by others (as, indeed, they have been)."

Sometimes the vocabulary generates a kind of double talk, such as the following remark about young American composers: "There will be at least one whose work will corroborate my criticisms at the same time that it makes them obsolete." Usually, the more pretentious Hodeir becomes—the more he exercises his role as "the Critic"—the more gas he spouts, so that though the journalist-historian is an accurate observer of the individual composers he favors, Hodeir as a critic can be a pernicious force. Indicatively, that pontifical tone becomes even more dominant where description requires less effort and evaluation has more opportunity—in his two books on jazz, *Toward Jazz* (1961) and *Jazz: Its Evolution and Essence* (1959)—neither of which, I should add, is as technically acute as *Since Debussy* or, better, as Gunther Schuller's essays on jazz. The basic problem with Hodeir's book on modern music is that whereas some parts are informative, it also has a high nonsense quotient. Thus, it is a threat to semiliterates, who by definition can separate truly critical concern from Hagginese but have trouble distinguishing real criticism from swashbuckling swordplay.

I gleaned a considerable amount of supplementary knowledge from a little anthology "edited" (apparently just pasted) by Paul Henry Lang, *Problems of Modern Music* (1962). Although the identity of the book is defined less by any overall purpose than its actual origin—a series of lectures at Princeton—I found it rich in stray comments that pertinently patched holes in my frame of knowledge, even though I sometimes did not entirely understand the context in which they were uttered. Whereas I could largely follow the contributions by Edward T. Cone and Vladimir Ussachevsky, two essays, Babbitt's and Ernst Krenek's, had portions I found indecipherable. That is, when a professional reader confronts a text in a field in which he is an amateur, he tends to pick up bits and pieces that he finds full of suggestive relevance, quite often because they unintentionally refer to areas more familiar to him.

Roger Sessions: "The current trend is to refer to such vertical conglomerates as 'densities' rather than as 'chords' or 'harmonies.' " That is, the quest for definitions of ordering principles in new music requires the development of a vocabulary that more accurately describes the unprecedented situation—more specifically, that identifies precise structures in what the untrained ear perceives as chaos; so rather than say that sound X is a chord that is not harmonic, let's call it a "density." Second, I interpret Sessions's statement as implicitly explaining how both contemporary music and post-symbolic poetry differ from traditional forms, for each creates a conglomerate of signs that violates traditional ideas of structure and yet develops its own discernible form.

Ernst Krenek: "Actually, the composer has come to distrust his inspiration because it is not really as innocent as it was supposed to be, but rather conditioned by a tremendous body of recollection, tradition, training and experience." This remark I find as applicable to the aleatory tradition of contemporary music as to the twelve-tone, as well as to tendencies in painting, poetry and intermedia art.

Milton Babbitt: "Schoenberg . . . established the means of a permutational musical system, as opposed to the combinational systems of the past." This suggests to me a similarity between twelve-tone technique and James Joyce's *Finnegans Wake,* where words form not sentences but aspects, echoes and transpositions of previous words.

Each of these sentences struck a familiar referent; and by working from my knowledge of the analogy, I could broach an understanding of technical phenomena in contemporary music. Although I know that formal analogies do not provide sufficient understanding and that comparisons based upon "content" invariably produce nonsense, the method is still, as Joyce's great book shows, a usable strategy for making the unfamiliar familiar.

George Perle's *Serial Composition and Atonality* (1962) I found the most thorough and ultimately useful introduction to that most difficult strain of contemporary composition that extends from Schoenberg through Webern through Babbitt. Its excellence lies in the author's ability to be at once general and technical; for as the book makes indubitably clear, this is a music where technical procedures must be understood if the music is to be comprehended at all. Pursuing this purpose, Perle outlines the basic concepts and compositional techniques, casting his explanations in prose that is at once direct and yet uncompromised by either condescension or false analogies. Moreover, he moves beyond the tasks of introduction; for as he points out early in the book, the true critical approach not only identifies the set—merely a descriptive process—but follows its various transformations in the course of the piece. (Perle: "*Every* twelve-tone work consists of variations of a twelve-tone set.") In this respect, the detailed character of his discourse makes the layman aware of the inherent complexity of serial procedure.

The book made clear to me, as nothing else did as well, the definitions of the basic terms, such as "serial," "free" atonality, "dodecaphonic," and the differences between them. Moreover, the entire book serves as an implicit demonstration of the achievement and usefulness of Babbitt's "consistent technical vocabulary," which I am finally beginning to find more agreeable than forbidding; for Perle succeeds, perhaps better than Babbitt, in clarifying all these new terms. He also explains more precisely than anyone else such important matters as how Schoenberg developed the twelve-tone language and why Webern might be considered more "advanced" than Schoenberg. The outlines of both Stravinsky's idiosyncratic twelve-tone procedure and "total serialization" are also the best I have seen, although both might have been longer and more specific.

In general, although its 149 pages are rich in useful knowledge, the book is far too short and sketchy, even for its introductory purposes. After reading Perle, I am not quite sure how to describe one piece as different from another, except by degree of serialization of the elements. To continue this exploration of differences, he might have broached the question of evaluative judgments. Once a piece fulfills such traditional criteria as originality, coherence, complexity, variety within unity, what other values become relevant? Does the twelve-tone language raise any intrinsic standards for esthetic judgment? These omissions perhaps explain why I do not fully understand how a composer's intelligence functions in a twelve-tone work. Perle's intentions may be merely descriptive; but I would think that these are concerns an introduction should broach. In addition, I wish he had discussed the question of Schoenberg's supposed abandonment of strict twelve-tone procedure in his later work. In the explanation of "free" atonal music, why does he restrict himself to art that attains an obvious coherence, rather than confront the issues raised by Ives, Varèse and Cage? (Indeed, why should we moderns consider internal coherence such a necessary value?) Finally, within its own development, Perle's book ends too abruptly, for it could use a summary conclusion which would, for one thing, enumerate all the essential differences between the new music and the old and, for another, discuss to what extent the new music demands different listening procedures of its audience. Still, all these suggestions are merely regrets that Perle did not go far enough; for of all the books I read, *Serial Composition and Atonality* exhibits the most intelligent introductory approach. If the literate reader should find Perle too difficult at first, I would send him back to Hodeir for more introductory reading; but to the latter's critical mistakes, Perle becomes the necessary antidote.

V

I hope that this survey reveals, both explicitly and implicitly, that a literate layman desirous of learning more about contemporary music should sooner read George Perle's book, the music columns of *The Nation* and *Perspectives of New Music,* two-thirds of which I assimilate with pleasure, than the more compromised, if not nonsensical, prose that appears in both the literary journals and between hard covers. Although the language of sophisticated music criticism may at first seem too difficult for the nonprofessional, this prose is hardly as inaccessible as some examples of contemporary poetry, experimental fiction or art criticism. The semblance of difficulty stems largely from what the literary gent would identify as "jargon," most of which succinctly describes technical procedures. Serial composition represents a conceptual revolution, and its ideas are thus so original that few people can grasp them the first time they are presented. I myself had read about them a few times and heard them explained several more before I started to comprehend the basic procedures, and there are dimensions that even now I do not begin to understand. One reason for its difficulty is its specialized character—it has no familiar precedent, and it does not lend itself, either truly or clearly, to extrinsic analogies. Precisely because it is both new and specialized, it creates its own language, both musically and critically. However, once a literate person penetrates this language, many articles in, say, *Perspectives* that once seemed difficult can become more accessible. Therefore, if twelve-tone composers want literate people to understand the new music, they owe it to their peers to communicate the new ideas wherever possible—in the classroom, in their articles, in informal conversations—until the new language becomes part of the common tongue.

BLUES CRITICISM (1968, 1963, 1968)

Most of the books published so far about Negro American music have suffered from a paucity of perceptive insight, if they made any consequential sense at all, because the writing combined failures endemic in the sociological study of black American life, on one hand, and the criticism of popular music on the other. If too many essays on Negro America are both excessively subjective and projective (foisting inapplicable generalizations or aspirations upon a *whole* people), most writing about popular music tends to indulge in uninterpreted facts (titles and dates) or platitudes that might be passable in magazines but seem ineluctably trivial in books. Both indulgences also evade more substantial commentary, such as the nitty-gritty of technical details; for as the great nineteenth-century critic Eduard Hanslick noted (and every good musician ultimately knows), musical art owes its great effects "not to the supposed extreme grief of the composer, but to the extreme intervals; not to the beating of his heart, but the beating of the drums."

Some books about Negro-American music (Nat Hentoff) gossip freely and frankly about the performers and their lives, at the expense of approaching with equal frankness their contributions to musical art; others (Marshall Stearns) report what any well-directed idiot savant could discover; some (Whitney Balliet) regard jazz as the inspiration for fancy and fanciful writing; others (LeRoi Jones) would exploit the music's eminence to corroborate a shoe-horned racist mystique; and yet others (Paul Oliver, who also misses most of the sexual allusions) are written by sympathetic white leftists who apparently feel that their sociopolitical good intentions implicitly empower them to make erroneous statements about Negro-American experience and art. Charles Keil's *Urban Blues* (1966), first of all, surpasses its predecessors—in scholarship, unlike art, definite progress is possible; but, likewise riddled by defects, it scarcely terminates the critical discussion.

Its opening words are pompous enough to alienate anyone hipper than a graduate student: "I am primarily concerned," he announces, "with an expressive male role within urban lower-class Negro culture— that of the contemporary blues-man." Thankfully, however, he talks more about the blues-man and his music than "roles" and other sociosexual-dramatic matters. Nonetheless, this opening reversal epitomizes the entire book, which is both knotty and nutty—diffuse in purpose, confused in argument, uneven in tone, sloppy in structure, mixed in style (combining both polemical journalese with an academic circumspection that reveals the book's origins as an M.A. thesis). His more perceptive observations fall sporadically throughout the book, rather than gathering in one place; and at times Keil seems inclined to record all the ideas in his mind, rather than separating the better from the worse.

Most of his problems stem from that great handicap of the young critic—his academic training; for instead of developing insights out of close, unbiased study of the music or even the current performers (only a few of whom, he admits, would grant him personal interviews), he approaches the urban blues with a classroom of sociological generalizations, which more than once seduce him into unpersuasively misinterpreting the songs he quotes. Unlike Paul Oliver, who is either a prig or a prude, Keil recognizes that sex is the root of most symbolism in the blues. However, after quoting the following lines from Muddy Waters,

> I can raise your hood.
> I can clean your coils.
> Check the transmissions.
> And give you the oils.
> I don't care what the people think
> I want to put a Tiger, you know, in you tank.

he apparently remembers what the psychosociologists have "discovered" about the emotional constitution of the Negro male and then rather ludicrously interprets that the "boastfulness is in some respects compensatory and defensive." (Where? Would Keil make such a condescending comment if the Caucasian rock star Jim Morrison, say, sang those same lyrics?)

Precisely because the author of *Urban Blues* has mastered so much of "the literature" about the blues, his attempts at theoretical definitions invariably disintegrate into choppy criticisms of the extant sources. Even then, his critique of Ralph Ellison's unfashionable interpretation of Negro culture as thoroughly American (and of much American culture as originally Negro) is glib and high-handed, while Keil's diametrically contrary thesis exemplifies the academic practice of bowing toward *all* current authorities and pseudoexperts. Keil's commentaries-on-commentaries eventually disintegrate into pointless nit-pickings.

Although one fears that Keil's background in anthropology might induce him to suggest that only bona fide lower-class American blacks can sing genuine blues, he notes in passing that various performers report they find "soul" in Frank Sinatra (!) and Japanese music. And Keil persuasively debunks the "moldy fig" advocates who would equate "authenticity" only with antique performers. (Besides, by 1968, such white Englishmen as Eric Clapton, Joanne Kelly and John Mayall, by mastering a complex of subtle techniques, have convincingly demonstrated that even non-U.S. palefaces can sing the Negro blues as "authentically" as blacks can.) Furthermore, Keil recognizes the relevance of Kenneth Burke's ideas to blues criticism; yet he seems totally unaware of Stanley Edgar Hyman's extremely perceptive, Burke-influenced forays into the subject [reprinted in Hyman's *The Critic's Credentials,* 1978]. Though he quotes Burke on the ritualistic bases of Negro gospel performance, Keil scarcely considers the theatrical qualities of blues performance.

Urban Blues is most valuable as unacademic reportage on the ways of contemporary urban bluesmiths generally unknown to the white community—self-taught musicians with largely self-made reputations; and although the sublime B. B. King, whom Keil interviews extensively and justly considers the master artist, has become a more familiar figure in the few years since the book was written, most of the other personages—American artists of peculiar pride and particular integrity—are still invisible to the white public's eye. Keil shows that the blues singer becomes a hero to his culture, not only because he is an accomplished artist but also because he reflects (rather than challenges) his audience and also articulates their complex truths in concise forms (which is not quite the same thing as the Beatles' acting out common aspirations that are normally repressed). Here, unlike elsewhere, Keil's commentary assumes that his subjects may as well be white, which is to say that they suffer, for instance, from existential predicaments whose essence transcends race; and at another point Keil conjectures that a major preoccupation of blues lyrics is those predicaments of the traveling life that have more to do with the performing life (and *its* sociology) than race.

Urban Blues is also valuable as an implicit introduction to the various questions that scholars and critics ought to be asking of Negro music; and in this respect, his appendix, "Talking About Music," is full of extraordinarily suggestive, critically intelligent hypotheses. In his preface, Keil lists the thinkers who have influenced his own ideas; and since he too is in his late twenties, I was amazed and then gratified to find that many of his choices correspond to my own—Kenneth Burke, Charles Ives, Ralph Ellison, Norman O. Brown, Marshall McLuhan. But let me conclude by noting that were I to do a book on Keil's subject instead of a review of it, I think their ideas would have been used differently.

II

Martin Williams has long struck me as the most profound and valuable of the regular jazz critics, for he attempts seriously to penetrate and dissect the mysteries of musical excellence and stylistic difference. Knowing that these artistic matters have less to do with the quality of a man's soul than his musical competence and fingerwork, Williams continually delivers technical explanations where his inferiors might offer pointless prose. This capacity for true criticism perhaps reflects his own extensive apprenticeship in academic English literature. Williams's essays on individual jazzmen, which have long appeared in *Evergreen Review,* rank among the very best of their kind.

Where's the Melody? (1966) is a more introductory work, however, especially destined for readers whose musical literacy is meager; for Williams explains all the basic technical phenomena in prose that is neatly constructed and rhetorically constrained. In addition to providing capsule notes on various major performers, he gives good advice on purchasing books and records. A final, not inconsiderable virtue is that Williams forgets that most of his jazzmen are black, and within the world of music that is the way it should be.

Negro blues have never received the objective, definitive study that their importance and excellence merits. Even the question of the art's precise definition has been more open than closed. To Jerry Silverman, in his *Folk Blues* (1958), "blues" is an honorific term bestowed rather indiscriminately upon all vocal music, both white and black, which he likes. Paul Oliver's *Blues Fell This Morning* (1961) had the elementary virtue of establishing which songs were the real blues—basically those twelve-bar structures in which both the third and seventh notes are flatted and the repeated first line is followed by a rhymed third line. Unfortunately, Oliver's blinding Marxist sympathies lead him to interpret, with a consistency verging on ludicrousness, themes of social protest in song after song of obviously sexual blues.

Just one chapter of Harold Courlander's fine *Negro Folk Music, U.S.A.* (1963) deals accurately and perceptively with the social origins, musical character, typical content and cultural development of the blues. He notes that the real blues, unlike "pop" music, attempt to deal realistically with experience and that the meaning of a blues song is conveyed not through plot (as in *John Henry*) but through a series of direct statements, usually about the singer's personal predicament. Courlander also knows that the prime extrinsic reference for blues symbolism is sexual, that in the classic blues the singer's voice becomes an accompaniment to the more expressive instrument and that the blues are not just a primitive stage in the development of Negro-American music (that culminated in jazz) but an art form of considerable intrinsic worth.

LeRoi Jones's *Blues People: Negro Music in America* (1963) is a curious farrago of comments on jazz, Negro history and the evils of white American society, for only sporadically do its pages lapse into a coherent argument. Whatever Jones has to say is marred by the gross carelessness of his presentation—excessive name-dropping, uncritical citation of inappropriate "authorities" (e.g., Oliver, a British blues buff who has never visited America, is cited as an expert on American migrations!) and a style that mixes technical jargon with the latest slang. Furthermore, Jones so constantly wanders to peripheral matters that his paragraphs frequently disintegrate into chaos. Since he has previously offered evidence of clear and sharp writing, one must suspect that this book was hastily written and inadequately edited.

At any rate, Jones has a simple story to tell: Negro music came to America as a pure art only to be corrupted every time it touched white culture and, in contrast, to be enriched by those few musicians who preserved its post-African character. This thesis provides him with the simplest criteria for his judgments: "Swing" is bad because white society accepted and imitated it; Ornette Coleman and John Coltrane are good because they affirm that jazz is separate from Western music; the Modern Jazz Quartet is best when least classical, etc. Anyone familiar with jazz history can write the rest of the argument. Precisely because his evaluations are so consistently based upon racial factors (and are so often wrong, as with the Modern Jazz Quartet), one doubts if Jones has much musical taste at all.

III

The Poetry of the Blues (1963) is a monumentally bad book, whose subject occasionally shines through the stultifying commentary, which persistently suggests that its author, the folk producer and writer Samuel Charters, neither cares much for or knows much about the first dimension of his subject—poetry. Though his wife, Ann, happens to be a sensitive Charles Olson scholar, Charters's own expositions epitomize the compromises and evasions of writers who hardly respond to poetry but somehow regard slick lyrics as containing more "true poetry" than the stuff taught in courses or praised in the book reviews. This pseudo-philistine position, whose early advocates were the folkniks of the late forties, has its current exponents in the rock-is-the-best-poetry publicists. The truth is that precious little in folk, blues or rock has approached the complexity, resonance and subtlety of the best modern poetry; and one major reason is that the conservative form of most pop-music lyrics—the couplet and its variations—puts a demanding, if not restricting, clamp on verbal expression.

Charters reveals his weak taste, or absolute lack of it, by regularly quoting couplets, such as the following clumsiness by Son House, that fail the most charitable tests of poetic interest:

> You, know, I fold my arms and I slowly walk away.
> Uumh, I slowly walk away.
> You a good old gal, I just can't take your place.

Uh-huh. The problems posed by poetry criticism make Charters so uncomfortable that rather than risk discussing blues lyrics as poetry, he consistently mentions other things. In practice, therefore, his commentary often makes blatantly obvious what was just slyly implicit in the original. Memphis Willie B. sings:

> Your clothes is wrinkled, little girl, your shade is
> pulled down low,
> There's a towel layin' cross the bed, and a pan of
> water on the floor.

And Charters's entire gloss reads: "As he stands in the darkened room he realizes that she has been in the arms of another man." Elsewhere, Charters speaks generally of "this directness of expression," which, one assumes, is meant to contrast with the indirect expression of professional poets; but blues are customarily an indirect, symbol-ridden art! Unable to say much of specific consequence, he often unleashes such unashamed platitudes as "The blues, as a poetic language, has still the direct, immediate relationship to experience that is at the heart of all art." (Why not "the liver" or "the root"?)

If Aristotle identified effective metaphor as a primary criterion of poetic talent (and some blues lyricists illustrate this proposition), Charters's own metaphors are often so inept that perhaps something other than poetry might be his real subject: "The verse, rather than the line or the couplet, is the poetic brick out of which the structure of the blues is built." (His subsequent examples, all of them couplets, render his distinction meaningless.) Then there are contorted sentences apparently intended for readers who prefer scanning from right to left: "The blues sometimes seem to have traveled a long way before the earliest recordings helped to settle it down in the 1920's.") Or liberal sociological sentimentality masquerading as cultural one-upsmanship: "No one who has not lived as a Negro in the Mississippi Delta can understand fully what the singer Son House meant to express when he sang. . . ." Charters then quotes an appropriate example. However, if a smart city boy has trouble understanding the experience portrayed in the song, then that blues is deficient as both art and communication. (And how, pray tell, does Charters propose to measure "fully"?) In case anyone should think I had to scour the whole book for the above inept examples, let me conclude with the revelation that they were all drawn from between pages 10 and 14 of *The Poetry of the Blues.*

This is not such a thoroughly useless book, nonetheless, mostly because it is saved by such passages of genuine poetry as Robert Johnson's couplet:

> I got stones in my passway, and my road seems dark
> at night,
> I have pains in my heart, they have taken my appe-
> tite.

Or Memphis Willie B's:

> I say I'm leaving in the morning, I'm going to travel
> 61 by myself.
> So's I get killed in my journey no one will know my
> death.

The book's best chapter deals with sexual imagery and metaphors, which are a dimension some commentators coyly neglect and which Charters, in his own reticence, saves for near the book's conclusion. In this section, the tone of his commentary indicatively gains some expository energy, as the critic enthusiastically lists numerous symbols for phallus and vagina, several metaphors for sexual pleasure, the double entendres, the occasional symbols of perversions.

Here, in the sexual references, are most of the blues' best poetry: Metaphors such as Blind Lemon Jefferson's "blacksnake" (though Charters apparently misses Jefferson's magnificent "crocheting" for fellatio), or "digging potatoes" and "coffee grinding," or the lemon in One-String's epithet:

> Well, you squeezed my lemon, baby, and you started
> my juice to run.

Perhaps the most subtle couplet, at once elaborate and ludicrous, is Robert Johnson's:

> I'm going to get down deep in this connection, keep
> on tangling with your wires,
> And when I mash down on your starter, then your
> spark plug will give me fire.

In the end, however, there simply is not enough first-rate poetry in blues lyrics, or at least not that kind of poetry I understand and appreciate in the best literary art. Contrast, for instance, that last Robert Johnson couplet with E. E. Cummings' more intricate, ingenious and witty "she being Brand." For another thing, in truly sublime blues singing, like that of Bessie Smith or B. B. King, the most profound "poetry" literally lies between the lines—beyond the range of verbal transcriptions that Charters pours into this book.

This observation, added to my long love of blues and rock, leads me to suggest yet another artistic category for genuine blues criticism—music-accompanied lyrics, or musical lyrics—to encompass blues, folk and nearly all rock (which in this and many other ways is indebted to blues traditions). Such a term would hopefully imply, by definition, that words, music and performance must be regarded together; and since music and lyrics artfully enhance each other, song without words would be emasculated and probably negligible as musical art. Similarly, most lyrics would have no artistic life without their music (or, more practically, their singers).

The real achievement of the blues is a powerful, tragic, concise, symbolic art that fuses words and music (with artistic domains between) about important common experiences—love, sex, frustration, emotional involvements, disappointments, unhappiness—all of which are treated profoundly enough to placate and perhaps influence a reflective person.

ON *PERSPECTIVES* (1969)

Perspectives of New Music has appeared twice each year for over seven years now; and it is such a superb periodical that I am continually surprised to discover how scarcely its name has spread outside professional-academic music circles. Perhaps this unfamiliarity should not be so surprising, for it is, I fear, a symptom of a larger general ignorance of modern music that afflicts literate Americans. There are many people who think themselves well educated in current culture—if not conversant with "all" modern thought—and yet remain thoroughly unaware, if not suspicious, of contemporary music. Indeed, when the composer Milton Babbitt is invited to address a general conference on "the arts today," he frequently opens by asking how many people in the audience have ever heard such-and-such piece by Arnold Schoenberg. As never more than a sprinkle of hands arise, he mutters, "That's where the problem starts," and indeed he is very right. Instead of amending this deficiency, too many American cultural journals, even those we consider among the best, perpetuate it, as much by intention as default. If Winthrop Sargeant can write superciliously in *The New Yorker,* "The avant-garde composers of today range a long way—from Mr. Stravinsky, the last of the great figures of the twentieth-century decadence, down to men like John Cage," he suggests that not only are those musicians no good but also that they are beneath interest; therefore, he has excused both himself and his readers from any confrontations with the difficult questions and perceptions raised by modernist music. Indicatively, when George Perle's *Serial Composition and Atonality,* surely the most important basic book on the subject, appeared in 1962, it completely escaped review in nonmusical magazines. Such neglect by the serious press might be more excusable if native music were prosaic and hackneyed; however, I would judge that few artistic scenes are, as a whole, as esthetically various, as abundant in major talents and as rich in originality. If only for ignoring the news, many critical media are evading their cultural responsibility.

Although *Perspectives* is surely intended for a musician more professional than myself—probably, as Ernst Krenek says, "an individual who has absorbed knowledge of music theory and history on the graduate level"—I still find it among the most consistently interesting magazines in America. First of all, like the best highbrow journals, it succeeds in making news out of the most serious criticism. When newspapers and magazines devote skimpy, usually deprecating coverage to certain important events in contemporary music, such as a premiere of a recent Stravinsky or Aaron Copland's *Nonet,* in *Perspectives* this new piece is excerpted and analyzed in detail, sometimes not in just one essay but two. Similarly, certain unknown works by young composers—pieces unavailable either on record or in published scores—receive individual articles, full of the necessary evidence of extensive musical quotations; certain older composers present ideas and preoccupations too slender for a book and yet too important for a short essay or book review; eminences unwilling to write are interviewed with sympathy and cunning; developments in the use of computers and other technologies for both composition and musicology are reported in abundant detail—all of which is to say that *Perspectives* executes those essential tasks that an occasional journal can best perform. Its standards are so high and strong that out of its pages are coming book-length anthologies of critical essays on a single modern subject—Schoenberg, Stravinsky, etc. In short, no other publication since the demise of *Modern Music* covers as broad a territory, probes important issues as deeply, approaches as intelligently the critical problems raised by certain strains of contemporary composition; and primarily for these reasons, anyone seriously interested in current music, particularly in America, should oblige himself to read it. I have more than once wondered if its subscribers may not include more non-musicians than its editors suspect—quite simply, how else are we to inform ourselves; and I for one will testify that *Perspectives* succeeds in educating its amateur readers to its discourse and interests.

One should add, however, that *Perspectives* stands for a certain kind of committed concern, perhaps even to the exclusion of other forms of seriousness. It insists that contributors talk as precisely as possible about the technical procedures of music, largely because in important contemporary compositions technical matters must be defined if the music is to be understood at all (and perhaps because the serious American composer can no longer pretend that music is something else). Most of its contributors respect the serial tradition of modern music—a canon that has thoroughly assimilated both Schoenberg and Webern and is at present considering differing directions posed by Babbitt, Stravinsky (in his pieces of the last fifteen years), Elliott Carter and Stefan Wolpe. Certain composers on the margin of this tradition—elder contemporaries such as Roger Sessions, Aaron Copland and the late Edgard Varèse—receive serious respect; but the neoclassical establishment—Virgil Thomson, Samuel Barber, Leonard Bernstein, Ned Rorem, et al.—have entered *Perspectives'* pages only once, when Bernstein's *Kaddish* received a short analysis by Jack Gottlieb, who shamelessly identifies himself as Bernstein's "General Music Assistant." This attitude to the present and the recent past seems to inform an implicit, approximate hierarchy of current reputations; and these ratings, although never explicitly charted, appear generally assimilated at the same time that they are continually questioned. Pop music, perhaps needless to say, goes as unnoticed as journalism does (and should) in a literary quarterly, one kind of ephemeral popularization being the esthetic equal of the other.

The second avant-garde of contemporary music, the Cagean wing, becomes an itch on the magazine's skin; for although most of its regular contributors reject this alternative, with varying degrees of vehemence, and Cage himself has never contributed to *Perspectives'* pages, he haunts its collective mind so deeply that an informal survey reveals that no living composer but Stravinsky is mentioned in its issues more often than Cage. His first book, *Silence* (1961), was reviewed by the poet-critic John Hollander, who exhibited a haughtiness more characteristic of literary polemic. ("My three-year-old daughter drew a smiling face in the margin of one of the pages of *Silence.*") Two articles by acknowledged Cageans, David Behrman and Roger Reynolds, have soberly elaborated upon the techniques and notation of indeterminate music; but the general coverage of its challenges and possibilities has not, in my opinion, been either just or adequate. The problem here, I think, is that Cage's ideas essentially escalate "music" into a theater of spectacle which has more to do with primitive conceptions of theatrical experience than either the concert tradition of post-Renaissance music or the conventional performance of dramatic literature. *Perspectives,* in contrast, belongs to that contemporary tendency, having its exponents in all the arts, that would preserve the attributes of each particular art. That is, whereas Cage would "combine," to use Robert Rauschenberg's coinage for his stand-up paintings, most of *Perspectives'* contributors would isolate; and in this respect, it is indicative that the serial revolution creates forms that have not been (and probably cannot be) successfully adapted to nonmusical purposes. Beyond that, a commitment to the serial tradition creates not only a bias favoring music's unadulterated integrity and pieces written primarily for other composer-musicians but also a certain language for critical analysis. However, neither this bias nor language can cope with serious Cagean activities, which in turn instigate a bias and language that are as insufficient with phenomena *Perspectives* takes seriously. My own proposal is to rule, by critical fiat, that Cagean performances hereafter be called "theater of mixed means," for only by separating them from the musical tradition can we recognize their radically different purposes and values. This neo-aleatory persuasion, based on artistic freedom, conceptual idiosyncrasy and a more popular appeal, informs another lively, imaginatively designed, but intellectually less rigorous magazine entitled *Source,* published in Davis, California; and its founding, in 1967, represents an implicit critical response to *Perspectives'* growing influence in the profession.

In devising a language suitable for critical discourse about music, the contributors to *Perspectives* favor explanations that identify verifiable phenomena in a verifiable prose; for both denotative language and esthetic empiricism are crucial ingredients in *Perspectives'* conception of seriousness. This position often demands the coinage of new words, or the precise definition of old ones; and the most useful guide to the magazine's lingo is the faintly ironic "A Budding Grove" that one of the editors, Edward T. Cone, contributed to the issue dated Spring-Summer 1965. Most of the language in its pages distinctly differs from the following sentences, which opened an essay, in a recent issue, on "Richard Strauss" by the widely praised German critic Theodor W. Adorno:

> That Strauss's flexibility never slips from the forming
> hand is his *tour de force,* truly a piece of magic
> become esthetic. Without granting the ear an instant
> to contemplate the total coherence, he tirelessly con-
> nects the unconnected.

Of course, nothing substantial could possibly be said in language so overblown with hot air; and another line on the following page generates even more heat: "Nietzsche criticized Wagner for allowing his music to perspire." Such metaphorical prattle suggests less a musical insight than the comic image of globules dripping down a score; and it is my conjecture that the editors probably published this essay to embarrass either Adorno and/or his American supporters. *Perspectives* is, to its credit, generally immune from such gush over the esthetic mysteries, as well as grandiose philosophical and sociological platitudes; for its discourse owes less to Middle-European philosophy than to Anglo-American empiricism. Indicatively, the opening issue published a physicist's attack on fallacious forms of scientific explanation in a sample of *die Reihe,* an earlier German counterpart and an implicit competitor since defunct; and in a more recent *Perspectives,* a New York composer called for an exposure of the under-the-music-stand politics of the European contemporary-music scene. This cultural patriotism might seem excessive were it not so deserved.

Indeed, quite often the language tends to emulate the convoluted precision of American analytic philosophy, a style which only Babbitt manages to use with energy and a peculiar grace:

> I eagerly anticipate detailed discussions of Varèse's music, which concern themselves with the analysis of total progression, the motion toward and from points of conjoined climax, by means of transformation of rhythmic components, particularly in the sense of the number of attacks per unit time, the pitch content and range of extrema, the dispersion and internal distribution of the elements of similitudes, the total spectrum, and other compound concepts, for the possibility of such discussion, if it is to be more than mere translation from musical to verbal notation, depends upon the formulation of scale to measure degrees of similitude applicable to such concepts.

So far, Babbitt's thought is not too obscure to follow, though I should add that his essays invariably progress beyond my capacities to understand them. Since I have more than once comprehended summaries that others have made of ideas I could not decipher at their source, there is reason to suspect that Babbitt makes everything sound more complicated than it really is. One of his protégés, Michael Kassler, contributed to the Spring-Summer 1967 issue an eighty-page essay so full of mathematical symbols that its readers were inevitably very few; but the criticisms contributed to a succeeding issue by Eric Regner, a less-favored Babbitt student, were considerably more comprehensible. Nonetheless, everything Babbitt writes deserves the most dogged attention; for solely to judge by how often other contributors quote him, he is obviously the most fertile theoretical mind in American neoserial composition. Not only were many of the contributors once his students, but what George Perle calls his "consistent technical vocabulary" permeates much of the discourse. One of the early issues contained a letter from the musicologist Joseph Kerman attributing the magazine to a "Princeton" cabal, and his charge makes more sense as a geographical insight than as devastating criticism. True, Babbitt has taught at Princeton for over thirty years, the magazine's publisher is the Princeton University Press and many of its contributors hold Princeton degrees (as, incidentally, does Kerman himself); however, such a curt dismissal neglects the fact that certain (though not all) Princeton music professors have long espoused a distinct approach to musical issues, very much as a certain Oxford teachers some years ago offered a new kind of philosophy and other Cambridge professors collectively revolutionized anthropology.

Historically, *Perspectives* represents yet one more sign of the efforts by composers to extend their values and concerns into other dimensions of the musical scene. The first editor was the composer Arthur Berger, a Brandeis professor, who was for a while, some time ago, a newspaper music critic; its present top editors are both practicing composers more noted for their critical writings, Edward T. Cone and Benjamin Boretz, the latter recently becoming the sole chief editor. The major individual backer is Paul Fromm, a Chicago wine merchant, whose Fromm Music Foundation has generously aided neoserial composers in various ways for over a decade. Its editorial board includes composers as different (within the neoserial ambience, of course) as Babbitt and Leon Kirchner, Elliott Carter and Gunther Schuller, Lukas Foss and George Perle. Most of these men currently have regular teaching jobs at major American universities—most, indeed, were founding members of the newly formed American Society of University Composers, another dimension of this tendency; and this academic affiliation distinguishes them not only from Cage, who has so far taken only short-term appointments as "composer-in-residence," but also from the major neoclassical composers who tend either to teach at "conservatories" or to live off commissions, royalties and other favors. Several of the younger contributors to *Perspectives* are also regular performers of new music in chamber ensembles that have recently, in yet another dimension, been organized at American universities. Therefore, the magazine stems from the recognition by those composers that critical writing about contemporary music would not improve unless they assumed the task themselves; and this means that many contributors fuse the practitioner's committed engagement to the critic's disinterested rigor and circumspection. This success of *Perspectives* may hopefully inspire ways of solving the next major professional problem bothering these composers, the prompter publication of their fresh scores.

Implicit in their program is a reform not only of criticism but also, finally, of music teaching. The unending, if not tiresome, attacks in *Perspectives* on inadequate textbooks justifiably deprecates discourse that rarely rises above listing names, dates, pieces and social connections. Behind this sniping is the same sort of motivation that, in literature, energized the New Criticism some thirty to forty years ago—a sense that the simplistic historical approach does little more than describe and classify a piece; it fails to inculcate either perceptive understanding or critical discrimination. This attitude to music insists that education must be based not upon "appreciation" and the accumulation of informational data but upon the comprehension and analysis of technical procedures. If *Perspectives* is now a cross, metaphorically, between *The Kenyon Review* and *Modern Language Notes* of twenty-five years ago, I suspect that the musical equivalent of *Understanding Poetry* will soon appear and that the kind of music criticism currently developed in *Perspectives* will have increasingly greater impact upon both the students and the audience of modern music.

TALKING WITH JOHN CAGE ABOUT HIS WRITINGS THROUGH *FINNEGANS WAKE* (1978)

In the 1960s, John Cage wrote poetry, initially in a series of notational "Diary" pieces which I regard as a rich extension of Black Mountain poetics. More recently, he has been rewriting poetry—to be precise, rewriting someone else's poetry. His principal literary project of the early 1970s was based upon the writings of Henry David Thoreau. Our conversation about it appeared first in the *New York Arts Journal* (no. 19, November 1980) and then in the recent collection of my essays on poetry, *The Old Poetries and the New* (Ann Arbor: University of Michigan Press, 1981). More recently, Cage has been working with James Joyce's *Finnegans Wake*. When we met for the following conversation, for SoHo Television in the spring of 1978, he had already finished two of his Writings Through *Finnegans Wake;* he was then beginning a third which, in fact, he subsequently put aside, so that the title *Writing for the Third Time Through Finnegans Wake* went instead to a piece composed in a different way. At last report, the piece begun during the following conversation is titled . . . *for the Fifth Time.* At any rate, my 1979 review of Cage's *Wake* project appeared first in *The New York Times Book Review* (December 2, 1979) and then in my book *The Old Poetries and the New* (1981).

As poetry radically unlike any written before, which is composed in ways original with Cage, it is, in the truest sense, avant-garde work important not only in itself but also for its status in Cage's continuing artistic adventure. It is not difficult poetry in the sense of something no one else can do. Rather, it is inventive poetry—better yet, audaciously inventive poetry. It was often said of Cage's music that no one else composes like this, because no one else would dare; the same might be said of his poetry. His Writings Through *Finnegans Wake* exist outside not only the mainstream of contemporary American poetry but its tributaries as well. It is not reviewed in poetry magazines; it is not anthologized or mentioned in the literary histories of native work. Nonetheless, on several grounds, it connects to advanced tendencies both in the other arts and in literature around the world—to tendencies that to various degrees and in various ways reflect Cage's influence.

I'm with John Cage. He is just beginning a new piece. What is it called, John?

Just a second. 41, 42, 43, 44, 45, 46, 47, 48, 49, 50, 51, 52, 53, 54, 55, 56. I was counting the letters in this line of *Finnegans Wake*. The text will be called *Writing for the Third Time Through Finnegans Wake*.

It follows, therefore, the pieces called Writing for the Second Time Through Finnegans Wake *and* for the First Time.

Right. But the first time didn't have that in the title. It just said *Writing Through Finnegans Wake*. Actually, the title of this third one may change because I'm not going through it. What I'm doing is, through chance operations, landing here and there in it: coming down on phrases, words, syllables and letters but not writing or riding or walking through it, but flying over it and landing here and there on it.

How did you do the first one?

For the first one I made mesostics. You know what an acrostic is, with the name down the edge. A mesostic is the name down the middle.

It's a form you have used before.

Right. I have made them for the names of Marcel Duchamp and Merce Cunningham and Mark Tobey and so on, but these are on the name James Joyce and this is the first page of them. The number 3 on the right refers to the opening page of *Finnegans Wake* which is page 3. It opens: "wroth with twone nathandJoe" which includes the words "wroth" and "Joe." "Joe" has a "J" in it and that "J" doesn't have an "A" after it, because the "A" belongs to the second line.

Because the mesostic spine here is J-A-M-E-S.

This is the first "J" that doesn't have an "A" after it. I think it's actually the first "J" in the book.

It seems to be, yes.

You know how you can tell—you can turn the page upside down and then if you look for the dots you can catch the "I"s and the "J"s that way very easily because the "J"s dip below the line whereas the "I"s don't. I had a friend named Hazel Dreis who was a fantastic proofreader, and she proofread the *Leaves of Grass* of Walt Whitman which she had bound for the Grabhorn Press in San Francisco. She proofread it upside down and backwards. That means—and this is something I think of as very close to my work—that means that we do very good work when we don't know what we're doing.

Anyway, here's "wroth with twone nathandJoe," and then my second line is "A" and I skip the word "rot" that lies between them. "A"—this is the first word that has an "A" that doesn't have an "M" after it. Then I leave out "peck of pa's" and here's the letter "M" in "malt." M-A-L-T doesn't have an "E" in it.

The "E" being the next letter in "James." The next "E" in the text appears in "Jhem."

And then "S" is in "Shen." Then we have the brothers Jhem and Shen.

Since brothers in various form are a continuing motif in Finnegans Wake, *you were lucky to get them into the opening mesostic of your own redoing of* Finnegans Wake.

Now we look for the next "J," and here's the first thunderclap, by the way—the hundred-letter word.

Right, but there's no "J" there.

No, we don't get a "J" until we come to this marvelous word right here: "pftjschute."

Which sounds like air going down a chute.

Right, the falling of Humpty Dumpty—"the pftjschute of Finnegan." He fell off a ladder, you remember.

So it's a neologism for falling. But here you broke the phrase into two lines, putting "pftjschute" and only it with the "J" and then "of Finnegans" for the "O." Why did you use "of Finnegan," rather than just "of" alone?

Because I was so delighted to get "Finnegan."

Ah, you made a decision of taste.

Well, you see, I'm not dealing with chance here, and I have the choice, I gave myself the liberty, of going up to forty-four characters to the left and forty-four to the right, so that the name would come down the middle.

Forty-four characters in measuring away from the letter on the mesostic axis.

Right, and sometimes I made a long line and kept quite a lot—except there was a tendency to omit and, in that way, to arrive at a different rhythm than was in the original, though all my words are words from the *Wake* itself. Anyway, for the next line I need a "Y": "that the humptYhillhead of humself." You see, we don't have any "C" there. Here we'll have it: "is at the knoCk out." You see I had to skip practically a whole line . . .

. . . to get the next "C."

Because the original reads this way: "that the humptyhillhead of humself promptly sends an unquiring one well to the west in quest of his tumptytumtoes: and their upturnpikepointandplace is at the knock out in the park . . ."

So you take the "c" from "knock."

Right, and the "e" is in "in the park."

So, in effect, you've completed one mesostic there—one vertical "James Joyce."

And we leave out the rest of the sentence, which is: "where oranges have been laid to rust upon the green since devlinsfirst loved livvy."

So what you did, in Writing Through Finnegans Wake, *is go through the entire* Wake, *writing up mesostics on the name "James Joyce."*

Then what I'm going to do, Richard, is distribute the punctuation by chance operations on the page like an explosion. Read just the text and you'll see the punctuation omitted. You can imagine it where you like. You can replace it where you wish. And I also have it oriented according to the twelve parts of the clock.

Which is to say that it isn't all horizontal—that the exclamation point on the first page, for instance, is tilted slightly like the tower of Pisa.

Right, and you know that the night hours are important in *Finnegans Wake.* So that's the first one. Anyway, my editor at the Wesleyan University Press found the text, which is about 125 pages, to be too long and boring, and he said I should make a shorter text and I didn't want to shorten that because that one is complete. It's like Schoenberg said: "A long work can't be cut because if it is cut it would be a long work that was cut." So I wanted to make a new work that wasn't cut but that was shorter. And what I did was to make a further discipline, keeping the ones I had of J-A-M-E-S J-O-Y-C-E but keeping an index—I actually kept a card index. And once I used a syllable, I put it in the card index.

How did you measure a syllable?

Well, like in the word "nathandJoe," I assume that it's the syllable "Joe" that has the "J" in it.

Why isn't "nath" the syllable?

Because it doesn't have the "J."

Oh, the only syllable you're counting is the syllable on the mesostic axis.

Right. So "Joe," J-o-e, represents the "J" of James which I don't identify as the "J" of Joyce. I keep it as the "J" of James. "A" represents the "A" of James and "malt" represents the "M" and they never do it again in the entire work. So the result was, following that discipline, that something like 125 pages here became something like 39 pages there. You can see that the word "just," for instance, which recurs and recurs in the *Wake,* only gets used twice here, once for the "J" of James and once for the "J" of Joyce, because "just" has neither "A" nor "O" after it. I did one thing that was, again, a question of taste. I knew, from having written that, that the final mesostic could be this one:

> Just a whisk
> Of
> pitY
> a Cloud
> in pEace and silence

And I admit to being very fond of that. Somehow, it's very evocative. And so I saved the word "just," representing Joyce, for the end. And even though it could have come up earlier, I didn't let it.

It seems to me that, here and elsewhere, one characteristic of your work is always this: yes, chance is a basic principle for doing things, but certain decisions of taste appear throughout. They govern quite a bit.

Well, they govern, for instance at the beginning, the decision to work with *Finnegans Wake.*

Which is a very key decision.

I'm actually glad that I made that decision, because I think that, living in this century, we live, in a very deep sense, in the time of *Finnegans Wake.* Don't you think so? And there I was, here I am rather, sixty-six years old almost, and I have never read *Finnegans Wake* through. I had read parts of it but this process of working with it and writing with it has gotten me deeply engaged in it and I've not only read it once, I've read it many times. And, as I pointed out to you, sometimes upside down.

And you're always discovering new things in Finnegans Wake, *as you're always going to discover new things in your own redoings of* Finnegans Wake, *because you've respected the basic richness and multiplicity of the text. Is your reworking of the* Wake *a work of literature or a work of music?*

Well, this is whether we pay attention to it as literature or whether we pay attention to it as music, and we're capable—that's one of the lovely things about being a human being—we're capable of turning one way or another. We can turn ourselves toward literature or we could turn toward music. One could take, for instance, the text, and say I sang it to you. Then would you say, "Is that literature?" You would rather think that it was music, if I sang it. Actually, reading is the process that takes place in time so that literature has an affinity for music, because they both take place in time. If the literature sits, so to speak, on the page and waits for you to come to it and doesn't itself move, as some concrete poetry does, then we might say it is not having an affinity for music; it's having an affinity for painting.

Are you going to publish this?

Certainly. This little one is actually going to be in my next book from Wesleyan [*Empty Words,* 1979]. And the big one is going to be published by the *James Joyce Quarterly* [and the University of Tulsa Press]. The two of them, together, are being published in a limited edition printed by the Steinhour Press.

What will that edition look like? Will it be multicolored like those special editions of your Diaries?

No, it's going to be black and white, but the punctuation, as I told you, is going to illustrate each page. It will be on fine paper. The Wesleyan edition and the *James Joyce Quarterly* edition will be reduced in size and not on fine paper.

Are you going to make a record of it as well?

I think that this is naturally something that one wants to do now, and Joyce himself wanted to do that and did—to make records of parts of *Finnegans Wake,* but we more and more like to hear something rather than just read it. On the other hand, the expenses of all our technologies, even though we have all their benefits, the expenses are still very great. And now that everything is so expensive, it's quite possible that we'll all eat dinner, rather than listen to records of my readings.

One question that constantly comes up with reference to your activity is whether you're now a composer who writes or, since you've done so much writing recently, a poet who also composes.

Well, this morning I was writing music and this afternoon I'm showing you how I'm starting "a Third Time."

So you've set up an existence in which you can do one thing at one time and another thing at another time, for they are simply options in your own life.

Which seems reasonable. One can also go to sleep.

Sure enough. Now that we know how the Second Time *was done, let me ask about the new piece.*

The new one is not going through the book but, as I told you, landing on it, so it's a mix of phrases, words, syllables and letters, and I omit sentences. That's perhaps again a question of taste. And if I kept sentences I might come out with something like *Mureau,* which is music/Thoreau; and this, instead of coming from *Finnegans Wake,* comes from the *Journal* of Thoreau, and this includes sentences. So it has sentences, phrases, words, syllables and letters, and it produces a sound like this: "sparrowsita grosbeak betrays itself by that peculiar squeakarieffect of slightest tinkling measures soundness ingpleasa we hear!"

This is, in effect, a prose, as Finnegans Wake *is prose.*

A kind of prose, yes. Now *Empty Words* begins this way and it doesn't have any sentences and yet it comes from the same material that *Mureau* came from and it goes this way:

>   notAt evening
>   right can see
>   suited to the morning hour
>
>   trucksrsq Measured tSee t A
>   ys sfOi w dee e str oais

So by avoiding sentences you approach poetry.

That first section that I just read to you has phrases, words and letters. Now if you have just those things, one, two, three and four—phrases, words, syllables and letters—you can use them singly, one two three four, or in combinations of two, phrases and words . . .

Which is to say singly—only phrases, only words?

Right, or you can use phrases and words, or phrases and syllables, or phrases and letters, or you can use words and syllables or words and letters—this is the principle of permutation—or syllables and letters; or phrases, words and syllables; or phrases, words and letters; or words, syllables and letters, or all four, phrases, words, syllables and letters. That means you have fourteen possibilities. A little bit before we began talking, I began this. I found out what I was to write through the chance operation—and this beside me is the printout of the *I Ching.* I no longer toss the coins. A young man named Ed Kobrin at the University of Illinois programmed for *HPSCHD* (1967–69) a simulation of tossing three coins six times, and I use the printout now instead of the coins.

So that the I Ching *process is now all coded.*

Right. And then I form the questions. Now I have a question dealing with the number 14. Which of these permutations am I going to involve myself in? And then we got, as you recall, the answer that led to words and letters. And then our next question was how many words and letters are we looking for? And the answer was 28.

You made twenty-eight lines there, to be filled.

Twenty-eight places, yes. Then I had to find out which were words and which were letters and that's a question having to do with the number 2, so that the table of 2 in relation to 64 is one to 32 is *one* and 33 to 64 is *two.*

That means, in this either-or question, if you get any number between 1 and 32, it is one choice; if you get between 33 and 64, you have the other choice.

I pick a word and the other way get a letter, and so I've gone through here and I get W, W, W, W, W, letter, letter, word, word, letter, etc., and now I know what I'm doing. Then the next question is what part of *Finnegans Wake* am I looking in? And here are the parts of the *Wake.* The first part about the father and mother has eight chapters and these are the page numbers and these are the numbers of pages. This is the second part about the children: 41, 49, 74, 17. This is the third part: 26, 45, 81, 36; and this is the last part which returns to the first: 36 . . . So there are 17 parts. And I ask that question, of course, in this case now for this first part of words and letters I asked it 28 times: which part are we in? And then which page of that part are we on? And then which line am I going to? And it turns out that the full pages have 36 lines.

And all these decisions are made by consulting the I Ching?

Right. And then I count the words or letters as the case may be, and I finally pinpoint a word.

Which you pull out or extract from the Wake?

Or I pinpoint a letter. And in this case I'm keeping a table of what pages and lines it comes from because the words in *Finnegans Wake* are so invented that there might come up later on some question as to their spelling. And I can refer back.

That is a very shrewd way of keeping track of Joyce's neologisms that are not only easy to misspell but easy to miscopy.

Right. Now when the program or when our conversation just now began—that's a question: is this a conversation or is it a program?—what do you think? It's according, as I said, don't you think, according to how we pay attention.

Or what you want it to be in your life?

Right. Anyway, I was looking for a letter which is on page 203; and when you asked me the first question, I was counting the letters and there are 56 letters in this line, and now I want to know which letter I've put in the text. So my next number here is the number 17. And I turn to the table for 56, because there are 56 letters, and 1 to 24 equals 1 to 24, so it will be the seventeenth letter: 1, 2, 3, 4, 5, 6, 7, 8, 9, 10, 11, 12, 13, 14, 15, 16, 17, which is an "I." And since it's surrounded by consonants, there's no question about it. I just plain take the "I."

If there were another vowel, you might take the other vowel?

If there were another vowel, I would then ask, shall I have them both or shall I have just one of them?

And what would govern your choice?

The *I Ching* again. The reason I did that was because of the vowels really more than the consonants, because of the diphthongs, which you know are important among vowels.

So what you've done here is develop a compositional method by which lots of choices are made by you by consulting the I Ching, *your chart there that you made before, the chart here, from which you thereby extract words from* Finnegans Wake, *a text by Joyce that you chose, just as you chose the* I Ching. *Now what is it going to look like in the end?*

Well, I don't know exactly.

How long will it take you to finish?

I have the habit, which I see no reason for breaking, of making a text of this kind until I have completed four thousand events. And this first business of mine has twenty-eight events; and I've now in an hour done eight of them. So you could divide eight into four thousand and could give me an estimate.

Five hundred hours.

But you see, I'm doing other things. Like this morning, I was writing music. So I don't know exactly when it would be through. But it's the sort of work that I can take with me; and when I'm waiting in line or riding in the bus or subway or plane or whatnot, I can continue this work.

If you can carry not only the Wake *but all your codebooks with you.*

Right.

AUTOBIOGRAPHICAL

ON BEING A COMPOSER WHO CAN'T READ MUSIC (1989)

> *The composer who lives by nonmusical work is rare,*
> *but still there are some. The chief mark of his work*
> *is its absence of professionalism. It is essentially naïve.*
> *It breaks through professional categories, despises*
> *professional conventions. . . . The professional makes*
> *esthetic advance slowly, if at all, progressing step by*
> *step, in touch at all times with the music world. The*
> *naïf makes up his music out of whole cloth at home.*
> *He invents his own esthetic. When his work turns out*
> *to be unplayable technically, it often gives a useful*
> *kick to the professional tradition. The music of*
> *Modest Moussorgsky, or Erik Satie, and of Charles*
> *Ives did that very vigorously indeed.*
> —Virgil Thomson, "Why Composers Write Now,"
> *The State of Music* (1961)

I've written books and articles; I have composed audiotapes that are sometimes classified as music. Some of my criticism deals with music; some of my experimental prose reflects musical principles of organization more than conventional language syntax. Certain audiotapes are based upon initially literary ideas that were realized in musical ways. Don't ask me to stand on one side or the other, because my general sentiment is that there is only one art, which is Art; but among its kinds are music, poetry, painting, etc. The qualities we admire in one art are largely the qualities we admire in other arts, whether they be invention, for those with avant-garde tastes, or the fulfillment of conventions, for conservatives; tastes of all kinds are always prepared to acknowledge a unique handling of the materials of any art.

My work as an artist takes many forms. If asked, as I am, how I divide my attention—how much to writing, how much to music—my reply is that to each and every art my devotion is always 100 percent. In my daily activity, I've tried to develop a situation where I can be working in any one of several areas, where I can move from one to another without undue anxiety. Two reasons my music might be more *experimental* than my writing are my incapacity and innocence. As a writer,

I'm a pro who can blend or deviate at will, through all kinds of situations; as a composer I've so far been a novice who can do only what I've done.

One reason why my music might seem less experimental is that, out of innocence and not unlike other under-trained composers, I tend to use obvious compositional solutions, of the simplistic sort that I would avoid in my writing, where the radical quality of my creative work depends not only upon a comprehensive awareness of what others are doing but upon eschewing their characteristic tricks. To put it differently, whereas the innovative moves of my poetry and creative prose depend upon a profound awareness of precedent, my composing proceeds in blissful ignorance.

When asked if I have "a need to compose," as distinct from doing other arts, my only reply is that I feel a need to make art; music composition per se is one of several alternatives (each of which can be put aside while I do other things). Though the materials of art may differ, the processes of creation are fairly similar: discovering inspiration, selecting the most suitable materials for the inspiration, working everything up, pushing an idea as far as it will go, judging the piece *finished* only when you can do no more. The same imagination works in all media; there are no compartments in my head. The reason I find it hard to identify my "earliest musical compositions" is that, it seems to me, I slid into "music" from doing creative work that was initially classified in other categories. I didn't so much "become a composer" as realize in retrospect that I had already been (and would continue) composing. I had to be told, and tell myself!

Perhaps because my compositional career is so unusual, I find it hard to get a neat form for these miscellaneous perceptions; there is no model known to me for the kinds of issues and experience I'm confronting here. (Did Paul Bowles ever write about the relations between his writing and his music?) One reason for discussing my music as I do is that I've always admired those artists who seemed to understand their work far better than their interpreters—artists such as Moholy-Nagy, Ad Reinhardt, John Cage—though I also believe that in discussions about an artist's art, the tale, in principle, has more authority than the teller.

II

Among the great techniques, music is all by itself an auditory thing, the only purely auditory thing there is. It is comprehensible only to persons who can

> *remember sounds. Trained or untrained in the*
> *practice of the art, these persons are correctly called*
> *"musical."*—Virgil Thomson,
> *The State of Music* (1961).

Just as I cannot remember a time when I was unable to read words, so there was no time when my ear couldn't recognize music.

As a young person, I had several formal trips through music, initially with piano lessons in elementary school, All-State Choir in high school, folk guitar in college and then harmony exercises when I was twenty-four. I always felt I should have been a musician, but somehow other interests captured me. Many years later, I find that I can read a line of pitches at a keyboard, but my sense of rhythm is inept; a more complex score is beyond me. As a composer, I belong to a truly underprivileged minority whose ability to read music is deficient, my company being B. B. King, the pioneering French tape composer Pierre Schaefer and, if his latest biographers are to be believed, even Duke Ellington. One difference between the kind of music that those guys made and what I do is that, as my music cannot be performed live, no scores need be made (and I have no need to learn traditional technicalities, except for showing off). The electronic music studio is my compositional instrument; audio-tape has been the principal medium for making my music not only public but permanent.

I think that just as my poetry and fiction descend largely from my reading experience, my music is based mostly upon my aural experiences. Everyone around me knows that I am always appreciating the acoustic qualities of things, whether the distinctive voices of people I meet (or radio announcers) or sounds peculiar to a certain place. That accounts for why each of the major tapes I have composed is of and about a sound that has long preoccupied me. For *Invocations* (1981, 1984, 61 minutes) the source was the sound of the language of prayer, which I vividly remember appreciating during a tour of Mt. Athos in eastern Greece in 1960; from that time forward for sure, perhaps before as well, I've always had a conscious affinity for religious music. (Beethoven's *Missa Solemnis* I first heard in the wake of JFK's assassination; soon afterward I discovered the J. S. Bach masses. For a long time the only Mozart acceptable to me was his requiem; the only Brahms, his *German Requiem;* the only Berlioz, his *Requiem.* The strongest argument I know for the existence of a higher presence called God is that much of the very best music is addressed to Him. Curiously, whereas I've composed music I think religious, I have never done religious poetry.)

For *The Eight Nights of Hanukah* (1983, 5:20), the inspiration was the sound of Hebrew spoken in the accents of the Diaspora (and behind that a residency in Jerusalem). For the text and then the tape of *Turfs/Arenas/Fields/Pitches* (1982 as a book; 1988 as a tape, 21:26), the source was the Robert Craft recording of the complete Anton Webern (to whom *Turfs,* etc. in all its forms are dedicated). For *Americas' Game* (1988, 60'), the source was that sound that makes the aural experience of that game (and, ultimately, life in America) so different from the acoustic experience of other games. For *New York City* (1984, three versions: 60', 87', 140'), the source was sounds I've heard all my life, which I associate with home, whose characteristic aggressiveness scarcely offends me. The inspiration was to compose music wholly of those sounds unique to New York. Divided into sections, my piece aims less to represent the city than to reveal acoustic qualities unique to it. For instance, in one section the shouting traders at the Commodities Exchange are mixed with aggressive street vendors, acoustically fusing similar selling sounds from radically different physical spaces. In another section are several people speaking languages other than English with the rhythm and mannerisms of New Yorkers, such as running words together. Once my work was composed, it became clear that some of my love of these indigenous, superficially chaotic sounds might be indebted to the musics of Charles Ives, Edgard Varèse and John Cage.

I suppose I could *write* an essay about the sound(s) of New York City, but it would never be anything more than a printout to read. Now that I consider the possibility, it might be interesting to write a visual-verbal representation, probably in nonsyntactic prose of words for sounds indigenous to New York, scattered across the space of a page, the spatial sequence approximating the lengths of my piece; but my suspicion is that while such a text might reflect my *New York City,* the result would still be something only to be read. To make similar points about auditory experience in New York I would now rather compose a tape.

One observable difference between my tapes and my creative writings is that the latter tend to be very short works, many of them a page or less in length, while my major audiotapes run to durations that are comparatively long even for music—one hour, two hours. This difference might reflect the greater focus of my acoustic ideas, or less restlessness (as my writing, unlike my music, is composed largely in my house, where distractions are many), or it could reflect another determining element not conscious to me. One development within my tapes has been away from pieces composed of discrete vignettes—there are sixty separate sections in one version of *New York City*—to the uninterrupted sound of *Americas' Game*. Whereas the first structure is more typical of literature or theater, the latter is pure music.

In my book *Autobiographies* (1981), I listed the milestones in the evolution of my musical taste: "Unchained Melody" (which I discovered in 1955), "Greensleeves" (1957), J. S. Bach's *Goldberg Variations* (1958), Willie McTell's "Statesboro Blues" (1963), Ludwig van Beethoven's *Grosse Fugue* (1964), Charles Ives's *Symphony No. 2* (1964), Edgard Varèse's *Ionisation* (1964), Elliott Carter's *Second String Quartet* (1966), Charles Ives's *Concord Sonata* (1967), J. S. Bach's *Art of the Fugue* (1968), Claudio Monteverdi's *Vespero della Beata Vergine* (1970), Charles Amirkhanian's *Seatbelt, Seatbelt* (1974).

Were I to compile a similarly chronological list for books it would include: Sinclair Lewis's satires (1954), Jean-Paul Sartre's "The Wall" (1956), George Orwell's *Selected Essays* (1959), Ralph Ellison's *Invisible Man* (1960), Harold Rosenberg's *The Tradition of the New* (1960), Norman O. Brown's *Life Against Death* (1961), Hannah Arendt's *Eichmann in Jerusalem* (1963), John Barth's *The Sot-Weed Factor* (1963), Marshall McLuhan's *Understanding Media* (1964), Buckminster Fuller's *Nine Chains to the Moon* (1966), L. Moholy-Nagy's *Vision in Motion* (1966), Ad Reinhardt's *Selected Writings* (1966), Sol LeWitt's *Arcs, Circles & Girds* (1973). I like to think that my audiotape compositions, as well as my poems and fictions, reflect the influence of both lists.

Regarding literary sources for music, consider this extraordinary passage from Alvin Lucier's memoir, "The Tools of My Trade":

> Mine was a New Hampshire childhood of creek-floats, canoe trips (with pungent experiences of wave motion), mountain hikes and woodland walks. Coupled with early readings of Robert Frost's poems, in which natural phenomena stand for states of mind, these experiences drew me toward the exploration of these phenomena for music purposes. Later my readings of Hemingway's works led me to the minimalism my pieces exhibit time and time again. Hemingway felt that if you knew your subject well enough, what you chose to leave out would still be present in your work.

Since there is only one art, even a fully accredited university composer, such as Lucier, is as likely to be influenced by literature (or visual art) as by music.

To test my relationship to the world of contemporary composition, a colleague asked whether, as I compose, I think about other composers or about a particular audience? The "audience" part was easier to handle. One difference between journalism and creative work is that for the former you necessarily have in mind a particular readership, that for the New York *Times,* say, being different from that of a literary review; and as a veteran writer for both of these, I instinctively adjust references and intellectual pitch to suit each audience. In making art, you simply try to do as well as possible within the premises of your work—what you've done and what you want to do—and hope that your conclusions will interest others. Though I assume that my journalism will be read, I don't expect people to listen to my music and am, in truth, surprised if anyone tells me that he or she does.

I have personally known many composers, of several schools, enjoying their company as well as their work; but since remarkably few inhabit the territory where I labor, there are few comparisons and few real competitors. (That accounts for why my music is less of a "threat" than my writing.) Nonetheless, I very much admire the complexity of Milton Babbitt and Elliott Carter (especially in my book whose text also informed my early composition, *Recyclings*), the freedom in the use of noise-making materials of Edgard Varèse and John Cage (reflected especially in *Americas' Game* and *New York City*) and the spirituality of Arvo Pärt and William Duckworth. I suppose that, most of all, I would like to realize a synthesis of all these qualities; but, hell, I have not gotten there yet.

One question intriguing me is whether I would have become a composer before the age of audiotape? Only in my dreams, I suspect. It was my good fortune to grow up in an era when audiotape replaced wire (which could not be so easily edited), multitrack tape replaced monophonic transcription and, most important, sound electronically channeled through speakers became acceptable. What initially attracted me to audiotape composition is its resemblance to writing, which is to say that you work up material, edit it, revise it, reconsider it all by yourself or with a technician until arriving at a definitive form that you then give to someone else to distribute. (Printing a manuscript thus resembles duplicating, or disking, an audiotape.)

After disappointing experiences in both live theater and filmmaking, I've come to the conclusion that my art is best made either by myself or in collaboration with no more than one other person. (Though I had an uncle who professionally conducted orchestras with several dozen players, the idea of working with a group of people creates in me feelings of anxiety; some tastes, or competences, are not inherited, I guess.) Given that bias, I should learn computer composition which would enable me to synthesize a whole cast of characters from few vocal sources.

To what extent is the music "American"—to what cultural provenance does it belong? The fact that I majored in "American Civilization" in college accounts for why as a critic I've often tried to define characteristics unique to American art. In the case of my composing, though, such definition seems problematic; for most of my composing has been done in studios abroad, initially for broadcast abroad. I didn't wish it to happen this way—I didn't consciously defect—but opportunities for work as idiosyncratic as mine were so limited here that I had to go abroad to discover that I was, indeed, a composer! (For extreme kinds of indigenous experimental music, the situation here today is comparable to that for American poetry in 1913.) If my music belongs to any country, however, it is to the New Acoustic World that appeared with the advent of multitrack tape.

Perhaps the most profound statement about music composition at present has come from John Cage. "I can distinguish three ways of composing music nowadays," he said recently. "The first is well known—that of writing music, as I do. It continues. A new way has developed through electronic music and the construction of new instruments of making music by performing it rather than writing it. And a third way has developed in recording studios, which is similar to the way artists work in their studios to make paintings. Music can be built up later by layer on recording tape, not to give a performance or to write music, but to appear on a record. This last, begun in popular music, will continue in serious music." I am clearly the third kind of the composer; indeed, in putting together some of my books, not only anthologies but *Conversing with Cage,* I had already exemplified this third way of working.

My sense of my musical past is that the compositions fall into three groups: (1) early realizations of literary texts whose writing preceded my involvement with audiotape, beginning with simple works made at WXXI-FM in Rochester in 1975 and including *Seductions* made at the Electronic Music Studio of Stockholm in 1981 and *Relationships* made at WGBH-FM in 1983, as well as *Turfs/Arenas/Fields/Pitches* (1980–88) and *Epiphanies* whose production is still in progress. In each case, the idea was to realize on audiotape a "reading" that could not be done live;

among the technical processes I used were overdubbing, voice resynthesis, multitracking and acoustic processing—only recently, as I have said, have I come to regard these as musical compositions; (2) tapes composed of and about the sounds of particular acoustic material, such as the language of prayer in *Invocations* (1981, 1984), the Jewish Diaspora in *The Eight Nights of Hanukah* (1983), *New York City* (1984) and *Americas' Game* (1988); (3) tapes composed of texts that were written after my exposure to a new technology, such as the Sampler in 1988; were I to master the computer, the result would probably draw upon other sorts of texts; (4) a new development, still very much in progress, of providing musicians with verbal texts that may be spoken aloud or played on their instruments, the experiment being whether words alone can serve as an exclusive substitute for musical notes.

NOTES ON *AMERICAS' GAME* (1988)

In 1981 I began to compose a series of audiotapes that were initially both of and about the *sound* of certain subjects in our experience. For the first *Invocations* (1981), about the sound of the language of prayer, I recorded over sixty ministers speaking in over two dozen languages, and from these tapes myself mixed a sequence of solos, duets, quintets and grand choruses roughly along the structure of J. S. Bach's *St. Matthew Passion.* My fundamental motive was to reveal acoustically that particular sound that transcends linguistic differences. Though these audiotapes lack introductions or other explanatory commentary and thus proceed as musical compositions do, they are not obscure. At every point in its length, each of them is fundamentally about its theme, which is the unique sound of itself.

Remembering that my initial idea for what became *Invocations* was to use sports announcers, who sound roughly alike around the world, apart from differences in language, I decided for my new composition to focus upon a sport that was acoustically distinctive. Tennis was possible, but too limited in its sounds. I thought about basketball and hockey, as well as soccer, but not only were these sports acoustically limited too, they prompted audiences to respond in unison ways that, to my ear, are uninteresting. Golf, needless to say, was quickly dismissed.

No, it became quickly evident that the best choice for me would be American baseball—*not* my favorite sport, to be sure, but aurally the most resonant. Not only do hardballs hitting bats and gloves resound distinctively, but a baseball crowd sounds like no other, mostly because, for most of its time together, it is audibly more chaotic than harmonious. A common joke holds that during a three-hour baseball game there are only seventeen minutes of action, and it is only in those rare moments that a baseball crowd begins to resound in unison. Otherwise, spectators are talking to one another, addressing players, buying edibles or excusing themselves to go to the bathroom. A German friend, more familiar with soccer and its pacing, judged that the most active, interesting element in even a professional baseball game is the audience! It not only makes music; it is much of the music unique to baseball.

Though disorganized, the baseball crowd is not unruly, in part because with so many games in a professional season—almost one each day—no one of them is absolutely essential to ultimate season victory. Precisely because there are no cheerleaders (while the attempts of the PA system to prompt cheers are so rarely successful), the audience generates enthusiasm spontaneously, sometimes for only a few seconds, among a few people, while at other times for several minutes among many people. Precisely because extended cheers are a music unto themselves, each attains a unique trajectory that, as Reynold Weidenaar pointed out, can be visually scored. (One is reminded of Marilyn Monroe telling her husband, Joe DiMaggio, about her visit to the troops in Korea. "You should have heard the cheering." He replied, "I have.") Another peculiarity of baseball is the emphasis upon individual performance, and upon the audience's responses to individual performers, down to addressing them as unresponding gods. It is for the chaos of the crowd, as well as this emphasis upon individualism, that I consider baseball acoustically reflective of America, all the Americas, and thus entitled my piece "Americas' Game." As Jacques Barzun, a Parisian-born American professor and critic once wrote, "Whoever wants to know the heart and mind of America had better learn baseball, the rules and realities of the game."

Another concern in my mind in beginning this piece was my colleague Frits Wieland's subtle criticism of my earlier long tapes *Invocations* and *New York City.* He judged them more *literary* than musical because they had discrete sections, like scenes in a play, rather than a sustained continuous flow. As my audio work has more and more approached the character of music, I decided that, first of all, the stream of sound in this new work must never be interrupted. Another difference between it and its predecessors was that the new work lacked a determining literary model comparable to *Finnegans Wake* for *Invocations* and both Dylan Thomas's *Under Milk Wood* and John Dos Passos's *U.S.A.* for *New York City,* which is to say that whatever particular literary example or experience might lie behind *Americas' Game* cannot be identified by me.

Even though my material has been exclusively speech and sounds recorded in the environment, I think it best for me to proceed with a musical model, if only to give structure and pace to my sounds. For *Invocations,* I had Bach's *St. Matthew Passion;* for *The Gospels,* Beethoven's *Grosse Fugue.* In searching for a musical guide for baseball, I looked first into the music of Charles Ives, who not only portrayed American chaos, but also appreciated baseball. No luck, however. Most of Ives's chaos is rapidly articulated, whereas baseball is a languid *summer* game. This last point reminded me of George Gershwin's masterpiece from *Porgy and Bess,* "Summertime"; and the more of it I heard, mostly in my head, the surer I became that it should guide my baseball piece, not by its explicit presence, but by informing its pace.

I recorded a universe of baseball sounds—in the seats of professional stadiums, on the practice fields of spring training, among the fans at a minor league park. I taped amateurs in Central Park, kids in an open field as well as Puerto Ricans, Dominicans, Chicanos, Panamanians and French Canadians. What and where I could not do or go myself, I got help. Thanks to Ceil Muller, I did spring training with the Los Angeles Dodgers; thanks to Reynold Weidenaar, who once recorded the Cleveland Orchestra, I got both the acoustic details of both batting practice and dense crowds. Other helpers included Jay Godfrey in New York and Thomas Hammar and Magnus Fredriksson in Stockholm, as well as the dedicatee, a Dutch artist long resident here, Jan Henderikse. A grant from the Media Arts Program of the National Endowment for the Arts made initial production possible.

All this recorded material was audited and evaluated and then summarized on forty pages of single-spaced notes. Remembering that I wanted not to portray a single game, but to reveal its sounds, I then composed, again at the Electronic Music Studio in Stockholm, overlapping shorter passages—acoustic essays, so to speak—of sounds distinctive to baseball, such as pitched balls hitting bats (both wooden and aluminum), balls thudding in leather mitts or striking the earth, the imprecations of individual players, heavy steps exploding in four-second bursts, umpiring decisions, players shouting at one another, audience expletives, collective cheering and groaning, hawkers of food and souvenirs moving through the crowd, etc., all of these elements fading over one another.

In composing I remembered not only my reportorial theme but musical and literary considerations. Whatever words are heard, for instance, are those I might have written for such a composition, had I not already recorded them on tape; and always evident is my appreciation of uniquely American language. Where sounds are placed in relation to one another customarily reflects my musical judgments. Since reel to reel tape moving at 15 inches per second is most conveniently composed in segments no more than a half hour long, I divided the hour into two—a doubleheader so to speak. Each segment has its own beginning and conclusion, and within that structure the piece then alternates roughly between sounds from the field and sounds from the crowd. The first part is 29:40; the second 29:55. As more than two hundred separate sources were used, another structural characteristic is combining games from a wide variety of venues, both professional and amateur, so that sandlot hobbyists appear, acoustically, alongside major league players. In its dense mix of sounds with speech *Americas' Game* most resembles, within my work and in contrast to others, my earlier *New York City*.

What follows is an illustrative documentation in the form of a visual-verbal score (prepared by Sarah Gleason). In the upper left-hand corners of each page are numbers identifying each minute within the two halves mentioned before. Thus, page 0, for instance, portrays not only the opening sixty seconds but the thirtieth minute. Along the top are numerals identifying ten-second periods. Along the left-hand margins are enumerated the tracks on the 24-track tape. (Because of a technical limitation peculiar to the EMS studio, tracks 19 to 24 were not used.) Tracks 9 to 18 contain the first thirty minutes, while tracks 1 to 8 contain material from the second half hour. The descriptions begin where each sound begins and end approximately where the sound ends; sometimes arrows are used in place of words to extend a sound's duration. The purpose of this experiment in scoring is discovering whether a composition like *Americas' Game* can be documented in print, much as a score with staves and clefs is a representation of musical experience; and just as a musically literate person can tell from "reading" an instrumental score what a piece is like, so someone reading this score might get a sense of my piece.

One critical question raised by my audio compositions is whether they should be considered "collage." Because they are composed from so many fragments separately gathered, some think that term appropriate. I think not. Collage, we remember, is about the fusing of dissimilars, or materials originally from separate sources, whether in image or sounds. In most of my sections, I fuse elements similar to one another, whether bat cracks in one section or vendors in another, albeit in ways more condensed than would be possible in reality; and in that respect, it could be said that I compose harmonies, though they hardly sound harmonious to the ear, and further that such kaleidoscopic harmonious composition of fundamentally nonharmonic materials is made possible only by audiotape. The relevant term is Mauricio Kagel's *metacollage*, which is defined as a collage-like composition using only a single source. In the overlapping pastiche of several versions of the song "Take Me Out to the Ballgame" is, of course, an allusion to Charles Ives, who remains a prime influence upon my music.

One quality I wanted for *Americas' Game* is that it be primarily acoustic. Though filled with details and cross-references for the cognoscenti, little in the appreciation of it should depend upon the listener's knowing English, and in this respect it differs scarcely from other avant-garde musical works whose words happen to be English. If its subtleties and complexity are sufficient to demand rehearing, then perhaps it is ultimately not for broadcast over radio or in a concert hall, but for media that can be easily reexperienced, such as records and audiocassettes. Perhaps it could become, like other audiotapes of mine, the sound track of a film or videotape. I also wanted *Americas' Game* to epitomize the kind of composing possibilities that are available, even to someone as musically limited as I am, in this late twentieth century.

Baseball · Americas' Game

isolated voices in stands. rabble from bleachers. — rhythmic clapping →→→→ →→→
(parents with Kids)

Canadian anthem →→→→

American Anthem →→→ →→→→ →
(flute playing)

Batters warming up
"what's happening"
"gonna a strike"
(birds in background)

American Anthem → →→→

Slow-voiced announcer "Cold for the Yankees"... Announces entire lineup with each →→→→
(sound of crowd in stadium with applause after individual names.

Pitcher warming up →→→ →→
(airplane flying in background)

10   20   30   40   50

1
2
3
4
5
6
7
8
9
10
11
12
13
14
15
16
17
18
19
20
21
22
23
24

10   20   30   40   50

Baseball · Americas' Game

10   20   30   40   50
10   20   30   40   50

1 crowd ambience continues
2
3 plane flying overhead
4 Announcer echoing lineup of Yankees
5
6 American anthem
7
8
9
10
11
12
13 played on organ as heard through deficient loudspeakers, audibly from a minor league venue
14
15 Player's position, number, name and then number again
16 kids talking, Father: "what do you want?"
17 isolated background applause
18
19
20
21
22
23
24

light applause + whistling   loud applause from crowd

Baseball: America's Game

10   20   30   40   50

1
2
3 Central Park players continue →>   →> →> →> →> →> →> →> ⟰⟰⟰
4
5 Players' running feet
6
7 Sirens   Loud manager: "Hustle Brian"
8
9 drums —> ba ba boom, ba ba boom   bat and response
10 organ: "Over There" ⌐
11
12
13   bat and response — low bat crack in distance
14   (prompts small cheer)
15 cheers to lull   >> >> > > >> > >> >>   crowd waiting to cheer with lull
16   > > > >   lots of whistles
17
18 cheers with whistles
19   crash - "Ohh."
20
21
22
23
24

10   20   30   40   50

Baseball: Americas' Game

10   20   30   40   50

"Foul ball"

Thump "strike"

Big cheers to even bigger disappointment screams →→→→→→→→→→

Middle American Family
yelp yelp "alright Dave" →
baby crying →→→→
Announcer →→→→→→

Announcer: "Ladies and gentlemen, the Red
Sox remind you that no alcohol will be sold after the seventh inning"   Glove thumps

SPIT

disjointed Pop Music →→→

"Cold beer"   "Cold bread, here, Cold beer!"   "hot pretzels!"

Get your hot pretzels here!

Ice cream! Ice Cream! Ice Cream! Ice Cream!
mit Thud   Spit
mit Thud →→→→→ mit Thud

Faint ducks

bat crack
commotion

1
2
3
4
5
6
7
8
9
10
11
12
13
14
15
16
17
18
19
20
21
22
23
24

10   20   30   40   50

Baseball: America's Game

Screaming and whistling

Boos

Kids trying to talk intelligently

Family chat stops abruptly for cheer

continued chat

low announcer

reply: "strong again" | Pop music

Yankee Stadium fades to sandlot ball in Central Park

glance over head

general dugout chat

arguing among players

he makes it?

"out out, two outs" → no orap — He Crack'd metal bat

little. Central Park kid Fan: "Yeh, he's out!" Older Kid: "Hey! What's a matta witchu?"

"move it" move it! move it!"

Baseball: Americas' Game

10   20   30   40   50

1 — "Take me out to the ball game" … Once, twice, three strikes, you're out at the old ball game"

2 — Restless crowd singing   lead male voice begins second verse audience joins in

3 — It's root, root, root for the home team, if they don't win, it's a shame" | Great cheer at song

4 — lead voice sings simultaneously "one, two, three strikes, you're out"

5 — "Never came back"

6 — organ repeats last refrain | Crowd begins another chorus of "Take me out to the ball game"   chaotic crowd

7 —

8 — Crowd   Boos   Crowd gets belligerent

9 —

10 — Yankee Stadium crowd build to consistent cheers   Crowd reacting to field turns to boos

11 —   inaudible chest in stands

12 —

13 — Manager reacts to field: "Run, Run, Run! That was good, that was nice!" He yells over runs and outs.

14 —

15 — | Plane flying overhead |

16 —

17 — Players in dugout banter: "last one, first strike, one down. NICE"

18 —

19 —

20 —

21 —

22 —

23 —

24 —

Baseball: America's Game

50

One out, two out, one out, two out — Players debating — two down, two down

Muffled preaching to fans against breaches of propriety

Yankee Stadium crowd booing

THUD

ball against wall

THUD at bat

For amateurs egging each other on.
Camaraderie that lacks in big leagues

Vero Beach Spring training: "Go Go Go" encouraging each other "get your hands in there mud"
"can those bases"
ducks barely in background
"C'mon Jay!"
"little bit"

10 20 30 40 50

1
2
3
4
5
6
7
8
9
10
11
12
13
14
15
16
17
18
19
20
21
22
23
24

Baseball: America's Game

Announcer: "Designated hitter" — Faint airplane — Fan: "strike one" "Two more, two more" "Two strikes, two strikes"

"Reggie, Reggie, Reggie, Reggie, Reggie, Reggie" — rhythmic clapping — clapping cheers

Announcer: "The 1984 Metfinauble And we thank you"

Large stadium crowd erupts — Rhythmic clapping

"drums, drums, drums, da da dum, da da dum..."

Cheers

Faint organ music — Mixed voices

COMPOSING MUSIC/
PERFORMING WORDS (1989)

Even though most of my days have been spent writing, I have wanted all my life to be a composer; instead I got distracted successively by sports, by folksinging, by literature and by art. Nonetheless, the ambition remained in the bottom of my head; for not unlike other critics sympathetic to the avant-garde, in contrast to those with conservative esthetics, I came to do creative work with a radical thrust, by now in more arts than I'd ever planned to make. As I had no ideas for prescribing pitches, I necessarily focused on words and sounds, composing audiotapes that exemplified the contemporary principle that music can be made by manipulating prerecorded sounds in a sophisticated multi-track-mixing studio. Among these were *Invocations* (1981, 1984), *The Gospels* (1982), *The Eight Nights of Hanukah* (1983), *New York City* (1984) and *Americas' Game* (1988). Some were broadcast over radio stations, sometimes in contexts reserved for music; some were mentioned in books about contemporary experimental music. Beginning in 1983, ASCAP began rewarding me with annual Standard Awards for "serious" composition.

Having long ago discovered that composers, of all artists, had the most fertile esthetic ideas, I have been writing semblances of music, making musical structures with materials other than notes, since the early 1970s. Some of my poems made exclusively with numerals reflect the influence of Milton Babbitt, while the sequences of abstract drawings that I call Constructivist Fictions echo not only J. S. Bach but more contemporary systemic, nonrepresentational music. In the nonsyntactic prose of *Recyclings* is the influence of John Cage, to whom the book was dedicated. In this abbreviated fictional text, for another instance, are echoes of Philip Glass's ideas of additive structure:

'Death. Death comes. To comes death. To everyone comes death. To everyone comes. Everyone comes. Everyone.

In *Foreshortenings and Other Stories* (1978), eighty-four discrete sentences were reorganized in several alternative ways, the reassemblings thereby making different stories from the same body of verbal materials—a technique resembling more the manipulation of musical phrases than any structure indigenous to language. (Charles Dodge used the text in 1981 to make a tape of his own computer-assisted music. The idea of my making music to or of my words never occurred to me at the time.)

For another fiction, *Seductions* (1981), I learned about the idea of musical parts. The text consists of sixteen different seduction stories, each interwoven among the others, one sentence at a time, in sixteen different typefaces. Invited to do a performance (and having nothing else to perform live), I recruited sixteen males from the audience and issued them sixteen different copies of the text, each with only one story (i.e., one typeface) marked continuously throughout. In that the speakers were reading individually marked parts of a single score, this resembled musical performance. During a residency at the Electronic Music Studio in Stockholm, I put this text on tape, using a similarly polyvocal structure for sixteen different amplifications of my own voice. It recently occurred to me to play this tape for sixteen instrumentalists, each with one of those marked parts mentioned before, asking them to improvise background music only whenever their character speaks, which is to say that the sixteen parts (of the ur-text) could serve as the score for sixteen duets for sixteen instruments and prerecorded tape.

Lovings is a manuscript composed of erotic stories each a single sentence long and none intentionally connected to any other. In offering them for periodical publication I suggest that editors select whichever ones they wish and then put their selections in whatever order they wish, ideally with spatial separations and different typefaces that would accent the assumption that each story should be perceived by itself, apart from others. (As all stories have equal weight and value, this is a Cagean structure, if ever there was one.) So in offering "Lovings" for performance I would suggest that performers choose whichever ones they want to recite and then that they, or a director working above them, choose in what order those selections should go, within the limitations that no one speaker recites two stories in succession.

However, to bring the recital of *Lovings* yet closer to *music,* I would add that the speakers could be instrumentalists who would be given the option of evoking by whatever means are available to their instruments the content and style of that particular sentence. It would also be permissible to mix speaking and playing within the performance of a single sentence. Singers could choose to sing the words to a melody of their own devising, or to vocalize the text, likewise to a melody of their own devising. What should be heard, in addition to words, is a wealth of eroticized instrumental sounds, some of them more elegant and complex than others (in response to the varying qualities of the sentences). One strategy I know from writing holds that in experimenting with unusual forms of communication it is wise to choose a plot everyone knows.

The best way to structure the performance of *Lovings* is to have the selected sentences numbered in sequence, and then to place in front of the performers, facing them, a silent LCD counter that would move forward one numeral immediately after the reading of a story was complete, the appearance of a new number thus becoming the signal to begin reading the next story. The individual interpretations, whether for speech or sound, should be as extreme as possible, even to the point of incomprehensibility. Since the sentences have no connection to one another, listeners could miss one or another of them without "losing their place," to so speak; for the theme of *Lovings,* which is to say the content that is continually expressed, is *varieties* of erotic experience. Therefore, it might be feasible to have the sentences performed in an overlapping fashion, one beginning before the others end; and the best way to realize this last effect would be to have the counter go to the next number *before* the current story is finished.

A further step, perhaps for a second reading of the text in a single performance, would be to use a spate of LCD counters to get several readers to speak at once, not by starting in unison but by a new reader's beginning soon after his or her predecessor, so that several stories could be going simultaneously, again making a speech music with different melodic lines, in this case asyntactical or dissonant in the relation among lines but utterly complementary, which is to say harmonic, in content.

Getting musicians to play words offers an initial advantage of removing the obstacles of notes; a second advantage is encouraging virtuosic, extreme display of their instruments. Remembering the great tradition of speech music pieces (for example, *Peter and the Wolf*), I thought it might be interesting to write a sort of "Adult Person's Guide to the Orchestra," in which would be played a taped text explaining the history and uniqueness of each instrument, while an individual performing on that instrument would be invited to improvise with (or against) it. As the texts would be separated by a pause, the performance could be modified to suit as many instruments as were available in any performance group; and as each taped part would be three minutes long, the piece could conceivably go on for a while.

What further ambitions do I have for my composition now? To do an opera on audiotape. One intention of *Invocations* was to avoid any hint of live theater—to eschew creating an acoustic environment that could be clearly visualized; so I never let any speaker define an individual presence in the mix. Later, in *A Special Time* (1985), a montage of voices and sounds evoking the 1960s, I let individual speakers assume seats in an acoustic spectrum, trying to create on audiotape alone the theatrical illusion of a symposium. With *Kaddish,* in progress, the voices of individuals will be given more theatrical presence; and in "live" performance, they will emerge from eight physically separated loudspeakers.

I also want to do a single very long piece of continuous sound, perhaps expanding *A Special Time* or beginning anew with creation myths, that would be six hours long and thus utilize the unprecedented acoustic capabilities of 1/2" hi-fi videotape. (Just think that only a half century ago, it was impossible to get more than five minutes of continuous sound on a home storage medium.) Speaking of videotape, I have also been using an Amiga computer, housed at the Experimental TV Center in Owego, New York, to synthesize lush visual settings for my audiotapes—fantasias, so to speak—partly to present them in concerts, where seeing complements hearing, ideally not on the small-screen monitors of traditional television but on a giant video projection screen which is more appropriate to their intricate imagery.

Perhaps because I have done less composing than writing, I feel that I now have many more musical ideas than schemes for writing. My sense is that access to new technologies, such as sampling synthesis, will inspire works that were inconceivable to me before. If I could take a long vacation from my writing activity, most of it would be devoted to making music.

INDEX

Abish, Walter, 124
Adorno, Theodor W., 268
Alexander, Johnny, Jr. (aka Johnny Ace), 154
Ames Brothers, the, 192
Amirkhanian, Charles, 289
Apollinaire, Guillaume, 26; *The New Spirit and the Poets* (book), 73
Arel, Bülent, *Music for a Sacred Service,* 170
Arendt, Hannah, 289
Armstrong, Louis, 67, 75
Arp (Tonus Synthesizer), 183–84, 187
Ars Nova, 192
Artaud, Antonin, 136
Ashbery, John, 82
Auden, W. H., 240
Austin, Larry, 234
Austin, William, *Music in the Twentieth Century* (book, 1966), 248–49
Ayler, Albert, 227

Babbitt, Milton, xiv, 21–30, 31–35, 58, 85, 92, 107, 114, 115, 125, 128, 197, 205, 206, 207, 209, 210, 214, 218–19, 225, 226–27, 234, 235, 250, 253, 254, 265, 266, 269, 270, 307; *Composition for Four Instruments* (1948), 26; *Composition for Synthesizer* (1961), 227; *Composition for Tenor and Six Instruments* 1959), 226; *Composition for Twelve Instruments* (1948), 226; *Correspondences for Strings and Tape* (1968), 118; *Du* (1951); *Ensembles for Synthesizer* (1964); *Phonemena* (1974), 31, 33; *Sextets for Violin and Piano* (1967), 108, 227; *Three Compositions for Piano* (1947), 226; *Vision and Prayer* (1961), 31, 227
Bach, Johann Sebastian, xiii, 3, 5, 7, 8, 63, 107, 111, 113, 123, 132, 139, 140, 143, 144, 145, 158, 164, 181, 182, 214, 225, 245, 287, 307; *Anna Magdalena* books, 111; *Art of the Fugue,* 121, 289; *Brandenberg Concerto No. 1,* 216; *Brandenburg Concerto No. 3,* 169; *Brandenberg* concerti, 182; *Goldberg Variations,* 6, 11, 12, 289; *Partita No. 5 in G major,* 12; *Saint Matthew Passion,* 293, 294; *Sinfonias,* 12; *Well-Tempered Clavier,* 8, 120, 139–40, 145
Bach, P. D. Q. (aka Peter Schickele), 120, 141–49; *The Abduction of Figaro,* 145;

Bach Portrait, 143; "A Ballet in One Selfless Act," 144; *Concerto for Horn and Hardart,* 143; *Einstein on the Fritz,* 145; "Hansel and Gretel and Ted and Alice," 145; *Iphigenia in Brooklyn,* 143; *Minuet Militarie,* 143; "New Horizons in Music Appreciation," 145; *P. D. Q. Bach on the Air,* 144; *Pervertimento for Bagpipes, Bicycle, and Balloons,* 144; *The Preachers of Crimetheus,* 144; *The Safe Sextette,* 144; *The Seasonings,* 141; *Serenude for Devious Instruments* (s. 36-24-36), 144; *Sonata for Viola Four Hands,* 144; *The Stoned Guest,* 144; *Toot Suite,* 144; *Traumerei,* 144
Baez, Joan, 193
Balliet, Whitney, 257
Barber, Samuel, 22, 221, 266
Barraqúe, Jean, 252
Barth, John, *The Sot-Weed Factor* (book, 1960), 289
Bartók, Béla, 17, 21, 95, 105, 109, 146, 199, 241
Barzun, Jacques, 294; *The Pleasures of Music* (book), 242
Bauer, Marion, *Twentieth Century Music* (second ed., 1947), 248, 249
Beachboys, the, 167, 194; "Good Vibrations," 181
Beardslee, Bethany, 32, 108, 230
Beatles, the, 14, 21, 155, 157, 167, 181, 185, 193, 194, 199, 259; "Strawberry Fields Forever," 170, 194; "Norwegian Wood," 194; *Sergeant Pepper* (record album), 228
Beethoven, Ludwig van, 4, 5, 7, 9, 62, 108, 115, 131, 164, 199, 214; *Fifth Symphony,* 11, 18, 145, 200; *Grosse Fugue,* 289, 294; *Missas Solemnis,* 287; *Sonata in E Major,* Op. 109, 12; *Variations on a Waltz by Diabelli,* Op. 120, 12, 132
Behrman, David, 55, 233, 267
Bellows, George Kent, with John Tasker Howard, *A Short History of American Music* (revised ed., 1967), 246
Berberian, Cathy, 230
Berg, Alban, 12, 86, 225, 241
Bergen, Edgar & Charlie McCarthy, 149
Berger, Arthur, 208, 270
Bergman, Ingrid, 193
Berio, Luciano, 210, 226
Berlioz, Hector, 115, 164; *Requiem,* 287
Bernstein, Leonard, 11, 107, 221, 266; *Third*

Symphony-Kaddish (1963), 211, 266, 267

Berryman, John, 32

Bettina, Judith, 34

Big Brother and the Holding Company, 194

Bill Haley and the Comets, "Rock Around the Clock," 193

Blackwood, Easley, 107, 110, 229; *Trio for Violin, Cello and Piano* (1968), 110

Blake, Eubie, 148

Blake, William, 250

Bland, Bobby Blue, 152, 153

Blitzstein, Marc, 250

Bloom, Hyman, 97

Bluesbreakers, the, 155

Blumberg, Valentin, 111

Boccherini, Luigi, 164

Böll, Heinrich, 133

Boretz, Benjamin, 26, 81, 209, 226, 227, 240, 270

Borges, Jorge Luis, 5, 128, 131, 133, 140; *Pierre Menard, Author of Don Quixote*, 140, 146, 148–49

Boulanger, Nadia, 86, 87, 121, 123, 125

Boulez, Pierre, 55, 208, 209, 226, 231, 251, 252

Bowie, David, 119

Bowles, Paul, 286

Brahms, Johannes, 7, 113, 164; *German Requiem*, 287

Brant, Henry, 17, 223, 234; *Millennium II* (1953), 223

Braque, Georges, 163

Britten, Benjamin, 164, 221

Broder, Nathan, with Paul Henry Lang, eds., *Contemporary Music in Europe* (1965), 248

Brophy, Brigid, 244

Brown, Earle, 55, 223, 224, 232; *Folio* (1952–53), 224; *Available Forms I* (1961), 224; *Available Forms II* (1962), 224

Brown, Norman O., 47, 259; *Life Against Death* (book, 1959), 281

Browne, Sir Thomas, xv

Bruce, Neely, 62

Buchla, Donald, 183; Buchla Synthesizer, 186, 187

Buckley, William, 243

Bühlig, Richard, 37

Bull, Sandy, 228

Buñuel, Luis, *Un Chien Andalou*, 129

Burghardt, Ursula, 127

Burke, Kenneth, 242, 259

Busoni, Ferrucio, *Concert for Violin and Orchestra*, 117; *Second Sonata for Violin and Piano* (1898), 113

Cage, John, xiii, xiv, xv, 18, 21–30, 35, 37–41, 43–45, 47–60, 61–65, 67–76, 77–83, 85, 89, 95, 97, 98, 103, 108, 112, 114, 115, 125, 127, 140, 196, 201–4, 221, 213, 217, 220, 222–23, 224–25, 228, 232, 234, 235, 241, 245, 246, 247, 250, 252, 255, 265, 267–68, 270, 273–81, 286, 288, 290, 291, 307, 308; *Amores* (1943), 22; *Notations* (1968), with Alison Knowles, 234; *Bacchanale* (1938), 38; *Cheap Imitation* (1969), 41; *Dance* (1944), 22; "Diary," 52, 273; *Dreams* (1948), 40; *Europera* (1987), 43, 67–76; *First Construction (in Metal)* (1939), 56; *Fontana Mix* (1958), 23, 247; *4'33"* (1952), 23, 40, 43, 44, 49, 51, 56, 57, 60, 78, 203, 222; *HPSCHD* (1969), 43, 57, 61–65, 71, 75, 224–225; *Imaginary Landscape IV* (1951), 202; *Indeterminacy* (1959), 23, 51, 53; "Juilliard Lecture" (1952), 52; *Metamorphosis* (1938), 38; *Music for Amplified Toy Piano* (1960), 57; *Music for Carillon No. 2* (1954), 22, 202; *Music for Marcel Duchamp* (1947), 40; *Music for Piano 64* (1956), 212; *Music Walk* (1958), 50; *Not Wanting To Say Anything About Marcel* (Sculpture, 1969), 55; *The Perilous Night* (1944), 39; *Prelude for Meditation* (1944), 40; *Roaratorio* (1979), 43, 71, 75; *Radio Music* (1956), 57; *Root of an Unfocus* (1944), 39; *Rozart Mix* (1965), 57; *Silence* (book, 1961), 30, 37, 49, 50, 51, 52, 53, 55, 247, 267; *Sonatas and Interludes* (1946–48), 39, 43, 44, 45, 57, 71, 139; *Suite for Toy Piano* (1948), 40; "Talk I" (1965), 52; *Theatre Piece* (1960), 50; *Third Construction* (1941), 22, 202; *31'57.1499"* (1954), 44; *34'46.776"* (1954), 44; *Tossed As It Is Untroubled* (1943), 39; *Variations V* (1965), with Merce Cunningham, 57, 182, 202; *Variations VI* (1966), 22; *Variations IV*, 58; *Variations VII* (1966), 65, 223, 245; *Variations III* (1964), 49; *Williams Mix* (1953), 43, 57, 71, 170, 202, 218, 222, 230; Writings Through *Finnegans Wake*, 273–81; *A Year from Monday* (book, 1967), 30, 37, 47–60; *0'00"* (1962), 44

Carlos, Walter, *Switched-On Bach*, 167, 169, 174, 181–82, 186, 187

Carter, Elliot, 58, 85–93, 115, 121, 125, 228–29, 234, 241, 249, 266, 270, 290; *Concerto for Orchestra*, 91; *Double Concerto for Harpsichord and Piano with Two Chamber Orchestras* (1961), 89, 229; *Eight Etudes and a Fantasy* (1950), 116; *First String Quartet* (1951–52), 88, 228; *A Holiday Overture* (1944), 87; *The Minotaur* (1947), 88;

Piano Concerto (1966), 89, 229; *Piano Sonata* (1946), 87, 93, 228; *Pocahontas* (1939; revised 1941), 87; *Second String Quartet* (1959), 89, 90, 229, 245, 289; *Sonata for Cello and Piano* (1948), 88; *Third String Quartet*, 91

Carter, Helen, 91

Casals, Pablo, 216

Cervantes, Miguel de, *Don Quixote,* 140, 146

Chakmakjian, Haroutiun & Madeleine, 96

Chamberlain, A. W., 174

Chambers Brothers, the, 194

Charles, Daniel, *Pour les oiseaux* (book, 1976; *For the Birds,* 1981), 83

Charles, Ray, 193

Charters, Samuel, *The Poetry of the Blues* (1963), 261–264

Chase, Gilbert, *The American Composers Speaks* (book, 1966), 248; *America's Music* (book, 1966), 251

Checker, Chubby, 193

Chopin, Fréderic, 12, 164

Christgau, Robert, 195

Clapton, Eric, 151 259

Clark, Petula, 14, 15

Cocteau, Jean, *Le sang d'un poète (Blood of the Poet),* 88

Cocyannis, Michael, *Electra,* 135

Coleman, Ornette, 227, 261

Coltrane, John, 261

Cone, Edward T., 241, 253, 268, 270

Conrad, Tony, 135

Conus, Julius, 113

Converse, Frederick, *The Mystic Trumpeter* (1905), 97

Cook, Bruce, *Listen to the Blues* (1973), 157

Copland, Aaron, 22, 75, 79, 85, 87, 95, 97, 107, 108, 121, 125, 144, 145, 208, 211, 214, 221, 244, 246, 247, 250; *Connotations for Orchestra* (1962), 208, 221; *Copland on Music* (book, 1963), 246; *Lincoln Portrait* (1942), 143, 164; *Music and Imagination* (book, 1952), 246; *Nonet,* 266; *Piano Variations* (1930), 125; *The Red Pony* (1948), 125; *Sextet for String Quartet, Clarinet and Piano* (1938), 116; *Vitebsk* (1929), 125

Corbusier, Le, 60

Corner, Philip, 62

Courlander, Harold, *Negro Folk Music, U.S.A.* (book, 1963), 260–61.

Cowell, Henry, 17, 18, 22, 37, 39, 40, 86, 103, 200–201, 221; *New Musical Resources* (book), 201

Craft, Robert, 288

Cream, 155

Creedence Clearwater Revival, 192

Creeley, Robert, 112

Crew Cuts, the, 192

Crumb, George, 108, 234

Culshaw, John, 215

Culver, Andrew, 67

Cummings, E. E., 112; "she being brand," 264

Cunningham, Merce, 24, 38, 40, 53, 57, 58, 77–83, 274; "The Impermanent Art" (essay, 1957), 83; *Variations V,* with John Cage (1965); *Untitled Solo* (1953), 80

Dallapiccola, Luigi, *Tartiniana Seconde,* 113, 115

Daniel, Oliver, 100

Dart, Thurston, 216

Davies, Peter Maxwell, 241

da Vinci, Leonardo, 105

Davis, Douglas, "Art & Technology—The New Combine" (1968), 167

Dayan, Moshe, 163

Debussy, Claude, 21, 108, 199

de Jong, Constance, 124

de Kooning, Elaine, 82

de Kooning, Willem, *Woman I,* 245

Denby, Edwin, xv

Denisov, Edison, 92

Der Hagopian, Yanouk, 97, 98

Des Roches, Raymond, 230

Deutsch, Herbert, 172, 177, 184–85

Deutsch, Otto Erich, 240

Diamond, David, 221

DiMaggio, Joe, 294

Dinesen, Isak, 148

Dodge, Charles, 307–8

Domino, Antoine "Fats," 193

Doors, the, 194

Dos Passos, John, *U.S.A.,* 294

Downes, Olin, 244

Druckman, Jacob, 112

Duchamp, Marcel, 16, 55, 76, 148, 274

Duckworth, William, 290; *The Time Curved Preludes* (1979), 44

Duncan, Isadora, 77

Duncan, Robert, 112

Durner, Leah, 71

Dylan, Bob, 193

Dymschitz, A. L., 159

Dymschitz-Tolstoya, S., 159

Edison, Thomas, 169

El Greco, 100

Eliot, George, 148

Eliot, T. S., 79

Ellington, Duke, 287

Ellison, Ralph, 67, 258, 259; *Invisible Man* (book, 1951), 289

Enesco, Georges, 111

Englert, Guiseppe Giorgio, 230

Eno, Brian, 119

Falla, Manuel de, 128
Faulkner, William, 3; *Absalom, Absolom,*
 245
Faust, Karl, 132
Feldman, Morton, 55, 223, 224, 232; *The
 King of Denmark* (1961), 224
Fennelly, Brian; *Divisions for a Violinist*
 (1968), 113
Fort, Syvilla, 39
Foss, Lukas, 270; *Time Cycle,* 109
Fredriksson, Magnus, 295
Frerch, Robert, 63
Fromm, Paul, 270
Frost, Robert, 31, 289
Fugs, the, 191
Fujihara, Hinako, 100
Fuller, Buckminster ("Bucky"), 24, 48, 53,
 60, 65; *Nine Chains to the Moon*
 (book, 1966), 289

Galamian, Ivan, 111, 112, 113, 117
Gandhi, Mahatma, 123
Gerbrant, Carl, 104
Gerhard, Roberto, 208
Gershwin, George, 164; "Summertime,"
 294–95.
Ghent, Emmanuel, 114
Gibbons, Orlando, 12
Gibson, Jon, 121
Ginsberg, Allen, 112, 191, 193
Giovanno, Herman di, 97, 100
Glass, Philip, 119–25, 140, 142, 145, 307;
 Akhnaten, 124; *Einstein on the Beach*
 (1976), 123, 124; *Music by Philip Glass*
 (book, 1987), 124; *Music in Changing
 Parts* (1970), 119, 120, 121–22; *Music in
 Contrary Motion* (1969), 119; *Music in
 Fifths* (1969), *Music in Similar
 Motion* (1969), 119; *Music in Twelve
 Parts* (1974), 120, 122, 123, 124, 125;
 Satyagraha (1980), 123, 124; *Strung Out*
 (1967), 119; *Two Pages* (1966), 123, 125
Glazunov, Alexander, 159, 164
Gleason, Sarah, 296
Globokar, Vinko, 230, 231
Glock, William, 88
Godfrey, Jay, 295
Goethe, J. W. V., 72
Goldman, Albert, 239
Goldstein, Richard, 195
Gottlieb, Jack, 267
Gould, Glenn, 3–16, 140, 182, 214, 215, 216;
 The Art of Glenn Gould (radio), 4;
 Idea of North, 14; *String Quartet,* 5;
 aka. Dr. Herbert von Hockmeister, 5;
 recording of J. S. Bach's *Goldberg
 Variations,* 6, 11; recording of Bach's
 Well-Tempered Clavier, 8
Graham, Bill, 151, 158
Graham, Martha, 77, 78, 79, 98, 105;
 Appalachian Spring, 77

Grass, Günter, 133
Grateful Dead, the, 192
Greenberg, Noah, 239
Grieg, Eduard, 38
Grofé, Ferde, *Grand Canyon Suite* (1931),
 211

Hagenau, Heinz, 75
Haggin, B. H., 240, 241–44, 248, 249;
 Music Observed (book, 1964), 241–
 43.
Hamilton, David, 222, 226
Hammar, Thomas, 295
Handel, G. F., 95, 103
Hanslick, Eduard, 257
Harrison, Lou, 97, 98, 103
Harris, Donald, 114, 115
Harris, Roy, 121, 147; *Third Symphony*
 (1938), 211
Hartog, Howard, *European Music in the
 Twentieth Century* (book, 1961),
 248
Haydn, Franz Joseph, 89
Heifetz, Jascha, 160
Hemingway, Ernest, 289
Henderikse, Jan, 295
Hentoff, Nat, 257
Henze, Hans Werner, 133
Hesse, Herman, 100
Heward, Leslie, 97
Hiller, Lejaren, 61, 62, 63, 64, 230;
 HPSCHD (1969), with John Cage,
 224
Hindemith, Paul, 140, 221; *Ludus Tonalis*
 (1943), 44, 113, 139
Hodeir, André, 251–53, 255; *Jazz: Its
 Evolution and Essence* (book, 1959),
 252–53; *Since Debussy* (book, 1961),
 251–53; *Toward Jazz* (book, 1961),
 252–53
Hoffnung, Gerald, 146
Hollander, John, 32, 267
Holst, Gustav, 86
House, Son, 262, 263
Hovhaness, Alan, 95–105, 223; *Armenian
 Rhapsody No. 1,* 98; *Bluebeard,* 96;
 Concerto for Accordion, 103; *Daniel,*
 96; *Duet for Violin and Harpsichord*
 (1954), 101; *Etchmiadzin,* 98; *Floating
 World—Ukiyo* (1968); *Khaldis,* Opus
 91, 102; *Lousadzek* (1944), 98;
 Magnificat, Opus 157, 102, 103, 104;
 Meditations on Orpheus, Opus 155,
 103; *Mysterious Mountain* (1955), 99,
 101, 102, 105; *Saint Vartan Symphony*
 (*Symphony No. 8,* 149–50), 99, 102;
 Symphony No. 1, 99; *Symphony No. 2,*
 99; *Symphony No. 8,* 99; *Symphony
 No. 23,* 104; *Symphony No. 24,* 104:
 Symphonies No. 27, 28, 29, 30 (1976),
 95; *Symphony No. 31,* Opus 296, 95:

Symphony No. 36 (1979), 95;
Symphony No. 40, 95
Howard, John Tasker, *Modern Music*
(book, with James Lyons, 1957o, 245;
Our American Music (Fourth ed.,
1966), 251; *A Short History of
American Music* (with George Kent
Bellows, revised ed., 1967), 246
Howe, Irving, 241, 243
H. P. Lovecraft (a band), 192
Hyman, Dick, 177, 180
Hyman, Stanley Edgar, *The Critic's
Credentials* (1978), 259

Ichiyanagi, Toshi, 233
Ives, Charles, xiii, 17–19, 21, 22, 39, 65, 75,
78, 86, 89, 108, 110, 128, 139, 158, 197,
199, 200, 201, 221, 234, 249–50, 255,
259, 285, 288, 294, 296; *Concord
Sonata*, 17, 18, 289; *Fourth Symphony*
(1910–16), 65, 200; *Second String
Quartet* (1907–13), 88; *Song for
Harvest Season*, 17; *Symphony No. 2*,
17, 200, 289; *The Unanswered
Question* (1908), 17, 18, 56, 116, 200;
Third Sonata for Violin and Piano,
113; *Three Places in New England*
(1903), 200; *Variations on a National
Hymn*, 18
Ives, George, 19

Jacobs, Paul, 116, 117
James, William, 140
Jarrell, Randall, 241
Jefferson, Blind Lemon, 155, 263–64
Jefferson Airplane, the, 192, 194
Joglars, 24
Johns, Jasper, 48, 82
Johnson, Robert, 155, 263, 264
Johnston, Ben, 62
Johnston, Jill, 49, 53, 80, 81
Jones, LeRoi, 257; *Blues People: Negro
Music in America* (book, 1963), 261
Jones, Spike, 145, 148
Jonson, Ben, 133
Joplin, Janis, 152
Joplin, Scott, 148
Joyce, James, 93; *Finnegans Wake*, 26, 43,
209, 253, 254, 273–81, 294; *Ulysses*, 86

Kafka, Franz, 133
Kagel, Mauricio, 127–134, 145, 146, 296;
Acustica (1970), 129, 130; *Aus
Deutschland* (1977–80), 127; *Ensemble*
(1967–70), 129; *Finale* (1980–81), 127,
133; *Hallelujah* (film, 1967–68);
Ludwig Van, 129, 132; *MM51* (film,
1976), 129; *Quodlibet* (1987–88), 131;
Oral Treason (1981–83), 129; *Pas de
cinq* (1965), 127; *Sankt-Bach-Passion*
(1983–85), 128; *Tanz-Schul* (1988), 131

Kalish, Gilbert, 117
Kaprow, Allan, 55, 135
Karajan, Herbert von, 11
Kassler, Michael, 269
Keil, Charles, *Urban Blues* (book, 1966),
155, 157–58, 257–59
Kelly, Joanne, 259
Kerman, Joseph, 241, 269
Kern, Jerome, *Mark Twain* (1942), 164
Khachaturian, Aram, 221
Kierkegaard, Soren, 5
King, B. B., 151–58, 259, 264, 287; "Every
Night I Got the Blues," 152; *Live at
the Regal* (record album), 157; "Three
O'Clock Blues," 154; "The Thrill Is
Gone," 153
King, Martin Luther, Jr., 152
Kingston Trio, the, 192
Kirchner, Leon, 270
Kirstein, Lincoln, 86
Klee, Paul, 115
Kleiber, Erich, 128
Klein, Howard, 108
Knowles, Alison, *Notations* (book with
John Cage, 1968), 234
Köchel, L. R. V., 99
Kodály, Zoltán, 107, 108
Koegler, Horst, 72
Komitas Vartabed, 95
Kontarsky, Alois, 129, 230
Kostelanetz, André, 159–65
Kostelanetz, Richard, *Americas' Game*
(1988), 288, 289, 290, 292, 293–305,
307; *Autobiographies* (book, 1981), 289;
Conversing with Cage (book, 1988), 83,
320; *The Eight Nights of Hanukah*
(1983), 288, 292, 307; *Epiphanies*, 291;
Esthetics Contemporary (book, 1978);
Foreshortenings and Other Stories
(1978), 307; *The Gospels* (1982), 294,
307; *Invocations* (1981, 84), 287, 292,
293, 294, 307, 309; "Kaddish," 310;
Lovings, 308–9; *New York City* (1984),
288, 289, 290, 292, 294, 296, 307; *The
Old Poetries and the New* (book, 1981),
273; *Recyclings* (book, 1984), 290, 307;
Relationships (1983), 291; 308;
Seductions (1981), 291; *A Special Time*
(1985), 309–310; *Turfs/Arenas/Fields/
Pitches* (book, 1982), 288, 291; (tape,
1988), 291
Koussevitzky, Serge, 86
Krenek, Ernst, 208, 253, 265; *Johnny
Spielt Auf* (1926), 208
Kubrick, Stanley, *2001* (film), 231

Lambert, Constant, 239
Lambranzi, Gregorio, *Neue und Curieuse
Theatricalische Tantz-Schul*, 131
Landry, Dickie, 121
Lang, Paul Henry, 249; *Problems of*

Modern Music (book ed., 1962), 253;
Contemporary Music in Europe, with
Nathan Broder (book ed., 1965), 248
Langer, Suzanne K., 78–79
Lassaw, Mr. and Ms. Ibram, 82
Lawrence, D. H., 251
Leavis, F. R., 249, 250, 251
Leigh, Shirley (Ms. Moog), 172, 173, 174,
177
Lesschaeve, Jacqueline, *The Dancer and
the Dance,* 82
Lewis, John, 227
Lewis, Sinclair, 28, 289
LeWitt, Sol, *Arcs, Circles & Grids* (1973),
289
Ligeti, Gyorgi, *Atmospheres* (1961), 231;
Lux Aeterna (1966), 231
Limon, José, *The Moor's Pavane,* 77
Liszt, Franz, 12, 115
Lovin' Spoonful, the, 194
Lucier, Alvin, "The Tools of My Trade,"
289, 290
Luening, Otto, 233
Lyons, James, *Modern Music,* with John
Tasker Howard (book, 1957), 245

Macdonald, Dwight, 29, 241, 244
Mallarmé, Stéphane, 26, 51, 252
Malraux, André, 10, 72
Mannes, David, 111
Mann, Thomas, 102
Marks, J, 170, 187
Martha & the Vandellas, 194
Martino, Donald, 210, 227
Martins, Joao Carlos, 139–40
Martinu, Bohuslav, 97
Martirano, Salvatore, 234; *L's GA* (1967),
234; *O O O That Shakespearean Rag*
(1958), 234; *Underworld* (1965), 234
Marx Brothers, 58; *A Night at the Opera,* 68
Marx, Josef, 230
Matisse, Henri, 163
Mauzey, Peter, 172
Mayall, John, 259
Mayer, Martin, 240
McCartney, Paul, 170
McLuhan, Marshall, 3, 5, 47, 48, 60, 63,
259; *Understanding Media* (book,
1964), 289
McTell, Willie, "Statesboro Blues," 289
Méliès, George, *Trip to the Moon,* 64
Mellers, Wilfrid, 249–51; *Caliban Reborn*
(1967), 251; *Music in a New Found
Land* (1965), 249–51; *Studies in
Contemporary Music* (1947), 251
Memphis Willie B., 262, 263
Menotti, Gian-Carlo, 221
Menuhin, Yehudi, 115, 163, 216
Messaien, Olivier, 115; *Vingt regards sur
l'enfant Jésus* (1944), 44, 139
Metzger, Heinz-Klaus, 71

Michener, James, 239
Mies van der Rohe, Ludwig, 49
Migliorotti, Atalante, 105
Miller, Robert, 230
Milstein, Nathan, 115
Miró, Joan, 163
Mitch Ryder & the Detroit Wheels, 194
Modern Jazz Quartet, 261
Moholy-Nagy, L., 127, 286; *Vision in
Motion* (1966), 289
Mondrian, Piet, 136
Monk, Meredith, 123
Monroe, Marilyn, 294
Monteverdi, Claudio, *Vespero della Beata
Vergine* (1970), 289
Moog, Robert, 167–88
Moore, Carman, 240
Morrison, Jim, 258
Mossolov, Alexander, *The Steel Foundry,*
22, 201
Mothers of Invention, the, 191, 228
Moussorgsky, Modest, 285
Mozart, W. A., 5, 26, 61, 62, 63, 72, 89,
95, 99, 108, 123, 145, 164, 199, 209,
225, 240, 287; A Major Sonata (for
violin), 113; *A Musical Dice Game*
(aka *Introduction to the Composition
of Waltzes by Means of Dice*), 62, 225
Muller, Ceil, 295
Munkasci, Kurt, 122
Munro, Thomas, xv
Murnau, F. W., *Nosferatu,* 129
Murphy, Arthur, 121

Nabokov, Vladimir, *Pale Fire* (1962), 146
Nameth, Ronald, 63
Neuhaus, Max, 224; *American Can* (1966),
233
Newlin, Dika, 240
Newman, Ernest, 241
Nietzsche, Friedrich, 268
Nikolais, Alwin, 172, 180–81, 187
Nono, Luigi, 210
Norton, Charles Eliot, 246
Novalis, 72

O'Hara, Frank, 82
Ohio Express, the, 192
Oldenburg, Claes, 17, 18; *Giant
Hamburger,* 18
Oliver, Paul, 257, 258; *Blues Fell This
Morning* (book, 1961), 260
Olson, Charles, 261
O'Neill, Eugene, Jr., 86
Orcutt, Sarah Gene, 164
Orwell, George, *Selected Essays* (book,
1959), 289
Owens, Calvin, 152

Paganini, Nicolo, 113
Parker, Charlie, 227, 249

Parris, Robert, 241
Pärt, Arvo, 290
Partch, Harry, 223
Pearls Before Swine, 192
Penderecki, Krzysztof, 92, 113; *The Passion According to St. Luke* (1965), 231; *String Quartet* (1960), 231; *Threnody for the Victims of Hiroshima* (1960), 231
Perle, George, *Serial Composition and Atonality* (book, 1963), 25, 254–55, 265, 269, 270
Perspectives of New Music, 248, 265–71
Pisarro, Camille, 163
Piston, Walter, 113, 121
Politics, 29
Pons, Lily, 160, 164
Ponselle, Rosa, 160
Pound, Ezra, xiv, 112
Pousseur, Henri, 225
Presley, Elvis, 193
Procter, Adelaide, 96
Prokofiev, Sergei, 105; *Peter and the Wolf*, 309
Proust, Marcel, 93
Purcell, Henry, 113
Putney (synthesizer), 183, 187
Pynchon, Thomas, 139

Randall, J. K., 227; *Lyric Variations for Violin and Converted Digital Tape* (1968), 113
Rauschenberg, Robert, 17, 82, 267
Read, Herbert, 47
Regner, Eric, 269
Reich, Steve, 120, 121, 123, 142
Reinhardt, Ad, 286; *Selected Writings* (1966), 289
Renoir, Jean, 163
Reynolds, Roger, 233, 267
Rhodes, Philip, 115
Richter, Hans, *Dreams That Money Can Buy* (film, 1948), 40
Riehn, Rainer, 71, 72
Riesman, Michael, 123
Riley, Terry, 121, 123, 135, 140, 233; *Harp of New Albion*, 139; *In C* (1964), 233, 234; *Poppy Nogood's Phantom Band* (1966), 233
Rimsky-Korsakov, Nicolai, 164
Robbe-Grillet, Alain, 48
Rodgers, Richard, 164
Rolling Stones, the, 155, 167, 194; "Let's Spend the Night Together," 171
Rorem, Ned, 246, 266; *Music from Inside Out* (book, 1967), 246; *Paris Journal* (book, 1965), 246
Rosen, Charles, 87, 88
Rosenberg, Harold, 82, 141; *Art on the Edge*, 141; *The Tradition of the New*, 289

Rossellini, Roberto, 193
Rostropovich, Mstislav, 91
Rubínstein, Arthur, 160
Rudiakov, Michael, 110
Rudin, Andrew, *Tragoedia* (1968), 187
Ruggles, Charles, 250
Russo, William, 230

Sager, Christopher, 12
Sahl, Michael, 115, 230, 234
Saint-Saëns, Camille, 113
Salzedo, Carlos, 86
Salzman, Eric, 224, 226, 230, 235; *The Nude Paper Sermon* (1969), 230
Sandburg, Carl, 32, 143, 163
Sandler, Irving, 82
Sarasate, Pablo, 113
Sargeant, Winthrop, 240, 265
Saroyan, William, 103
Sartre, Jean-Paul, "The Wall" (1956), 289
Satie, Erik, 21, 41, 57, 113, 199, 245, 285
Schaefer, Pierre, 287
Scheffer, Frank, 71
Scherchen, Hermann, 216
Schickele, Peter (aka P. D. Q. Bach), 120, 141–49; *Last Tango in Beyreuth*, 147; *O Calcutta* (with others), 147; *P. D. Q. Bach (1807–1742?)*, 142; *Quartet*, 147; *The Definitive Biography of P. D. Q. Bach* (1976), 141
Schnebel, Dieter, 230
Schoenberg, Arnold, 4, 5, 8, 10, 11, 12, 23, 24, 25, 25, 29, 38, 40, 45, 56, 77, 78, 85, 86, 89, 107, 113, 204–9, 214, 225, 226, 239, 240, 242, 245, 251, 252, 253, 254, 255, 265, 266, 276; *Moses und Aron* (1932), 206; *Opus 23*, 4; *Pierrot Lunaire* (1912), 113
Schon, Donald A., *Technology and Change* (1967), 176
Schonberg, Harold, 108, 242
Schöning, Klaus, *Roararorio* (book, 1982), 83
Schubert, Franz, 12, 120
Schuller, Gunther, 116, 118, 227, 229, 253, 270
Schuman, William, *New England Tryptich* (1956), 164
Schumann, Robert, 12, 129
Scott, Howard, 12
Sear, Walter, 180, 185
Searle, Humphrey, 225
Seawright, James, 177; *Electronic Peristyle* (sculpture, 1968), 182–83
Sessions, Roger, 85, 110, 115, 125, 208, 225, 253, 266
Shankar, Ravi, 97, 121, 194;
Shankar, Ude, 97
Shapey, Ralph, 115, 229; *Evocations* (1959), 229

Shattuck, Rogert, *The Banquet Years* (1958), 245
Shifrin, Seymour, 115
Shirali, Vishnu, 97
Shostakovitch, Dmitri, 113, 140, 164, 211, 221; *Fifth Symphony* (1937), 211; *Preludes and Fugues* (1950–51), 44, 139
Sibelius, Jan, 95; *Fourth Symphony, The Swan of Tuonela, Luonnotar for Soprano & Orchestra,* 95
Siday, Eric, 173
Silver Apples, 228
Silverman, Jerry, *Folk Blues* (book, 1958), 260
Silverman, Stanley, 230
Sinatra, Frank, 192, 193, 228, 258
Skalkottas, Nikos, 208
Slonimsky, Nicolas, 40
Sly and the Family Stone, 194
Smith, William O., 227
Smokey Robinson & the Miracles, 194
Snyder, Ellsworth, 69
Sollberger, Harvey, 229, 230
Sorabji, Kaikhosru Shapurji, 140; *Opus Clavicenbalisticum,* 139
Spector, Phil, 195
Stearns, Marshall, 257
Stein, Gertrude, 18
Steinberg, Michael, 117
Steinberg, Saul, 141
Steiner, George, 241
Steppenwolf, 192
Stern, Isaac, 115
Sternfield, F. W., *Music in Shakespearean Tragedy,* 241
Steuermann, Edward, 12, 113, 208
Stockhausen, Karlheinz, 17, 55, 90, 133, 140, 196, 208, 210, 225, 226, 230–232; *Carré* (1960), 231; *Gesang der Jünglinge* (Song of Youths, 1956), 170, 218, 231; *Gruppen* (1959), 231; *Hymnen* (1967), 231; *Kontra-Punkte* (1953), 231; *Mikrophonie I* (1964), 232; *Mikrophonie II* (1965), 232; *Momente,* (1965) 232; *Solo für Melodie Instrument mit Rückkopplung* (1966), 231; *Zyklus* (1961), 231;
Stokowski, Leopold, 98
Strauss, Richard, 10, 268
Stravinsky, Igor, 17, 21, 25, 37, 78, 85, 89, 90, 108, 112, 142, 145, 146, 147, 158, 208, 214, 221, 235, 239, 240, 241, 249, 252, 254, 265, 266, 267; *Agon* (1957), 208; *Canticum Sacrum* (1956), 208; *Requiem Canticles* (1966), 208; *Thereni* (1958), 208;
Subotnick, Morton, 186
Sumsion, Calvin, 63
Supremes, the, 194
Suzuki, D. T., 30, 78
Swansen, Chris, 181

Swed, Mark, 72
Sweelinck, Jan Pieterszoon, 12
Sydeman, William, 108
Synket (synthesizer), 183, 187

Takahishi, Yuji, 62
Taylor, Cecil, 227
Tchaikovsky, Peter Ilich, 113, 164
Tenny, James, *Meta + Hodos* (book, 1964), 248
Tharp, Twyla, 124
Theobald, Robert, 24
Thomas, Dylan, 31, 32; *Under Milk Wood,* 294
Thomson, Virgil, xv, 22, 40, 88, 121, 240, 246, 249, 266; *The State of Music* (revised ed., 1962), 246, 285, 286–87
Thoreau, Henry David, 73, 273, 278
Tillich, Paul, 5
Tobey, Mark, 274
Tristano, Lenny, 147
Trotsky, Leon, 243
Tudor, David, 23, 49, 51, 62, 203, 222, 247

United States of America, the, 192, 228
Ussachevsky, Vladimir, 173, 187, 233, 253

VanDerBeek, Stan, 57
Van Doren, Mark, 241
Vanilla Fudge, the, 192
Varèse, Edgard, 18, 40, 78, 86, 89, 90, 100, 202, 204, 221, 228, 249, 252, 255, 266, 269, 288, 290; *Déserts* (1954), 218; *Ionisation* (1931), 22, 39, 40, 56, 108, 201, 221, 289; *Poème élèctronique* (1958), 170, 218
Vischer, Antoinette, 64
Vivaldi, Antonio, 144, 199

Wagner, Richard, 21, 239, 268; *Tristan and Isolde,* 251
Walton, William, 221
Waters, Muddy, 152, 153, 258
Webber, Lynn, 34
Weber, Ben, 250
Webern, Anton, 86, 113, 208, 210, 214, 224, 225, 241, 251, 252, 254, 266, 288
Weidenaar, Reynold, 145, 294, 295
Weinberg, Henry, 227
Weiss, Adolph, 37
Weiss, Jonathan, 181, 183
Welles, Orson, 26
Welty, Eudora, 28
Westergaard, Peter, 210, 227, 248
White, Bukka, 154
Whitman, Walt, 97, 250; *Leaves of Grass,* 274
Whittington, Elizabeth, 104
Who, the, 194
Wieland, Frits, 294

Williams, Jonathan, 112
Williams, Martin, *Where's the Melody?*
  (book, 1966), 260
Williams, William Carlos, 112
Willis, Ellen, 195
Willson, Meredith, 239; *The Music Man*
  (1957), 239
Wilson, Edmund, xiv, 93
Wilson, Robert, *Einstein on the Beach*
  (with Philip Glass), 124
Wolfe, Tom, 195
Wolff, Christian, 55, 223
Wolpe, Stefan, 229, 245, 252, 266
Wouk, Herman, 239
Wuorinen, Charles, 115, 229–30; *Chamber
  Concerto for Flute and Ten Players*
  (1964), 230; *Chamber Concerto for
  Oboe and Ten Players* (1965), 230;

Janissary Music (1966), 230; *Time's
  Encomium* (1969), 187

Xenakis, Iannis, 181

Yater, Peter, *Twentieth Century Music*
  (book, 1967), 248
Young, La Monte, 55, 108, 135–37, 140,
  232, 234; *The Tortoise, His Dreams
  and Journeys,* 135–37, 217, 233, 245;
  Well-Tuned Piano, 139
Young, Stark, 241
Ysäye, Eugene, *Sonata No. 6,* 113

Zazeela, Marian, 135, 233
Zukofsky, Louis & Celia, 111, 112
Zukofsky, Paul, 107–18, 230

ABOUT THE AUTHOR

Richard Kostelanetz (1940-) has written and edited scores of books of and about contemporary literature and art. His previous Limelight book is *Conversing with Cage*. As a composer he has received annual Standards Awards from ASCAP; as a media artist he has received many grants and residencies for his work in radio, video, holography and film. His visual art has been exhibited around the world. He lives in New York City.